THE ARCHITECT

THE ARCHITECTURE OF FREEDOM

HEGEL, SUBJECTIVITY, AND THE POSTCOLONIAL STATE

Hassanaly Ladha

BLOOMSBURY ACADEMIC
LONDON · NEW YORK · OXFORD · NEW DELHI · SYDNEY

BLOOMSBURY ACADEMIC
Bloomsbury Publishing Plc
50 Bedford Square, London, WC1B 3DP, UK
1385 Broadway, New York, NY 10018, USA
29 Earlsfort Terrace, Dublin 2, Ireland

BLOOMSBURY, BLOOMSBURY ACADEMIC and the Diana logo are
trademarks of Bloomsbury Publishing Plc

First published in Great Britain 2020
This paperback edition published in 2021

Cover design by Maria Rajka
Cover image: Memnon's Statue, 1731 (engraving), Picart, Bernard (1673-1733)
© Private Collection / The Stapleton Collection / Bridgeman Images

A catalogue record for this book is available from the British Library.

A catalog record for this book is available from the Library of Congress.

ISBN: HB: 978-1-3501-0579-9
       PB: 978-1-3502-6743-5
       ePDF: 978-1-3501-0578-2
       eBook: 978-1-3501-0580-5

Typeset by Integra Software Services Pvt. Ltd.

To find out more about our authors and books visit www.bloomsbury.com
and sign up for our newsletters.

For Ayla

"Philosophy is its time grasped in thought"

– G. F. W. Hegel

CONTENTS

LIST OF ILLUSTRATIONS

PREFACE

Hegel has plausibly been called the "inaugural thinker of the contemporary world."[1] And yet foundational elements of his thought have escaped attention—not only those buried in neglected manuscripts, marginal notes, and obscure literary and political allusions, but also those hiding in plain sight. This book attends to a constellation of such moments across Hegel's work. Ranging from Egyptian "architectonics" to the logic of borders, from Persian poetry to the sublimity of representation, from "beautiful" democracy to forced labor, and from African history to international "right," the book offers a new reading of Hegel's related theories of architecture and language, aesthetics and history, mastery and slavery, and subjectivity and the state.

I wrote this book for scholars in philosophy as well as those in other fields impacted by Hegel's thought, including architecture, postcolonial studies, political theory, and the history of slavery. I would recommend that readers resist the urge to pass directly to chapters most relevant to their area of study. The argument of the book proceeds methodically from beginning to end; the later sections will make little sense if read out of sequence. My hope is that the payoff will have been worth the effort of a patient reading.

This book has had a long gestation, and I have accrued more debts along the way than I could possibly acknowledge. I wrote and completed Part One of this book in 2004; this section appears here in essentially the same form. I am deeply grateful to Claudia Brodsky and Michael Wood for reading the manuscript at that time, just as I was going on academic leave for personal reasons. I am indebted to both for their early encouragement and insistence that I continue with my work. Since then, I have had the privilege of tapping the prodigious intelligence and friendship of both Claudia and Michael on numerous occasions. Barbara Johnson served as a mentor during my years at Harvard. I will never forget her steadfast passion, generosity, and commitment to excellence, even as writing and speaking became difficult for her: I continue to feel her loss keenly. Walter Johnson shared his encyclopedic knowledge of the history and theory of slavery; to him I also owe the book's title. Tom Conley, Ann Smock, Sebastian Wogenstein, Sarah Johnson, and Peter Constantine provided invaluable feedback on various aspects of the manuscript. While I have benefitted from the generosity and erudition of these and other scholars, all shortcomings and errors in this book, including those of fact, interpretation, and translation, are mine alone.

I am grateful to the journal *October* for generously granting permission to reprint material that appeared in my essay entitled "Hegel's *Werkmeister*: Architecture,

---

[1] Jean-Luc Nancy, *Hegel: L'inquiétude du négatif* (Paris: Hachette, 1997), 5.

Architectonics, and the Theory of History."[2] I am particularly thankful to the Humanities Institute at the University of Connecticut for support as I completed research for the final chapter of this book. Michael Lynch, Brendan Kane, and other fellows at the Institute created a collegial and fertile intellectual environment. I am deeply appreciative of my other colleagues at the University of Connecticut, especially Roger Célestin, Anne Berthelot, Eliane DalMolin, Valérie Saugera, Jennifer Terni, and Gustavo Nanclares. Their support has meant more to me than they could know. A number of scholars have played a formative role in my intellectual development, including Suzanne Nash, Gerhard Böwering, Alan Trachtenberg, and Langdon Hammer, as well as David Underdown and Wolfhart Heinrichs, whose memories I honor here. I am humbled to have benefitted from these scholars' instruction and example. Mary Gaylord, James Irby, John Hamilton, Karen Feldman, Luis Girón-Negrón, Fernando Rivera-Díaz, Fermin Rodriguez, Paola Cortes-Rocca, Pablo Ruiz, Ana Yáñez Rodriguez, Amr Shalakany, Katherine Stevens, and Yamila Hussein have each had a hand in this book in ways large and small. Susan Holman proved a most generous and valuable proofreader. No one deserves more appreciation than my beloved wife, Emily. To my parents, siblings, and children, I owe simply everything. This book is dedicated to Ayla, who as an infant slept on my shoulder while I labored over Hegel, who taught me the meaning of unconditional love, and who made me a Daddy.

[2]Hassanaly Ladha, "Hegel's *Werkmeister*: Architecture, Architectonics, and the Theory of History," *October*, 139 (Winter, 2012), pp. 15–38. © 2012 by October Magazine, Ltd. and the Massachusetts Institute of Technology.

INTRODUCTION

In the 1820 preface to the *Philosophy of Right*, Hegel argues that freedom through "ethical life," shaping a polity into a "well-formed building" [*gebildeten Bau*], constitutes "the architectonic [*Architektonik*]" of the state's "rationality."[1] In 1824 he likewise characterizes the state as "a great architectonic building or hieroglyph of reason that presents itself in reality."[2] Hegel here echoes the *Lectures on Aesthetics*, where the "architectonic" emerges from the interpenetration of built and linguistic form or, in their respective aesthetic modes, architecture and poetry. As I will show, for Hegel the opposition of these two "arts"—one principally material, the other verbal—defines the dialectic of the aesthetic and propels what he calls, engaging Kant, the "architectonic" unfolding of history. For Hegel the "architectonic" manifests in particular as the Egyptian "hieroglyph," a term he applies not only to written signifiers engraved in stone, but also to pyramids and obelisks arranged in rows over the desert, like inscriptions on a page. Most quintessentially, the architectonic and hieroglyphic converge in the colossus of Memnon, an African warrior appearing in ancient Egyptian architecture and in Greek myth and art from Homer to the Hellenistic period. As non-referential, built form voicing only the poetic signifier, the colossus marks the circulation of the architectonic across dialectical limits, hence the coimbrication of concept and matter, aesthetics and logic, and East and West. Moreover the Memnon, bearing the "African element" into history, isolates the subject's possible freedom from dialectical stasis. In the *Phenomenology of Spirit*, the Memnon, as embryonic self-consciousness, appears as the enslaved "work-master" [*Werkmeister*] laboring for freedom. This "statue in

---

[1] G. W. F. Hegel, *Werke*, 20 volumes, eds. E. Moldenhauer and K. M. Michel (Frankfurt am Main: Suhrkamp, 1969–1971), 7: *Grundlinien der Philosophie des Rechts*, 19. All translations of Hegel are mine, unless otherwise noted. Following customary scholarly practice, I will designate "additions" and "remarks" in the various versions of the *Philosophy of Right* or the *Encyclopedia of the Philosophical Sciences* with a simple "A" or "R" after the paragraph citation from the text. For the sake of economy, in this book I will refer to Hegel's *Outlines of the Philosophy of Right* as simply the *Philosophy of Right*. I refer to Hegel's *Encyclopedia of the Philosophical Sciences* by its full name or as simply the *Encyclopedia*, and to its constituent parts as the *Encyclopedia Logic*, the *Philosophy of Nature*, and the *Philosophy of Spirit*. In the same vein, I also refer to the *Phenomenology of Spirit* as simply the *Phenomenology* and to the *Lectures on Aesthetics* as simply the *Aesthetics*. I use the same method of abbreviation for his other lecture courses.

[2] Hegel, *Werke* 7: §279A, 449. The term "architectonic" in Hegel ultimately signifies the unstable entanglement of conceptual and material form, hence language and phenomenality, that gives rise to apparently enduring objects of experience. I examine Hegel's relation of architecture to architectonics in Part One of this study.

human form" hypostatizes the twin aesthetic operations through which the slave in Hegel's system struggles for emancipation: first, through the "formation" [*Formierung*] of material form, or of the objectified "thought" through which he attempts to produce and know himself as a subject; and second, through the poetic dissolution of inherited form, which will ultimately enable the recognitive and thus discursive reconciliation of the self-liberated slave and ousted master in the state.[3]

The aesthetic articulation of freedom underwrites the political theory advanced through the critique of the "architectonic" state in the *Philosophy of Right*. In its most immature conception, the state posits itself as a sealed "building," a self-sufficient totality predicated on the "ideality" of "right" only within its borders. By contrast the free state, endlessly superseding its territorial or other material boundaries, attains to a coherence of "internal" and "external" right. Polities at the telos of history—effecting the reciprocal recognition of their concrete freedom—realize "universal right" everywhere and for "everyone."[4]

Astonishingly, scholars of Hegel have overlooked the architectonic and its implications in his work, resulting in significant distortions in the interpretation of his corpus.[5] Partly to blame is the critical tendency to view Hegel's works in isolation, neglecting their dialectical place in the system set forth in the *Encyclopedia of the Philosophical Sciences*,

---

[3]Hegel, *Werke 3: Phänomenologie des Geistes*, 510. As I will show in Part Two of this book, for Hegel the activity of *Formieren* or *Bilden* underpins the relation between aesthetics and political economy.

[4]Hegel, *Vorlesungen über die Philosophie der Weltgeschichte*, ed. G. Lasson (Leipzig: Felix Meiner, 1920), 761; Hegel, *Vorlesungen über Natturecht Staatswissenschaft*, 247, 280. Since all dialectical oppositions are unstable, they articulate the principle of their own undoing, hence the possibility of freedom from given signs and their referents. I use the phrase "telos of history" as a heuristic to refer to this idea of freedom paradoxically internal to the dialectic, not to a chronological "end of history" as the positive outcome of a temporal process. As we will see, history for Hegel does not bend to chronology or the arbitrarily linear conjunction of purported causes and effects, but rather emerges from the dialectical structure of logic: indeed, historical concepts emerging after a "fact" can be shown to have constructed its always belatedly attributable "causes" and "effects." (Cf. Alexandre Kojève's reading of "reason" [*Vernunft*] as a "teleological action" in *Introduction à la lecture de Hegel* [Paris: Gallimard, 1947], 531.)

[5]An important exception is Claudia Brodsky Lacour, the only scholar who considers seriously the dialectic of architecture and poetry in Hegel's *Aesthetics* (see her "Architecture in the Discourse of Modern Philosophy: Descartes to Nietzche," in *Nietzche and "An Architecture of Our Minds,"* eds. Alexandre Kostka and Irving Wohlfarth [Los Angeles: Getty Research Institute, 1999], 19–34 and "From the Pyramids to Romantic Poetry: Housing the Spirit in Hegel," in *Rereading Romanticism*, ed. Martha B. Helfer [Amsterdam: Rodolpi, 2000], 327–66, two studies to which this book must make continual reference). Informing my general approach to the aesthetic in Hegel are Jacques Derrida's "Architecture Where the Desire May Live," in *Domus*, vol. 671, 1986, 17–25; "Point de folie—maintenant l'architecture," in *Psyché* (Paris: Galilée, 1987); "From Restricted to General Economy: A Hegelianism without Reserve," in *Writing and Difference*, transl. Alan Bass (Chicago: University of Chicago Press, 1978); "The Pit and the Pyramid: Introduction to Hegel's Semiology" and "White Mythology," in *Margins of Philosophy*, transl. Alan Bass (Chicago: University of Chicago Press, 1982); and *Glas*, transl. John Leavey Jr. (Lincoln: University of Nebraska Press, 1986); the seminal essays on Kant and Hegel in Paul de Man's *Aesthetic Ideology*, ed. Andrzej Warminski (Minneapolis: University of Minnesota Press, 1996), including especially the discussion of the "architectonic" in Kant (ibid., 125ff.); de Man's *The Resistance to Theory* (Minneapolis: University of Minnesota Press, 1986); and Jean Hyppolite's *Logique et existence* (Paris: Presses Universitaires de France, 1961).

the purported armature for all of Hegel's work, including his lectures.[6] Failing to connect the pyramidal sign in the *Encyclopedia* with the architectonic delineation of form in the *Aesthetics*, scholars have misconstrued key elements of Hegel's theory of language. In turn, commentators on Hegel's theory of art have failed to notice his definition of the aesthetic as the dialectic of architecture and poetry—and, consequently, the foundational place of their covalence in his system.[7] They have thus not accounted adequately for the impingement of the aesthetic on Hegel's theories of logic, subjectivity, and history. Most readers of the *Phenomenology* have ignored the slave's aesthetic fashioning of "form"; they have accordingly missed the relation between the dialectic of master and slave in the section on "Self-Consciousness" and the necessarily aesthetic appearance of the servile self-consciousness in the section on "Religion." The latter section, uncoupled from its complementary passages in the *Aesthetics*, has thus remained largely impenetrable. Scholarship on the theory of recognition tends to focus on only the phenomenological iteration of "self-consciousness," abstracting it from the dialectic of subjective and objective spirit. Scholars engaging Hegel's critique of political economy and the state in the *Philosophy of Right* and the *Encyclopedia* have accordingly not registered the aesthetic mediation of person and property, the resulting centrality of slavery in political economy, and the movement from the slave's recognitive agency to the reconciliation of states in universal right. Most damaging to Hegel's reputation, readers of the *Lectures on the Philosophy of History*, seduced by its deceptive accessibility, have missed its governing principle—namely that there is no history independent of the aesthetically mediated "narration of history" [*Geschichtserzählung*]."[8] Embracing precisely the positivism Hegel eschews, these readers have not fully grasped his conception of "world-history" as the

---

[6]This understandable tendency results from the critical rejection of any claim to systematicity binding the works to each other. I am, of course, not suggesting that the *Encyclopedia* subsumes or converges neatly with the *Phenomenology*, the *Science of Logic*, the *Philosophy of Right*, and the lecture courses—or that there is only consistency or even complementarity across Hegel's works. Even so, the reworked encyclopedic versions of the *Phenomenology*, the *Science of Logic*, and the *Philosophy of Right* connect these texts to the *Encyclopedia*, to each other, and to the lecture courses on world-history, art, religion, and philosophy in a manner that at least merits consideration. The intertextualities to which we will attend across the "works" will indeed undermine the notion that any of them stands apart as an independent totality. Ultimately Hegel's system, subject to endless revision and reiteration, will reveal its components as fragments of a paradoxically ungraspable whole; accordingly I suggest they should be read alongside each other. On the relation of the *Phenomenology* to the *Encyclopedia*, see Martin Heidegger, *Gesamtausgabe* (Frankfurt: Vittorio Klostermann GmbH, 2009), 68: 69ff. Heidegger demonstrates that Hegel established the encyclopedia system between 1808 and 1811, hence within a few years of the publication of the *Phenomenology of Spirit* (ibid.). In a salutary turn, scholars like Robert Pippin, Slavoj Žižek, Catherine Malabou, Frederic Jameson, Rebecca Comay, and Frank Ruda—to name a few—have taken more comprehensive approaches to Hegel's oeuvre. On the relation between the *Phenomenology* and the *Science of Logic* see, *inter alia*, Hyppolite, *Logique et Existence*; Robert Pippin, *Hegel's Idealism: The Satisfactions of Self-Consciousness* (Cambridge: Cambridge University Press, 1989), 91ff.; Frederic Jameson, *Valences of the Dialectic* (London: Verso, 2009), 75ff., and Rebecca Comay and Frank Ruda, *The Dash—The Other Side of Absolute Knowing* (Cambridge: MIT Press, 2018), 29ff.

[7]This oversight has unfortunately clouded views of Hegel among scholars of architecture. I present Hegel's theory of architecture in Part One of this book, in the hopes of supplementing such texts as Denis Hollier's seminal *Against Architecture: The Writings of George Bataille*, transl. Betsy Wing (Cambridge: MIT Press, 1992).

[8]Hegel, *Werke* 12: *Vorlesungen über die Philosophie der Geschichte*, 83.

discursive reconciliation of "internal" and "external" right in the state and, accordingly, the overcoming of geographical and anthropological determinism.

As a consequence, scholars referencing Hegel continue to circulate reductive and, indeed, non-dialectical readings of certain sweeping claims made in his lectures on history—notoriously, that illiterate peoples, especially Africans, "in spite of their achievements in the realm of linguistic development, do not possess a history"; and that "world-history progresses from East to West, for Europe is absolutely the end of history, Asia the beginning; in the West the sun of self-consciousness rises, spreading a superior luminosity."[9] Studied in isolation and outside of their dialectical context, such statements have been universally dismissed, even as their superficial content, fully misinterpreted, continues to inflect historiography across the humanities and social sciences. This state of affairs is particularly deplorable given that Hegel's statements, understood in the terms of his dialectical system, ultimately subvert the very claims imputed to him by his detractors.

Indeed Hegel's insistence on the architectonic fluidity of historical categories in "world-history" is entirely at odds with his legacy, which Paul de Man describes as follows:

Whether we know it, or like it, or not, most of us are Hegelians and quite orthodox ones at that. We are Hegelian when we reflect on literary history in terms of an articulation between the Hellenic and the Christian Era or between the Hebraic and Hellenic world. We are Hegelian when we try to systematize the relationships between the various art forms or genres according to different modes of representations or when we try to conceive of historical periodization as a development, progressive or regressive, of a collective or individual consciousness. Not that such concerns belong exclusively to Hegel; far from it. But the name "Hegel" stands here for an all-encompassing vessel in which so many currents have gathered and been preserved that one is likely to find there almost any idea one knows to have been gathered from elsewhere or hopes to have invented oneself. Few thinkers have so many disciples who never read a word of their master's writing.[10]

De Man goes on to attribute to a distorted Hegelianism such "historical fallacies" as "the ideologically loaded genealogy of the modern as derived from the classical, Hellenic past," "responsible for a good deal of poor historiography from the early nineteenth century to the present."[11] De Man's brief but seminal essays on Hegel lay the groundwork for a rereading of the latter's conception of the aesthetic. But even de Man does not register the persistent implication of the aesthetic across the entire dialectic of "subjective" and "objective spirit" in Hegel's system. As we will see, de Man mistakenly

[9]Hegel, *Werke* 12: 133–4.
[10]De Man, *Aesthetic Ideology*, 92–3.
[11]Ibid., 108.

uncouples the pyramidal sign from the aesthetic "symbol," the articulated voice from the materiality of written inscription, and the aesthetic in history from what he also incorrectly considers the "definitive" and "non-dialectical" moment of the "sublime." In fact, Hegel's view of the "architectonic" translation of the concept in history reflects precisely the sublimity and thus performative violence of all representations, including of such categories as "Western," "Eastern," or "African" "culture."

Hegel's centrality for modernity owes much to his delineation of the dialectical nature of thinking. Less familiar, especially to non-specialists, is the aesthetic interpenetration of concept and materiality, or sign and referent, internal to the dialectic.[12] Usefully, Hegel offers a basic exposition of the dialectic in the first section of the *Phenomenology*.[13] He presents his argument in the context of a broader discussion of the movement between the universal and the particular in the act of indication:

1. In order for language to refer to a sensuous object, it must move from a universal to a particular element subsisting in space and time.

2. The indicative or deictic marker "this," marking the attempt to particularize the universal, underlies any referential gesture, even if implicitly.

3. "This" means "here" and "now," but these markers of spatial and temporal presentness nonetheless remain universal: if I say "this" rose "now," the moment I utter the word "rose," it has aged, subsisting in a different "now."

4. The "this" underlying language thus reveals any act of indication as a cancellation of the particular.

5. In the absence of any referential anchor for the sign, binaries between oppositional terms cannot hold.

6. Each binary thus yields to other, equally unstable and thus dynamic oppositions.

The determination of a thing in a particular place and time, pointing to its absence, empties the name of content; the name, negating the particular, thus reverts to universality until once again made to indicate the real. This cycle from the determination of a thing to its negation and then displacement by a newly determined particular comprises the movement of the dialectic:

---

[12]Even some specialists have not registered the aesthetic dimension of the dialectic, in part because of the progression of the dialectic through (and thus apparently beyond) its aesthetic and religious toward its philosophical modalities. But as we will see, philosophy does not completely strip away the aesthetic; rather, the former dialectically cancels and preserves the latter. Thus, philosophy in the *Encyclopedia* is the "unity of art and religion": "this knowledge [of philosophy] is the thinkingly cognized [*denkend erkannte*] concept of art and religion, in which the sundry content [produced through the aesthetic] is recognized as necessary, and this necessity is recognized as free" (Hegel, *Werke* 10: *Die Philosophie des Geistes*, §572: 378). In the same vein, the aesthetic, expressing itself as religious artifice, bears the "revealed religion" as the immanent "future" of art (ibid., §563: 372). In the *Phenomenology*, as we will see, Hegel subsumes this movement from the aesthetic to the revealed religion under the category of "religion." The differences between the *Encyclopedia* and the *Phenomenology* accounts of this movement will not concern us; we will, however, study the relation between the aesthetic and religion in the *Phenomenology* in Chapter 6.

[13]"Sense-Certainty, or the This and What Is Meant" (Hegel, *Werke* 3: 82ff.).

[T]he *This* is posited as something sublated [*aufgehoben*], or as not *This*; and hence not as nothing, but as a determinate nothing, the nothing of a content, namely, of the *This*. As a result the sensuous aspect is still present, but not as it was intended, [subsisting] in immediate certainty or as the single thing that is meant, but as a universal, or as that which will be taken as a quality. Dialectical overcoming [*Das Aufheben*] evinces its true double meaning which we have seen in the negative: it is negating and preserving at the same time.[14]

This "double meaning" of the term *Aufhebung*, meaning both "cancellation" and "preservation" and often translated as "sublation," captures for Hegel the dual movement of the dialectic: as the instrument of logic, the dialectic cancels existing categories and binaries of thought but preserves their internal features, subsuming them within the categories of a new and substituting binary. These paradoxically "canceled" and "preserved" features, as the actual or potential residue of earlier binaries, constitute the emergent categories and inflect their dialectical trajectory:

> The concept's moving principle, which both dissolves and produces the particularizations of the universal, I call "dialectic" … This dialectic is not an activity of subjective thinking oriented externally, but rather the very soul of the matter producing its branches and fruit organically … To consider a thing rationally means not to bring reason to bear on the object from without and so work it through; rather it means that the object is rational on its own account. Here it is spirit in its freedom, the highest peak of self-conscious reason, that gives itself reality and produces itself as an existing world. The sole task of the philosophical science is to bring into consciousness this proper work of the reason of the thing itself.[15]

Or elsewhere:

> [T]hinking gets caught up in contradictions; that is, it loses itself in the rigid nonidentity between thoughts, and thus does not reach itself, but rather remains trapped in its opposite. The higher need goes against this result of thinking at the stage of understanding; it is grounded in the fact that thinking does not relinquish thought, but remains faithful to itself even in this conscious loss of its being at home with itself, "so that it may overcome," and even accomplish in thinking itself the dissolution of its own contradictions. The insight that the nature of thinking in essence is the dialectic, that it must, as understanding, come into the negative of itself, into contradictions, marks a crucial element of logic.[16]

---

[14]Hegel, *Werke* 3: 94.

[15]Hegel, *Werke* 7: §31: 84–5. On *Aufhebung*, see also the discussion in Hegel, *Werke* 5: *Wissenschaft der Logik*, 113–6.

[16]Hegel, *Werke* 8: *Enzyklopädie I: Wissenschaft der Logik*, §11: 55.

Mediated by language and marking a "crucial element of logic," the dialectic both unfolds discursively and delineates materially the "object" or referent that is "rational on its own account." Here the contradiction internal to the term *Aufhebung* emerges: the contingency of objects on their dialectical and hence logical articulation both belies and proves their "rational" necessity. In the first place, the "sensuous 'this' that is meant [*gemeint*] *cannot be reached* by language"; the thing itself slips endlessly away from the grasp of the discursive concept.[17] By the same token, the verbal delineation of the "this," even as it negates the thing, shapes and thus already constitutes what is "meant," traversing the gulf between language and matter. The dialectic paradoxically articulates even as it negates the limit between concept and thing and, by corollary, between the linguistic temporality of the "now" and the "becoming" of the real.

In order to have meaning, Hegel adds, any concept must accord with its object; so, too, the concept as such (i.e., the concept of the concept) "must have a content which conforms to its form."[18] But this more fundamental "content" of the paradigmatic concept accords only inadequately with its "formal" articulation and dissolution in time.[19] As we will see, Hegel calls any such imperfect conjunction of content and form "aesthetic" and more particularly—in the latter's quintessential, dialectical mode—"architectonic." This aesthetic entanglement of form and content, concept and matter, or language and reality—in other words, the self-negating, performative delimitation of the concept—marks the dynamic "frontier" of "freedom": unfolding by virtue of its instability, the architectonic exposes both concept and thing to dissolution, rearticulation, and thus possible liberation from inherited mediations of "history." Thinking thus frames the latter as the endless narration and process of its own undoing. Only through "vulgar" mystification—the dogmatism and positivism of mere "understanding"—can consciousness blind itself to this internal fluidity of the given and cling to the fiction of given, unmediated time.[20]

Driven by the possibility of freedom from the inherited category, Hegel's historiographical methods remain exemplary for postcolonial thinkers, including Africanists, resistant to dependence on a purportedly "Western" epistemological frame. Understandably, Hegel's comments on Africans remain controversial. On the one hand, his comments on their "barbarism"—cited in the United States Congress in 1860 to justify slavery—have cemented his reputation as a racist for many across the humanities and social sciences, not least in African studies. On the other hand, such views do not reconcile with Hegel's explicit critique of racism, his insistence on the innate rationality and freedom of all human beings, his consequent condemnation of the "barbarism" of slavery, and his approbation of Haiti, a state born of the successful revolt of transplanted and enslaved Africans against their European masters.

---

[17]Hegel, *Werke* 3: 91–2. Emphasis in original.
[18]Hegel, *Werke* 6: *Wissenschaft der Logik*, 267.
[19]Ibid., 266–7.
[20]Hegel, *Werke* 8: §41A: 115.

Adducing valuable archival evidence, a few historians and postcolonial thinkers have linked the Haitian revolution to Hegel's ensuing articulation of the dialectic of master and slave, or *Herr* and *Knecht*; but many Hegelians remain unconvinced of the value of any such concrete referents on the reading of the *Phenomenology of Spirit* or of the *Philosophy of Right*.[21] Participants in the "Hegel and Haiti" debate tend either to strip the *Knecht* of any historical specificity or to reduce the figure to a literal type of servant, serf, or slave; in this respect, such scholars ignore the necessity internal to Hegel's "narrative" of the movement between sign and referent, including between the conceptual *Knecht* and its historical manifestation as slave, serf, and wage laborer in the progression toward freedom in self-consciousness.

With all the controversy, the apparent contradiction arising from Hegel's view of the universality of freedom and his denigration of Africans remains unresolved. Approaching this problem contextually, I argue that the emergence of concrete freedom out of the dialectic of the "internal" and the "external" "right" of the state in Hegel's system cannot be understood without reference to the theory of Africa as the non-historical and non-dialectical incipit and telos of "freedom"; the relation of the aesthetic and history; the critique of the "understanding"; the theory of recognition emerging from the dialectic of *Herr* and *Knecht*; and the implication of slavery in modern political economy.

Hegel's view of the non-historicity of "Africa proper"—the unpenetrated interior that produces no accessible archive for him as he writes and thus eschews representation—stems from his radical view of history as a contingent narrative based on available, circulable written materials. The marginal place of "Africa" in Hegel's system thus underscores its significance; for "Africa" marks the dialectical limit of the system and the limit of the dialectic. Grasping his historical moment philosophically, Hegel identifies the slave's historical appearance as a movement out of Africa: the African's subjection to slavery marks its "essential" connection to European mastery and thus—from the latter's standpoint—to history.[22] In Hegel's system, a non-historical people must live in a "state of nature," which he characterizes as the "barbaric" fight to the death between self-consciousnesses prior to the subjugation of the slave, her entry into history in the age of the modern state, and her ultimate reconciliation with the ousted master in ethical sociality. Hegel's exaggerated and at times invented view of life in Africa (for which he deserves critical opprobrium) may well reflect an underlying racial prejudice;

---

[21] I discuss the scholars who have written on Hegel's relation to Haiti in Part Two.

[22] Hegel's argument here is a matter of definition. From the perspective of the racialist economic paradigm then prevalent on his continent, "slavery" marks the "essential" [*wesentliche*] relation between the European and African (*Werke* 12: 128): given the lack of European access to the (accordingly) non-historical interior, the African, from the European "standpoint," "appears" historically as the slave. For Hegel, however, the "essential" relation between subjects emerges from the "essence" of self-consciousness—namely the human capacity to reflect back into itself and out of its immediacy. The "essential" relations of self-consciousness thus reveal its innate capacity for freedom in sociality and thus its historicity. To a reader of the *Science of Logic*, Hegel's formulation—contingent on his relative and thus provisional "standpoint"—discloses the contradiction internal to any "essentializing" view of the African as a slave. As we will see, Hegel identifies the African as the slave to reiterate, critique, and ultimately subvert the reduction of the "African" to thinghood, the foundational assumption of race-based slavery in European political economy.

on the other hand, he states clearly that his narrative, based on what he insists is a thin archive of European accounts of Africans that spill over the edges of the non-historical "interior," follows only from the "idea" of the state of nature as the dialectical opposite of freedom, not from positive "facts" that "truthfully" represent a reality.[23] By definition, Hegel's explicitly "non-historical" account of Africans thus does not represent what he calls their innate "aptitudes" or "capacity." As I have intimated, he in fact attacks judgments of peoples based on skin color, skull size, and other biological features, and he holds up the example of Haiti to indicate the capacity of Africans for the spiritual development that leads to the ethical sociality of the state and its inflection of world-history.

Crucially, Hegel attributes the absence of ethicality in "Africa proper" to the fact that some are transplanted from Africa and sold into slavery; and it is "Europeans," he reminds us, that "lead" Africans into the "savagery" of "historical" bondage. Hegel's purpose is to demonstrate to his European audience that slavery begets a state of nature; and that a state of nature begets slavery. Any references to the miserable condition of Africans, whether true or false, thus cannot justify the reduction of humans to property. On the contrary, Hegel's view of Africa as the "non-historical" "state of nature" underwrites a devastating critique of the relation of race-based slavery, political economy, and the European state based on mere "understanding"; in this context, he justifies the radical right of enslaved peoples to overthrow their masters, establish independent states, and seek recognition from former imperial powers as equals. As I will demonstrate, the mere "understanding" of Africa as a land of "unconscious" humans immersed in "sense-certainty" undergoes complete "inversion" in Hegel's narrative through the manifestation, however embryonic, of self-conscious freedom in the Haitian state; so, too, geographical and anthropological determinations, revealed as mere "idealities" of "understanding," unravel before the "architectonic" movement of universal spirit through the endlessly self-canceling categories of "world-history." The non-historical African thus discloses for humanity the capacity to free itself from inherited history.

This book traces Hegel's history of freedom from its aesthetic articulation in and by the slave to the recognitive reconciliation of humanity in the state. In Hegel's narrative, the African as enslaved self-consciousness ultimately overcomes his interpellated otherness, including his identification with the "servitude" he has suffered. The Haitian experience, from slavery to the demand by "mulattoes" and blacks for racial equality in the late 1780s in France to the recognition of Haiti by France in the 1820s, instantiates—like no other example historically to that point—the entire cycle in Hegel's work from *Knechtschaft* to the "recognition" between modern states, hence to the concrete realization of the "architectonic" of the state's rationality.

Through this study of Hegel, I attempt an intervention in contemporary debates on the idea of freedom and its implications for political theory. To begin with, I analyze what Hegel posits as two competing views of the state: first, as a polity based on the increasingly "cosmopolitan" interest of atomized "persons" and their property and,

---

[23]Without foreclosing the critique of Hegel's use and abuse of the archive, my purpose will be to shift the focus from indeterminate authorial intentions to the performative power of his texts.

second, as the enclosed, violently defended territory of a "people." This opposition comprises what may be the dominant political dialectic of our time. Reading the *Philosophy of Right* in light of Hegel's constellation of theories centered on the aesthetic, I analyze the signifying economy that gives rise to both visions of the state. Following Hegel, I also critique internationalist alternatives to the realization of right in the "particular" state, including supranational unions and global legal regimes based on abstract doctrines of human rights. In the end the aesthetic production of the state and its symbology, culture, and territoriality in Hegel's text underwrites the "architectonic" process through which "universal right" actualizes itself in time: through dynamic narrations of "reconciliation," the reconstruction of world-history leads, discursively and materially, to the "recognition" of states through the concrete paradox of the open border. As the architectonic limit of the state, the self-canceling frontier sublates the opposition between "inner" and "external" "right" and between human polities toward the realization of universal right on earth.

Part One, "Hegel's Memnon," examines Hegel's relation of architecture and poetry as the defining dialectic of the aesthetic. Figured as the Memnon, the co-implication of built and linguistic form further underwrites Hegel's conception of the dialectic as the very form of critical thought. In particular, the Memnon articulates any dialectical delimitation as an apparently enduring but actually fluid "architectonic" line or binary between opposed terms, including those of "East" and "West." In the form of the poetic sublime, this architectonic line underwrites all linguistic operations, inflecting the telling and thus production of history.

Chapter 1, "The Figure of History," centers on Hegel's figuration of the progress of history from East to West as the sun's daily arc through the sky. While readers of Hegel have registered this narrative frame across his oeuvre, they have not accounted for its figural mode. Reading the neglected but crucial section on "Religion" in the *Phenomenology of Spirit*, the chapter identifies the historical advent of the aesthetic with the birth of history itself through the aestheticized sign. Through this radical inversion, Hegel argues that only the verbal figure mediates phenomenal form in time. Instantiating this relation of linguistic and material form, Hegel appropriates and emblematizes a mysterious architectural structure, identified elsewhere as the historical Memnon, that issues meaningless but recognizably discursive sound when struck by light at the dawn of history. The chapter thus sets forth the methodological and theoretical stakes of reading such figural elements in Hegel's dialectical history of the phenomenal.

Chapter 2, "Naming Building," interrogates the relation between architecture and language evoked by the Memnon in the *Phenomenology of Spirit* and in complementary passages in the *Lectures on Aesthetics*. The chapter relates the voice of the Memnon at dawn to Hegel's theory of linguistic "performance" or "action," understood as the dialectical materialization or "building" of form in the real.

Chapter 3, "From Memnon to Mnemosyne," examines Hegel's poorly understood theory of language, focusing in particular on his critique of the linguistic sign. Reading his relation of building and language in the *Encyclopedia* for the first time alongside corresponding passages in the *Phenomenology* and the *Aesthetics*, the chapter argues that the necessary kinship of symbol and sign, figured as the relation between Memnon and Mnemosyne, subverts inherited and necessarily discursive categories of logic, hence all attempts at referentiality.

Chapter 4, "Architecture and the Poetry of Light," analyzes Hegel's foundational but neglected definition of the aesthetic as the dialectic of the apparently nonverbal and material art of architecture and the verbal and immaterial art of poetry. I then relate this dialectic to Hegel's conception of the sublime as the attempt to render discursively what eschews articulation. Closely reading his largely overlooked texts on "Oriental" literature, the chapter examines the relation between the delimitation of the aesthetic and the poetic delineation of the referent in historical time.

Chapter 5, "The Architectonic in Time," examines Hegel's conceptualization of the "architectonic" as the impingement of the aesthetic on thought and hence on history. Figured as the Memnon, the architectonic actively reconstructs the lines of received historical narratives, contributing to the aesthetic materialization of history itself. The chapter thus studies Hegel's philosophically grounded and explicit subversion of the very categories of "East" and "West" that structure his historical narratives, not least through the figure of the African Memnon.

Part Two, "Africa and the Idea of Freedom," studies the implications of Hegel's theories of the aesthetic, language, and history on his conception of subjectivity, freedom, and the state, arguing for a reassessment of these foundational concepts in scholarship on Hegel and in philosophy and political theory in general. This second part of the book, offering a new reading of the *Phenomenology of Spirit* and the *Philosophy of Right* in light of Hegel's entire oeuvre, centers on the relation between architectonics, the master–slave dialectic, sovereignty, and the conception of "Africa" as the origin and telos of freedom in Hegel's system.

Chapter 6, "The Structure of the *Phenomenology*," finds that the long-standing confusion over the organization of the *Phenomenology* stems from the misreading of the relation between conceptual and historical form in Hegel's work. I demonstrate that the section on "Religion," rather than evoking an extraneous term within the tripartite conceptual scheme of consciousness, self-consciousness, and reason, marks their historical appearance. The section on "Self-Consciousness," the birth of the subject as slave, must therefore be read in the context of both this triad and its phenomenal materialization in "Religion," which charts the appearance of spirit as the architectonic in time.

Chapter 7, "The World Turned Upside Down," argues that the dialectic of master and slave emerges from the logic of Hegel's famously resistant critique of mere "understanding" and its "inverted world" in the final section on "Consciousness" in the *Phenomenology*. Hegel's critique of the "state based on understanding" in the *Philosophy of Right*, too, requires a grasp of the difference between "understanding" and "reason" in the *Phenomenology*. I adduce contemporary German literature, Hegel's other writing, and other moments in the *Phenomenology* to contextualize and elucidate his critique of the static "categories," "laws," and "creeds" of the positivist understanding. Discursively mediated and unmoored from objectivity, such dogmas for Hegel succumb to inversion and "perversion." The chapter relates Hegel's view of the ultimately ironic dimension of all "understanding" to his theorization of race and slavery, evident implicitly in the *Phenomenology* and explicitly in other texts that have not received adequate scholarly attention.

Chapter 8, "Slavery and the Subject," analyzes the celebrated section on the master-slave dialectic in relation to Hegel's theory of the aesthetic. Closely reading the entire section on "Self-Consciousness" from the beginning up to the slave's first contact with freedom, the chapter attends to the dialectic of "perversion" plaguing the attempt merely to "understand" subjectivity and its relation to objectivity. In this context, I argue that commentators have missed the central problematic in the dialectic of master and slave, namely the nature of subjectivity given the dissonance between agency and embodiment. For Hegel the problem of agency—or of the free will—must center on the subject that, reduced to a slave and thus corporeal thing, surrenders his will to another. Only the labor of the aesthetic, initially in the form of the slave's architectonic delineation of an alien object and later in the form of the poetic dissolution of form, will begin to liberate him from the illusory permanence or fixity of the given.

Chapter 9, "Africa, Agency, and Freedom," revisits the master–slave dialectic in light of the slave's historical "appearance" in "Natural Religion" in the *Phenomenology* and of the centrality of slavery in the *Philosophy of Right*. Through a cognitive separation from objectivity, the slave as the *Werkmeister* or Memnon in the *Phenomenology* isolates the principle of the recognitive will. In Hegel's work on history and political theory, the aesthetically mediated cohesion of individual and collective agency—including through shared narratives resignifying historical violence—underwrites the reconciliation of master and slave through the social body of the state. Hegel's interrelated theories of agency and the aesthetic frame his view of the slave's indisputable right to revolt to achieve emancipation. Through architectonic labor—material and discursive—the slave initiates and propels the history of freedom toward its telos in the politically mature state, realized as the social cohesion of the endlessly dispossessed subject in the non-dialectical place Hegel calls Africa. Adducing several neglected texts from the Hegelian corpus, I further argue that the slave [*Sklave*] marks the quintessential, but not exclusive historical form of Hegel's conceptual *Knecht*; and that the *Knecht* in the *Phenomenology* and the *Sklave* in the *Philosophy of Right*, as initially abstract paradigms, gesture at the modern African transplanted to the New World. In this vein, I contend that reductive readings of Hegel's claims about Africans misconstrue or ignore his theories of agency, history, and freedom.

Chapter 10, "The Postcolonial State," examines the implication of aesthetics in political economy and therefore on the realization of freedom in the state. Born of slavery, aesthetic production drives the innovation, commodification, and circulation of objects in political economy. That cycle also results in excess goods and labor and thus trade and colonization. These cross-border activities subvert the primitive conceptualization of the state as violently defended and bordered ground. As they become habituated to a universal law tied to overlapping territories, subjects increasingly recognize each other as free, sloughing off racial, religious, educational, linguistic, and other differences as rigid markers of identity. In this context, the chapter sets forth new perspectives on the importance of the Haitian revolution in the interpretation of Hegel's work. I suggest, first, that the self-emancipation of Haiti marks a concrete corollary of the movement toward freedom in Hegel's dialectic not only of master and slave, but also of the "recognitive" state; and second, that Hegel's work performatively articulates the slave's progression toward the state as a retrospective and thus prototypical narrative of resistance and recognitive reconciliation. Finally, I assess Hegel's decoupling of sovereignty and ground, the implications of his critique of "ground" on the free or postcolonial state at the telos of history, and the actualization of the "architectonic" state through the self-cancelling and paradoxically open border.

The conclusion, "Aesthetics and Sovereignty," considers the relation between Hegel's "state" and the problem of freedom in the contemporary international order. In particular, the chapter examines how Hegel's conception of Africa as a recognitive and aesthetic phenomenon inflects its current discursive construction and prospects for sovereignty. Instantiating the relevance of Hegel's argument for postcolonial African thought, the book concludes with a study of the radical modes of sovereignty articulated in the art of Barthélémy Toguo. In "The Last Supper," Toguo conceives of Africa as the dialectic of the subject and state, each endlessly trespassing its limit, whether corporeal or territorial. As the paradoxically concrete idea of no-place, Toguo's Africa marks the freedom from the statically arbitrary and particular, overcoming what Hegel would call the subjective demarcations of culture and the objective delimitations of territory. A postcolonial Africa thus emerges as the freedom internal to the dialectic and its architectonic unfolding in time.

PART I
HEGEL'S MEMNON

For Hegel the material, nonverbal art of architecture cannot be conceptualized without the discursive medium of language, particularly in its aesthetic manifestation as poetry. Similarly, the immaterial, verbal art of poetry, suspending referentiality and so isolating the pure form of phenomenality, cannot be thought without reference to the apparently enduring division and ordering of space through the act of building. Material, nonverbal buildings and immaterial, verbal figures, the latter a defining characteristic of poetry, thus mark oppositional forms of the aesthetic; even so, they share a common aesthetic function, both generating an infinite range of possible meaning.

Architectural historians have studied buildings as figures of religious, political, aesthetic, or other meaning in diverse traditions and periods. Similarly literary historians have investigated the ways in which architecture functions as a figure for meaning in poetry across languages and cultures. Scholars in both disciplines have assumed that architecture can serve as a figure without interrogating the relation between built and verbal figures as radically different forms of the aesthetic. The task, for scholars in architecture and literature alike, is to define their object of study in relation to the aesthetic. How does the dialectic of architecture and poetry, as formally oppositional but functionally similar modalities of art, inflect the category of the aesthetic? Given their entanglement within the field of the aesthetic, How do each of these two art forms inform the conception of the other?

The most comprehensive treatment of these questions occurs in Hegel's *Aesthetics*, where he explicitly identifies architecture and poetry as "oppositional arts" marking the conceptual limits of the "aesthetic." Hegel opposes these two art forms particularly in their relation to matter: in its essential mode as an "enclosure" for a body, architecture materializes a line that divides externality and interiority, doubling and displacing its corporeal demarcation; by contrast, poetry posits the dissolution of this line through an attempt at rarefied, incorporeal articulation. In its characteristic or "proper" pyramidal form, architecture reproduces the "corporeal shell" of a preserved corpse forever sealing off a dark, interior space of departed soul and mind, hence referring to lost and indeterminate spiritual or intellectual meaning; by contrast, poetry posits the dissipation of a living body in the exteriorizing and immediately vanishing voice of enunciated or written signs. But architecture nonetheless finds "articulation" in the verbal signs of present, living interpreters; thus, ancient, enigmatic monuments attain to an infinite succession of brief and partial meanings. Likewise poetry, even as it aims to dispense with the living body, ultimately reasserts and accentuates its corporeal foundation and materiality.

Together performing the dialectical production and cancellation of the body as an "architectonic" line, architecture and poetry propel the circuit of the aesthetic, making possible its historical progression as a materialization and dissolution of such lines over time. Surfacing in non-verbal buildings gesturing at indeterminate content and in the poetic disassembly and "reconstruction" of discursive, given structures of meaning, the architectonic isolates the spatial and temporal difference and also the "mechanical," but nonetheless unstable arrangement underlying all human productions. Associated in Hegel's oeuvre with both the "instinctive" work of building and the symbolic manipulation of the "psychophysiologically" resonant voice, this mechanical function of the intellect, which Hegel calls "memory" [*Gedächtnis*], makes possible the externalization of thought, whatever its content, as the non-representational, fluid line of the architectonic.

Under the name of the "work-master" [*Werkmeister*], the architectonic in Hegel's work takes the form of the spirit as laboring hand, builder, and logician—and of spirit in its wholeness as the artificer of narrative history [*Geschichtserzählung*] across its artistic, religious, and philosophical dimensions. Above all, the architectonic marks the aesthetic basis for the delimitation of any category of thought, hence its internal heterogeneity and potential for evolution. Hegel's narratives identify the *Werkmeister* with Egyptian architecture and the "architectonic" memorial to Memnon, a colossal structure producing a wordless "voice" when struck by the light of the sun. As the bridge from symbolic architecture to sublime poetry in the *Aesthetics*, the Memnon—in its interplay of monumental building and the human voice and, equally, of light and sound, respectively, the media of architecture and poetry—figures the coimbrication of the two art forms and hence the essential dialectic of the aesthetic. And as a mythopoeic figure, the Memnon instantiates the impingement of aesthetics upon history, marking the self-conscious and self-reflective symbolism of Hegel's own historical narratives.

Reading the lecture courses alongside his written texts, we will trace Hegel's relation of architecture, the quintessence of seemingly static and enduring form, to the "architectonic" as the principle of dynamism that, traversing the physical and discursive realms, underwrites a mode of resistance to entrenched forms and categories of history, proving concepts and categories identifiably Hegelian in inspiration to be, in fact, falsely so in their rigidity and endurance.

CHAPTER 1
THE FIGURE OF HISTORY

In the *Phenomenology of Spirit* and the published text of the *Encyclopedia of the Philosophical Sciences*, Hegel frequently dispenses with historically specific proper names, reserving references to actual religions, cultures, and material artifacts for his more provisional and supplementary remarks and lectures.[1] The elision of proper names and their geographic, cultural, and periodic specificity in favor of more general, figuratively suggestive terms lends a polysemic quality to the written texts, where the narrative mode traverses a wide range of religious, ethnic, linguistic, and cultural categories. For instance, Hegel figures his narrative of spiritual progress from East to West—through anthropological and psychological forms and aesthetic and religious history—as the sun's daily arc through the sky. Readers of Hegel have noted this central narrative frame, but have not accounted for its obviously figural nature or for the relation of figure and history as mutually inflected aesthetic forms. Such oversights reflect a frequent blindness to the aesthetic dimension of Hegel's writing and, more seriously, critical misunderstanding of his painstakingly developed position, foundational for any reading of his work, on the relation of aesthetics, language, and history.[2]

A decisive instance of Hegel's narrative mode is the section in the *Phenomenology of Spirit* entitled "Religion," which marks the birth of artifice in religious history. In a series of beautifully crafted passages, Hegel characteristically figures the evolution of spirit as a diurnal movement from the "light of sunrise," associated with "*immediate consciousness or sense-certainty*," to the "depth of night," which belongs to the inward-turning and "self-knowing" spirit freed from externality and contingency.[3] The diurnal figure in Hegel's

---

[1]Hegel's lectures on world-history, religion, art, and philosophy, as well as a number of additions [*Zusätze*] to and remarks on various paragraphs of the *Encyclopedia of the Philosophical Sciences*, were all published after his death, compiled from his own lecture notes and from those of his students. On Hegel's view of his lectures, Boumann remarks in the foreword to the 1845 edition of the *Zusätze* that Hegel, who "lectured with great freedom," "thought that one should for the most part give a freer and, in part, a more profound rein in one's lectures than in the printed text," which Hegel was satisfied to write with "extreme compression" [cited in J. N. Findlay's "Foreword" to *The Philosophy of Mind, together with the Zusätze in Boumann's text (1845)*, transl. W. Wallace and A. V. Miller (Oxford: Clarendon Press, 1971), vi].

[2]Günter Wohlfart, one of a few exceptions, articulates a view of the aesthetic nature of Hegel's writing quite different from my own (cf. Günter Wohlfart, *Der Punkt: ästhetische Meditationen* [Freiburg: Karl Alber, 1986] and Günter Wohlfart, *Der spekulative Satz* [Berlin: De Gruyter, 1981]).

[3]Hegel, *Werke* 3: 505–6, emphasis in original. For further references to light and darkness in the section on religion, see Hegel, *Werke* 3: 495, 516, 520, 526–7, 537. Hegel addresses the emergence of the "self-knowing" spirit from the "depths of night" at the end of the section on religion (*Werke* 3: 572); the roots of this "spirit" are already present in the dialectic of illuminated determinations and nocturnal essence at the beginning of

text accords with at least the initial progress of historical religion from the worship of "formless" light at dawn to the reverence of lit and shadowy forms objectified by the light of the sun.[4] But the relation of figure and history in Hegel's text evolves from any apparent congruity as spirit moves through various modes of religious expression: from "Luminous Essence" [*Das Lichtwesen*] to "Plant and animal" [*Die Pflanze und das Tier*] to, finally, "The Work-master" [*Der Werkmeister*], where religious artifice, in the form of architecture, first divides spiritual from physical light and, consequently, figural meaning from the illuminated matter and external forms of history.[5] How does this admittedly difficult text, interrogating its own figurative mode, relate its use of figures to its status as a history?

To begin with, artifice, which Hegel defines broadly as the "formation of material at hand" [*das Formieren eines Vorhandenen*], originates with instinctive or pre-conscious construction akin to the activity of "bees building their cells."[6] The medley of the organic and inorganic in the latter phrase marks aptly the transitional moment between the worship of plants and animals and the construction of inorganic forms such as pyramids and obelisks. These "crystal" forms, manifesting the pure lines and planes of geometric space, contrast with the "formless" space of deified light posited

---

this section: "This concept is, against the day of this [external] development, the night of its essence—against the [outer] existence of its moments as independent shapes, the creative secret of its birth" (ibid. 3: 505). The diurnal progression from "sunrise" to "sunset" is one of Hegel's most frequently cited figures for the movement of history: I will examine this figure at length in Chapters 4 and 5, particularly its famous formulation in the *Philosophy of History* (Hegel, *Werke* 12: 133–4).

[4]Spirit initially takes on the "shape of shapelessness" [*Gestalt der Gestaltlosigkeit*]: "this 'shape' is the pure, all-encompassing and all-saturating rising *light*, which preserves itself in its formless substantiality. Its otherness is the equally simple negative, *darkness*; the movements of its own externalization, its creations in the element of its otherness, which lacks resistance or opposition, are downpours of light [*Lichtgüsse*] … streams of fire [*Feuerströme*] consuming all structures of form" (Hegel, *Werke* 3: 506). But the negativity which dissolves the transient, vanishing lines between forms, as the principle of immediate being, endows those forms with enduring presence: thus, "pure light" itself disperses into an "infinity of forms," each form becoming an individual substance (ibid., 3: 506–7).

[5]The standard English translations of the *Phenomenology* give "artificer" or "artisan" for both *Werkmeister* and *Arbeiter*. French translations typically give "*l'artisan*." And yet *Werkmeister* also means "overseer" or "foreman," while *Arbeiter* also means "worker." While Hegel does appear to use *Werkmeister* and *Arbeiter* interchangeably, he subtly distinguishes the two when he argues that "the work-master himself, the spirit in its wholeness, has not yet appeared, but is still inner, concealed essence which, as a wholeness, is present only as fractured into active self-consciousness and the object it has produced" (Hegel, *Werke* 3: 509). At least here, Hegel differentiates between the spirit as a supervising power that remains concealed "in its wholeness" and the fractured, manifest spirit as laborer and underling. While *Werkmeister* in this section refers to both the concealed, entire spirit and the manifest, laboring spirit, *Arbeiter* only refers to the latter. Translating *Werkmeister* as "overseer" and *Arbeiter* as "worker" would preserve the potential distinctness of concealed spirit in its absence, wholeness, and power and maintain, too, the rhythmic pulse of the German text as it moves between *Werkmeister* and *Arbeiter*. But to retain the ambivalence of *Werkmeister* as "artificer," "artisan," and "overseer" as well as the paragrammatic suggestion of a certain "mastery" over the work, I have chosen not to translate *Werkmeister* or to render it as "work-master"; by contrast I use "worker" or "laborer" for *Arbeiter*. Over the course of this book, I will address the ambivalent power and agency of the *Werkmeister* as an "overseer" and also as a slave attaining to limited "mastery" (see Chapter 2 and especially Chapter 9).

[6]Hegel, *Werke* 3: 508.

in the first moment of religion, where God as light, or the indeterminate matrix of space, contrasts with darkness, or pure negativity and nothingness.[7] Opposed to this formless, indeterminate position, abstract, geometric architecture ends the identity of spirit and light, drawing meaning only from the absence or shadows of the sun: the pyramids, in their sealed darkness, house the spirit only negatively as departed spirit; and obelisks translate the sun's spiritual significance only into shadowy forms cast in the sun's external light:

> Either the works produced receive the spirit only as a foreign, departed spirit that has abandoned its living penetration of reality, and, being itself dead, enters into these lifeless crystals [as with the pyramids]; or they have an external relation to spirit as something which is itself there externally and not as spirit—they are related to it as to the rising light which throws its significance on them [as with obelisks].[8]

Dividing spiritual meaning from externality and illuminated matter, these structures locate meaning neither within nor outside their confines, since both interiority and externality lack intellectual content. By materializing a division that betrays the loss or instability of meaning, architecture dispels the accord and continuity of content with historical substance, fact, or form.

Hegel's narrative then turns to the entanglement of organic and inorganic forms in the stylized and geometric shapes of ancient columns and temples.[9] The artificial work at this stage, even though it includes animal images and statues, remains architectural, falling under the rubric of "habitation" and "dwelling" [*Behausung, Wohnung*] because, like all architecture, it cannot fully harmonize its external form with its content, the form of the house to what is housed.[10] Form blends partially with content, but remains

---

[7]Hegel, *Werke* 3: 508.

[8]Hegel, *Werke* 3: 509. Where light originally takes its meaning from the equation of God with physical light, as in Zoroastrianism, here the dominant sense recalls the Egyptian view of Ra, the sun-god, as either separated from the atemporal and non-historical abode of the dead inside the pyramid or, reduced to the realm of time and history, striking the obelisk externally to convey only shadowy meanings.

[9]Spirit emerges as a fashioner of material objects at the end of *Die Pflanze und das Tier* in the transition leading up to *Der Werkmeister*. Here nations identifying themselves with animal spirits manifest *Geist* as "destructive being-for-self" divided into forms of existence that prey on the negativity of things as such; these nations thus hate and fight each other to the death. As it begins to produce objects, the self finds itself in the object: thus the production is also "the produced self, the self depleting its self in its productive activity, that is, the self become a thing" (ibid., 508), marking the birth of the spirit as *Werkmeister*. In this diremption spirit grasps itself as being that is *for itself*, and sees nature as material to be used, altered and fashioned into artificial productions. He then returns to the form of being-for-self, namely the animal, but this time constituting himself as the producer of the work incorporating the animal element (ibid., 510–11).

[10]Ibid., 510. The worker attempts to harmonize form and content, or externality and thought, by blending organic and inorganic forms. He lifts nature from its transitory, particular existence and "brings its organic forms nearer to the more rigid and more universal forms of thought" (ibid., 509). The resulting architecture materializes thought into the world, thus bringing "nearer to actuality the spirit that previously was separated from existence, and was external or internal to it," while still maintaining the difference between thought

always superfluous to any particular meaning.[11] From the architectural "formation [*Formierung*] of material" emerges the producer's knowledge of itself as a self distinct from plant and animal life; this self-consciousness remains limited, however, since the resulting work "still" "lacks speech."[12] Here speech is the discursive channel for meaning that, fully rarefied, overcomes the difference between interiority and exteriority—the very difference first separating meaning and fashioned matter.[13] While Hegel alerts us to a potential dialectical progression from engraved stone to spoken language, he predicates any such progression, crucially, on light:

> Diese Wohnung, die Seite des *allgemeinen Elements* oder der unorganischen Natur des Geistes, schließt nun auch eine Gestalt der *Einzelheit* in sich, die den vorher von dem Dasein abgeschiedenen, ihm inneren oder äußerlichen Geist der Wirklichkeit näherbringt und dadurch das Werk dem tätigen Selbstbewußtsein gleicher macht. Der Arbeiter greift zuerst zur Form des *Fürsichseins* überhaupt, zur *Tiergestalt*. Daß er sich seiner nicht mehr unmittelbar im Tierleben bewußt ist, beweist er dadurch, daß er gegen dieses sich als die hervorbringende Kraft konstituiert und in ihm als *seinem* Werke sich weiß; wodurch sie zugleich eine aufgehobene und die Hieroglyphe einer anderen Bedeutung, eines Gedankens wird. Daher wird sie auch nicht mehr allein und ganz vom Arbeiter gebraucht, sondern mit der Gestalt des Gedankens, mit der menschlichen, vermischt. Noch fehlt dem Werke aber die Gestalt und Dasein, worin das Selbst als Selbst existiert;—es fehlt ihm noch dies, an ihm selbst es auszusprechen, daß es eine innere Bedeutung in sich schließt, es fehlt ihm die Sprache, das Element, worin der erfüllende Sinn selbst vorhanden ist. Das Werk daher, wenn es sich von dem Tierischen auch ganz gereinigt [hat] und die Gestalt des Selbstbewußtseins allein an ihm trägt, ist die noch tonlose Gestalt, die des Strahls der aufgehenden Sonne bedarf, um Ton zu haben, der, vom Lichte erzeugt, auch nur Klang und nicht Sprache ist, nur ein äußeres Selbst, nicht das innere zeigt. ... Die Seele der menschlich geformten Bildsäule kommt noch nicht aus dem Innern, ist noch nicht die Sprache, das Dasein, das an ihm selbst innerlich ist ...[14]

---

and world, spirit and actuality (ibid., 510). This work partially blends form and content since the form "includes within it the shape of individuality"—namely the human body, the sensual form corresponding to and expressive of self-consciousness (ibid., 509–10). But the harmony remains incomplete since natural and geometric shapes are still inadequate and superfluous to the human body (ibid., 512). In this sense, Hegel's use of *Behausung* and *Wohnung* to describe hieroglyphs and statues suggests that as long as works do not embody the human form as the expression of the self, they remain in the realm of architecture. As we will see, Hegel will make this argument explicitly in the *Aesthetics*.

[11] If the mixture of organic and inorganic forms in architecture results in superfluous material, we are made to wonder whether by extension Hegel's own mixture of these elements in his figure of bees building their cells is likewise merely superfluous to his "meaning," and thus marks independently rather than doubles figurally a moment in religious history. And since his figure is both about architecture and like architecture in its superfluity, we further wonder how far the complicity of architecture and figurative language extends.

[12] Hegel, *Werke* 3: 510.

[13] Hegel, *Werke* 3: 511.

[14] Hegel, *Werke* 3: 510–1.

This dwelling [*Wohnung*], the aspect of the *universal element* or inorganic nature of spirit, now also includes within it a shape of *individuality* that brings nearer to actuality the spirit that had previously been only internal or external to existence and thus separated from it; thereby the work becomes more like the active self-consciousness. The worker first seizes upon the form of *being-for-self* in general, the form of the animal. He shows that he is no longer conscious of himself immediately in animal life by establishing himself as the producing force in relation to it, and he knows himself in it as in his *own* work, whereby the animal shape at the same time is one which is superseded and becomes the hieroglyph of another meaning, the hieroglyph of a thought. Hence this shape is no longer used solely and as a totality by the worker, but becomes blended with the shape embodying thought—the human form. Still, the work lacks the form and existence where self exists as self: it also fails to express in its very nature that it includes within itself an inner meaning; it lacks speech, the element in which the sense and meaning contained are actually present. The work done, therefore, even when quite purified of the animal aspect, and bearing the form and shape of self-consciousness alone, is still the soundless shape that needs the rays of the rising sun in order to have a sound—sound that, when produced by light, is only noise and not speech, and shows merely an outer self, not the inner self … The soul of the statue in human form [*Bildsäule*] does not yet emerge from the inner being, is not yet speech, the outer existence that is intrinsically interior …

Here the sun promises a dialectical advance from "soundless" stone to meaningless noise, but "not yet" to fully expressive language. By this point, light draws its significance less from the symbolic system internal to any specific historical religion and more from the symbolic relation of art, light, and meaning [*Bedeutung*] as it evolves over the course of Hegel's own narrative. That is, the meaning of light in the history of the spirit as work-master follows from Hegel's appropriation of light from various religious traditions and its subsequent resignification within his narrative account of religion. To all appearances, figure and history initially cohere in Hegel's narrative, which locates the "dawn" of religion in the religion of light; they likewise accord at the opening of "The Work-master," where Hegel's figure of bees building their cells occupies and, on first reading, rhetorically represents the transitional point between naturalist pantheism and inorganic construction. The congruity of figure and history unravels explicitly, however, once Hegel, without reproducing any given or antecedent interpretation, instead attributes his own symbolic meaning to the light that will give soul to the statue. Similarly it is the increasing independence of figuration from history that structures the larger narrative movement from "Luminous Being" [*Das Lichtwesen*], which refers to an historical object of worship, to "The Work-master" [*Der Werkmeister*], which accrues meaning only from the figural significance given by Hegel and not from the tenet of any historical religion.

Thus figuration here does not serve as a mere embellishment to a conceptually prior and independent history. Moreover the imperfect coimbrication of figure and history in

Hegel's treatment of light develops the tension he creates throughout the text on natural religion by figurally appropriating but not naming historical forms of religious expression. To begin with, Hegel implies (and elsewhere states explicitly) that, past its opening diremption, "natural" religion is fundamentally symbolic or figural to the extent that it intermingles form and meaning.[15] And while he also insists that spirit's "progression" is "not to be represented as occurring in time,"[16] distinguishing the philosophical from the

---

[15]Hegel recounts explicitly the evolution from the non-symbolic worship of light to symbolic pantheism and monotheism in the *Aesthetics* (Hegel, *Werke* 13: *Vorlesungen über die Ästhetik I*, 418–85). I will have occasion to examine Hegel's dialectic of the symbol and sign at length; for now it suffices to say that the symbol for Hegel is the imperfect confluence or "intermingling" of sensual form and abstract meaning: thus the symbol or figure is a type of sign, in that it involves a relation of form and content that is to some extent arbitrary, but as a symbol it "should not be fully inadequate to its meaning; at the same time to remain a symbol it must not be made entirely adequate to that meaning" (ibid., 395–6). In the *Phenomenology* Hegel offers only a general description of semiosis: a "sign" [*Zeichen*] is "something unconcerned with the content it is supposed to designate [*bezeichnen*], just as that which posits the sign for itself is unconcerned with it" (Hegel, *Werke* 3: 259). But in reference to natural religion, Hegel uses the term *Zeichen* to refer loosely to a range of signs, from those indicating the closest associations of form and content (in which cases *Zeichen* can be taken to mean "symbol" in the sense of the *Aesthetics*) to those assigning the most arbitrary relations of form and content (in which case *Zeichen* can be taken to mean a "pure sign"). Thus in the context of the cult, for instance, "the animal sacrificed is the symbol [*Zeichen*] of the god" (ibid., 523); but once stripped of its association with the divine it becomes reduced to a "pure sign" [*bloßen Zeichen*]: "The human form strips off the animal shape with which it was mixed; the animal is for the god merely an accidental form; it moves aside, next to its true shape, and no longer counts for anything in itself, but has sunk down to signifying something else, reduced to a pure sign" (ibid., 516). (For Hegel's use of the word *Zeichen* in the *Phenomenology*, see also, tentatively, ibid., 186, 233, 236, 239, 243, 244, 251, 253, 261.) In any event, Hegel conveys the figurality of the natural religions quite clearly in the *Phenomenology*. In the monotheistic phase of religion, for instance, the determinations or forms of spirit, though still subject to dissipation as in the worship of light, become "embellishments" of spirit in the form of "names" that take the place of self or substance: "Hence the content developed by this pure *being*, or its perceptive activity, is an unreal, superficial play in this substance which only *rises* without *coming down* into itself to become a subject and thus bind together its differences. The determinations [of spirit] are only attributes that do not achieve self-subsistence but remain merely names of the many-named One. This One is clothed with the manifold powers of existence and with the forms of reality as with jewelry or an adornment that lacks a self; they are merely messengers, having no will of their own, messengers of its might, visions of its glory, voices in its praise" (ibid., 506). These superfluous forms and names have an affinity with spirit (as its outer garment and "messenger"), but mark only the absence of substance rather than inhere in or express it (ibid., 506). As we will see in Chapter 4, to take "forms of reality" as "names," "adornments," and "clothes" for spirit is, in Hegel's later terminology, to take those names (or substances displaced by names) as symbols of spirit. The figural displacement of fact extends also to the pantheistic "flower" and "animal" religions, which are essentially figural in that they attempt to "take from the things of perception the deadness of abstraction" and consider "particular forms of animals as their essence," confusing them with spiritual meanings (ibid., 507). Finally, architectural production, in an attempt "to clothe and give form to the soul in its self, and to imbue the body with soul," will aim but fail to remove the "division of soul and body" posited by monotheism (ibid., 509). All three phases of natural religion are thus characterized by the continuing coimbrication of form and content through the mode I call, interchangeably, a "symbol" or "figure." Strictly speaking, a figure in the *Aesthetics* is only a discursive symbol; nonetheless all symbols for Hegel, even material artifacts, are discursive since they require interpretation and thus linguistic mediation. The equation of symbol and figure here serves to isolate their common discursive dimension and, through contrast, the non-discursive or material aspect of architecture—prompting an investigation of the latter's relation to the external form of figural language. This problem, which Hegel treats at length in the *Aesthetics* in the dialectic of the symbol (especially in the section on "symbolic architecture"), is a central preoccupation of Part One of this book.

[16]Hegel, *Werke* 3: 498.

chronological use of historical materials, his treatment of these materials goes beyond mere disregard for temporal succession: his account suppresses all explicit historical references, withholding proper names for religions, cultural contexts, and material artifacts and, instead, weaving together multivalent symbols drawn from or evocative of the Zoroastrian worship of light and darkness, the Jewish and Islamic worship of a monotheistic God "clothed" with purely ornamental shapes of reality,[17] the Indian worship of nature, the worship of plants and animal spirits, and the Egyptian commemoration of nature and death. In other words, Hegel abstracts these symbolic religions from their historical specificity as he appropriates their figures into his dense and elliptical narrative. To merely reduce these symbols or figures to specific historical referents, as have several eminent Hegelians, would be to assume a harmony of figure and history, where figures mediate, without inflection, the philosophical appropriation of history, and history mediates, without burden, the philosophical use and interpretation of figurative language.[18]

But the above passage introducing the "statue in human form," without foreclosing the possibility of decoding its referent, implicitly cautions against hastily supplying missing names or history merely to circumvent dense and elliptical figures. Human-like but for its evident and animal-like lack of speech and interiority, the statue lies along the evolutionary trajectory of the hieroglyph, a form of writing that, according to the passage, begins with animal and part-animal shapes and then proceeds to forms increasingly human. As a dwelling, the statue houses but does not manifest or express its inner soul, just as a hieroglyph gives the external or material shape of thought rather than its rarefied, "intrinsically interior" dimension. By likening the nameless, near-human statue to a hieroglyph, Hegel relates the work to a form of language he views as disconsonant with meaning. Indeed the unidentified "statue" [Bildsäule] awaiting the

---

[17]Hegel alludes cryptically to the oneness or unity of God and his infinite external accidental attributes, the multiple names of Allah, and the angels and prophets appearing in both the Old Testament and the Qurʾān (Hegel, Werke 3: 507). Influenced by German translations of especially Sufi poetry, Hegel in the Aesthetics will differentiate between the Judaic and Islamic attitude to the relation of God as ornament or accident; he will further relate Islam and Christian mysticism in their common blurring of the difference between ornament or accident and an independent God. Hegel views these modes as contrasting (and ultimately architectonic) delimitations of the sublime, which we will study at length in Chapter 4.

[18]Thus Findlay, in his paragraph-by-paragraph analysis of the Phenomenology, strictly identifies Das Lichtwesen with "Persia"; Die Pflanze und das Tier with "India"; Der Werkmeister with "Egypt"; and Die Kunstreligion with "Greece" (Findlay, J. N. "Analysis of the Text," in Phenomenology of Spirit, transl. A. V. Miller. Oxford: Oxford University Press, 1977, 578–80). But the reduction of Hegel's dialectical religious categories in the Phenomenology (natural religion, the religion of art, the revealed religion, and their subsidiaries) to the world-historical categories of the Philosophy of History at least merits justification, especially since Hegel takes pains to avoid proper names in the entire section entitled "Religion" in the former text. In any event, his religious categories by no means accord with Findlay's: hence the cryptic, but nonetheless plausible, references to Semitic monotheism in Das Lichtwesen; the animist religions of all nations, not just India, in Die Pflanze und das Tier; and the "motionless black formless stone," which Baillie and Findlay both identify as the Kaʿbah (Hegel, The Phenomenology of Mind, transl. J. B. Baillie [Mineola: Dover, 2003], 411 and Findlay, "Analysis," 423), in Der Werkmeister and in Das abstracte Kunstwerk (Hegel, Werke 3: 511, 516). Any identification of particular artifacts, as in Baillie and Findlay, should at least acknowledge the multiple referential possibilities of Hegel's text and its symbolic traversal of national, cultural, linguistic, and religious lines.

rays of the sun acts like a hieroglyph in this text, a cryptic figure that Hegel does not gloss here or anywhere else in the *Phenomenology*. As a compound of "figure" [*Bild*] and "pillar" [*Säule*], the term *Bildsäule* emphasizes paronomastically the figurality of the built structure. Architecture can be read just as figures can be read; Hegel implies, however, that both forms are fundamentally hieroglyphic, intermingling with but ultimately superfluous to their connotations.[19]

How then do we read the relation of figure and history in this crucial passage? Like architecture, figurative language remains ostensibly discontinuous with the event it would memorialize; and yet this passage presents the first stirrings of language in the history of artifice not through the vocabulary of a strictly identifiable event in time, but through the figural terms of Hegel's own symbolic system. What sense can be made of the statue before the sun, an architectural "figure" that refers both to its own inadequacy to meaning and to the future birth of meaningful speech? How does the work of building, the craft apparently furthest from verbal art or figuration, inflect the figural determination of history, or the historical determination of figures? Answering these questions will require a thorough interrogation of the relation of architecture and language in Hegel's work, after which we will turn to the implications of architecture on the symbolic mode of Hegel's own historical narrative—and on the telling and making of history in general.

---

[19]As previously indicated, the hieroglyph, as a type of dwelling [*Wohnung*], generates form superfluous to content. By contrast for spoken language, rarefied as an "outer existence that is intrinsically interior," voice and meaning—or sound and its "contained" sense—appear to be "present" to and temporally continuous with each other (ibid., 510). With the hieroglyph and architecture, there is no such continuity of form and meaning, for they remain physically manifest whether or not meaning is conveyed. The temporal incongruity between these forms and their meanings extends generally to figurative language and specifically to the trope of the statue before the sun, where the figural play of architecture and light exceeds the strict dialectical meaning given by Hegel: "the soul of the statue in human form does not yet issue forth from the inner being, is not yet speech" (ibid., 511). The figure of light is also temporally discontinuous with the dialectic here, since as readers we do not immediately reduce the figural relation to the prosaic meaning given by Hegel, but may take it as productive of numerous other meanings. Again, we will see later that, in the *Aesthetics*, Hegel will explicitly make the case for the superfluity of figurative language to particular meanings and, accordingly, the endless displacement of those meanings by other possible significations.

CHAPTER 2
NAMING BUILDING

The statue before the sun appears in various texts in the Hegelian corpus, including several lecture courses published after his death. Where in the written *Phenomenology of Spirit* Hegel does not identify this structure, in his spoken lectures he names it explicitly:[1]

> Especially remarkable are those colossal [statues of] Memnon which, resting in themselves, motionless, the arms joined to the body, the feet together, rigid, stiff, and lifeless, are set facing the sun in order to await its ray to touch them, animate them, and make them sound. Herodotus at least recounts that the [statues of] Memnon gave a sound at sunrise. More advanced criticism has cast doubt on this, yet the fact of this sounding has recently been established again by Frenchmen and Englishmen; and if the sound is not produced by contrivances, it may still be explained in that, as there are minerals which crackle in water, so the sound of these stone figures comes from the dew and the cool of the morning and then from the falling of the sun's rays on them, making small rifts arise and vanish again. But if the colossi are taken as *symbols*, the meaning to be ascribed to them is that they do not have free within themselves an intellectual soul and that—rather than being able to draw animation [*Belebung*] from within, from what bears symmetry and beauty in itself—they require light from without, which alone draws out of them the sound of the soul. The human voice, by contrast, resounds out of one's own feeling and one's own spirit without any external impetus, just as the height of art in general consists in letting the inner shape itself from itself. But the interior of the human form is still mute [*stumm*] in Egypt and in its animation [*Beseelung*] only considers the natural moment.[2]

This passage, appearing in the section on symbolic architecture in the *Aesthetics*, refers to the statue as a specific and historical Egyptian artifact. By providing the name, Hegel must also acknowledge the historical multiplicity of the statues of Memnon, where in the *Phenomenology* the reference to the single, nameless artifact accords with the condensed and elliptical mode of the text. In this passage from the *Aesthetics*, Hegel further insists that

---

[1] It bears remembering that while the posthumously published texts give us mediated access to the lecture material, they do not erase its originally spoken character. And the emergence of standardized forms of this course material, even where some versions from different years have been published, belies the multiplicity inherent in any course given orally numerous times over the years.

[2] Hegel, *Werke* 13: 462. For an image of the colossal statues of Memnon in the wake of the Napoleonic invasion of Egypt, see Figure 1, *The Colossi of Memnon*, published in the *Monuments de l'Egypte* in 1809.

it makes no difference whether the sound produced at dawn is an effect arising mechanically from a human contrivance or accidentally from temporary rifts in the structure; in this manner, he distinguishes the historical or physical explanation from his own symbolic reading of the sunlit colossi. Where "The Work-master" section in the *Phenomenology* evokes history only obliquely for its own figural purposes, providing no names and limited, if any, context for its allusions to historical religions, cultures, or artifacts, here the figural or symbolic sense explicitly displaces what Hegel insists is a documented historical "fact." And though Hegel overtly refers to the architecture as a figure whose meaning he reduces to spoken prose, that prosaic meaning concerns the very incommensurability of architecture and speech. Where the statues of Memnon cannot speak, Hegel speaks for them in his lectures, and his voice, disappearing the moment it is uttered, further instantiates its contrast to architecture and to the unspoken text of the *Phenomenology*, both enduring as fashioned matter or inscription.[3] Speech, even if it refers to the written historical record, articulates history only provisionally; beyond displacing certain "facts," speech subjects the contingent history it expresses to the vanishing suffered by the voice itself.[4] In the end the effect in both texts is the same: the Memnon could not be named in the *Phenomenology* without compromising the figural displacement of history; and in the lectures the Memnon as a spoken figure remains as fleeting and provisional as the history it disarticulates.

In the context of its dialectical circuit, the statue in both the *Phenomenology* and the *Aesthetics* marks not only the difference, but also the convergence of architecture and speech. In the *Phenomenology*, Hegel develops their relation through his notion of the *Werkmeister* and its particular manifestation as the statue before the sun. As the "work-master," the spirit instinctively manipulates given materials through the activity of its hands. Hegel first associates the *Werkmeister* with the laboring hand in the context of a critique of palmistry earlier in the *Phenomenology*[5]:

---

[3]It is, indeed, in the written *Phenomenology of Spirit* that Hegel claims that writing, produced by the hand, is "given a more durable existence" than speech (Hegel, *Werke* 3: 238). Compare the account of the voice in the "Anthropology" section of the *Encyclopedia*: "Thus in the voice, sensation acquires a corporeity in which it dies away just as fast as it is expressed. This is the ground of the higher power present in the voice of externalizing what is internally felt ..." (Hegel, *Werke* 10: §401: 115–6). Hegel then points to the example of wailing at a funeral to externalize feeling. Just as crying out disembodies the grief following death, Hegel's voice, uttering the name of the Memnon, frees the statue from the death it memorializes, the history it represents. We will return to Hegel's view of the voice in this and other texts in the *Encyclopedia* below.

[4]For Hegel only writing, and not speech, comprises and produces history: "Speech is the action of the theoretical intelligence in the real sense, because it is its external manifestation ... But in general this theoretical act, as with its further development, and the more concrete elements linked with it—the spreading of peoples over the world, their separation from each other, their interchange, their wandering—remain enveloped in the murkiness of a voiceless past ... Because they do not take up this truthful element [in enduring phenomenal form, i.e. in written records], those peoples, in spite of their achievements in the realm of linguistic development, do not possess a history" (Hegel, *Werke* 12: 85–6). I will address the narrative mediation of history in Chapter 5.

[5]The discussion of palmistry appears as part of a larger analysis of psychological observation, physiognomy, and phrenology (*Hegel, Werke* 3: 199–262). These sections, as Eric von der Luft notes, are the least read of the *Phenomenology*, despite the fact that they mark the crucial transition from the dialectic of inner and outer to the first explicit appearance of spirit (Eric von der Luft, "The Birth of Spirit for Hegel out of the Travesty of Medicine," in *Hegel's Philosophy of Spirit*, ed. Peter G. Stillman [Albany: State University of New York Press, 1987], 25–42).

next to the organ of speech, it is the hand most of all by which a man manifests and actualizes himself. It is the living work-master [*Werkmeister*] of his fortune. We may say of the hand that it is what a man does, for in it, as the active organ of his self-fulfillment, he is present as the animating soul [*Beseelender*].[6]

As a mediating term, the hand potentially differentiates producer and product. But the description of the hand as *Werkmeister* complicates such a reading, especially since, in the section entitled "The Work-master," Hegel reserves the term not for any mediating instrument, but for the spirit as artificer or producer actualizing itself in its production.[7] The description further contrasts with a passage that appears moments earlier in the same discussion of palmistry, where Hegel characterizes the hand as *arbeitende Hand* and not as *Werkmeister*:

> The speaking mouth, the laboring hand [*arbeitende Hand*], and, if you will, the legs too are the organs of performance and actualization [*verwirklichenden und vollbringenden Organe*] which have the action as action or the inner as such within them. The externality which the inner attains through the action, however, is the deed as an actuality separated from the individual. Speech and labor are external expressions [*Äußerungen*] in which the individual no longer preserves and possesses himself within himself, but lets the inner escape outside him, surrendering it to something other than himself. Consequently we might just as truly say that these expressions express the inner too much as that they do so too little: too much, because the inner itself penetrates through them, effacing the opposition between them and it; they give not merely an expression of the inner, but the inner itself immediately; too little, because in speech and action the inner transforms itself into something else, thus yielding itself to the whim of the element of change, which distorts the spoken word and the performed act into meaning something other than what they are in and for themselves, as actions [*Handlungen*] of this determinate individual … The organ [of speech or action, eg. the mouth or hand] in view of this opposition does not therefore give the expression that is sought.[8]

The movement from the working hand in this passage to the hand as work-master moments later—from *Arbeiter* to *Werkmeister*—occurs in the larger context of the dialectic of inner and outer, and more particularly of man and his external expression. Here the organs of the mouth and hand perform the self, producing it via its externalization, but not in this manner recuperating the self as a stable entity. In this sense the dialectic of the particular self and its speech or action can also be framed in terms of mastery and servitude, insofar as what is at issue in the entanglement of self and its expression are control, dominion, and definition. The dubious position of the hand as partly master

---

[6]Hegel, *Werke* 3: 237.
[7]Hegel, *Werke* 3: 508.
[8]Hegel, *Werke* 3: 235–6.

of and partly servant to man would be reinforced in this case by the term *Werkmeister*, meaning overseer or foreman. An overseer both directs workers and serves the master who governs them all; at the same time, the overseer's authority can be overruled and he may not fully convey or represent the will of his master. Hegel thus critiques the notion in palmistry that a hand abstracted from its deeds reveals something of the inner character: accordingly the hand as *Werkmeister* occupies only an ambiguous or fluid position in the dialectic.[9] Indeed the adage "the hand is what a man does" [*die Hand ist das, was der Mensch tut*], leaving open whether man governs the hand or vice versa, suggests a reciprocal relation that could preserve and undermine, for instance, both the agency of man and the unconscious or instinctive work of the hand.

This unresolved ambivalence extends into the later dialectic of architectural production. In the section introducing the "work-master," the hand appears subtly in a position of apparent servitude. Hegel refers to the activity of the work-master as the fashioning of "what is available" or (to surface the pun) "what is already at hand" [*Vorhanden*], where "hand" is associated with presumably slavish external material.[10] In this sense the nominalized *Vorhanden* materializes man by anthropomorphizing materiality, achieving its effect not through the action of the "working hand" [*arbeitende Hand*], but through the figurative effect of paronomasia. Indeed the working, physical hand represents the figural excess or superfluity of the term that contains it. And as a figure itself, *Vorhanden*, beyond just bringing hand and matter into a dialectical relation, inscribes the hand into matter before the hand fashions it, a temporal priority accentuated by the presence of the prefix *vor*. For a moment, language assumes the place of action in its dialectical relation to matter: Hegel's figure refers to its own verbal fashioning of material as precursory to and dialectically implicated in the act of building, at least insofar as figuration recognizes the malleability of matter in human hands.

Taken together, the passages from the *Phenomenology* suggest that, far from being merely or only servile, the figurative hand, as a rhetorical figure and also like the physical hand, produces the subject as an actor but then exceeds and transforms him in order to actualize him in the world. Just as the "spoken word" [*gesprochene Wort*] becomes an "action" [*Handlung*] in the transformation from inner to outer, so *Handlung* connects

---

[9]The hand does briefly assume a mediating position in the dialectic: "Now if the organs in general proved themselves incapable of being taken as expressions of the inner, since the action as [process of] action is present in them and so internal to them, whereas the action as [accomplished] deed is merely external, and inner and outer in this way come apart and are mutually foreign or can be [foreign to each other], then the organ must now, by virtue of its determination, be taken again as also a *middle term* of both [inner and outer]" (Hegel, *Werke* 3: 237). This middle term includes not only deeds, however, but also the more contingent expressions of the inner. Because these expressions, being contingent, can be manipulated or misinterpreted, they again throw into doubt the continuity between intention and deed, hence the agency of the actor over organs like the hand (Hegel, *Werke* 3: 237–8).

[10]"This production, however, is not a perfect, but a conditioned activity, the fashioning of what is already available, of material already at hand [*das Formieren eines Vorhandenen*]" (Hegel, *Werke* 3: 508). In Part Two of this book, we will study the relation of the *Werkmeister* to the dialectic of master and slave, to the formation of form [*Formieren*], and to Hegel's theory of agency.

figurative language and action, again through the pun on *Hand*. By extension, both the mouth and hand produce and then traverse the division of inner and outer that, in part, grounds the distinction between speech and action, saying and doing. Thus the passages at once insist upon and subvert the mediating power of the hand, the rhetorical spillage pointing up and displacing the categories of producer, instrument, and material—and other such categories upon which the epistemology of linguistic acts ("performances" or "actualizations") or physical actions depends.

Likening the mouth and hand and then further blurring the line between the figurative and physical hand—and, accordingly, rhetorical play and physical work— Hegel opens the space even as he challenges the basis for a theory of language as action, or action as language. If we are prepared to accept this blurred line or intersection in Hegel as the site where language becomes action—where words "actualize," "realize," or "manifest" something in the real—to use common Hegelian terms—we can without anachronism refer to a dialectical theory of linguistic action or, in contemporary terms, "performativity" in his text. Hegel critiques not only the case of the speech-act, but also the very concept and limit of the performative; anticipating contemporary critical theory, he locates the power of linguistic "performance" in the dialectical subversion of any stable delineation of discursivity, materiality, or corporeality.[11] The external form of thought— its sensuous reality—cannot be fully separated from the formative activity of thought itself: language, as the medium of thoughtful activity, does not demarcate itself as the absolute "outside" of matter. Hegel's text thus implicitly ties linguistic action to artificial productions blending intellectual meaning and fashioned matter. Indicatively, the term *Vorhanden*, as rhetorical play, produces and cancels the distinction between figurative language and action; by referring to its own figural power of inscription, the term evokes even as it subverts the category of the performative. In the self-contradiction intrinsic to

---

[11]I mean "performative" here in its broadest sense, where language exceeds referentiality to change the real. Hegel identifies the mouth as an organ of "performance and actualization" and, by extension, spoken words as performative actions. But the performative, subverting the line between the self and its exteriority, only contradicts the conceptual basis of the self's "performance and actualization." Here it bears noting that Hegel's account of the collapse of the line between language and action depends upon the self-referential presentation of the instability of the limit that would make the concept of linguistic action thinkable in the first place. This notion of linguistic "performance," which we will study at length below, relates to the contemporary view of performativity as a referentiality that undermines the very concept of referentiality. Shoshana Felman, in her study of the performative in both Austin's seminal *How to Do Things with Words* and Benveniste's *Problèmes de linguistique générale*, formulates this contradiction internal to the performative as follows: "The performative has the property of subverting the alternative or the opposition between referentiality and self-referentiality. If the language of the performative refers to itself, produces itself as its own reference, this language effect is nonetheless an act, an act that exceeds language and modifies the real: self-referentiality is neither perfectly symmetrical nor exhaustively specular, but produces a *referential excess*, an excess on the basis of which the real leaves its trace on meaning" (Shoshana Felman, *The Literary Speech Act: Don Juan with J. L Austin, or Seduction in Two Languages*, transl. Catherine Porter [Ithaca: Cornell University Press, 1983], 79–80). Thus understood, the self-referentiality of the performative, which Benveniste and many contemporary linguists take as its determining characteristic, should not be too quickly dismissed. We will return to this issue when we develop Hegel's relation of aesthetics and language in Chapter 4.

linguistic action lies not only its potency, Hegel implies, but also the impossibility of its articulation as a stable category.[12]

For Hegel speech and labor serve as the "animating soul" of man, guaranteeing presence to a self even as it abolishes the continuity of the same self, or self-presence as such.[13] It is the absence of this "animation" or "soul" that accounts for the mute and "motionless" statues of Memnon in the *Aesthetics*. Meaningless sound issues from the statues out of a brief opening in stone, the only interior space the forms possess: but voice and interiority "arise" and "vanish" in the same instant. This fleeting interiority of the Memnon, as a manifestation of the *Werkmeister*, specifies the relation of architecture and speech: architecture externalizes man, seizing what is "at hand" to materialize the labor of his hands, but in the process canceling interiority; likewise speech manifests man externally, inscribing him materially even as it effaces his individuality.

But the blurred boundary between the mouth and hand, the organs of speaking and building, suggests that the relation of architecture and speech extends beyond similarity to complicity through their dialectical entanglement in material production. Here again it is the *Aesthetics* that is explicit where the more figurative section on "Religion" in the *Phenomenology* is suggestive. According to the former text, architecture and language are not just analogous externalizing expressions: as a form of linguistic action, architecture is a language because it materializes meaning symbolically:

The relation between content and sensuous reality by which the content should come from [the producer's] conception into [a viewer's] can only be of a symbolical kind. At the same time, a building which is to convey a universal meaning to viewers stands for no other purpose than to articulate this elevated meaning in itself, and is thus an independent symbol of an absolutely essential and universally valid thought, or a language [*Sprache*], present [*vorhandene*] for its own sake, though it be soundless, for spiritual beings. Thus the productions of this architecture should give rise to thought and universal ideas by themselves without being merely an enclosure and setting for meanings given shape through other means. But the form that lets such a content

---

[12]By framing the intersection of speech and action as a dialectical movement of inner and outer, Hegel goes farther than J. L. Austin in critiquing the concept of linguistic action or "illocutionary" speech-acts (see J. L. Austin, *How to Do Things with Words*, eds. J. O. Urmson and M. Sbisà [Cambridge: Harvard University Press, 1975], 98–132 *passim*). Austin's seminal analysis and critique of various types of performative utterances remain enormously productive for contemporary theoretical projects relating, for instance, to legal concepts like hate speech (see, for instance, Judith Butler, *Excitable Speech: A Politics of the Performative* [New York: Routledge, 1997]). Austin's privileging of speech as the principal form of linguistic action has drawbacks, foreclosing an interrogation of the lines between the various material forms of language, including speaking, writing, and gesturing—and hence of the boundary between language in this broader sense and potentially meaningful actions like physical labor, including the act of building. (On Austin's refusal to acknowledge the performativity of poetry, see Barbara Johnson, *The Critical Difference: Essays in the Contemporary Rhetoric of Reading* [Baltimore: John Hopkins University Press, 1980], 52–66.) Hegel, I am arguing, takes up this concern with language in its multivalent sensuousness: already in the palmistry section of the *Phenomenology*, he positions writing—an act of the hand and yet related to speech—as a dialectical subversion of inner and outer, such that the movement between language and action applies, by extension, both to the spoken word and to script (*Werke* 3: 238).

[13]Hegel, *Werke* 3: 237.

shine through it may not be regarded as merely a sign in the way that, for instance, crosses are set up on graves, or piles of stones in commemoration of a battle. For although such signs are suitable for giving rise to ideas, a cross and heap of stones do not themselves indicate [*deuten*] the idea they were meant to bring to mind, since they can just as easily be reminiscent of all sorts of other things.[14]

Though it lacks spoken form, architecture is a language because it manifests externally a "symbolic" relation between sensuous reality and thought. Here *vorhandene* modifies *Sprache*, explicitly attributing material presence to language, but in this case not to language as merely vocalized sound. Recalling the interplay of building, speech, and *Vorhanden* in the *Phenomenology*, the passage implies that though speech does materialize language the way, for instance, the hand materializes thought, language externalizes itself regardless of any audibility. If architecture is a "soundless" language, so too language, before its vocalization, materializes thought architecturally, that is, by externalizing a necessary but imperfect affinity of shape and thought.[15] Bereft of sound, language still exercises the inscriptional power of the working "hand." The use of "vorhandene" to modify "Sprache" conveys that inscriptional power figurally, instantiating both the architectural force of language and the linguistic power of architecture, both of which exert themselves through the modality of the symbol.[16] As a

---

[14]Hegel, *Werke 14: Vorlesungen über die Ästhetik II*, 273.

[15]For Hegel the architectural dimension of language lies precisely in this exteriorizing function; for this reason he calls hieroglyphs "dwellings" in the *Phenomenology* and co-implicates the fundamentally linguistic symbol with architecture in the *Aesthetics*—a dialectical entanglement reaching its crisis in the figure of the Memnon.

[16]Here we must take brief note of a recent critical debate over Hegel's use of the terms "symbol" and "symbolic." In Paul de Man's reading, Hegel views art as fundamentally symbolic, where "the symbol is the mediation between the mind and the physical world of which art manifestly partakes, be it as stone, as color, as sound, or as language" (*Aesthetic Ideology*, 93). Rodolphe Gasché, attributing to de Man the argument that Hegel's use of "symbolic" is "purely linguistic" and theoretical, accuses de Man of applying the term "linguistic" in its contemporary sense and therefore anachronistically. Gasché further insists that the "symbolic" for Hegel is in fact "prelinguistic," and as such refers only to "one of three art forms" and not, as de Man claims, to a modality fundamental to all art (Rodolphe Gasché, "In-Difference to Philosophy: de Man on Kant, Hegel, and Nietzche," in *Reading de Man Reading*, ed. Wlad Godzich [Minneapolis: University of Minnesota Press, 1989], 269–70). Most unusually for so astute a reader and thinker, Gasché seriously misreads de Man on several levels, of which I can only mention two. First, de Man explicitly acknowledges the historical register of the symbolic (*Aesthetic Ideology*, 187–8), and indeed his entire argument turns on the impossible confluence, in the symbol, of its historical and theoretical dimensions (*Aesthetic Ideology*, 102). Second, de Man contends that both linguistic *and* non-linguistic forms ("be it as stone, as color, as sound, or as language") interplay, in the symbol, with varying and fleeting meaning; and that it is because such meanings are only accessible through language that the symbol must ultimately be understood linguistically. Far from being anachronistic, de Man rather allows for only this general discursivity of the symbol. Hegel, in fact, builds precisely this interplay with discursivity into the dialectic model of the symbol, which moves between the "soundless language" of architecture and the discursive mode of poetry to produce, in dialectical synthesis, verbal figures of "comparative art." De Man and Gasché each cite a few of the best-known passages on the symbol in Hegel, but neither provides a sufficiently sustained, dialectically contextualized reading of the sections devoted to the symbol. We will, in Part One of this book, patiently follow Hegel through his theoretical history of the symbol and its dialectical recuperation in romantic art to vindicate some of de Man's basic claims and nuance or challenge others. On Hegel's semiology, cf. *inter alia*, T. Bodammer, *Hegels Deutung der Sprache: Interpretationen zu Hegels Äußerungen über die Sprache* (Hamburg: Meiner, 1969); J. Derrida, "The Pit and the Pyramid," in *Writing and Difference*, transl. A. Bass (Chicago: University of Chicago Press, 1978); and D. J. Cook, *Language in the Philosophy of Hegel* (The Hague: Mouton, 1973).

language that is not yet voiced, the symbol finds its proper expression in architecture.[17] Does the symbol, then, serve as the particular modality through which "words" become the work of the hands or "actions" [*Handlungen*]? Conversely, to what extent is symbolic architecture a modality of linguistic action? Confronting these questions will require extensive analysis of Hegel's concept of the symbol and of symbolic architecture, as well as of the dialectical movement of the aesthetic from architecture to language, specifically in poetry and verbal figures. Only after completing this somewhat lengthy itinerary will we then be able to engage critically the relation of the performative—as a self-referential, figural inscription that Hegel will ultimately call "architectonic"—to the act of building.

In the above passage from the *Aesthetics*, Hegel distinguishes between merely arbitrary relations of form and content in "signs" like crosses or cairns and the necessary but inadequate medley of form and content in the "independent symbols" of architecture proper.[18] Where a cross can indicate, for instance, a church or an intersection as well as a grave, truly independent symbolic architecture cannot be divorced from a particular meaning, even if that meaning is "general" or "universal." The "prototype" for properly symbolic art is another marker for a grave, the Egyptian pyramid:

> The pyramids present visually the simple image [*einfache Bild*] of symbolic art itself; they are enormous crystals which hold within themselves an inner meaning and, as external forms produced by art, they enclose that meaning such that it is apparent that they are there for this inner meaning which they have separated from pure nature and only in relation to this meaning. But this domain of death and the invisible, which here makes up the meaning, has only one side, a formal one, of the true content of art, which is to be carried away from immediate existence; and so this domain is first of all only Hades, not yet a life which, even if relieved of the sensuous as such, is still and at the same time self-existent and thereby in itself a free and living spirit. Thus the shape for such an inner meaning remains an utterly external form and covering for the definite content of that meaning. The pyramids are such an external setting in which an inner meaning rests concealed.[19]

---

[17]Hegel, *Werke* 13: 459.

[18]The task of architecture "consists in fashioning external inorganic nature in such a way that, as an artistically shaped external world, it enters into a relation with mind or spirit. Its material is matter itself in its immediate outward appearance as a mechanical heavy mass, and its forms remain the forms of inorganic nature, shaped according to the relations of the abstract understanding, that is, in relations of symmetry. In this material and in these forms the ideal, as concrete spirituality, cannot be realized: the outward reality presented in them remains an impenetrable externality opposed to the idea or relates to it only abstractly; thus the fundamental type of the art of architecture is the *symbolic* form of art" (Hegel, *Werke* 13: 116–7). The "idea" is the "absolute unity of the concept and objectivity," while the "ideal" refers to the "presentation" [*Darstellung*] of the idea in time as a convergence of spiritual content and form, or self-conscious spirit and its sensual appearance (Hegel, *Werke* 8: §213: 367). As we will see, Hegel's insight that the "ideal" articulation of the "idea" cannot be realized in time will have enormous consequences for political theory, linking democracy, political economy, and slavery (see Chapter 10).

[19]Hegel, *Werke* 13: 459–60.

The "obvious" meaning of the pyramids lies in this purposeful "concealment" of their meaning: they "put before our eyes" their removal of the dead from the visible world of the living.[20] As in the *Phenomenology*, what these buildings as a material division enclose is not spirit, but departed spirit—a body bereft of mind. The pyramids present themselves as a "shell" containing and preserving a corpse as its "kernel"; and by concentrating meaning on that embalmed corpse as the "enduring body and form" of a "departed spirit," they imply that the body is also a "shell," in this case for a lost "kernel."[21] Just as the pyramids preserve corpses removed from the world of life and light, so those bodies, by being preserved, refer to their former function as houses for souls removed from the world of nature. Concealed and preserved, "the dead acquires the content of the living. Divested of immediate existence, the dead, in its separation from life, still maintains its relation to the living, and in this concrete form it is made independent and preserved."[22] Indeed the "houses for the dead" [*Behausungen für Tote*] not only enclose, but symbolize corpses as houses for departed spirit: each pyramid is a "corporeal shell" [*leibliche Hülle*] placed round the dead person as an "architectonic enclosure."[23] While the pyramids and the dead both become "independent" symbols, they remain architecturally and linguistically entangled: as an enclosure of the negative, each depends on its physical position "inside" or "outside" the other, just as the houses for corpses and the corpses as houses can each be articulated only in terms of the other.

Moreover the two symbols negate each other's demarcation of the negative. The mutual entanglement of these symbols and the movable boundaries of the negative do not, however, belie the independence of either spirit or its symbols. For "independence" here does not arise from rigorous division, but from a simultaneous separation *and* relation of the sensuous and negative—in this case of the living and the dead, the visible and the invisible, body and soul, and nature and spirit. The barrier interposed between any two

---

[20]"With the Egyptians, however, the antithesis of the living and the dead comes out powerfully; the spiritual begins separating from the unspiritual. It is the advent of the concrete individual spirit. The dead are therefore held on to as something individual and equipped and preserved against the idea of dissolving into the natural … This honoring and safekeeping of the dead must mark for us the first important moment in the existence of spiritual individuality since here, instead of being given up, this individuality appears preserved, in that the body is esteemed and respected as this natural immediate individuality. As previously mentioned, Herodotus reports that the Egyptians were the first to have said that the souls of men were immortal … there is in the embalming of the body a strong sense of physical individuality and an actual existence separated from the body" (Hegel, *Werke* 14: 291).

[21]Pyramids are just "simple crystals, shells which enclose a kernel, a departed spirit, and serve to maintain as permanent its body and form. The whole meaning is focused on the sheltered dead, achieving representation for its own account; but architecture, which up to now had its meaning independently in itself as architecture, now becomes separated from meaning and, in this division, subordinate to something else" (Hegel, *Werke* 14: 294). The shell and its kernel, though counterparts making up a formal and conceptual whole, are temporally discontinuous, since the kernel belongs to an unrecoverably "departed" spirit. This temporal discontinuity of form and content represents, of course, the structure of the symbol.

[22]Hegel, *Werke* 13: 458.

[23]"It is therefore also of importance for architecture that [with the pyramids] there occurs at once the separation of the spiritual as the inner meaning which is represented for itself, while the corporeal shell is fashioned about it as a purely architectonic enclosure" (Hegel, *Werke* 14: 291–2).

of these terms cannot be traversed, as the pyramids close in upon themselves, offering neither opening nor passage into its interior realm of death.[24] But the true content of the pyramids does not lie on the other side of its walls, since the souls being remembered are not sensual and cannot be physically contained. Indeed, the "independence" of the pyramid as a symbol arises from a double negation: the removal from sight of what has already departed. The pyramids symbolize this capacity for revealing the force of what has been removed, for giving conceptual life to the dead, or for quickening what has ossified; more broadly, they emblematize the conceptual attempt to negate the exclusionary force of any binary. They erect a barrier between inside and outside, but derive meaning by further shifting interiority, attributing it to the corpses they conceal from view.[25] By materializing the binary, the pyramids reveal not only the negative, but also the power of the negative to subvert its defining binary. The pyramids thus reveal the "freedom" of the negative from the sensual world without fixing that division in a manner that would again abolish the negative; at the same time they reveal the negative as the very principle of fluidity that propels the dialectic. Discovering the freedom of the limit, the Egyptians accordingly reach the limit [*Schwelle*] of freedom.[26]

Hegel conveys this same relation of architecture, division, and freedom more generally in the *Encyclopedia*:

> All consciousness contains a unity and a dividedness, and therefore a contradiction [*Widerspruch*]; thus, for instance, the idea of "house" is completely contradictory to my "I" and yet [this contradiction] is endured. But mind endures contradiction because it knows that it contains no determination that it has not posited [*gesetzte*] itself, and that it cannot in turn cancel and sublate [*aufheben*]. This power over all content subsisting within the mind forms the basis of its freedom ... [A]ctual

---

[24]Hegel points out that the pyramids were sealed shut, with all entrances hidden; "this proves that the pyramids were to remain closed and not to be used again" (Hegel, *Werke* 14: 293).

[25]Architecture has its conceptual roots in enclosures that divide externality from interiority; architecture begins where such divisions are not merely functional, however, but rather supplanted by a larger division of external *form* and interior *meaning*. This *symbolic* division occurs in independent architectural works that hold their meaning in themselves, separating out and accenting their exteriority as enigmatic form (Hegel, *Werke* 14: 268–9). It is in this sense that, for Hegel, the task of architecture is to fashion exteriority such that it enters into relation with mind or spirit (Hegel, *Werke* 13: 116–7).

[26]For Hegel the Egyptians discover or reach "the threshold or frontier [*Schwelle*] of the realm of freedom"; while the pyramid's "liberation" of departed spirit "from sensuous nature" is not tantamount to life that is in itself "free and living spirit," the Egyptian pyramids come "very close" to being a true conception and symbol of freedom: with these structures "there first emerges in this higher way too the separation between nature and spirit, since it is not merely the natural which acquires independence for itself. The immortality of the soul lies very close to the freedom of the spirit, because [the conception of immortality implies that] the self comprehends itself as withdrawn from the naturalness of existence and as resting on itself; but this self-knowledge is the principle of freedom" (Hegel, *Werke* 13: 458–9). For a brilliant discussion of Hegel's relation of the pyramids to "freedom," see Claudia Brodsky Lacour, whose reading of the *Aesthetics* begins with the observation that the pyramids and Kantian philosophy, each isolating and preserving "freedom," are parallel moments in Hegel's history of the aesthetic ("From the Pyramids to Romantic Poetry: Housing the Spirit in Hegel," 332).

freedom [*die wirkliche Freiheit*] does not ... belong to mind immediately but emerges from mind's own activity.[27]

The interiority posited by the walls of a house does not accord with the interiority of an "I": the lines dividing "inside" and "outside" conflict. But this contradiction of binaries, because it arises from the mind, reveals the mind's power over all binaries. The mind's freedom lies precisely in this recognition of its ability to replace or overlay the lines demarcating forms, concepts, and names.

If the house in this passage from the *Encyclopedia* figures only incidentally in the elaboration of the mind's "freedom," the pyramid in the *Aesthetics* both symbolizes that freedom and heralds the freedom of the symbol. The pyramids, we found, make visible their demarcation of a space that cannot be seen, while relating the unseen, or more specifically the negative, to a sensual corollary. In other words, by housing an embalmed corpse and bringing to mind its departed spirit, the pyramids relate spirit and the bodies of living men; at the same time, the pyramids separate spirit from nature, affirming that the body, or any house, remains a form fundamentally inadequate to spirit. Like true symbols, the pyramids manifest externally their division of form and content even as they inextricably yoke the two together.

Moreover the pyramid, as the image [*Bild*] of the symbol, gives symbolic expression to the entanglement of inner and outer and, more specifically, of sensuous externality and spiritual negativity that lies at the core of the symbol. Thus Hegel explains the advent of the symbol proper in terms that echo the symbolism of the pyramid:

Inner and outer [or thought and external shapes] link up to form a closer bond, since every determining of the absolute is in itself already a beginning of an externalizing movement into expression. Every determination is inherent differentiation; but the external as such is always determinate and differentiated, and there is, therefore, a facet in which the external accords more with the meaning than in the phases we have looked at thus far. The first determination and negation of the absolute in itself, however, cannot be the free self-determination of the *spirit* as spirit, but is only the immediate negation. The immediate—which is also to say the natural—negation in its most comprehensive mode is *death* ... death has a double significance: on the one hand, it is precisely the immediate passing away of the natural; on the other it is the death of the *solely* natural and therefore the birth of something higher, something spiritual to which the merely natural dies in such a way that the spirit has this moment [of death] as belonging to its essence.[28]

The inherent differentiation of the external lends itself to closer affinities with "inner" determinations formulated by thought. But the initial positing of the "absolute," or spirit as a principle beyond mere sensuous externality, requires the negation of that externality in its

---

[27]Hegel, *Werke* 10: §382: 26–7.
[28]Hegel, *Werke* 13: 450–1.

immediate determination as nature. Thus the apprehension of the absolute in the sensuous world must occur by way of the symbol, a close but imperfect affinity between sensuous form and intellectual content, in which that intellectual content must moreover be negative.

The resulting relation of the symbol to division and death suggests a more essential relation between the symbol and the pyramid as its "simple image" [*einfache Bild*].[29] Amongst all tombs and mausoleums, pyramids are the "simplest constructions" [*einfachsten Konstruktionen*] because they externalize the purely abstract and mathematical principles of point, line, and plane:[30]

> [With the pyramids] there enters the line proper and essential to architecture, namely, the straight one; thus geometric regularity and abstract forms in general make their appearance. For architecture as a mere enclosure and as inorganic nature (i.e., nature that is not in itself individualized and animated by its indwelling spirit) can take shape only in a manner external to itself; but this external form is then not organic, but abstract and mathematical. And yet however much the pyramid already begins to have the character of a house, still the right angle does not dominate, as in a house proper; rather the pyramid has the purpose of containing itself within itself and thus, eschewing utility, runs in a line directly from the base to its point or tip [*Spitze*].[31]

While architecture in general draws its fundamentally symbolic character from the fact that it must manipulate "external inorganic nature" into mathematical "relations of symmetry,"[32] the pyramid specifically manifests the straight line as a movement from the plane of its "base" to the "point" of its apex.[33] The point, straight line, and plane as "inorganic" forms, by definition, do not occur in nature; for the same reason, they are also "external" to matter fashioned architecturally. Though they are external to externality (i.e., foreign to the sensual world), as dialectical forms of the limit [*Grenze*], they manifest and also provide an image of the differentiation of externality. Elsewhere Hegel glosses the limit as follows:

> [T]he limit [*Grenze*], as the negation of something reflected into itself, contains *ideally* within it the moments of something and other ... the limit is the non-being of the other, not of the something itself: at its limit, the something limits its other. But the other is itself a something in general; the limit which something

---

[29]Hegel, *Werke* 13: 459.

[30]Hegel, *Werke* 14: 295.

[31]Hegel, *Werke* 14: 295.

[32]Hegel, *Werke* 13: 117.

[33]So, too, the *Phenomenology*: "The crystals of pyramids and obelisks, simple [*einfache*] connections of straight lines with plane surfaces and equal proportion of parts, in which the incommensurability of the round is eliminated—these are the works of this work-master of strict form" (Hegel, *Werke* 3: 508–9). For Hegel it is the representation of the "simple" forms of abstract geometry that distinguishes the pyramids at Giza from mere step-pyramids; so essential is the line and "smooth surface" to the Egyptian spirit that Hegel surmises the step-pyramids in Egypt must have been left unfinished (Hegel, *Werke* 14: 294).

has against the other is also the limit of the other as a something, its limit by which it holds the first something as its other away from it, or is a *non-existence of that something*; hence it is not only the non-existence of the other, but also of the one and of the other something, therefore of the something in general ... the limit [*Grenze*] is simple [*einfache*] negation or the *first* negation, while the other is, at the same time, the negation of the negation ... It is in conformity with this difference of something from its limit that the line appears as line only outside its limit, the point; the plane as plane outside the line; the [animate or inanimate] body [*Körper*] as body only outside its limiting surface. This is the facet [*Seite*] of the limit that pictorial representation [*Vorstellung*] first grasps—the self-externality of the concept—particularly with respect to spatial objects.[34]

Conceptually the limit demarcates a concept or thing as a negation of its other; but by also demarcating the other, the limit at the same time negates the initial concept or thing. The limit marks the dialectical progression from undifferentiated self-externality to concrete space through the movement between point, line, plane, and solid [*Körper*],[35] each term negating and negated by the preceding or succeeding term.[36] Now, the limit as difference, or the negation and double negation that constitute the demarcation of a spatial thing, cannot be reproduced faithfully in sensuous form, since difference itself has no exact sensual corollary. Similarly, point, line, and plane as images externalize, but also negate their conceptual negativity as the thought of non-dimensionality or dimensionality. In this respect, point, line, and plane, inorganic and so unprecedented in nature, are strictly and fundamentally non-representational, imitating or reproducing

---

[34]Hegel, *Werke* 5: 136ff.

[35]For a discussion of point, line, and plane in terms of the differentiation and concretization of externality, see Hegel, *Werke* 9: *Die Naturphilosophie* §256: 44–7 and §312: 204.

[36]"The point is therefore the limit of the line, not merely in the sense that the line only ceases in the point, and as a determinate being outside it; neither is the line the limit of the plane merely in the sense that the plane only ceases in it—and similarly with surfaces as limit of the solid; on the contrary, in the point the line also *begins*; the point is its absolute beginning. Even when the line is represented as unlimited on either side, or, as it is put, is produced to infinity, the point still constitutes its *element*, just as the line is the element of the plane, and the surface that of the solid. These limits are the *principle* of that which they limit ... the other determination is the unrest of the something in its limit in which it is immanent, an unrest which is the *contradiction* which impels the something out beyond itself. Thus the point is this dialectic of its own self to become a line, the line the dialectic to become a plane, and the plane the dialectic to become total space ... That point, line and plane by themselves are self-contradictory, are *beginnings* which spontaneously repel themselves from themselves, so that the point, through its Notion, passes out of itself into the line, *moves in itself* and gives rise to the line, and so on, lies in the Notion of limit which is immanent in the something. The application itself, however, belongs to the consideration of space; to give an indication of it here, the point is the wholly abstract limit, *but in a determinate being*; this is taken as still wholly abstract, it is so-called absolute, that is, abstract *space*, a purely continuous asunderness. But the limit is not abstract negation, but is *in this determinate being*, is a *spatial* determinateness; the point is, therefore, spatial, the contradiction of abstract negation and continuity, and is, therefore, the transition, the accomplished transition into the line, and so on; just as also, for the same reason, *there is* no such thing as a point, line, or plane" (Hegel, *Science of Logic*, transl. A. V. Miller [Amherst: Humanity Books, 1969], 128–9).

nothing in the world: "*there is* no such thing as a point, line, or plane."[37] Regardless, Hegel implies a distinction between conceptualizing the point, line, or plane as abstract, mathematical, and non-existent principles and drawing a point, line, or plane.

Any such illustrative representation or image [*Vorstellung*], as the positive or concrete corollary to a negative or abstract form, could only be said to be symbolic of the dialectical and differentiating movement of the limit. Likewise the pyramid, as an expression of all these forms and especially of the straight line "proper and essential to architecture," "seizes a representation" of the differentiating limit not as its mimetic reproduction, but as its symbol.[38] Erecting not just a wall or enclosure, the pyramid is the "simplest" manifestation of the symbol because it externalizes the limit as "simple negation" [*einfache Negation*], the first differentiation of pure space; likewise as the "simplest construction" [*einfachste Konstruktion*], it manifests architecture essentially and in its most essential, symbolic mode. Inner and outer, thought and sensuous externality, spirit and nature, and life and death are brought into symbolic affinities most fundamentally through the sensory manifestation of the pyramid because the pyramid is the sensory manifestation of the limit. Since it is also the "image" of the symbol "proper" (where "proper" signifies an impenetrability of the limits of the concept), the pyramid can be called the symbol of the symbol,[39] the symbol of the limit, and indeed the limit of the symbol, to the extent that it marks, in Hegel's theoretical history of art, the "beginning" of the symbol "proper."[40]

In accordance with the dialectical movement of Hegel's narrative, the human form concealed by the pyramid must find sensuous expression. Thus symbolism proper proceeds from (i) pyramidal structures to (ii) animal forms (in Egyptian death-masks and hieroglyphic writing) to (iii) near-human statues (such as Memnons and sphinxes) that still represent "the inner element of subjectivity" outside themselves.[41] As Hegel

---

[37]Hegel, *Science of Logic*, 129. Hegel's italicization of "*there is*" in this negative phrase asserts both the existence and non-existence of these forms of the limit, in accordance with its own double inscription of being and negation.

[38]It is worth noting, incidentally, that the pyramid could equally serve as a symbol for the progression of art, as Hegel describes it, from a three-dimensional solid in architecture and sculpture to a two-dimensional "plane" in painting and finally to a vanishing "point" in music and poetry (Hegel, *Werke* 13: 121–3).

[39]Here Hegel likens the pyramid and the sphinx, respectively the beginning and end of "proper" unconscious symbolism. Where the pyramid is the visual symbol of the symbol, the sphinx is "the symbol of the symbolic itself" (Hegel, *Werke* 13: 465). Posing the riddle "What walks on four legs in the morning, two in the afternoon, and three in the evening?"—the solution being "man"—the sphinx verbally articulates the problematic of symbolic art as such—the relation of architectural form or linguistic expression to self-conscious man. But it is the pyramid that emblematizes essentially the form or structure of the symbol.

[40]Hegel carefully stakes out the limits of the symbol, arguing that "for the more specific classification [*Einteilung*] of the symbolic form of art, here we must ascertain the limits [*Grenzpunkte*] within which the development progresses" (Hegel, *Werke* 13: 407). While he attempts to settle on broader or "narrower" (Hegel, *Werke* 13: 408) boundaries, ultimately the limit must come from within the concept of the symbol. And with respect to the symbol "proper," the limit lies precisely with the architectural manifestation of the limit in the form of the pyramid. Only the pyramid—appearing to erect impenetrable limits and to stand non-dialectically against dissolution and history—underwrites the proper limits of the symbol.

[41]Hegel, *Werke* 13: 462. Here again we should note the symbolic structure of Hegel's own narrative, centering as it does on the appearance of self-consciousness in human form: the human body thus emerges first as a dead corpse hidden in a tomb, then in animal form, and gradually in shapes increasingly human.

intimates in the *Phenomenology* and will make explicit in the *Aesthetics*, all of these forms remain architectural because of their symbolic and hence imperfect relation of form and content: indeed, only a sculptural representation of the human body as an expression of the individuality and self-conscious spirit would harmonize form and content and so attain to the rank of pure sculpture, which Hegel associates with classical, Greek art.[42]

Hegel argues, by way of a famous claim that has been properly understood only recently, that such a congruity of form and content cannot find any temporally sustainable exterior expression; form and content must remain temporally discontinuous.[43] Thus Hegel asserts in the *Aesthetics* that "art in the form of its highest determination [*nach der Seite ihrer höchsten Bestimmung*] is and remains for us a thing of the past."[44] Rather than declaring art as such dead for all time, Hegel here refers specifically to art "in the form" (or literally "on the side") of its "highest" or "ideal" determination in classical Greek art. This art must be "past" not only in the historical sense, but also in the more radical sense that the ideal unity of form and content cannot be seized in the present any more than, in Hegel's analysis of sense-perception, the "This" can be taken "now."[45] The universal and particular, the "idea" of self-conscious spirit and its sensory appearance, meaning and shape, form and content remain always fundamentally incommensurate. The term "classical," one might add, already suggests the intrinsic pastness of a work: newly made art is usually only called "classical" if it rehearses more than it breaks from the art of the past.

Hegel's statements on the "end of art" as such[46] have been misread in part because of a misunderstanding of what he frames as the conceptual "advance" of spirit past art toward religion and philosophy—a dialectical movement that has everything to do with history but nothing whatever to do with chronology: as Hegel writes, "chronological difference holds no interest at all for thought" [*der Zeitunterschied hat ganz und gar kein Interesse für den Gedanken*].[47] Though it is easy to be misled by his seemingly nostalgic tone, Hegel makes quite clear that he is not devalorizing the present: "No Homer, Sophocles, etc., no Dante, Ariosto, or Shakespeare can emerge in our time … Only the present is fresh, all else is paler and paler."[48] Moreover the pastness of classical or "proper" art—indeed of the art of the past—does not negate the future possibility of symbolic or romantic forms of art—or indeed of some higher imbrication of these. While the "form

---

[42]Hegel, *Werke* 14: 298, 275.

[43]For further discussion of Hegel's views on the pastness of art proper, see de Man, *Aesthetic Ideology*, 102–3 and Brodsky Lacour, "From the Pyramids to Romantic Poetry: Housing the Spirit in Hegel," 346–7.

[44]Hegel, *Werke* 13: 25.

[45]Hegel, *Werke* 3: 82–92. Hegel identifies the "ideal" Greek attempt to render God as man, or man as God, in the mimetic art of sculpture as the quintessentially classical attempt to realize the "idea" of self-conscious spirit in time (see the discussion of "ideal artists" of Greece "shaping themselves" through statues of the human body in Hegel, *Werke* 14: 374). But this "ideal" articulation of the idea cannot constitute a sustainably present articulation of the aesthetic.

[46]As we will see, the notion of an "end," ultimately indistinguishable from a "beginning," remains an immanent element in every historical moment, including the moment in which history is written.

[47]Hegel, *Werke* 9: §249: 32.

[48]Hegel, *Werke* 14: 238.

of art," in its proper articulation in classical statues, is no longer "of spiritual interest,"[49] the present possibilities of art lie precisely in its freedom from restrictive forms and in the heterogeneity of its materials: writing at the moment of what, from his relative contemporary perspective, must be the provisional end of aesthetic history, Hegel writes that

> all materials, regardless of what they are and from what time and nation they arise, receive their artistic truth only when filled with living and present interest … It is the appearance and work of imperishable humanity in its many-sided significance and infinite all-round development that, in this vessel of human situations and sensations, can now make up the absolute content of our art.[50]

Classical art "finds" a "complete unity of inner meaning and outer form" in the "representation of substantial individuality," but then loses that harmony by unveiling the fundamental incommensurability of sensuous externality to spiritual content.[51] By contrast symbolic architecture, built to withstand the passage of time, continues to seek that unity by making its "highly varied and changing" meaning contingent on the interpretation of any present observer.[52] The symbol lacks any specific "content, fixed in itself": its outward form, despite its material fixity, thus maintains a necessarily imperfect affinity with any particular content.[53] More to the point, as we have seen with its quintessential, pyramidal articulation, the symbol proper manifests that imperfect affinity by revealing the unstable limit or self-negating binary between form and content. Classical art, by "finding" what cannot be temporally maintained, arrives at a dialectically untenable point of finality and stasis; it belongs therefore to an unrecuperable past. By contrast symbolic architecture expresses the fluidity of the binary, marking the necessity of a future, interpretive observer even as it banishes hermeneutic finality. Thus the limit, in its architectural expression as straight line and plane, informs all expressions of "proper" symbolism: Egyptian statue works "cannot do away with the straight and regular in walls, gates, beams, obelisks, etc.," but must have recourse to an "architectonic [*architektonisch*] arrangement," namely the "uniformity of size, regularity in distance from one another, a rectilinear arrangement of rows, and generally to the order and regularity of architecture proper"; likewise Hegel writes that these shapes are extended "into colossal and massive forms, lined up into rows, embellished with added walls, divisions, gates, and passages, such that what is sculptural about them is treated utterly

---

[49]See Hegel, *Werke* 13: 61, 141.

[50]Hegel, *Werke* 14: 239.

[51]"In this way symbolic art *seeks* that complete unity of inner meaning and outer form which classical art *finds* in the representation of substantial individuality for sensory observation" (Hegel, *Werke* 13: 392). But by finding the external shape adequate to spirit, classical art reveals sensuous externality as such to be fundamentally opposed to spiritual content (Hegel, *Werke* 14: 127).

[52]Hegel, *Werke* 14: 275.

[53]Hegel, *Werke* 14: 275.

architecturally. The Egyptian sphinxes, Memnons, and enormous temples belong to this group."[54]

What then, of the middle term in Hegel's three-part progression of the symbol proper? What would be the relation of the limit and the animal form of the hieroglyph? Here again the surviving version of Hegel's lectures can be read profitably alongside the *Phenomenology*. According to "The Work-master," after the pyramid's elimination of "roundness"[55] in favor of straight lines and rectilinear forms, buildings begin to resemble nature, melding inorganic regularity and organic "curvature" [*Rundung*], a dialectic resolved in the straight and curved lines of the animal hieroglyph.[56] But the hieroglyph progresses from the representation of natural forms to the expression of conceptions: the animal shape becomes "the hieroglyph of a thought" [*Hieroglyphe ... eines Gedankens*]. By implication, through this process the hieroglyph subverts the organic character of its form: as the animal hieroglyph no longer represents an animal, the straight and curved lines making up its image take on increasingly independent force as the external expression of thought. What is at stake in this dialectical progression is the status of writing as drawing and engraving: on the one hand, its lines serve to reproduce shapes in the world; on the other hand, these material shapes externalize the non-representational dimension of thought itself. Reflecting its first, representational mode, the hieroglyph evolves to take on the shape apposite to thought, the round, human form of the statues before the sun. But since the hieroglyph also externalizes thought in non-representational form, this organic expression remains inadequate.[57] Ultimately the dialectical tension between its non-representational and organic modes manifests itself in the architectonic, linear arrangement of the round, human Memnons. Thus Hegel instantiates how this evolved and now explicitly discursive work, despite its mimetic character and roundness, remains architectural and not sculptural.

In what sense does the hieroglyph materialize the non-representational dimension of thought? Because the lines of the hieroglyph become superfluous to the represented animal, even its curves, as forms of the line, take on an architectonic quality. As we have seen, Hegel already characterizes the hieroglyph as a dwelling [*Wohnung*] in the *Phenomenology*; in his later lectures, he explicitly identifies the hieroglyph as a form of symbolic architecture, and symbolic architecture as a kind of hieroglyph:

---

[54]Hegel, *Werke* 14: 298, 275.

[55]Hegel, *Werke* 3: 508.

[56]Hegel, *Werke* 3: 509–510.

[57]Since the work-master recognizes the animal shape as his own work, it is "superseded and becomes the hieroglyph of another meaning, the hieroglyph of a thought. Hence this shape is no longer solely and entirely used by the worker, but becomes blended with the shape embodying thought—the human form" of the Memnon (Hegel, *Werke* 3: 510). Just as the hierolgyph manifests the material externality of thought, so too, with respect to the Memnon, the outside sun will trigger a sound that will be a merely physical, "outer" expression of thought (Hegel, *Werke* 3: 510). The hieroglyph, the sound issuing from the statue, and the statue itself all remain inadequate to thought.

The excellence of the Egyptian spirit lies in the fact that it stands before us as a prodigious work-master [*Werkmeister*]. It seeks neither splendor, diversion, nor pleasure, but is instead compelled to comprehend itself; and it has no other material or ground to work on, in order to teach itself what it is and realize itself for itself, than this working out its thoughts in stone. And what it engraves on the stone are its riddles—these hieroglyphs. They are of two types: hieroglyphs proper, which aim at expressing language and relate to subjective conception; the other hieroglyphs are those enormous masses of architecture and sculpture with which Egypt is covered.[58]

Conceived as a sheer engraving in stone, and no longer as a mere image "designed to express language," the hieroglyph can be identified with other essentially non-representational work in stone—the massive symbolic architecture and architectonic sculpture that cover Egypt. Laid out in rows over the landscape, the symbolic buildings of Egypt appear as a text spaced carefully across a page. Not only do these productions give the landscape the form of a book, but the architectural works, covered with hieroglyphs, are themselves "pages of a book" or even "*substitutes* for books."[59] More than just eluding representation, architectural and linguistic hieroglyphs as "engraving" actively subvert mimesis: as books within books, hieroglyphs within hieroglyphs—these works subvert the limits and unity of purported totalities of knowledge. The physical demarcations of script—the form of the book, the space around a hieroglyph—give only the impression of unity, as the content necessarily exceeds the strict limit implied by the form.

Furthermore, as both symbols and surfaces for symbols, buildings point to the negativity of material inscription or engraving: thoughts "worked out in stone" or upon any physical surface both leave a mark and clear a space—material effects that are not in themselves representational but that may, for instance, efface earlier marks or inflect other hieroglyphs "designed to express language." As parts "substitute" for the whole, so too hieroglyphs upon architectural surfaces substitute for buildings, and the buildings again for the land they cover as a book. Architectural and linguistic hieroglyphs displace each other both in stone and in the language of Hegel's text, further blurring the line between "engraving" and "expressing": indeed "engraving," as a form of negative expression, "expresses" as much as it merely accompanies a representation. Thus the hieroglyph, in its architectural dimension, makes visible the material or non-representational dimension of language, revealing the cancellation, displacement, and subversion that attend and actively contaminate any representation.

The hieroglyph becomes, then, the symbol *par excellence* for the conflation of architecture and language: "In Egypt, overall, almost every shape is a symbol and

---

[58]Hegel, *Werke* 12: 265.

[59]Hegel, *Werke* 14: 283–4 (emphasis mine). The Egyptian temple-precincts, Hegel continues, proliferate "en masse": "this prodigious architecture," "enclosed by walls," is "without roofing, gates, or passages between divisions"; "whole forests of columns" form "labyrinths" that "substitute for books because they convey their meanings not by their mode of configuration but by the writings, images engraved on their surface ..." The walls, with Memnons leaning on them, are "bedecked all over with hieroglyphs or huge pictures in stone ... like the pages of a book" (ibid.).

hieroglyph not signifying itself but indicating something else with which it has kinship and therefore a relation."[60] But while the hieroglyph, whether architectural or linguistic, functions principally as a symbol, still at a certain level it retains the accidental character of a sign. Now, Hegel defines the sign as a purely "arbitrary connection" of expression and meaning, or form and content.[61] And most hieroglyphs, he writes, represent an animal not to denote it, but to indicate the first sound of the animal's name: "the hieroglyphic script of the Egyptians is largely symbolic … more often [than designating a concept], in its so-called phonetic element this writing indicates the particular letters by depicting an object whose initial letter, when spoken, has the same sound as the one to be expressed."[62] The hieroglyph functions "largely" as a symbol since the image relates necessarily but imperfectly to the animal, but also in part as a sign, since the relation of the animal's image to its sound is purely arbitrary. As a dialectical advance over the pure symbolism of the pyramid, the hieroglyph in fact marks, in the course of Hegel's theoretical history, the emergence, however partial, of the discursive sign. In this respect, the hieroglyph marks the entanglement of not only architecture and language, or inscription and speech, but also the symbol and the sign.

To be sure, Hegel insists on the distinctness of the symbol and the sign as modes of relating form and content. But from the beginning of the *Aesthetics*—and we would expect no less of a dialectical system—he recognizes points of fluidity between the symbol and the sign:

1. Now the symbol is in the first place a sign [*Zeichen*]. In a pure designation [*Bezeichnung*], however, the connection between meaning and its expression is totally arbitrary. In this case, the expression, this sensuous thing or image, represents not itself, but rather a foreign content with which the image need not stand in a relation of particular affinity. So in languages, for instance, sounds are a sign of some conception, feeling, etc. but with respect to content, the predominant part of the sounds in a language is linked by accident with the ideas they represent, even if it can be shown, by an historical development, that the original connection was of another sort; and the difference among languages consists particularly in the fact that the same idea is expressed by different sounds … When the symbol is considered in this sense of indifference between meaning and designation [*Bezeichnung*], [i.e., as a sign], we may not take account of it in reference to *art*, since art in general consists in the relation, kinship, and concrete coimbrication [*konkreten Ineinander*] of meaning and form.

2. It is different, then, when a sign is to be a *symbol* …. The symbol is no merely arbitrary sign, but a sign which in its externality [consists of and] relates at the same time the content of the idea to which it gives outward form.[63]

---

[60]Hegel, *Werke* 13: 461.
[61]Hegel, *Werke* 13: 394.
[62]Hegel, *Werke* 13: 461.
[63]Hegel, *Werke* 13: 395–6.

While the "predominant part" of the sounds of a language has no affinity to the thoughts they express, Hegel leaves room for the exceptions: any sign that retains its historically determined affinity of sound and thought (as with onomatopoeia or paronomasia), and any sign that generates meaning through an artistic exploitation of sound (as with euphony or rhyme).[64] Where history or art implies a "kinship" or genetic relation of form and content, the "purely" and properly "formal"[65] sign relates sound to an absolutely "foreign" content. Far from marginalizing the symbol in language, Hegel indicates that any sign can become a symbol by virtue of an artistic determination: thus he lays out the condition for a sign to be a symbol. Indeed, to begin with he ascribes semiotic purity to a "predominant part" not of the signs, but of the sounds of a language. Only usage determines or motivates a sound, and most sounds in their prevalent rather than artistic usage relate arbitrarily to meaning. Nowhere stating that specific names, as sounds, remain impervious to symbolic use, Hegel on the contrary acknowledges the symbolic capacity of the sign, as well as the signifying capacity of the symbol.

In the course of Hegel's theoretical history of the symbol, it is the hieroglyph that first manifests discursively the interpenetration of the symbol and sign. The hieroglyph, both a symbol for a name and a sign for a sound—that is, a letter—presents the name and letter as internally subversive, dialectical counterparts. Now, the letter as a sign at once depends upon and replaces the name of the animal symbolically evoked by the image. Etched in lines upon a material surface, the hieroglyph in its architectural dimension—as an inscribed letter—suspends the articulation of the animal name: thus the letter displaces the name, sign displaces symbol, inscription displaces speech, architecture displaces language. Nonetheless, the animal persists: even with the concatenation of hieroglyphs in a phonetically written word, the hieroglyphs remain names and symbols—names that haunt each letter in the phonetic chain, symbols that inhabit, manifestly, the deciphered sign.

If the pyramid marks the birth of the symbol, and the hieroglyph the partial birth of the sign, the statue before the sun marks the sign's attempt to overcome its subjection to the symbol.[66] Standing dumb before the horizon, unable to articulate meaningful sound, the "dwelling" that Hegel does not name in writing but identifies in his lectures manifests the temporal discontinuity of architectonics and speech. At the same time,

---

[64]For discussions of or references to onomatopoeia, see Hegel, *Werke* 10: §459: 271–2; for puns, see Hegel, *Werke* 8: §96: 204–205; for euphony, see Hegel, *Werke* 15: *Vorlesungen über die Ästhetik III*, 228–9; for assonance, alliteration, and rhyme, see Hegel, *Werke* 15: 303–18. Hegel discusses each of these cases in relation to semiotics in general or to the symbolic interplay of form and content.

[65]Hegel, *Werke* 13: 396.

[66]True enough, as Derrida points out, "the Egyptian hieroglyph will furnish the example of that which resists the movement of dialectics, history, and logos" in the *Encyclopedia* and in the *Philosophische Propädeutik* (*Margins of Philosophy*, 83). But in such texts Hegel, in the course of a polemic against a universal, ideogrammatic language, considers the hieroglyph only as a pictorial representation and not as a phonetic referent (Hegel, *Werke* 10: §459: 273–6; *Philosophische Propädeutik*, in *Sämtliche Werke* [Stuttgart: Frommans, Verlag, 1957], 3: §161: 211). In his reading of the hieroglyph in Hegel, Derrida ignores its explicitly dialectical appearance in the *Phenomenology* and hurries through its appearance in the lectures on art and history, where, as I have shown, the hieroglyph initiates the dialectical history of the discursive sign and its emergence from the symbol.

the Memnon as a dialectical evolution of the pyramid and hieroglyph gestures at the possibility of reconciling the symbol and the sign, or buildings and names. As a three-dimensional hieroglyph approximating the human form, the Memnon thus strains to translate the power of symbolic architecture—of the engraved letter, the chiseled figure—into the human language of signs. Such a synthesis of symbol and sign, rather than reducing the former to an impalpable articulation, would harness into spoken language the power of the laboring hand as it razes the ground, carves stone, and erects its masonry. Indeed it is the "unique purpose" of architecture "to show an inorganic nature built by human hands."[67] In this sense, the architectonic Memnon, laboring to speak, holds forth the promise of a name that builds.

Figure 1 *The Colossi of Memnon*. Etching by Baltard. Based on a drawing by Dutertre. *Description de l'Egypte* (Paris: Imprimerie impériale, 1809), Vol. II, Plate 20, 1809.

---

[67] The pyramids in particular reveal this "unique purpose" of architecture: "Dazu gehört nun wesentlich, daß die Architektur sich nicht nur eingrabe und Höhlen bilde, sondern sich als eine unorganische Natur zeige, von Menschenhänden da hingebaut, wo man ihrer, um ihres Zweckes willen, nötig hat" (Hegel, *Werke* 14: 294).

CHAPTER 3
FROM MEMNON TO MNEMOSYNE

Declaiming before the sun, the Memnon utters apparently incomprehensible noise. Its abortive sign still draws symbolic significance, however, from Hegel's narrative. In this respect, the sounding Memnon figures the failure of the sign and its subjection to the symbol. How does the resurgence of the symbol inflect the status of the symbolic narrative in Hegel's corpus and in general as a mode of philosophy? What are the implications of this narrative of the failed sign on Hegel's theory of language?

Answering these questions will ultimately require following the dialectics at play—of light and sound, of spirit and body—as they move past the Memnon in Hegel's theoretical history of art. But we must first pause over another dialectic of the sign, this time in the *Encyclopedia*, that rehearses the progression from symbol to sign and, indeed, from pyramid to Memnon in the *Phenomenology* and the *Aesthetics*:

> Now the general idea, freed from the content of the image, in making its *arbitrarily* selected external materials into something intuitively perceivable, produces what has to be called a *sign*—in particular distinction to the symbol. The sign must be declared something great, a major advance. Intelligence, in designating something by a sign, has finished with the content of intuition, and has bestowed upon the sensuous material a soul or signification *foreign* to it … The *sign* is some immediate intuition that introduces significance totally different from what the sign has for itself materially; it is the *pyramid* to which a foreign soul [*eine fremde Seele*] is translated [*versetzt*] and preserved.[1]

For Hegel the sign marks a new level of intellectual freedom—the freedom to choose from a range of sensory material to express a particular idea. If that freedom is limited by an unsuspected aptness or affinity of sound and content, Hegel continues, the intelligence may nonetheless treat the material "as its own property," "erasing the content which properly and particularly belongs to it and granting it a different content for its soul and significance. This sign-creating activity may be specifically termed *productive* memory [*Gedächtnis*] (the principally abstract Mnemosyne), since memory, which is commonly mistaken for or taken as synonymous with recollection [*Erinnerung*], and even conception and imagination, has in general to do only with signs."[2] This dense

---

[1]Hegel, *Werke* 10: §457–8: 269–70. Emphasis in original.
[2]Hegel, *Werke* 10: §458: 270–1.

account of the sign prompts another round of questions: Why does Hegel, in the course of distinguishing the sign from the symbol, emblematize the sign as a *pyramid*, the very prototype of the symbol itself?[3] Why does he attribute to memory the capacity to appropriate sensuous material and strip it of antecedent connotations? How does this power enable memory to produce the pyramidal sign? And how does this account of the advent of the pyramidal sign compare to the abortive symbolic narratives from pyramid to spoken sign, as I have bracketed them, in the *Phenomenology* and in the *Aesthetics*?

Here we must patiently follow Hegel through his dialectical narrative, involving as it does one of the "most difficult points" of his system—namely, the relation of memory, via the sign, to thought.[4] Now, Hegel distinguishes recollection, in the sense of a mental souvenir or image taken from a particular time and place, from the faculty of memory.[5] Rather than associating signs with images, memory separates the sign from the thing to which it refers. Thus to understand the name lion, "we require neither the physical sight of the animal, nor even its image."[6] The sign, reduced to a mere name in which the sound and meaning are perfectly conjoined, thus takes the place of the thing. But the sign becomes totally interiorized by the subject through this process, such that its meaning loses its independence and becomes entirely contingent on the subject. At the same time, the name remains purely independent in its external, material form; and since this materiality inhabits the mental faculty of memory, the name in effect alienates the mind from its interiority and subjectivity:

---

[3]It is this passage from the *Encyclopedia* that prompts Paul de Man to state incorrectly that the pyramid "connotes, to a reader of Hegel, the emblem of the sign as opposed to the symbol ... the deliberate forgetting of substantial, aesthetic, and pictorial symbols" (*The Resistance to Theory*, 69–70). To a reader of the *Aesthetics*, anyway, the pyramid is, as I have already shown, the quintessential emblem or symbol of the symbol; it can further be said to be the symbol of the sign or, for that matter, the sign of the symbol only retrospectively, in light of their discursive coimbrication in later moments of the dialectic. For a discussion of the relation of the pyramid to Hegel's semiology, see Derrida's "The Pit and the Pyramid: Introduction to Hegel's Semiology", in *Margins of Philosophy*, transl. Alan Bass (Chicago: University of Chicago Press, 1982), 71–108. While Derrida's essay has the considerable merit of pointing out many of the important texts relevant to a discussion of Hegel's theory of language, he focuses principally on Hegel's valorization of speech over writing, and of phonetic over other forms of writing. My purpose, taking cues from Derrida here and from de Man's "Sign and Symbol in Hegel's *Aesthetics*" in *Aesthetic Ideology*, 91–104, is to follow Hegel's dialectical procedure in the history of the symbol in the *Aesthetics* and of both symbol and sign in the "Anthropology" and "Psychology" sections of the *Encyclopedia* in order to flush out Hegel's theory of language, which will be shown to be much more nuanced than at least Derrida allows.

[4]Hegel, *Werke* 10: §464: 283. My review of Hegel's relation of memory and thought here rehearses and then takes as its point of departure Paul de Man's brief but remarkable discussion of memory [*Gedächtnis*] in "Sign and Symbol in Hegel's *Aesthetics*," in *Aesthetic Ideology*, 101–2.

[5]Hegel echoes the Aristotelian distinction between *mnēmē*, memory or the possession of the past, and *anamnēsis*, or the recollection of the past; as Aristotle writes, "it is clearly possible to remember what is not presently recalled" [*phaneron hoti mnēmoneuein esti mē nun anamnēsthenta*] (*Peri Mnēmes kai Anamnēseōs*, in *Aristotle's On the Soul; and On Memory and Recollection*; transl. Joe Sachs [Santa Fe, New Mexico: Green Lion Press, 2001], 450a 31). See also *On Memory* 449b *passim*.

[6]Hegel, *Werke* 10: §462: 278.

Thus in filling itself with the word, intelligence takes into itself the nature of the thing. But this assimilation [of the thing] has, at the same time, the sense that intelligence thereby makes itself objective, taking on the quality of a thing, and in such a way that subjectivity, in its distinction from the thing, becomes something quite empty, a mindless [*geistlosen*] container of words—that is, a *mechanical memory* [*mechanischen Gedächtnis*]. In this way the *excess* [*Übermaß*] of remembered words can, so to speak, turn around to become the total surrendering and *relinquishing* [*Entäußerung*] of intelligence. The more familiar I become with the meaning of the word, and the more that this merges with my inwardness, the more, then, can the objectivity and definiteness of meaning disappear—and consequently the more can memory [*Gedächtnis*] itself, and with it the word, become something bereft of mind [*Geistverlassenem*].[7]

At first, the sign maintains the division between interiority and exteriority: the meaning of the sign rests with the subject, while the objective "thing" to which the sign refers remains in the world. Ultimately, however, the sign marks the radical break between subjectivity and the mental function of memory: once words become so deeply internalized as to be mechanically instrumentalized, the memory no longer subsists in subjective determinations of meaning. And since the words, in the process of interiorization, have already sloughed off their objective referents, the memory harboring them consists in nothing but the words bereft of meaning: thus the memory and its words become "mindless."

The dialectical argument here accords with the psychological phenomenon through which the repetition of a word can lead to a moment of radical alienation from its meaning, as with the use of a mantra to enter into a state of trance.[8] Hegel's explicit example of the estranging effect of memory is the psychological "miracle" of memorization. When we memorize texts, we register the names or words not according to their individual meaning, but based on their position within a series of words, whether in a spoken chain or on a page. Thus memorization registers words independently of their meaning, reducing them to their materiality:

As everyone knows, a text can be completely learned by heart [*auswendig*] only when one connects no meaning to the words. A recitation of something learned by heart therefore becomes monotonous or accentless by its very nature. The right accent, if it is brought in, evokes the meaning: but the interjection of the meaning or idea upsets the mechanical connection [between mind and text] and therefore easily confuses the reciter. The ability to memorize rows [*Reihen*] of words, where no law regulates their sequence, or which are individually meaningless (as with a succession of proper names), is so miraculous, because it is the very essence

---

[7]Hegel, *Werke* 10: §462: 280.

[8]The example is mine, not Hegel's. The mind acquires a language precisely through this process of repeating unknown words.

of the mind to inhere in itself; whereas in this case the mind is alienated from itself, and its action is that of a machine. It is only as a unity of subjectivity and objectivity, however, that the mind inheres in itself; while here … [the mind] as memory makes itself external to itself.[9]

Droning through a composition by rote, a reciter must abandon his presence of mind, relinquishing it to the mechanical competence of the faculty of memory. Processing an aural chain of sound or visualized rows [*Reihen*] of written names, the mind not only reduces those names to objects, but itself becomes a mechanical "thing," subsisting only in the sheer materiality of names, the exterior objectivity of material sound or script.[10] As sound or script mechanically rather than meaningfully arranged, memorized names are the instruments of thought; indeed "it is in names that we think."[11] But memory, effacing the subject and emptying thought of all but the material form of names, in turn instrumentalizes thought: for memory alone is the "external mode or existential moment of thought."[12] Thus when Hegel writes that the mechanical memory, consisting of only meaningless words, takes on "the quality of a thing" or becomes "objective,"[13] he literally identifies—in the material remnant of words bereft of meaning—the external manifestation of mind.[14]

For Hegel the reduction of the subject to an automaton or machine in the course of memorization discloses not only a particular capability of the mind, but also the fundamental bridge between thought and externality.[15] In other words, the mental function of mechanical memory, though more evident in certain psychological states, underwrites the quotidian "familiarity" with language and its routine, habitual use.

---

[9]Hegel, *Werke* 10: §463: 281.

[10]In his reading, de Man emphasizes the inherence of the mechanical mind in the writing of words: "Memory, for Hegel, is the learning by rote of *names*, or of words considered as names, and it cannot therefore be separated from the inscription, or the writing down of those names. In order to remember, one is forced to write down what one is likely to forget. The idea, in other words, makes it sensory appearance, in Hegel, as the material inscription of names" (*Aesthetic Ideology*, 102). Here de Man ignores the materiality of the voice, hence the dialectic of voice and inscription central to Hegel's argument and to his dialectic of symbol and sign. But de Man's statement that memory requires the *physical* act of writing—aside from being superfluous to the logic of his argument, and at least contestable in the case of oral cultures—misrepresents Hegel, who emphasizes the objective inherency of the voice and of writing in each other and *in* the mechanical memory. Memory does not "require" writing; rather writing, no less than the voice, *is* and hence *always was* memory. These claims will be supported and developed in detail below.

[11]"Es ist in Namen, daß wir denken" (Hegel, *Werke* 10: §462: 278).

[12]"Das Gedächtnis als solches ist selbst die nur äußerliche Weise, das einseitige Moment der Existenz des Denkens" (Hegel, *Werke* 10: §464: 283).

[13]Memory "is itself this externality"; it is "mechanical" (Hegel, *Werke* 10: §463: 282).

[14]As de Man points out, this external manifestation of mind corresponds to the sensuous manifestation of the idea in the *Aesthetics* (*Aesthetic Ideology* 102–3). As we have seen, the claim, not only in the *Aesthetics* but also in the *Phenomenology*, that the human body is the only shape adequate to thought—indeed, the form of thought [*Gestalt des Gedankens*]—must be read alongside Hegel's larger claim that "art, in its highest determination" as the form of the human body, "is for us a thing of the past." As the "sensuous manifestation of the idea," art, if it is to occur at all, can only do so as the symbolic externality of thought, of the mind as machine.

[15]Hegel, *Werke* 10: §463: 281–2.

The ability to memorize names stems from the sign's arbitrary relation of sensuous material (sounds or letters) and meaning; and it is this severability of the sensuous material from its meaning that justifies Hegel's claim that the faculty of memory, instantiating precisely this divisibility of the sign, "has to do with signs only." As the sign-producing capacity, memory leaves the impress of thought upon the world— as the sensuous "mark" or *Zeichen* of the name.[16] For this reason memory constantly works to "erase" the content particular to the material it appropriates. This content consists in the "psychophysiological" resonance of sound, a symbolic relation of voice and meaning evident in onomotopoeia and associated with the "unconscious" register of language: "With regard to the elementary *material* of language ... the principle of imitation has confined itself to the limited area of sonorous objects ... The raw material [of language] itself is based not on a symbolic reference to external objects, but rather on an inner symbolism—namely, of anthropological articulation, the body's external utterance as almost a gesture or action [*Gebärde*]"; but "having been originally sensuous intuitions," Hegel continues, these utterances "are reduced to signs, and their original meaning is rendered vestigial [*verkümmert*] and extinguished [*ausgelöscht*]."[17] Now, *verkümmert* is not the same as *ausgelöscht*, and their juxtaposition here suggests an historical progression that must accord with the dialectical progression from symbol to sign. Hegel makes clear that the "hundreds" of German words retaining the trace of symbolic effect—*Rauschen, Sausen, Knarren*, and so on—comprise only a small portion of the language; but the acknowledgment of operative onomotopoeia suggests that the progression from *verkümmert* to *ausgelöscht* has not reached its dialectical culmination, that language has not attained to a state of rarefied synchrony.

Upon the dialectical advent of the sign, it is in fact the still persistent "vestiges" or "unconscious" remnants of the diachronous "psychophysiological" register of language

---

[16]Compare Aristotle's relation of memory and thought: "Memory is not perception or conception, but a state or affection connected with one of these, when time has elapsed." But this "state or affection," he continues, is "like" an "imprint" or "drawing" impressed upon us and then arising out of "that part of the body which contains the soul." Crucially, his image is the sealing of things with "signet rings" or an "imprint" on a building, which can again fade under stress or with time. This "image" within us is, for Aristotle, both a "something" or "object" "in its own right" and a "copy" derivative of the thing originally producing the state or affection. This dual status of the "change" attending a remembered state enables it to occur as both a "thought" and as a "reminder." Thought, however, like a spatial "drawing" or object, must exist in time and hence materially. Similarly memory, traversing the boundaries of inner and outer, is "like" a non-imitative "drawing" or "imprint" upon us: and it is the temporal and hence external subsistence of these non-imitative impressions, associated with "magnitude," "determination" and "change," according to which "memory will belong to thought." Thus Aristotle links memory to thought not only because the content of memory is a species of thought, but also because that content subsists as a temporal object within the subject in possession of the remembrance (*On Memory*, 449b 25–450a 30, in *A New Aristotle Reader*, ed. J. L. Akrill [Princeton: Princeton University Press, 1987], 206–8). This movement of the imprint or change across inner and outer in Aristotle sets the stage for Hegel's conception of memory, one of the "most difficult" moments in the dialectic. Further discussion of Hegel's relation to Aristotle's conception of memory is required; here it will suffice to note that Hegel goes further than Aristotle in acknowledging the bi-directionality of the imprint or change across inner and outer and the role of linguistic mediation and inflection in the relation of thought and representation. On Hegel and Aristotle generally, see Alfredo Ferrarin, *Hegel and Aristotle* (Cambridge: Cambridge University Press, 2007).

[17]Hegel, *Werke* 10: §459: 271–2. See also Hegel, *Werke* 10: §401: 100–17 *passim*.

that must be expunged. And yet the sign emerges from mechanical memory, the instinctive mental faculty that indelibly preserves the materiality of the sign as corporeal sound or physical mark. For only as a machine can the mind process what Hegel, referring to the sensory material of sound [*Ton*], insists is a physical, but nonetheless "mechanical" movement or vibration [*die mechanische Erschütterung*] penetrating the body.[18] For that matter, only in its mechanical and unconscious mode can the mind engage in the quintessential symbol-making craft—the "instinctive" work [*instinktartiges Arbeiten*] of building, which requires the manipulation of what Hegel elsewhere terms "mechanical" heavy mass [*mechanische schwere Masse*].[19] Hegel's use of the term "mechanical"—in his sense of "mindless" or "lacking consciousness"—to characterize memory as well as sheer substance like sound or stone reflects the extent of the mind's "objectivity" at the moment it produces signs.[20] It further reflects the persistence of the psychophysiological and hence symbolic properties of language. As mechanical memory effaces interiority, so the unconscious and latent power of the symbol bears upon the externalized sign. As the single and only bridge from thought to external expression, mechanical memory, rather than rarefying the sign as a thought-bearing medium, exposes the sign as a symbol, an unconscious "gesture" or action akin to the activity of building.

The initial characterization of the sign as a "pyramid" already betrays this latently symbolic mode of the sign. Like the pyramid, the sign houses a foreign and ethereal content, another "soul or meaning"; and just as the pyramid "preserves" as it marks the absence of the body, so the sign depends on the resonance of a voice that must also vanish. More precisely, the sign gives a "foreign soul" or universal meaning to the dead corporeality of its "material"—that is, to the rarefied sound of the voice—but nonetheless retains traces of the "psychophysiological" and corporeal dimension of language. Now the sign, in its symbolic form as voice or script, *is* objectified mechanical memory; thus the "pyramid" characterizes both the sign and the sign-producing memory. And indeed mechanical memory, like the pyramid, "effaces" [*tilgt*] both the history associated with corporeal material and the individual subject, but "preserves" their remnants in the form of a body "bereft of mind." In his lectures Hegel refers to the pyramids as "memorials to the dead" [*Totenmäler*]; these structures memorialize not by remembering a specific individual, but rather by preserving his individuality in the abstract, removed from any particular features.[21] The pyramid, like mechanical memory, remembers by forgetting—effacing particular content "proper" to corporeal matter and evoking the specter instead of only a departed "soul" or absent meaning. Last, the pyramid marks a certain "freedom" of the spirit from nature, or—as with the sign and with mechanical

---

[18] Hegel, *Werke* 10: §401: 105. Here Hegel does not exclude speech from the category of "mechanical" sound entering the body; where he does refer to speech in the *Encyclopedia*, he refers usually to its near-rarefied status.

[19] Hegel, *Werke* 3: 508, 13: 116.

[20] The term *geistlos* also means both "mindless" and "mechanical," in the sense of a mechanical mode of thinking or doing.

[21] Hegel, *Werke* 14: 295.

memory—of intellectual content from external form; but this "freedom" hinges, in all of these cases, on the form of a "mindless" body.

Hegel thus establishes, at all of these levels, a rigorous affinity or strictly symbolic relation of the pyramid and the sign. The pyramid, as a symbol for the sign, reveals its fundamental instability: for indeed the sign can only make a sensuous appearance symbolically—in the psychophysiologically resonating material of voice and script. As we have seen, Hegel consigns vocal sounds to the "dull unconscious" and dialectical "beginnings" of language. But the dialectic harnesses and rechannels rather than expunges its "vestigial" terms; and the psychophysiological dimension of language cannot be fully extinguished while language retains remnants of its symbolic corporeality.[22] Indeed, far from dispelling vestigial and non-arbitrary relations of sound and content, Hegel explicitly invokes the symbolism of the German language at the very moment of transition from memory to thought: "Already our language gives to memory [*Gedächtnis*], which it has become customary to deride, the high position of immediate relationship with thought [*Gedanke*]."[23] Just when language is to become an instrument of thought, Hegel appeals to the agency of language over against the interpretive volition of those subscribing to common prejudices. Before meaning, externalized thought confronts itself in the linguistically "given" form of mechanically repetitive material, whether of voiced homophony or reiterated letters. The origin of what is given cannot be known with certainty; hence the relation of *Gedächtnis* and *Gedanke*, Hegel insists, depends not on linguistic history or a determinate meaning, but on "immediate" formal correspondence. Buried under consciousness, meaning surfaces unpredictably out of the sonorous and paragrammatic kinship of signs.[24] The same immediacy confronts us with specifically written language: thus at the initial emergence of the still pyramidal sign, the dialectic proceeds to the ideational or hieroglyphic dimension of script. While Hegel valorizes phonetic over ideogrammatic writing, he nonetheless recognizes that "hieroglyphic writing takes place within alphabetic writing, as in our signs for the numbers, planets, chemical elements, etc."; and that, more subversively, internalization renders alphabetic writing "a sort of hieroglyphic to us, so that to use letters we need not

---

[22]According to the *Encyclopedia*, the "symbolical nature of sense impressions" [*die symbolische Natur der Affektionen*] (Hegel, *Werke* 10: §401: 108) is evident in the fact that people associate, for instance, a certain wail or the color black with grief. Hegel calls this an "inward symbolism" (Hegel, *Werke* 10: §459: 272) because, relating more to "mood" and "instinct," it remains an "unconscious relation," that is, one of which the subject is not fully cognizant (Hegel, *Werke* 10: §401: 106). Thus the sound of the pure voice as a symbol, while not the external, "proper" symbol emblematized by the pyramid, belongs, like all forms of symbolic architecture, to the unconscious or "anthropological" moment of the dialectic: "strictly speaking a symbol is an external object distinct from us in which we are conscious of an inner determination, or which we generally relate to such an inner determinateness. In a mood incited by an external sensation [as with the sound of the voice] we are not yet in a relation of distinctness from an external object, we are not yet [in the realm of] consciousness" (Hegel, *Werke* 10: §401: 106).

[23]Hegel, *Werke* 10: §464: 282.

[24]Hegel thus anticipates Lacan's formulation of the relation between the unconscious and the signifier in "The Instance of the Letter in the Unconscious, or Reason Since Freud," in Jacques Lacan, *Écrits*, transl. B. Fink (New York: W. W. Norton, 2006), 412ff.

be conscious of the mediating sounds [or phonetic referents]."[25] In other words, as the memory interiorizes alphabetic signs, it achieves a level of familiarity that then exposes their hieroglyphic materiality: for language to be used conventionally and instinctively, mind and sign must become "external and mechanical."[26]

This progression from pyramid to hieroglyph, in the context of a larger dialectic of symbol and sign, evokes the analogous narratives of the *Phenomenology* and the *Aesthetics*. While the pyramidal and hieroglyphic signs in the dialectic of the *Encyclopedia* take on the form of mechanical memory, "the principally abstract Mnemosyne," the pyramid and hieroglyph in the dialectic of religious and artistic expression take on the form of the statue of Memnon. Like Mnemosyne [*Gedächtnis*], the memorial [*Denkmal*] to Memnon relates to thought [*Gedanke*], in the *Aesthetics*, via the symbolic agency of language:

> Of the huge Memnon statues at Thebes, Strabo saw one preserved and intact, carved in its entirety out of a block of stone, while the other which rang out with the sunrise had already been mutilated: these had a human form. They were two gigantic sitting figures, in their grandiose and massive quality more inorganic and architectonic [*architektonisch*] than sculptural; for Memnon columns are found in rows [*reihenweise vorkommen*] and, since they draw their value only from such regularity of order and size, descend from the purpose of sculpture to that of architecture ... Hirt interprets this statue not as a divinity but rather as a king who had his memorial [*Denkmal*] here, like Ozymandias and others. These massive constructions should, however, suggest a more or less definite idea of something universal. The Egyptians and Ethiopians revered Memnon, the son of the goddess of the dawn, and sacrificed to him when the sun emanated its first rays, and the built image in turn greeted the adoring with its voice. The figure of [Memnon] is thus of import or interest not merely [as a figure of] sounding and giving voice [*stimmegebend*], but because it is in itself living, significant, and revealing, even if at the same time it indicates its meaning only symbolically.[27]

Where the pyramid, as *Totenmal*, represents only a mute mark [*Mal*] of the dead [*Toten*], the sounding Memnon, as *Denkmal*, promises a transition to thinking [*Denken*] via the mark [*Mal*] of the spoken sign. Since *Mal* means both "mark" and "time," the Memnon as *Denkmal* further promises a marking or preservation of time—or indeed a "thinking" of time or history. As a "memorial," the Memnon engages in this thinking

---

[25]Hegel, *Werke* 10: §459: 272, 277: "Acquired habit also erases the peculiar manner in which writing letters appears, in the interest of vision, as a detour to ideas through audibility; thus habit reduces alphabetic letters to hieroglyphs, so that to use the letters we need not be conscious of the mediating sounds [or phonetic referents]" (ibid., 277).

[26]Hegel, *Werke* 10: §451: 251.

[27]Hegel, *Werke* 14: 281–2.

of time as a physically external or "mechanical" mark of human memory. Arranged in lines over the landscape, the statues of Memnon appear as the hieroglyphs of a text accessible to memory by virtue of its alignment in "rows" [*Reihen*]—meaningless script, that is, arranged "according to no law" but the architectonic necessity of sequence.[28] Likewise mechanical memory relies on the mnemonic power of linear arrangement, and furthermore objectifies itself in such geometric, architectonic delineations.[29] In this respect the Memnon, as a "memorial" externalizing thought in hieroglyphic lines, converges with memory or Mnemosyne: and *Gedächtnis* refers to nothing more nor less than the edifice of memory—or, in the fullest etymological sense of *Denkmal*, the marking of thought in time.

Now, thought occurs in signs, and indeed Mnemosyne, the mythological inventor of words, and the Memnon, sounding before the sun, both attempt to produce properly meaningful language. But the former can only produce thought-bearing language in mechanical, objective form, while the latter only externalizes the voice as the symbolic medium of the sign. Rather than producing pure, which is to say incorporeal signs, Mnemosyne and the Memnon evoke each other paragrammatically, revealing through a *mise en abyme* the ungovernably mnemonic character of the sign, subject always to the psychophysiological agency of language. Lodged in memory, the letters *of* memory—Mnemosyne—link Memnon and Mnemosyne *through* the mechanical function of memory, that is, in an instinctive, and thoroughly symbolic relation of the otherwise disparate signs.

Or not entirely disparate: for Mnemosyne (*Μνημοσύνη*) includes, amongst its cognates, *mnēmosynon* (*μνημόσυννον*), meaning a funerary monument; *mnêma* (*μνῆμα*), a mound or building in honor of the dead, a monument or tomb, or memorial; and *mnēmatophylakia* (*μνηματοφυλακία*), the guardianship of cemeteries. And Memnon (*Μέμνων*), meaning steadfast and resolute, relates to *menō* (*μένω*), which means to lodge, to remain, and, most pertinently, to endure in time. As semantically close as Mnemosyne and Memnon appear, they are, according to all standard Greek lexicons, etymologically distinct: Mnemosyne derives from Greek *men*, to think, and Memnon possibly from Old Persian *man*, to wait.[30] Even so, as Hegel could not have known, the

---

[28]Hegel, *Werke* 10: §463: 281.

[29]Hegel does deride mnemonic learning in the narrow sense of "transforming names to images" (Hegel, *Werke* 10: §462: 280). But the mechanical function of memory or Mnemosyne remains fully mnemonic to the extent that it relies on the architectonic rather than meaningful arrangements of letters or words to facilitate memorization. "Mnemonic" is of course related etymologically to Mnemosyne: moreover the Greek and Indo-European root *men*, meaning "to think," includes amongst its derivatives, according to the *Oxford English Dictionary*, the words "mind," "music," and "automatic," thus placing "mnemonic" within the dialectical constellation of mechanical memory, external sound, and habit-driven or instinctive thought.

[30]*A Greek-English Lexicon with a revised supplement*, compiled by Henry G. Liddell and Robert Scott, revised Henry S. Jones. Oxford: Clarendon Press, 1996. For *mnēmosynon* (*μνημόσυννον*) see the revised supplementary notes. One scholar has also suggested the "chance" interplay, in the emergence of Greek *Memnon*, of *menō* with Egyptian *mn*, meaning "to be firm, remain, be established" (R. D. Griffith, "The Origin of Memnon," *Classical Antiquity*, 1998, 17: 2: 214).

genealogies converge in the same Indo-European root: *men*, meaning both to think and to wait.[31]

Hinting at only the possibility of such a genealogical relation, the text in fact challenges and blurs the line between etymology (*Gedächtnis* and *Denkmal*) and paragram (Mnemosyne and Memnon). An etymology, as a "story of origins," must contend with origins lost to history, buried in the body and inaccessible to consciousness.[32] Incorporating or eliding the possible sonorous or paragrammatic connections between signs, an etymology cannot avoid an implicitly symbolic mode of analysis and explanation.[33] Hegel identifies in this modality of linguistic research—continuous from his day to the present—the artifice and wit common to the reading of ancient myths:

> Yet if the ancient Greeks [*die Alten*] did not see in their mythology the thoughts we now see there, it in no way follows that their ideas are not *latent* or *implicit* [*an sich*] symbols, and indeed they must be taken as such … The fact that this is the case is something which here we have essentially to uphold and accept, even if we must admit the possibility that, in such a symbolic mode of explanation, purely artificial and witty interpretations will often creep in, as happens with etymologies.[34]

The relation of Mnemosyne and Memnon instantiates the "artificial" or "witty" hermeneutics of etymologies reaching fancifully toward historical origins—the same "wit" that for Hegel underlies felicitous "plays on words."[35] If the etymological relation of

---

[31]Indo-European *men* generates a broad range of terms relating architecture and memory, relating, for instance, English "mansion" and "mind." For the various meanings and forms of the Indo-European root *men*, see *The American Heritage Dictionary of Indo-European Roots*, ed. Calvert Watkins (Boston: Houghton Mifflin, 2000). The dictionary, intended for non-specialists provides a useful list of Indo-European roots, but focuses almost exclusively on the path from reconstructed Indo-European to Greek, Italic, Germanic, and modern English. It provides a highly limited number of references to Sanskrit roots, and practically no references to any offshoots and cognates in any Asiatic Indo-European language groups. All projects must face limitations of scope, but Watkins' systematic exclusion of non-Germanic and non-Greek languages is both unfortunate and telling, rehearsing the division already inherent in the nineteenth-century term "Indo-European."

[32]See the entry on "Lexis," in *The Princeton Encyclopedia of Poetics*, eds. A. Preminger and T. V. F. Brogan (Princeton: Princeton University Press, 1993), 690. C. T. Onions defines etymology as the "origin, formation, and development of a word" (*Oxford Dictionary of English Etymology*, ed. C. T. Onions [Oxford: Oxford University Press, 1966], v).

[33]The "comparative method" of historical linguistics, formulated over the nineteenth-century and essentially unchanged since, consists in the "reconstruction" of sound equivalences by establishing systematic correspondences of sounds—or, in the case of attested dead languages, graphemic signs of sounds—between words or other lexical units of two or more foreign languages. For a review of reconstruction, see the introductory essay in *The American Heritage Dictionary of Indo-European Roots*. See also Oswald J. L. Szemerenyi, *Introduction to Indo-European Linguistics* (Oxford: Oxford University Press, 1999) and Robert S. Beekes, *Comparative Indo-European Linguistics* (Amsterdam: John Benjamins Publishing: 1995), 98–119.

[34]Hegel, *Werke* 13: 404.

[35]Hegel, *Werke* 13: 511. For Hegel "wit" involves "subjective whim which, to escape from the ordinary, gives in to a piquant charm, not satisfied until it has succeeded in discovering related qualities in the seemingly most

Gedächtnis and *Denkmal* does not seem controversial, the relation of their mythological counterparts—Mnemosyne and Memnon—in fact hinges on the "wit" of mythopoeia: for indeed, as if in parody of the etymology that binds *Gedächtnis* and *Denkmal* to thought, the link between Mnemosyne and Memnon is, mythically speaking, genetic: Mnemosyne is Memnon's great-aunt.[36] The relevance of this kinship becomes apparent in Hegel's discussion of Greek mythology in the above passage. To begin with, Hegel's use of the word "mythology" rather than "myth" to describe the Greeks' accounts of their origins conflates the interpretation or study of myth with the original mythic text. Myth cannot be interpreted in any manner that does not produce another symbolic narrative, another myth. Tracing back the history of mythic traditions, mythology exposes each myth in a genealogical path to be nothing but mythology: as a reading of antecedent symbols, "myth" is "mythology" from the beginning.[37]

As with the history of myth, so too the history of words proves indeterminate, as an etymology cannot be made historical without the "symbolic mode of explanation" characteristic of both myth and its interpretation. The history of words cannot be recuperated, nor the words of history articulated through pure and proper signs. Mediating history and mediated by history, words always reverberate symbolically and hence cannot be historically fixed or reduced, pertaining ultimately to the order of mythopoeia. It is no wonder, then, that Hegel, in his history of signs, evokes Mnemosyne, the mythic origin of words and history.[38] Her appearance in the *Encyclopedia* punctuates the mythopoeic character of Hegel's history of the sign and, since the mother of the Muses both inspires and creates, underscores the endless entanglement of etymology

---

heterogeneous elements and therefore, in an astonishing way, in combining things utterly distant from one another" (Hegel, *Werke* 13: 522). Modern linguists still recognize the necessary place of wit in the work of etymology: thus C. T. Onions, discussing the limits of lexicographical methodology, remarks that the etymology for "each word needs to be judged on its own merits, from its form and context. It is hoped that the conclusions arrived at will be as correct as probability and human wit can make them" (*Oxford Dictionary of English Etymology*, vi).

[36]Mnemosyne is brother to Hyperion, the sun—and aunt to his daughter Eos, the dawn, who is the mother of Memnon. For the genealogy of Hyperion and Eos, see Apollodorus, *The Library of Greek Mythology*, transl. Robin Hard (Oxford: Oxford University Press, 1997), 1.2.2.

[37]"The other view, in contrast, does not find satisfaction with the purely external aspect of mythological figures and stories, but rather asserts that a general sense lies deeper in this material, and that to penetrate through and recognize that sense is the real business of mythology as the scientific consideration of myths. In this respect mythology must be a grasping of symbolism. For the term 'symbolically' here means only that the myths … still contain meanings, including general thoughts about the nature of god and implicit philosophemes" (Hegel, *Werke* 13: 402).

[38]Hegel references Mnemosyne as the origin of names and signs as early as the Jena lectures (Hegel, *Jenenser Realphilosophie, Die Vorlesungen von 1803–1804*, ed. J. Hoffmeister [Leipzig: Felix Meiner Verlag, 1932], 211) and again in *Philosophische Propädeutik*: §158: 209–10. And he explicitly refers to Mnemosyne as the producer of history in the *Philosophy of History* (Hegel, *Werke* 12: 83–5) and the *History of Philosophy* (Hegel, *Introduction to the Lectures on the History of Philosophy*, transl. T. M. Knox and A. V. Miller [Oxford: Clarendon Press, 1980], 92). For the mythological background on Mnemosyne as the organizer and chronicler of time, see Hesiod: *The Homeric Hymns and Homerica*, transl. Hugh Evelyn-White (Cambridge: Harvard University Press, 1936), 915.

and the paragram, of authorial mythopoeia in symbolic invention and the "given" symbolism of language.[39]

Hegel also gestures here at the disciplinary entanglement of etymology and mythology: from the time of William Jones' revelation, in 1786, of the common basis of Greek and Sanskrit, through Franz Passow's publication, in 1819, of a landmark etymological dictionary of Greek based on mythological texts, ancient myth serves as a primary source for etymology, and etymology as the basis for speculative reconstructions and interpretations of ancient myth.[40] To the practitioners of comparative and historical linguistics—no less in Hegel's day than ours—a complete etymology conceptually evokes and potentially ranges across the boundaries that separate, for instance, old, middle, and high phases of a language; branches of a language group; living and dead languages; and linguistic families.[41] That is, etymologies require the invocation or suppression of the category of "foreignness." To the extent that this category must be historically mediated, the "foreign," as a radical principle of difference, becomes a mythological construct. Indicatively, the mythic kinship between Memnon and Mnemosyne traverses the divide of foreignness, most obviously between Egypt and Greece. How does this kinship via mythopoeia inflect the larger organization of history into categories seemingly foreign to each other?

Kinship [Verwandtschaft] and foreignness [Fremdheit], of course, are crucial terms in Hegel's history of the sign: where kinship marks the structure of the symbol, foreignness marks the structure of the pyramidal sign.[42] Both the pyramid and sign lodge and conceal a "foreign" content or ethereal "soul" of meaning; but this foreign content must remain

---

[39]In the *Aesthetics* and the *History of Philosophy*, Hegel defends the hermeneutic engagement of mythology especially as practiced by Creuzer (see Hegel, *Werke* 13: 404 and Hegel, *Introduction to the Lectures on the History of Philosophy*, 150–1). In the *History of Philosophy* he further claims that myth in philosophy is, or ought to be, a merely "superfluous ornament" (ibid., 37, 157) that "does not advance philosophy" proper (ibid., 157) because mythology is a "sensuous presentation of the concept" (ibid., 151). On the other hand, in world-history or the study of art or religion, the use of mythic materials is indispensable, for however much "contingency and caprice may intervene" in the hermeneutic process, "there is reason in these forms" and hence they must be considered (ibid., 151). By the same token, the study, in aesthetics, of mythic coimbrications of sensuous form and religious, philosophical, and other meanings, as we will see, will throw into crisis the concept of a "superfluous ornament." Thus while Hegel writes in the *History of Philosophy* that "Mythical language has intentionally been used to evoke sublime conceptions" (ibid., 156), in the *Aesthetics* the sublime marks the apparent immanence of spiritual meaning in linguistic form, hence the convergence of adornment and adorned. Hegel's notion of the linguistic ornament and of sublimity—a crucial element in his theory of language—will be examined at length in Chapter 4.

[40]*Johann Gottlob Schneiders Handwörterbuch der griechischen Sprache: nach der dritten Ausgabe des größeren Griechischdeutschen Wörterbuchs mit besonderer Berücksichtigung des Homerischen und Hesiodischen Sprachgebrauchs und mit genauer Angabe der Sylbenlängen,* revised and expanded by Franz Passow (Leipzig: Friedrich Christian Wilhelm Vogel, 1819).

[41]The relation of *Gedächtnis, Denkmal,* and *Gedanke,* for instance, surfaces an etymological system with possible references, more or less hypothetical, to a vast array of Indo-European Old and Middle German roots as well as Frisian, Scandinavian, Dutch, Norse, and English sources, cognates and offshoots. Being speculative, linguistic genealogies cannot determine meaning; thus Hegel argues that whereas with living languages usage can differentiate between literal and metaphoric meanings, the recourse to "mere etymology" in the case of dead languages (or, by extension, archaisms) "cannot ultimately decide the question" of meaning (Hegel, *Werke* 13: 518).

[42]See Hegel, *Werke* 13: 395 and *Werke* 10: §459: 269.

attached to a preserved body, for only the body, whether an embalmed corpse or "vestigial" voice, can symbolically convey radically "foreign" spiritual or linguistic meaning. Thus the corporeality or materiality of the sign relies, paradoxically, on "foreignness" as grounds for the symbolic kinship of the sign and pyramid. Just as kinship marginalizes without banishing foreignness, so too foreignness marginalizes without banishing kinship. Hegel frames the failed suppression of the foreign as a problem of "translation": the sign, it will be recalled, "is the *pyramid* to which a foreign soul [*eine fremden Seele*] is translated [*versetzt*] and preserved." The first "foreign" element moved to and preserved in a pyramid is the body to which a soul is putatively attached. A linguistic sign, then, is the physical "translation" [*Versetzung*] of a body that must be removed to underwrite the purity of the sign, and yet without whose corporeality the sign cannot materialize.[43] In this case, *Versetzung* is like *Übersetzung*: just as a textual translation faces the task of rendering so perfectly as to dispense with the foreign original from which it derives, the sign, equally impossibly, aims to bury and extinguish the foreign body from which it originates and upon which it remains dependent. As a pyramid, the sign is thus an incomplete or even failed translation of its original, for its body still haunts the foreign and material surface of language, like the conceived specter of a corpse that indicates symbolically the meaning of a pyramid viewed from the outside. True enough, the "original" body, belonging to the mute Orient, does not attain to speech in Hegel's narrative, or may as well have never spoken, for its foreign language belongs only to the "dead." But just as the sign cannot become a "pure designation" freed of its "anthropological," "corporeal," and "unconscious" roots, so the history of a sign cannot dispense with what is dead, foreign, or lost: as much as an etymology aims at defining and categorizing so as to excise words "foreign" to its family, Hegel points out that no etymology can ever ascertain with certainty the meanings of dead and so necessarily foreign tongues. For Hegel a word's roots remain forever lost, its familial scope or limit undecidable.

In this sense, the mythic kinship of Mnemosyne and Memnon mythologizes the persistence of kinship in signifying structures. Already as Greek words imported into German, they traverse a linguistic and cultural divide. But it is the name "Memnon," as Hegel inherits it, that crosses lines of "foreignness" most spectacularly: linguistically, as a Greek corruption of an Egyptian name,[44] and above all mythopoetically, as the king of the Ethiopians who, in Greek myth, becomes a Persian hero and leads an African army into the Trojan War before being memorialized in Egyptian and

---

[43]In medieval usage the Latin *translatio* refers both to the rendering of a text into a different language and to the physical transfer of a corpse from one site to another.

[44]The point is not essential, but Hegel may have noticed the multiplicity, in Greek texts, of Egyptian names for Memnon, or for the builder of the complex known as the Memnonium: for instance, Diodorus Siculus gives several variants, including *Ammenemēs* (Ἀμμενέμης) and *Mendēs* (Μένδης) (Diodorus Siculus, *The Library of History*, transl. C. L. Sherman [Cambridge: Harvard University Press, 1985], 1.61.1), while Strabo claims that the Egyptians called Memnon *Ismandēs* (Ἰσμάνδης), also referred to as *Imandēs* (Ἰμάνδης) (*The Geography of Strabo*, 8 vols., transl. Horace L. Jones [Cambridge: Harvard University Press, 1960–1970], 17.1.42, 113 and 17.1.37, 105). The profusion of names, each phonemically resonant with the Greek *Memnon*, makes his figure and name a site of repeated linguistic corruption. Tellingly, the etymology of Memnon remains a mystery: for a contemporary philological account of the name "Memnon," along with useful bibliography, see Griffith, R. D., "The Origin of Memnon," 12–32.

Ethiopian architecture.[45] A central figure in Hegel's history of the sign, Memnon utterly tramples the categories of Orient and Occident, not only as a Persian hero with a Greek or Egyptian name, but also as an African king fighting at the divide of Europe and Asia. True enough, the symbol "belongs primarily to the Orient," and art history, like world-history, "begins in the East" and passes through Greece before ending in the West.[46] Furthermore, the entire dialectical history from pyramid to the statues of Memnon, or from symbol to sign, can be read as a crisis of "foreignness," to the extent that "pyramid," "hieroglyph," and "Memnon" are all Greek "signs" and thus strictly "foreign" to the "symbols" they name.[47] But the Memnon, as the transitional point between the architectural symbol and the linguistic sign, subverts the "Orientalness" of the symbol and places the first stirrings of the sign beyond the received categories of world-history: indeed, this dead, dark-skinned hero addresses not the Oriental sunrise, but his divine mother, the Greek goddess of the dawn.[48]

The persistence of foreign ghosts—of pyramidal spirits and the "living" [lebendig] Memnon—in the history of signs also subverts the superficial exclusion of the foreign within the signifying structures of Hegel's philosophical system. The symbolic relation and

---

[45]Classical sources refer to Memnon as some or all of the following: king of the Ethiopians, founder and builder of Susa in Persia, and nephew to Priam of Troy; they also refer to his sepulcher in Troy, his memorial in Egypt, and his palace in Ethiopia. Indicatively: "So Memnon, although being king of the Ethiopians, came to Troy, not from what today is called Africa, but from Susa, not far away from the river Tigris, in the land that later became Persia. And when he made his march to the west, he subdued all the peoples that lived between Susa and Troy" (Diodorus Siculus, *The Library of History*, 4.75.4). Moreover in discussions of Memnon's provenance, Ethiopia is a place of ambiguous or even plural geography, located in either Asia or Africa or in some cases straddling the two continents: Pliny, for instance, insists that Memnon was king of the Ethiopians in Africa (Pliny the Elder, *Natural History*, 10 vols., transl. H. Rackham [Cambridge: Harvard University Press, 1940], VI.35.181–84, 475). On Memnon as an "Ethiopian king," see also Hesiod, *Theogony*, 984. On Memnon's entanglement with both Ethiopia and Persia, see Daniel Potts, "Between Myth and History: Susa and Memnon through the Ages," *The Digital Archive of Brief Notes & Iran Review*, 2017, 1: 4: 15–35.

[46]Hegel, *Werke* 12: 133–4.

[47]The etymology of "pyramid" instantiates the difficulty of separating out Greek and Egyptian "origins." For instance according to the *Oxford English Dictionary*, English "pyramid" derives from Greek *pyramis* (πυραμίς), "perhaps of Egyptian origin, but anciently explained by some as a derivative of πῦρ—fire, by others as from πυρός—wheat, grain, as if a granary." Several explanations refer to the conical shape of a wheaten cake called *pyramis* in Greek. Scholars have proposed Ancient Egyptian *periemusi*, meaning "straight up" or referring mathematically to the "height" of a pyramid, as the source for the Greek *pyramis* (Rainer Hannig, *Grosses Handwörterbuch Ägyptisch-Deutsch: die Sprache der Pharaonen* [Mainz: P. von Zabern, 1995], 214, 285). Derivations from the Ancient Egyptian word for the pyramidal structures, *mr*, with metathesis of the consonants, have also been proposed.

[48]Derrida incorrectly reads Hegel's Memnon as made of "white stone" (*Glas*, transl. John Leavey, Jr. [Minneapolis: University of Minnesota Press, 1986], 255). Hegel never mentions the color of the statue, and in fact inherits a long tradition of dispute over the shade of both Memnon's skin and memorial. Thus in *Eikones*, Philostratus, one of Hegel's sources (see Hegel, *Werke* 13: 356 and 15: 39), describes a classical representation of the dark-skinned Memnon as follows: "You would not say that Memnon's skin is really black, for the black of it shows a trace of ruddiness. As for the Deities of the Sky, Eos mourning over her son causes the Sun to be downcast and begs Night to come prematurely and check the hostile army, that she may be able to steal away her son, no doubt with the consent of Zeus. And look! Memnon has been stolen away and is at the edge of the painting. Where is he? In what part of the earth? No tomb of Memnon is anywhere to be seen but in Aithiopia he himself has been transformed into a statue of black marble" (Philostratus the Elder, *Eikones*, in *Elder Philostratus, Younger Philostratus, Callistratus*, transl. A. Fairbanks [Cambridge: Harvard University Press, 2000], 1.7: 31). Strabo,

mythic kinship of Memnon and Mnemosyne reveal the fluidity and hence provisionality of the principal categories of the narratives of the *Encyclopedia* and the *Aesthetics*, structured as they are around the distinction between, on the one hand, anthropology and its African or Oriental subjects; the mute body; and symbolic architecture—and, on the other hand, psychology and its Western subject; the "soul" of pure meaning; and the linguistic sign. In this vein, Hegel's mute evocation of the Memnon in the *Phenomenology* and the *Encyclopedia* casts light on his elliptical narrative strategy in both texts. In the case of the *Phenomenology*, Hegel's heterogeneous symbolism, dispensing with culturally disparate proper names, gives rise to a narrative register including and traversing a wide range of religious, ethnic, linguistic, and cultural categories. In this mode, difference stems not from the exclusionary force of historically burdened proper names, but rather from the provisional and movable binaries and trifurcations of the dialectic. Hegel achieves a similar effect in the "extreme compression" of the published *Encyclopedia*, reserving as he does most references to historical religions, cultures, and material artifacts for the "improvisations"[49] of his spoken and, indeed, provisional and supplementary remarks or lectures.[50]

---

another of Hegel's sources, does not specify the color of Memnon or his memorial (Strabo, *Geography*, 17.1.46, 122–3). Catullus considers Memnon Ethiopian; Virgil and Seneca describe him as black; and Ovid refers to him as the black lover of Aurora (Frank Snowden, *Blacks in Antiquity: The Ethiopians in Greco-Roman Experience* [Cambridge: Harvard University Press, 1970], 153). There were varying representations of the color of Memnon in the eighteenth and early nineteenth centuries: for a black Memnon, see Figure 2, Bernard Picart's *Memnon*, an engraving dating from the 1730s. That Greek artists may not have actually represented Memnon as black African (Snowden, *Blacks in Antiquity*, 152) is beside the point; what cannot be contested is the historical ambiguity around Memnon's origin. For likely Greek representations of Memnon, see Figure 3, *The Departure of Memnon for Troy, c.* 6th century BC; Figure 4, *Memnon and His Ethiopian Warriors. c.* 530 BC; Figure 5, *Eos Tearing Her Hair in Grief over the Body of Memnon, c.* 5th century BC, a Greek vase showing Memnon next to his mother, Eos; and Figure 6, *Achilles Battles Memnon as Thetis and Eos Watch*, Attic red figure volute krater *c.* 490 BC. Hegel's silence on the color of Memnon only reinforces the indistinctness of his racial provenance, or at least the racial and cultural indeterminateness or heterogeneity of the mythological figure.

[49]We can here consider more fully the implications of Boumann's account, in the foreword to the 1845 edition of the *Zusätze*, of Hegel's view of his own lectures: "Hegel lectured with great freedom, and what he said had all the enchanting freshness of a new thought-world created at the moment, but such more or less total improvisation unfortunately led to unwitting repetitions, vaguenesses, divagations, and sudden jumps. These defects had to be carefully avoided in my revision. But the necessary changes remained within the authentic, indubitable sense of Hegel. I believe that I have been true to this sense since I have not left out from the *Zusätze* what constituted the *soul* of Hegel's lectures: the dialectical movement to which Hegel thought that one should for the most part give a freer and, in part, a more profound rein in one's lectures than in the printed text; in the case of the latter, extreme compression often gave an impression of externality and of mere asseveration" (cited in J.N. Findlay's "Foreword," *The Philosophy of Mind, together with the Zusätze in Boumann's text (1845)* transl. W. Wallace and A.V. Miller [Oxford: Clarendon Press, 1971], vi). Of Boumann's edition of the *Zusätze*, Findlay rightly asks: "Who shall say that more of Hegel has not survived in Herr Boumann's reconstruction, based on a living memory of a living performance, than in what will ultimately be served up to us, in all its dismembered repetitiousness, by the *Hegel-Archiv*?" (vi.) That Hegel would have left the "performance" of his spoken remarks to be "reconstructed" by "memory," however, implies multiple reconstructions by multiple minds over time; that likely accounts for why he did not publish them. In any event, the link between performance, reconstruction, and production from memory in Findlay's comment is revealing, reflecting the relation of these concepts in Hegel's own text.

[50]Of several exceptions, particularly notable is §459 of the *Encyclopedia*, where Hegel refers explicitly to a whole range of cultures, but principally to insist on the impossibility of a universal language and on the necessity of linguistic heterogeneity.

The figures of Memnon and Mnemosyne thus represent a turning point in Hegel's history of the sign, which begins with symbolic architecture and moves full circle to the sensuous appearance of the sign, or the manifestation of thought as the symbolic and architectonic object of mechanical memory. Unlike the proper sign, the language of mechanical memory and architecture endlessly intercalates the foreign, traversing and negating its categorical limits. In this respect the symbols of memory and architecture, already unintelligible in themselves, do not require translation. Because the mechanical memory produces thought in the form of an externalized voice or letter free of meaning, memory in fact isolates the universal in language. Thus Hegel had argued as early as Jena:

> Memory, the Mnemosyne of the ancients, in its true significance consists not in the fact that intuition or some such thing, the products of memory itself, are in the universal element and provoked by this element, [where memory is] particularized in a formal way which does not concern content; rather it is memory that produces thought, as a thing-of-memory [*Gedächtnis-sache*], or what we have called sensuous intuition ... The name exists as speech—this is the existing concept of consciousness—which is not fixed, and immediately dies away when it takes the form of existence; it exists in the element of air, as an outward appearance of formless and free fluidity, while it is so absolutely outside itself in that it has universal communicatory existence. The empty animal voice receives a significance infinitely determinate in itself. The pure sounding of the voice, the vowel, differentiates itself, while the organ of the voice reveals its differentiated arrangement as its own, as a unique articulation. This pure sounding is interrupted by dumb [consonants], the proper repression of sheer sound, the principal means by which every tone has a significance for itself, since the differences of the pure sounding in song are not determinate for themselves, but are rather determined only by virtue of their relation to the preceding and following sounds. Sounded, structured, and articulated, language is the voice of consciousness in that every sound has significance—that is, that in language a name exists, the ideality of an existing thing, and the immediate non-existence of the same.[51]

Before the name bears meaning as a sign, it exists materially as an "empty animal voice." Though free of articulated content, this empty voice nonetheless attains to "universal communicatory existence" by referring to itself as the universal modality of communication—universal precisely by virtue of the plurality of its structure. Here Hegel opposes and co-implicates the "pure sounding of the voice" or "vowel" and the "dumb," individually inarticulable "consonant." As a conceptual letter, the consonant negates the vowel or pure voice, but in this respect differentiates it and thus gives it an individual shape that can ultimately bear meaning. In the same manner, the voice, by articulating the consonant, negates it as a pure and mute letter, but thereby differentiates it as a vocalized tone capable of significance. Admirably, Hegel anticipates the twentieth-century notion

---

[51]Hegel, *Jenenser Realphilosophie, Die Vorlesungen von 1803–1804*, 211–2.

of the phoneme as a unit structured negatively by virtue of its differentiation along a chain[52]; and in one sense, he goes further, conceiving of the material or corporeal side of language as a coimbrication of the empty voice and abstract letter, of animal sound and architectonic arrangement. Before the name, as a universal, negates the particular thing, memory achieves universality by externalizing the differentiated phonemic structure of language as such, where the universality and "free fluidity" of the voice consist precisely in its basis in difference and negation. Reading its structure symbolically, Hegel contends that the universality or sameness [*Gleichheit*] of the pure voice lies in its subversion of homogeneity and its implicit consciousness of plurality and contradiction: "Voice is active hearing, pure in itself, posited as universal; [expressing] pain, desire, joy, contentment, it is the sublation of the univocal, the particular-itself [*Aufheben des einzelnen Selbst*], and the consciousness of contradiction, returning here to itself and attaining sameness [*Gleichheit*]."[53] Furthermore, the pure and animal voice, externalizing what is internal, empties out interiority and frees individuality of itself. In this respect, the voice articulates the lack internal to the subject, hence the negation or death of the individual: "Every animal has a voice in its forced death, expressing itself as negated, as a sublated self. (Unlike other [beasts], birds [have] song because they belong to the element of air—articulating voice, a liquified or dissolved self.) In the voice, meaning returns into itself; it is negative—yearning. It is absence, lack of substance itself."[54] Like Mnemosyne, Hegel's Memnon, too, produces "mere sound" that is "not yet speech" but nonetheless refers to itself as the medium of language; in this respect the colossus, "sounding and giving voice" [*tönend und stimmegebend*] at dawn, isolates the voice of language before it bears meaning. But for Hegel the Memnon's significance lies not only in the voice it produces, but also in the fact that "it is in itself living, significant, and revealing, even if at the same time it indicates its meaning only symbolically." Presumably only the voice of the Orient and of the dead, the "living" Memnon utters the universal voice of language, though marked always with the memory of difference and negation.

By eliding foreignness, neither Mnemosyne nor Memnon yearns for the monolithic language of Babel. On the contrary such a "universal language" is impossible, since "the progress of thought and the ongoing development of logic result," capriciously and locally, "in changed views of the inner relations [of intellectual objects] and, accordingly, of their nature."[55] Mnemosyne and Memnon thus express the impossible desire not

[52]For a review of theories of the phoneme from Saussure to the present, see Roman Jakobson, *Selected Writings* (Berlin: De Gruyter, 1988), 8 vols., 8: 7–82, and 125–9.

[53]Hegel, *Jenenser Realphilosophie, Die Vorlesungen von 1805–1806*, ed. J. Hoffmeister (Leipzig: Felix Meiner, 1931), 161.

[54]Hegel, *Jenenser Realphilosophie, Die Vorlesungen von 1805–1806*, 161. Agamben makes this passage the unlikely center of his argument that, for Hegel, the voice is the "expression and memory of the animal's death ... in dying, the animal finds its voice, it exalts the soul in one voice, and, in this act, it expresses and preserves itself *as dead*. Thus, the animal voice is the *voice of death* ... [that is,] the voice is death, which preserves and recalls the living as dead, and it is, at the same time, an immediate trace and memory of death, pure negativity" (Giorgio Agamben, *Language and Death: The Place of Negativity*, transl. Karen E. Pinkus [Minneapolis: University of Minnesota, 1991], 45).

[55]Hegel, *Werke* 10: §459: 273.

for permanent and universal names, particularly untenable in the case of intellectual objects, but for the "universality" of the "sensuousness of speech."[56] In its universality, the Memnon's voice is akin to the mute language of the symbol as it indicates its own symbolic modality of expression, where indication marks the preservation and cancellation of the particular.[57]

As a "memorial" belonging to "unconscious symbolism," the Memnon aims to preserve and, like the Mnemosyne of mechanical memory, "give voice" to the historical and unconscious vestiges of symbolic meaning. For, as Hegel makes clear elsewhere, only architecture preserves and reveals the otherwise "voiceless and mute" pre-history of language:

> [T]he growth, diffusion, development, and building up [Ausbildung] of the empire of [meaningful] sounds has remained voiceless and mute, an almost imperceptibly gradual development. It is a fact revealed by monuments, that languages, during the illiterate or ignorant [ungebildeten] period of peoples that have spoken them, have been built up [ausgebildet] to great heights, and that the understanding had developed on this theoretical ground [Boden] with elaboration and ingenuity.[58]

The "building up" and cultivation [Ausbildung] of a system of meaningful sounds, in the case of the invariably rich languages of "illiterate" or "ignorant" [ungebildeten] peoples, are evidenced only by architectural "monuments."[59] Substituting for books, architecture, as a mute language of symbols, memorializes the history of unlettered people lacking signs for sounds—or in the case of merely "ignorant" people who have left written inscriptions in stonework—architecture preserves the history of language through hieroglyphs engraved on erected surfaces. Here the transition from Unbildung to Ausbildung—from ignorance to education, or the lack of writing to the building up of language—occurs through etymological and paronomastic play. Likewise the architectural references—to empire, monument, ground, and development to great heights—suggest an etymological pun on bilden, to form, shape or construct, and through macaronic play, on English

---

[56]Hegel, Werke 10: §459: 275.

[57]Hegel discusses the "act of indicating" in detail in the first section of the Phenomenology of Spirit. The relation of the symbol to indication will become clearer in the next chapter.

[58]Hegel, Werke 12: 85.

[59]Hegel makes this point repeatedly; for a detailed discussion, see Hegel, Werke 12: 85-6 and Hegel, Werke 10: §459: 272. In the latter text he cites Humboldt's essay Über den Dualis [Berlin: Druckerei der Königlichen Akademie der Wissenschaften: 1828], I: 10–1), which points to the finer distinctions conveyed in the grammar of classical Arabic in comparison to the grammar of contemporary Romance and Germanic languages. Humboldt's thesis regarding the relative complexity of classical Arabic in comparison to these languages remains essentially uncontested; but some critics also rehearse Hegel's antiquated gradations of the "civilization" of the peoples speaking these languages: thus for Michael Inwood the view that the languages of "less civilized peoples" are more developed than those of "more civilized peoples" is "essentially correct" (Michael Inwood, A Hegel Dictionary [Malden: Blackwell Publishers, 1999], 159). Such elements of Hegel's provisional and outdated narrative of history remain remarkably persistent, even where they are not explicitly attributed to Hegel and even where his philosophy teaches us to move past them. I address the neglect of Hegel's philosophical conception of history in Chapter 5.

"building," from Middle English *bilden*: through this intercalation of the foreign, the construction of language as a linguistic edifice parallels and rhetorically mirrors the movement from empty "ground" to the building of an architectural "monument."[60]

Architecture preserves a "dead" language freed from its living usage and historical context, but not from history as such: on the contrary, architecture isolates the force of history in language, the inhuman agency exerted through the "given" relations of its surface symbolism. In this sense architecture only preserves linguistic history dialectically, where to "preserve" something is to produce it anew—first negating it and showing it as dead, but then drawing on its history to expose and assimilate excluded elements into what dialectically emerges. As the quintessential type of symbolic architecture, the pyramid, for instance, preserves a soul by embalming and concealing its corpse in order to incorporate its departed and thus "foreign" soul. More generally "preservation," a foundational concept in Hegelian dialectics, occurs through negation and "sublation," the work of the paronomastic *Aufhebung*, to produce a new term or concept.[61] The entanglement of paronomasia and "preservation" in the *Aufhebung* instantiates the continuity of speculative dialectics or logic with the heterogeneous symbolism of language. Thus Hegel writes of the term *Aufhebung*:

> This doubleness common to language, according to which the same word has a positive and negative meaning, is not an accident, nor does it afford any basis for reproaching language for causing confusion, but rather should be recognized as an instance of the speculative spirit of our language stepping beyond the mere either-or of understanding.[62]

The dialectic, as the movement of logic and thought, not only functions by exploiting the excess within the categories of seemingly static binaries, but also turns on the rhetorical excess formally and conceptually internal to the *Aufhebung*. Like architecture and memory, the dialectic only preserves by producing—and, by the same token, only produces what was, as latent material excess, already there, where production amounts rather to a preservation of something that has been forgotten. In this sense stasis or synchrony is only an illusion attending repressed diachrony and forgotten history. The inflexible mind is thus one that has forgotten the historicity of language, the unconscious and symbolic vestiges that subvert the relation of names to things, inner to outer, and

---

[60]German *bilden* shares a proto-Germanic root with Middle English *bilden*, to build, to erect a structure; to lodge, to stay, to reside (*Middle English Dictionary*, eds. H. Kurath and S. Kuhn [Ann Arbor: University of Michigan Press, 1952–2001]). Hegel uses *bilden* to mean "to shape a building" in *Werke* 12: 133–4.

[61]To recall, *Aufhebung* means both "cancellation" and "preservation"; the now canonical translation in English is "sublation." On *Aufhebung* see the discussion in Hegel, *Werke* 5: 113–116, Hegel, *Werke* 8: §11: 55; and *Hegel's Philosophy of Right*, transl. T. M. Knox (Oxford: Clarendon Press, 1942), 34–5.

[62]The lines preceding this important passage are also worth citing: "On this occasion we will note the double meaning of our German expression *aufheben*. By this term we understand, first of all, to remove, negate, or annul: in this sense we say a law or regulation is annulled; second of all, the term also means to preserve or keep, and we speak in this sense of the fact that something ought to be preserved" (Hegel, *Werke* 8: §96: 204–5).

representations to thoughts; similarly a mind committed to one history is a mind that has forgotten the rhetorical nature of the material from which that interpretive history presently emerges.

For Hegel, architecture—as the catholic language of buildings and markings—preserves and externalizes this symbolic and historical dimension of language, which is also the mechanical dimension of memory, and thus the material of history available to thought. In this manner, the Memnon, as an architectural "memorial" related to thinking [*Denken*] and the production of a sign, only preserves history by ceaselessly and mythopoetically rebuilding it. Laboring to speak architecturally, unconsciously, universally—the colossus marks the thinking of time through endlessly new lines of thought that efface the boundaries of foreignness, exclusion, and historically ossified understanding.

Figure 2 *Memnon.* Engraving by Bernard Picart. *The Temple of the Muses*, 1731.

Figure 3 *The Departure of Memnon for Troy*, Greek, 6th century BC. Courtesy of Royal Museums of Art and History, Brussels.

Figure 4 *Memnon and His Ethiopian Warriors,* Greek, *c.* 530 BC. Courtesy of British Museum, London.

Figure 5 *Eos Tearing Her Hair in Grief over the Body of Memnon*, 6th century BC. Courtesy of Gregorian Etruscan Museum, Vatican City.

71

Figure 6 *Achilles Battles Memnon as Thetis and Eos Watch.* Attic red figure volute krater, 500–480 BC. Courtesy of British Museum, London.

CHAPTER 4
ARCHITECTURE AND THE POETRY OF LIGHT

How does the performative marking of thought in time, the linguistic operation emblematized by the Memnon, inflect Hegel's theory of the aesthetic? The statue before the sun, in order to "give voice," requires "light from without, which alone draws out … the sound of the soul." In the *Aesthetics* light functions as the visual matrix of architecture ("art in the external," *die Kunst am Äußerlichen*) and spoken sound as the medium of poetry ("the art of speech," *die redende Kunst*).[1] The interplay of vocal sound and light in the figure of the Memnon evokes not only the aesthetic media of architecture and poetry, but also their conceptual interrelation or even dependence, not least given the statue's transitional position, in the *Aesthetics*, between symbolic architecture and the poetry of the sublime. This relation, which we will examine at length in this chapter, will underwrite the aesthetic mediation between language and materiality, serving as the epistemological foundation for Hegel's theory of history, subjectivity, and ethicality in the state.

The symbolic interplay of sound and light in the Memnon retains the charge of their dialectical relation in the *Encyclopedia of the Philosophical Sciences*, the armature for all of Hegel's courses including the lectures on art. In the terms of this system, the statue in human form does not utter the purely "human voice" of a self-conscious individual, but only the "abstract corporeity of the voice" produced by the "anthropological" subject. Hegel glosses this "abstract" voice in the "Anthropology" section of the *Encyclopedia*:

> An even more perfect corporealization and also clearing out of the internal sensations than what occurs through laughter or crying is produced by the *voice*. For the voice involves not just the formation of something external and at hand [*vorhandenes*] as in laughing, nor the discharge of real material as in crying, but the generation of an ideal substance, an incorporeal corporeity [*unkörperliche Leiblichkeit*], so to speak—a material in which the inwardness of the subject preserves in all events the character of inwardness and, furthermore, the self-existent ideality of the soul acquires for itself a suitable external reality—a reality immediately sublated, hence dissipating as it appears, since the materialization of sound is just as much the dissipation of it … Now indeed the abstract corporeity of the voice can become a sign [*Zeichen*] for others who recognize it as such; here, however, from the standpoint of the natural soul, it is not as yet a sign issuing from the free will [*freien Willen*], not as yet articulate

[1]Hegel, *Werke* 14: 271, 15: 224.

speech originating from the energy of intelligence and will, but merely a sound produced immediately out of sensation.[2]

Like Hegel's anthropological subject, the African or Oriental Memnon issues "mere sound" that is "not yet speech"; but while this producer of sound remains unconscious of its linguistic power, we can "recognize" in its "abstract corporeity" the sign-bearing medium of language. Similarly, though the statue lacks even a "natural soul," we can nonetheless "recognize" the voice of the "living" Memnon as the medium of the soul's self-production: for "beyond art, a sound as an interjection, as the cry of pain, as a sigh or a laugh, is the immediate, most living expression of states and sensations of the soul .... Within [such a sound] lies the self-production and objectivity of the soul as soul, an expression mediating between, on the one hand, the unconscious immersion and returning into self and internal specific thoughts—and, on the other hand, a production that is not practical but theoretical: the bird has this pleasure and production of itself in song."[3]

For those who "recognize" it—that is, for those who "take the [Memnon] as a symbol"—the statue's voice occupies precisely this straddling position between unconsciousness and pleasure, since in its voice the colossus, as a memorial to a departed soul, unconsciously exteriorizes itself, expressing and producing the natural soul that it lacks internally. Though fundamentally articulating the Egyptian spirit, "which seeks not pleasure," the Memnon thus reaches into the "theoretical," avian state of pleasure in sonorous self-production: indeed in the mythological accounts of Memnon, his "black ashes" or those of his "dark-skinned Aethiops" are transformed into birds named "Memnones" or "Memnonides," which fly yearly from his palace in Ethiopia to his tomb at Troy to fight each other, dying only to spring up again from the ashes.[4]

---

[2] Hegel, *Werke* 10: §401: 115–6.

[3] Hegel, *Werke* 15: 150.

[4] These black birds appear in Bernard Picart's engraving of Memnon (see Figure 2). The classical references to Memnon and his death are abundant, ranging from the earliest Greek sources to late antiquity. On the transformation of Memnon's army into "birds of Memnon," the Hellenistic poet Quintus Smyrnaeus writes: "Swiftly the dark-skinned Aethiopes from her sight buried their lord lamenting. As they wailed unceasingly, Erigeneia (the Dawn-queen) lovely-eyed changed them to birds sweeping through air around the barrow of the mighty dead. And these still do the tribes of men 'The Memnones' call; and still with wailing cries they dart and wheel above their king's tomb, and they scatter dust down on his grave, still shrill the battle-cry, in memory of Memnon, each to each. But he in Haides' mansions, or perchance amid the Blessed on the Elysian Plain, laugheth. Divine Eos comforteth her heart beholding them: but theirs is toil of strife unending, till the weary victors strike the vanquished dead, or one and all fill up the measure of their doom around his grave" (Quintus Smyrnaeus, *Epicus*, translated as *Quintus Smyrnaeus: The Fall of Troy*. A. S. Way [Cambridge: Harvard University Press, 1913], 2: 790–806). In Ovid's *Metamorphosis*, Memnon's own "black ashes" are transformed into birds: "Memnon's pyre fell to the leaping flames. Black billowing smoke obscured the daylight, as a stream exhaling mist that lets no sunlight through. Up flew black ashes, clustering thick into a single shape, taking form and drawing heat and life out of the fire. Its lightness gave it wings and like a bird at first, and then the actual bird, its wings whirring and in the neighboring air countless sister-birds whirring, all of the same birth. Three times they flew around the pyre; three times the sound accordant of their fluttering wings went swift upon the soft breeze. Their fourth flight divided them; thus in two hostile legions, they clashed in warfare, with beaks and crooked claws in rage, until their weary wings and battling breasts could not sustain

74

The empty voice, liberating the subject of his interiority, achieves its highest articulation in poetry, the human corollary of the animal cry or bird-song:

> Thus in the voice, sensation acquires a corporeity in which it dies away just as fast as it is expressed. This is the ground of the higher power present in the voice of externalizing what is internally felt. That is why the Romans, who understood this power, intentionally let women wail in lamentation at funerals so that they might externalize the pain they felt within ... Animals, in giving external form to their sensations, voice them only inarticulately, producing only cries of pain or pleasure; and some animals achieve this ideal utterance of their inwardness even in their direst need ... [For man] it is especially the writing of poetry that has the power to free him from internal anguish. Goethe, for example, recovered his spiritual freedom several times by pouring out his sorrow in a poem.[5]

In the Jena lectures, Hegel had made clear that the "direst need" giving rise to the "ideal utterance" of the voice for some animals is the encounter with death, the memory of which forever marks the ideality of the voice. The emptiness of the animal voice reflects the negativity not only of the voice itself but also of the dying animal. Thus Hegel explains the effectiveness of wailing as the human response to death: in a double negation, the voice, as the voice of death, eradicates the subjectivity the individual already and continually loses—both in his temporal discontinuity with himself and in his ineluctable march toward death. Cries of pain or pleasure, insofar as they void the voice and subject, are thus equally "ideal" forms of the voice of death. In the same passage from the Jena lectures Hegel had specified bird-song as a more rarefied "articulation of voice" and hence equally a liquidation and dissolution of the self. This movement from the "animal" to the vocalizing capacity of the "human" in the *Encyclopedia*, the *Aesthetics*, and the Jena lectures illuminates the rapid evolution in the *Phenomenology* from the work-master's identification with the animal to his erection of the sounding "statue in human form." Indeed, in the *Phenomenology* the human statue, evolving out of the animal hieroglyph, merges with "the formless black stone,"[6] symbol of interiority and pure thought, to produce the "ambiguous being" and "monster" evocative of the half-man, half-animal sphinx:

---

them; then they fell, like memorial offerings, upon their parental ash, belonging to brave Memnon buried in that place ... when the sun has passed through the twelve signs of the zodiac, they war to perish in his memory again" (Ovid, *Metamorphoses*, 2 vols. transl. Brookes More [Francestown: Marshall Jones Co., 1978], 13.576ff., 1042; translation modified). On the birds' movement between the palace and tomb of Memnon, Pliny the Elder writes: "Some authorities state that every year birds fly from Ethiopia to Troy and have a fight at Memnon's tomb, and consequently they call them Memnonides, or birds of Memnon. Cremutius records having discovered that every four years they do the same things in Ethiopia around the palace of Memnon" [*Auctores sunt omnibus annis advolare Ilium ex Aethiopia aves et confligere ad Memnonis tumulum, quas ob id Memnonidas vocant. hoc idem quinto quoque anno facere eas in Aethiopia circa regiam Memnonis, exploratum sibi Cremutius tradit*] (Pliny, *Natural History*, X.37.74, 339; translation slightly modified).

[5]Hegel, *Werke* 10: §401: 115–6.

[6]Hegel, *Werke* 3: 510.

Hence the *Werkmeister* combines the two, intermingling the natural and the self-conscious shape, and these equivocal and ambiguous beings, a riddle even to themselves—the conscious struggling with the unconscious, the simple inner with the multifarious outer, the darkness of thought coupled with the clarity of expression—break out into the language of a profound, almost incomprehensible wisdom … [Then, ending this phase,] these monsters in shape, speech, and action resolve into the [true] shape of spirit … The *Werkmeister* has given up the *synthetic* works *intermingling* shapes, foreign to each other, of thought and nature; having won the shape and form of self-conscious activity, he has become a worker for spirit.[7]

The voice of the statue before the sun, blending with the interiority and pure thought of the black stone, yields the enigmatic speech of the sphinx, which punctuates the theoretical history of the work-master and of "instinctive" art in the *Phenomenology* and, correspondingly, of symbolic architecture and unconscious symbolism in the *Aesthetics*. Whereas the former text proceeds with the history of religious expression, the latter moves, in the three-part history of the symbol, from symbolic architecture to "sublime" poetry and, last, verbal "comparison" or figuration.[8]

The movement in the "Anthropology" section of the *Encyclopedia* from the animal to the human voice articulated in poetry parallels the movement in the *Aesthetics* from the animal shapes of symbolic architecture to the externalizing human voice of sublime poetry. How does the Memnon of the *Aesthetics*, "giving voice" and producing meaningless sound, mediate this movement from architecture to poetry? The Memnon (or for that matter the sphinx) does not produce poetry as such, but like poetry isolates the voice in its "abstract corporeity," indicating its power to externalize "what is inwardly felt" and thus void the subject of his sense of loss. By taking the Memnon as a symbol, we can recognize its animal voice as not just the medium of the sign, but "as a sign" itself: a production utterly estranged from its corporeal origins. And this reduction of the voice, via symbols, to a sign is, in the *Aesthetics*, the defining work of poetry:

Sound, the last external material which poetry uses, is in poetry no longer the sensation of sound itself [as in music], but a sign, meaningless by itself: a sign, that is, of the idea [*Vorstellung*] which has become concrete in itself, and not just of indefinite sensation and its nuances and gradations. Sound thereby becomes a *word* as the articulated voice as such, the meaning of which is to designate [*bezeichnen*] ideas and thoughts … Indeed to express [ideas, poetry] avails itself of sound, but only as a sign worthless in itself and without content. Thus the sound

[7]Hegel, *Werke* 3: 511–2.
[8]Hegel organizes these three forms under three types of symbolism: "unconscious symbolism" [*Die unbewußte Symbolik*]; "symbolism of the sublime" [*Die Symbolik der Erhabenheit*]; and "conscious symbolism of the comparative art-form" [*Die bewußte Symbolik der vergleichenden Kunstform*].

may just as well be a pure letter, since the audible, like the visible, has been reduced to a pure indication [*Andeutung*] of spirit.[9]

Poetry isolates the voice as an "idea" or concept of materiality, hence an "incorporeal corporeity." This "idea" of the voice in its "concrete" materiality bears no significance other than the act of designation [*bezeichnen*] or indication [*Andeutung*] as such. In other words, the content of the idea remains empty, consisting of nothing more nor less than "pure indication," or what Hegel also calls the demonstrative "*This* of meaning."[10] Since this meaning of the idea of the voice relates arbitrarily to its corporeal form, the voice as such is structured as a sign. As a "word" with no referent other than the act of reference itself, however, it may as well only be a conceptual "pure letter," the external manifestation of thought itself. And as the product of the sign-producing Mnemosyne, mother of the muses and font of poetry, the verbal "art of speech" isolates the material of speech only to rarefy it as the pure thought of its own act of referring.[11] In this sense the voice, a conceptual letter, is rather a *pyramidal* sign, a sepulcher containing no meaning other than the negation of meaning itself in the act of indication. Or better, a hieroglyph, conceived negatively only by virtue of the difference between letters in architectonic arrangement. In this respect the poetic product of Mnemosyne equates not only to the "meaningless sound" of the Memnon but also to the Memnon itself as a symbolic memorial [*Denkmal*], the thought of its own externalized thought, and as a hieroglyph architectonically arranged. Thus to recognize the voice as a meaningless sign is already to know the voice as a symbol, a corporeity exceeding the strict limits of meaning, just as earlier we saw that to recognize the voice as a sign-bearing medium is to know it as a symbolic instrument, a tomb, or storehouse of the psychophysiological vestiges of language.

As a material indication of its own substantiality, the voice as such collapses the line between the interiority of the body from which it originates and the externality of things apprehended outside the body. But for Hegel any knowledge of differentiated, substantial

---

[9]Hegel, *Werke* 13: 122–3.

[10]Hegel, *Werke* 3: 82–94. For a discussion of the "emptiness" of the deictic marker "this," see Roman Jakobson, "Shifters, Verbal Categories, and the Russian Verb," in *Russian and Slavic Grammar*, eds. L. Waugh and M. Halle (Berlin: Mouton, 1984), 41–58 and Emile Benveniste, *Problèmes de linguistique générale*. 2 vols. (Paris: Gallimard, 1966), 251–6.

[11]Hegel's view of the Memnon as a figure for the linguistic construction of a referent, the simultaneous negation thereof, and thus of the self-referentiality of the verbal action anticipates Barbara Johnson's formulation of the performative in her seminal "Poetry and Performative Language": "if a performative utterance is originally a self-referential speech act, its production is simultaneously the production of a new referent into the world. This, however, is tantamount to a radical transformation of the notion of a referent, since, instead of pointing to an external object, language would then refer only to its own referring to itself in the act of referring, and the signifying chain would end in an infinitely self-duplicating loop. A variant of this difficulty has, in fact, been pointed out by Paul Larreya, who, in attempting to fit a performative utterance into a Chomskyan tree diagram, finds that 'to develop the tree it would be necessary to repeat the symbol [designating the performative] an infinite number of times.' The performative utterance is thus the *mise en abyme* of reference itself" (Barbara Johnson, *The Critical Difference: Essays in the Contemporary Rhetoric of Reading* [Baltimore: John Hopkins University Press, 1980], 57).

things outside the body depends primarily on the faculty of seeing and hence on the light of the sun. Thus he writes, again in the "Anthropology" section of the *Encyclopedia*:

> Sight is the sense of that physical ideality which we call light. From this we can say of light that it is physicalized space. For light, like space, is indivisible, a transparent ideality, extension absolutely free of determination—lacking self-reflection and hence inwardness. Light manifests a something-other, and this manifesting externalizes light in its essence; but in itself light is an abstract identity with itself ... immaterial matter. Thus light puts up no resistance [*leistet das Licht keinen Widerstand*], has no limit in itself ... The real material aspect of corporeity ... does not as yet concern us in seeing. Therefore the objects we see can be remote from us ... In opposition to sight, the sense of ideality devoid of any inwardness, hearing emerges as the sense of the pure inwardness of the corporeal. Just as sight relates to physicalized space, to light, so hearing relates to physicalized time, to sound. For sound is corporeity posited in time, the movement and pulsing of the body itself, a trembling and mechanical vibration in which the body, without having to change its relative position as a whole body, moves only its parts, posits its interior space as temporal, and thus negates [*aufhebt*] its indifferent differentiation, and by this negation [*Aufhebung*] allows its pure inwardness outwardly to manifest itself, but nevertheless immediately restores itself [to its formerly integral corporeity]. The medium through which sound comes to our hearing, however, is not just the element of air, but with even more force the concrete corporeity measuring the space between the sounding object and us.[12]

Sight and hearing both belong to the first, "theoretical" category of the senses, corresponding to, respectively, light as the matrix of materiality and sound as the negation of materiality. Hegel privileges sight as the marker for externality because sight measures distance without physical impact on the body, whereas hearing involves the body viscerally, even though the sonorous material—and hence the induced sense of corporeal movement—dissipate immediately. Taste and smell, the second group of the senses, mark the "decomposition and dissolution" of materiality and in particular of the body in its natural process of physical decay. The third group consists only of touch, "the sense affected by gravity," and marks the propensity of bodies to offer resistance rather than merely dissolve.[13] According to the *Aesthetics*, "the sensuous facet of art relates only to the two theoretical senses of sight and hearing."[14] The other senses "have to do with matter as such" and thus "cannot have to do with objects of art, which are meant to keep themselves in their real independence and exclude any purely sensuous relation."[15] The art of building, for instance, consists not in the mere physical resistance of built material

---

[12]Hegel, *Werke* 10: §401: 104–5.
[13]Hegel, *Werke* 10: §401: 104–117 *passim*.
[14]Hegel, *Werke* 13: 61.
[15]Hegel, *Werke* 13: 61.

or production by the laboring hand, though these are the essential conditions for any building; rather it consists in the symbolic separation and then entanglement of what is *seen* and what is *indicated*: thus the "indicative symbol" [*andeutenden Symbol*][16] in its proper, architectural form diverts meaning away from its visible exterior shape to the interiority of a preserved and negated body: for "the proper symbol [for instance, the pyramid] allows the determinate shape … to persist or endure in the same form, because symbolism does not seek to *see* [*anschauen*] in that shape the immediate existence of the meaning in its universality, but rather to indicate the meaning in the qualities of the object cognate [*verwandten*] to that meaning."[17] Or again: "The particular existents [of symbolism proper] are not meant actually to *be* the absolute meaning for vision [*Anschauung*], but rather to *indicate* [*andeuten*] it."[18] In the pyramidal symbol, external positedness or materiality is related to meaning only deictically, where deixis implies an imperfect correspondence of what is seen at a distance and what is fleetingly interiorized or taken in as meaning—by the tomb or body.

Now, visual matter—especially in architecture, whose "shapes are made visible by external light"—cannot posit a spiritual content in the absence of a body present to receive that meaning.[19] Since sonority penetrates the body and renders corporeal the space between sounding objects, within the category of the aesthetic the body, like architecture, can only mark the line between interiority and externality *visually*. Thus architecture, remaining a "soundless language" so long as spiritual meaning attaches to a hidden corpse, becomes, in the living bodies of external viewers, the "articulation" of diverging and changing "opinions" as to a work's multiple meanings.[20] In the same manner, the sound of the voice—especially in poetry—cannot posit itself as a corporeality removed from the body in the absence of an illuminated externality.

This relation of light and sound and, accordingly, of architecture and poetry underpins Hegel's symbolic reading of the sounding statue before the sun. The Memnon, we recall, falls short of the self-conscious subject that, knowingly possessed of an intellectual soul, requires no "external impetus" to produce meaningful speech, only the inner "free light of spirit."[21] Though the progression from architecture to poetry marks the increasing independence of the aesthetic from external light, this final and absolute interiorization of light falls outside the category of the aesthetic, since it would require a permanent separation of form and content—of the body from spirit, or of linguistic materiality from meaning. As we have seen, the history of aesthetics beginning with the pyramid—the first

---

[16]Hegel, *Werke* 15: 235.

[17]Hegel, *Werke* 13: 438. Emphasis mine.

[18]Hegel, *Werke* 13: 436.

[19]Hegel, *Werke* 14: 260.

[20]Thus Hegel asserts that to "articulate an opinion" [*sprechen die Meinung*] about symbolic architecture contributes merely to its infinite and endlessly dissipating content, unless governed by the reasoned or dialectical—which is to say, self-negating—categories of the aesthetic (Hegel, *Werke* 14: 275). This statement follows his formulation, previously cited, that symbolic architecture, as a "soundless language" [*lautlose Sprache*], "gives rise" to discursive "ideas" to present "viewers" (Hegel, *Werke* 14: 273).

[21]Hegel, *Werke* 12: 246.

attempt literally to free the spirit from the external light of day and, accordingly, spiritual content from material form—indicates the unstable division of form and content to be the defining condition of the aesthetic.[22] And for the aesthetic to be historical, it must move from its opening, pyramidal articulation: thus history sees the pyramids breached, the sepulchers opened, and the bones exposed.[23]

The light of day thus marks the vital corporeity of the aesthetic. Moreover as "immaterial matter," light occupies the space or, better, demarcates the sensuous difference between visual externality and the invisible infinite, between embodied space and incorporeal substance. Words that would attempt to free their corporeity from the demarcations of the body, achieving a condition of "incorporeal corporeity," would have to take up and expunge their dependence on illuminated externality. This encounter of language and the invisible characterizes what Hegel terms the "sublime"[24]—the second, mediating stage in the history of the symbol:

> The sublime is in general the attempt to *express* [*auszudrücken*] the infinite without finding in the *visual* realm an object that turns out to be apposite for this presentation [*Darstellung*]. The infinite—precisely because it is removed from the whole complex of objectivity and is made inner, as an *invisible* [*unsichtbare*] meaning lacking shape—remains, by virtue of its infinity, *unpronounceable* [*unaussprechbar*] and *sublimely above any finite expression* [*Ausdruck*].[25]

The infinite remains specifically "invisible" and "unpronounceable" because it subsists without light or voice, the media of architecture and poetry. The sublime attempt to present [*darstellen*] the infinite is not mimetic, but involves rather the struggle to "express" or "pronounce" it linguistically. Putting aside its grammatical formation, here the verb *auszudrücken* (to express), by coupling the exteriorizing and interiorizing prepositions *aus* and *zu* only through the corporeal violence of *drücken* (to strike, to press together), punningly instantiates the difficulties of transcending the corporeally marked categories of interiority and externality; and the loss of *zu* in the movement from *auszudrücken* to *Ausdruck* signals, in the same vein, the failure to interiorize matter through linguistic "expression."

---

[22]As we have seen, classical art by contrast "remains" in the "past" due to the impossibility of attaining a stable or "ideal" conformity of form and content in any present.

[23]Hegel, *Werke* 14: 293.

[24]Here I am building on Paul de Man's reading of the sublime in Hegel's *Aesthetics* ("Hegel on the Sublime," in *Aesthetic Ideology*, 105–18). Crucially, de Man ignores the initial, "pantheistic" moment of the sublime, which leads to two misreadings of Hegel: first, de Man claims that "the moment Hegel calls sublime is the moment of radical and definitive separation between the order of discourse and the order of the sacred" (*Aesthetic Ideology*, 111); and second, de Man argues that the sublime, thus defined, marks a non-dialectical moment in the aesthetic. For Hegel, the "definitive" separation of discourse and the sacred in fact characterizes only the second, negative articulation of the sublime in Hebraic poetry. As will become clear, the sublime in its "pantheistic" moment passes through the "immanence" of word and God: and it is precisely this sublime coimbrication of linguistic form and content that persists dialectically in the aesthetic.

[25]Hegel, *Werke* 13: 467. Emphases mine.

This division of interiority and exteriority marks the most general feature of sublimity, common to both symbolic architecture and sublime poetry:

> where the symbol is developed independently in its own proper form [as in the symbolic architecture of the Pyramids], it has in general the character of *sublimity*, because at first it is in fact only the idea, still limitless and lacking free determination in itself, that is to take shape, and thus it cannot find in concrete appearances [*Erscheinungen*] any specific form that corresponds entirely to this abstraction and universality. But in this lack of mutual answerability and nonconformity [*Nichtentsprechen*] [of concrete form and universal content], the idea lies totally above external existence instead of having merged or perfectly agreed with it. This elusion of the determinacy of appearance [*Erscheinung*] comprises the general character of the sublime.[26]

In symbolic architecture the sublime consists of the mute "nonconformity" or unanswering silence between outer stone and inner spiritual content, or the physical form of a corpse and the removed interiority of a departed soul—a muteness again conveyed punningly here by the presence of *nicht* and *sprechen* in the word *Nichtentsprechen*. To the extent that these divisions of interiority and exteriority emerge from artificial stone or a lifeless body, the architectural sublime, whose language remains "soundless" and incorporeal, does not proceed beyond the silent entanglement of its parts. To express or pronounce the infinite through language, the sublime must traverse corporeal and conceptual demarcations of interiority: corporeal, because language must slough off the finite body from which it originates; and conceptual, because language must linguistically give voice to what lies beyond exteriority.

In language, poetry alone, isolating the voice in its dissipation, can posit and attempt to negate the body; but a poetry that reaches for the incorporeal and invisible infinite would also have to posit and then negate illuminated externality. This "sublime" poetry, according to Hegel, has two types or modalities. In the first, "affirmative" or "pantheistic" mode of the sublime, associated with Indian, "Mohammedan," and Christian mystical poetry, divine "substance is envisioned [*angeschaut*] as immanent in all its created accidents, which are therefore not yet reduced to serving and merely adorning the absolute for its glorification, but rather affirmatively maintained by the substance inhering in them."[27] This mode of the sublime operates through the immanence of the

---

[26]Hegel, *Werke* 13: 393–4. I have translated *Nichtensprechen* as both "non-conformity" and, in view of the overall contextual concern with linguistic articulation, more loosely as "lack of mutual answerability."

[27]Hegel, *Werke* 13: 469. For a collection of Hegel's writings on "India," see Aakash Rathore and Rimina Mohapatra, *Hegel's India: A Reinterpretation, with Texts* (Oxford: Oxford University Press, 2017). Ignoring the "sublime" as a central philosopheme in Hegel's engagement of Indian thought, the authors read Hegel as a "racist" who was confused and "threatened" by the "sublimity of Indian religion" and the "complexity of Indian philosophy" (ibid., 79–80).

absolute in phenomena. By contrast the second, "negative" or "proper"[28] mode of the sublime, associated with Hebraic poetry, "cancels the positive immanence of the absolute in its created appearances and puts the *one* substance on one side, alone, as the Lord of the world; on another side, in utter distinction, there stands the totality of his creatures."[29]

The difference between affirmation and negation here turns on their respectively "implicit" and "explicit" modes of representation. In the affirmative mode of the sublime, "the accidental is not posited *expressly* as negative and servant, as in proper [Hebraic] sublimity; on the contrary the substance becomes *implicitly* particular and accidental, because it is the One inhering in everything particular."[30] Both modes of the sublime, however, require poetic articulation and a mode of presentational "envisioning." Thus Hegel says of Indian, Muslim, and Christian sublimity: "such a way of looking at things [*Anschauungsweise*] can express itself artistically only in poetry, not in the visual arts which bring before our eyes [*vor Augen bringen*] determined and single objects only as existent and enduring, which in turn dissipate by virtue of the substance present in such existents"; hence "the presentational mode [*Darstellungsweise*] of [pantheistic immanence] excludes visual art."[31] But for Hegel the affirmative sublime, while *implicitly* asserting the accidental nature of the created, *explicitly* "envisions" substance as "immanently" present in externalities, where "envisioning" marks this poetry's own representational intermingling of the universal and particular, or God and created accident.

Hegel's selection of texts instantiating the sublime moment of the aesthetic is extraordinarily revealing. The citations betray remarkable relations and tensions with each other and with the rest of Hegel's text on the sublime; and yet few studies have given any serious consideration to these texts or to Hegel's use of them.[32] His discussion of the sublime begins with Indian poetry, which "first surfaces the immanence of the divine in particular things as they appear and disappear to the mind's eye [*für die Anschauung*]."[33] As an example Hegel cites from the *Bhagavad Gita*, where Krishna intones:

---

[28]For Hegel a "proper" [*eigentlich*] aesthetic moment first arises with the pyramids, whose demarcation and separation of the negative creates an apparently impenetrable space, hence symbolically a self-enclosed concept standing non-dialectically against the evolving processes of thought. But the pyramids at the same time mark the fluidity of the binary, of demarcations of the negative, hence the mind's freedom from its own exclusionary and apparently self-sufficient concepts. These concepts in Hegel's *Aesthetics* are thus only provisionally "proper" or non-dialectical, rejoining ultimately the fluid currents of the mind's progress.

[29]Hegel, *Werke* 13: 469.

[30]Hegel, *Werke* 13: 471. Emphasis mine.

[31]Hegel, *Werke* 13: 471. Hegel's view here recalls Kant's conception of hypotyposis as a mode of presentation [*Darstellung*] in §59 of *The Critique of Judgment*. On hypotyposis see Rodolphe Gasché, *The Idea of Form: Rethinking Kant's Aesthetics* (Palo Alto: Stanford University Press, 2003), 202–20 and my "From Bayt to Stanza: Arabic Khayāl and the Advent of Italian Vernacular Poetry," forthcoming in *Exemplaria*.

[32]The principal exceptions are de Man, who examines Hegel's use of Hebraic scriptural verses, Michel Hulin, *Hegel el l'Orient* (Paris: J. Vrin, 1979), and Rathore and Mohapatra, *Hegel's India*.

[33]"[A]lso with [the Indians] there emerges the pure representational mode of the aforementioned pantheism, which surfaces the immanence of the divine in particular things as they appear and disappear in the mind's eye" (Hegel, *Werke* 13: 472).

ich bin in der Sonne und im Monde Glanz, das mystische Wort in den heiligen Schriften … der Glanz in den Flammen … im Glänzenden der Glanz; welche Naturen … scheinbar und finster sind, sind aus mir, nicht bin ich in ihnen, sondern sie in mir … Unter den Gestirnen bin ich die strahlende Sonne, unter den lunarischen Zeichen der Mond, unter den heiligen Büchern das Buch der Hymnen, unter den Sinnen das Innere … unter den Buchstaben bin ich der Vokal A.[34]

I am the glimmering of the sun and moon, the mystic word in the holy scriptures … the glow of the flame … the glimmering of the glow … natures luminous and dark are from me, I am not in them, they are in me … Amongst the stars I am the shining sun, amongst the lunary signs the moon; amongst the holy books the book of hymns, amongst the senses the inward … amongst the letters I am the vowel A.

Here Krishna, as both the phenomenal manifestation and the origin of "glimmering" or "luminous" phenomena—"they are from me"—at once posits and subverts the identity of light and the absolute. Moreover his recitation blurs the line between light as the condition of an object—its "glimmering"—and objects like the sun or moon, a flame, or a glow whose objectivity consists only of their luminosity. As the condition of matter, light, like the "immanent" absolute, collapses the distinction between predicate and subject, or created accident and substance as such. But in Hegel's reading the "One" manifests itself as a phenomenal part relating incongruously to the whole: thus Hegel reads the series of synecdoches—"Amongst the stars I am the sun," and so on—as Krishna's assertion that he is "the most excellent" [*Vortrefflichsten*] of any category.[35] Moreover as the origin of light, the absolute maintains a priority in immanence: "I am not in them, they are in me," where the chiasmus marks the ultimately hierarchical relation of the mirrored elements. Thus Hegel reads divine "immanence" here as "transient" or "transcendent," and it is precisely this unstable presence of the absolute that marks its sublimity.[36]

Immanenz—deriving from Latin *manere*, "to dwell," and Greek *menō*, "to remain"—relates etymologically to *Memnon*—"the steadfast, he who remains." But where the outward Memnon remains architectonically fixed, the "indwelling" absolute moves fleetingly through the phenomenal. Moreover for Hegel the "indwelling" of the absolute is only symbolically visual: repeatedly he insists that in this poetry the vanishing presence of the absolute "is brought before our mental vision" [*zur Anschauung gebracht werden*].[37] We do not *see* the absolute, but see it *as* physically present. In accordance with the transition from the "visual art" of architecture to sonorous poetry, visual

---

[34]Hegel, *Werke* 13: 472–3.

[35]Hegel, *Werke* 13: 473.

[36]Hegel reads Krishna's lines as expressing the One's "immanence in what is present and also [its] transcendence over the particular" (Hegel, *Werke* 13: 473). Meriting a separate investigation, sublime poetry here sublates the scholastic difference between "immanent" and "transient" acts, as well as Kant's distinction between the "immanent" and "transcendental" principle. On this same poetry, see also Hegel, *Werke* 10: §573: 381–6 *passim*.

[37]Hegel, *Werke* 13: 473.

light is displaced here by verbal, symbolic light: thus the text initially juxtaposes the "glimmering" of the sun with the "mystic word" of sacred texts; unifies light and word in the "lunary signs" of the heavens; and then asserts the immanence of divine "glimmering" not in the written word, but in the sung poems of the scriptures or the vocalized letter that begins the alphabet. Now, the "mystic word" or "lunary sign" is not a sign proper, but a symbol hinting obscurely at variable meaning. "Mystic" derives from Greek *mystikós*, meaning "symbolic," "mysterious," "esoteric," and "spiritual"[38]; moreover, "mystic word" would have intimated for Hegel the Christian sense of the logos immanent as spirit in the flesh. But here that immanence is transient, since the absolute manifest as hymn or vowel—as the symbolic medium of the human voice—must negate and transcend its fleeting corporeity.

As both a "mode of seeing" [*Auffassungsweise*] and the human articulation of Krishna's word, this sacred poetry must, like the absolute passing through it, exploit the duplicity of light—its status as both the condition of matter and material object and, equally paradoxically, as both the transparent medium of referentiality and a "mystic" or symbolic word—to bring before our mental vision the transient immanence of the divine.[39] Divine immanence can only be represented if light is taken as a symbol, a "lunary sign" traversing its double meaning as necessary and divine condition of externality and as created accident—that is, as holy word and as human articulation. Only then can the mind *see* externality *as* divine. It is in this sense that this poetry principally deploys not pictorial reproduction or mimesis, but rather synecdoche or chiasmus, the rhetorical and symbolic "presentation" of the disparity of related terms. Furthermore, given its dwelling in the symbolic medium of the voice—or alternately, given that Krishna passes only through the vowel and only through the songs of holy books—this sacred and sublime poetry must be understood as a vocalized text. Flouting or confusing the categories of "change" and "repetition," this human echo of the divine word presents speech as the imperfect corollary of the divine luminosity that brings objects to light.[40] In the transition from the outer sense of sight to the "inwardness" of the voice, from *seeing* to *seeing as*, verbal light must be uttered, as it were, through the dissipating sound of a vowel or song—for poetry to intimate, however fleetingly, the true incorporeity of the divine.

This poetry, exposing through its voice the transient movement of this divine power, already hints at the "emptiness" of "mystic" utterances and, correspondingly,

---

[38]*Oxford English Dictionary*, "mystic."

[39]Hegel, *Werke* 13: 472.

[40]"This enumeration of its [qualities of] excellence [within categories of phenomena], as well as the mere change of forms in which only the same thing should be brought to our mental vision over and over again, despite the wealth of fancy which at first sight appears to burgeon there, still remains—by virtue of just this equality of its contents—highly monotonous and on the whole empty and tiring" (Hegel, *Werke* 13: 473). Here the conflation of change and repetition or sameness, as well as of imagistic profusion and vocalized "monotone," reveals the deceptiveness of appearances and the ultimate "emptiness" of a vocalized presentation of the divine. Since Krishna only passes through the voice, rather than dwelling or remaining there permanently, this sublime poetry also gives voice to and hints at the ultimate negativity of the divine.

the negativity of the sacred. Contrasting with the multiplicity of its images and the appearing-disappearing movement of the divine, the vocal "monotone" of this poetry nonetheless continues without end, belying its corporeal finitude.[41] The emptiness of the voice is not yet death. It is in the sublime poetry of the "Mohammedans," especially the Persians, that Hegel finds this knowledge of death, the poet's consciousness of himself as a perishing "subject":[42]

> While the poet longs to see the divine in everything and really sees it, before the divine he also surrenders his own self, but then grasps or conceptualizes [*faßt*] the immanence of the divine [as inhering] within his expansive and freed interiority; and thus there arises within him that serene warmth, that free felicity, and that festive bliss distinctive of the Oriental who, with the abnegation of his own particularity, immerses himself completely in the everlasting and absolute and recognizes [*erkennt*] and feels [*empfindet*] in everything the image [*Bild*] and presence [*Gegenwart*] of the divine.[43]

Aware of his own selfhood, the poet willingly surrenders it through his poetry; and the verbal transcendence of subjective limitation results in what Hegel terms a "subjectively free" poetry.[44] Here again it is the desire to "see the divine" or "recognize" the "image" of the divine that prompts the fluidity of interiority and exteriority; and the subsequent vision of the divine—the poet "really sees it"—occurs in the form of a physical grasping or conceptualization of its immanence across the disappearing boundaries of the poet's necessarily corporeal subjectivity. Here the equivocal verb *fassen*, meaning to grasp or conceptualize, and the juxtaposition of the verbs *erkennen*, to recognize, and *empfinden*, to perceive and to feel, mark the ambivalent corporeity of this experience of the "absolute."

Instantiating this transcendence of the body through poetic seeing, Hegel cites Hafiz, the fifteenth-century Persian poet:

> Aus Dank, weil dich die Gegenwart
> Des Freunds erhellt,
> Verbrenn der Kerze gleich im Weh
> Und sei vergnügt.[45]

> Out of thanks—that the presence
> Of the Friend enlightens you,
> Burn in woe like the candle
> And be joyful.

---

[41] Hegel, *Werke* 13: 473.
[42] Hegel, *Werke* 13: 474.
[43] Hegel, *Werke* 13: 474.
[44] Hegel, *Werke* 13: 473.
[45] Hegel, *Werke* 13: 476. Hegel cites Rückert's translation.

Here the "Friend"—which Hegel takes as the multivalent Persian trope for the worldly and divine "beloved"—metaphorically enlightens but also literally illuminates [*erhellt*] the poet: as a symbol for both the illuminating God and illuminated poet, the burning candle metaphorizes their intermingling.[46] Hegel, reading the light-producing candle as, in the first place, a symbol for the Friend, emphasizes its "enlightening" or pedagogic value:

> die Kerze lehrt lachen und weinen, sie lacht heiteren Glanzes durch die Flamme, wenn sie zugleich in heißen Tränen zerschmilzt; in ihrem Verbrennen verbreitet sie den heiteren Glanz.

> the candle teaches us to laugh and cry, it laughs through the flame's cheerful glimmering even as it melts away in hot tears; in its burning it spreads cheerful light.

The flaming candle further symbolizes the self-dissolving poetic subject "burning in woe." On this score Hegel's remarks just prior to his citation of the Hafiz verse are revealing:

> [Die] mohammedanischen Persern … offen und froh ihr ganzes Selbst wie an Gott so auch allem Preiswürdigen hingeben, doch in dieser Hingebung gerade die freie Substantialität erhalten, die sie sich auch im Verhältnis zu der umgebenden Welt zu bewahren wissen. So sehen wir in der Glut der Leidenschaft die expansivste Seligkeit und Parrhesie des Gefühls, durch welche bei dem unerschöpflichen Reichtum an glänzenden und prächtigen Bildern der stete Ton der Freude, der Schönheit und des Glückes klingt.[47]

> The Mohammedan Persians … openly and gladly surrender their whole selves to God and to everything praiseworthy, yet in this self-abandon they preserve just that free substantiality which they know how to preserve in relation to the surrounding world. Thus we see [*sehen*] in the glow of passion the most expansive bliss and parrhesia of feeling by which, in the inexhaustible wealth of luminous [*glänzenden*] and splendid images, the steady tone [*Ton*] of joy, beauty, and good fortune sounds out [*klingt*].

Here the visually discernible "glow" external to the subject finds expression in the poet's verbal "parrhesia": the light of passion becomes the word of feeling. This uninhibited language remains "luminous" only in the form of verbal "images" that "sound out" the "tone" of feeling. In this sense, this poetry only preserves "free substantiality" in the form of free utterance, whose sound translates the visual glow of the body into the symbolic glow of poetically vocalized "luminous images."

---

[46]Hegel, *Werke* 13: 475.
[47]Hegel, *Werke* 13: 475.

In the Hafiz poem, the burning candle symbolizes the dissolution not only of the self in God, but also of the lit candle as a multivalent symbol for man, God, and their intermingling. The candle "melts away in hot tears," its fire consuming its substantiality, just as the subject, "enlightened" or aflame with the "glow of passion," loses its body in its involution in the divine. This "enlightenment" marks both the negation or death of the self as it vanishes into the absolute and also the self's preservation in the form of light—that is, the symbolic or tropological light of the poem's burning candle. As the surviving form of substantiality, the poetic candle "teaches us to laugh and cry," first by laughing through the flickering flame and then as a symbolic word. Only this vocal or verbal light remains of the visual "glow of passion," which we in fact only "see" through mental vision.

According to Hegel, in "Mohammedan" poetry the world's phenomena are not a "mere adornment" of God, but are rather celebrated for their own glory, even if this glory results from the immanence of the divine in all phenomenal objects. This modality contrasts with the proper sublimity of Hebraic poetry:

> Now, in proper [Hebraic] sublimity ... the best objects and most marvelous configurations are treated only as a mere adornment of God and serve to declaim the splendor and glorification of the one, since they are posed before our eyes [*vor unsere Augen gestellt*] only to celebrate him as master of all creatures; by contrast in [this] pantheism, worldly, natural, and human existence is lifted—by virtue of the immanence of the divine in all [created] objects—into a more independent glory of its own.[48]

In the same manner, symbols like the rose and the nightingale in this pantheistic verse are "no mere ornament" to an otherwise prior and independent idea; on the contrary these symbols are more than symbols, in that they pervade and partake of the presented idea:

> Bei den Persern aber ist die Rose kein Bild oder bloßer Schmuck, kein Symbol, sondern sie selbst erscheint dem Dichter als beseelt, als liebende Braut, und er vertieft sich mit seinem Geist in die Seele der Rose.[49]

> However, with the Persians the rose is no [explicit] image or pure adornment or jewel, no [explicit] symbol, but itself appears [*erscheint*] to the poet as inspired, a loving bride, and he becomes engrossed and absorbed spiritually in the soul of the rose.

---

[48]Hegel, *Werke* 13: 474.

[49]Hegel, *Werke* 13: 476. Here Hegel indicates that the rose is not an image or symbol in the sense of a "pure adornment," a form related to an utterly independent content. In the third section on symbolic art, Hegel calls this explicit independence of form and content in verbal figures the "conscious symbolism" of verbal "comparisons." Such relations in pantheistic poetry do not expressly posit the independence of their terms, but rather "envision" their interpenetration, the immanence of one in the other. But these sublime relations, positing the imperfect affinity and hence *implicit* difference of form and content, are nonetheless symbolic:

The phenomenal rose, in other words, is not an image for a withdrawn divinity—that is, no mere or pure [*bloßer*] adornment for a radically separate God—but rather bears that divinity immanently within it. Similarly, it is only an adornment of the lover in the sense that a jewel or rose belonging to her partakes of and conveys her body and soul; the same adornment, understood as a totally separate object and hence a "mere" adornment, by itself symbolizes only her absence. The difference between an ornament and an independent form depends upon a visual distinction between jewel or rose and body—or illuminated phenomena like the body and an invisible soul or divinity. Unlike a jewel, rose, or human lover, a separate divinity cannot "appear" [*erscheint*] visually; rather it is seen, like the "inspirited" rose, in the light of the mind's eye. As "luminous images" bearing only this inner light, phenomena cannot be "mere ornaments" or utterly derivative and dependent, but rather blur and confuse the line between ornamentation and independence.

In this sense a symbol for the beloved could only be called an ornament if it were taken as already blended with the body and soul of the beloved. As an example of this interpenetration of symbol, body, and soul, as well as the associated utter "freedom" and "abandon"[50] of semiotic and subjective limits, Hegel cites Goethe's description in the *West-East Divan* [*West-östlicher Divan*][51] of his poetic figures as jewels of the beloved:

> Dichtrische Perlen,
> Die mir deiner Leidenschaft
> Gewaltige Brandung
> Warf an des Lebens
> Verödeten Strand aus.
> Mit spitzen Fingern
> Zierlich gelesen,
> Durchreiht mit juwelenem
> Goldschmuck,
>
> nimm sie, *ruft er der Geliebten zu,*
>
> Nimm sie an deinen Hals,
> An deinen Busen!

"In the imagination of pantheism, however, as in [Hebraic] sublimity, the proper content, i.e. the universal substance of all things, could not be visualized independently without being related to an existence not necessarily compatible to the character of this content. Nonetheless this relation belonged to the [universal] substance, which in the negativity of its accidents gave proof of its wisdom, goodness, power, and justice. Therefore, in general at least, here too the relation of meaning and form is of a still *essential* and *necessary* kind, and the two connected sides have not yet become exterior to each another in the strict sense. This externality, however, because it is *implicitly* present in the symbolic [proper], must also be posited [expressly] ... [in] the conscious symbolism of comparative, verbal art" (Hegel, *Werke* 13: 486). To make clear that the Persian rose is a sublime and not an "explicit" symbol in the conscious and comparative sense, I have added the word "explicit" before "image" and "symbol" in the translation.

[50] Hegel, *Werke* 13: 477.

[51] Writing a *Divan*, Goethe casts himself as a "Mohammedan" poet, a characterization Hegel makes explicit (for the calligraphy-laden frontispiece of the *Divan*, see Figure 7, *Goethe as "Mohammedan Poet"*).

Die Regentropfen Allahs,
Gereift in bescheidener Muschel.[52]

Poetic pearls
Which the immense surf
Of your passion cast
Upon the deserted beach of my life.
Read deftly and gathered
With meticulous sharp fingers
On a necklace of jewels and gold,

Take them, *he calls to his lover,*

Take them to your neck,
Unto your bosom!
Raindrops of Allah,
Finished in a modest shell.

This "song to Suleika," inspired by "the breath of the East" and in particular by Goethe's readings in medieval Persian poetry, rehearses the traditional Arabic and Persian image of the poetic stringing of words as pearls upon a necklace.[53] Here "poetic pearls" [*Dichtrische Perlen*] are ornamental symbols or symbolic ornaments that nonetheless remain independent of the beloved, "cast" off of her and onto the seemingly disembodied space or "deserted beach" of the poet's life. But the pearls begin to fill this blank space and furthermore draw the poet's "fingers" to manipulate them, the image insisting upon the corporeity of his arrangement of words into a row upon a previously blank page. The double meaning of the verb *gelesen*, meaning both to "read" and physically to "gather," accents this renewed meeting of verbal jewel with the body—if only the poet's. But after the poet "reads" the pearls, suggesting they were first written by and belong originally to the lover, he asks her to "take them" back—literally "to" her "neck" and "bosom." In the last lines, the poet signals both the pearls' detachment from the lover as he offers them to her ("take them to your neck") and the immanence of the divine within the pearls (they are "raindrops of Allah"). As much as the lover's neck and bosom contrast with an insubstantial divinity, the reference to the pearls' watery origin as "raindrops of Allah" found in a "shell" recalls their original provenance in the oceanic "surf" of the lover's passion, thus blurring the line between the earthly and celestial lover, Suleika and God. What is at stake here is thus not "mere adornment" of the lover's body: the divine raindrops already assert the immanence of the beloved—the fleshly lover or divine spirit—in the poetic pearls, whether or not she "takes" them.

Hegel concludes the section on "Mohammedan" poetry with Goethe's lines, again to Suleika, insisting upon the body's immanence in phenomena and in poetry:

---

[52]Hegel, *Werke* 13: 477.

[53]Hegel, *Werke* 13: 477. The poem is from the *Buch Suleika*: "Die schön geschriebnen …"

Einer Welt von Lebenstrieben,
Die in ihrer Fülle Drang
Ahneten schon Bulbuls Lieben,
Seelerregenden Gesang.[54]

A world of vital instincts, bursting shoots—
In its urgent fullness
Anticipated already the *Bulbul*'s lovemaking,
Its soul-arousing song.

Here the plant-shoots are like the buds of new roses waiting to burst after a storm. Insisting upon their vitality and corporeity, *Lebenstrieben*—through the compression of *Leben* and *Trieb*, meaning "plant-shoot" but also "desire"—becomes *Lieben*, marking the desiring body's verbal consummation in lovemaking. With the Persian *Bulbul*, meaning "nightingale," Goethe evokes the "representation of the nightingale as the bridegroom of the rose,"[55] but only to insist, in another poetic compression, on their symbolic involution: for the urgent thrust [*Drang*] of the shoot suggests not the rose as a "loving bride," but rather the bird in its male sexuality. The "anticipatory" shoot is temporally and spatially displaced by the bird, which makes love with no present partner: its lovemaking accordingly takes the form of song summoning or awakening an absent interlocutor. While bird-song for Hegel marks the rarefied corporeity of the voice, here the "soul-arousing song," as a form of "lovemaking," remains both physical and ethereal, as erotically as it is spiritually arousing. If these verses mark the poet's own song "to Suleika," they thus indicate rather her displacement as a detached being—and consequent involution in the symbolic and articulated corporeity of these very lines.

This "Mohammedan" notion in Hafiz and Goethe of the positive immanence of God in phenomena, or of the body in the symbol, is similar to the Christian mystical notion of "pantheistic unity with respect to the subject who feels [*empfindet*] *himself* physically in this unity with God."[56] This mode of sublimity in turn contrasts with the "negative" notion of "strict" sublimity that Hegel finds in ancient Hebrew poetry, where phenomena are "posited expressly as negative and as a servant," or accidental and supplementary to a completely withdrawn divinity. But like Indian, Mohammedan, and Christian sublimity, this negative sublimity can only represent the divine through poetic rather than visual representation or phenomenal illumination:

This type of sublimity we find in its first original form especially in the vision of the Jews and in their sacred poetry. Visual art cannot appear here, where it is impossible to sketch any suitable picture of God; rather only a poetry of representation [*die Poesie der Vorstellung*] expressing itself through the word can appear.[57]

---

[54]Hegel, *Werke* 13: 477. The lines are from *Buch des Timur*.

[55]Hegel, *Werke* 13: 476.

[56]Hegel, *Werke* 13: 478.

[57]Hegel, *Werke* 13: 480. As we will see, this poetry of "representation" consists not in picture-thinking, however, but in the performative "presentation" or positing of difference.

And again this sacred poetry must "illustrate" the divine through "mental vision":

> In sublimity [proper] the external existence, in which the substance is brought to the mind's eye [*zur Anschauung gebracht wird*], is depreciated and degraded in opposition to substance, where this depreciation and servitude is the only mode according to which the One God—without form and expression in his positive being in anything worldly and finite—can be illustrated by art.[58]

But unlike pantheistic sublimity, which unifies inner and outer light through its "subjectively free" "substantiality," this verbal representation must reduce illuminated phenomena to a "mere adornment":

> When the power and wisdom of the One comes to be presented as the finiteness of physical things and human destinies, we find then no Indian distortion to excessive formlessness; rather the sublimity of God is brought nearer to mental vision [*Anschauung*] by the fact that what is in the world with all its glimmering [*Glanz*], splendor, and magnificence is shown [*dargestellt ist*] only as a serving accident and a passing glow [*Schein*] in comparison [*Vergleich*] to God's being and fixity.[59]

Crucially, the human "presentation" or showing [*Darstellung*] of God's sublimity occurs not through a referential sign, but through the verbal mode of simile [*Vergleich*], which compares illuminated phenomena to the pure negativity of an invisible God. Following Longinus, Hegel cites as an example of sublimity the verse from Genesis: "God said: Let there be light; and there was light."[60] This verse emphasizes the "thought of *creation* by spiritual might and activity," where that power is enacted through the positing force of the creative word. Here the word "light" exists as a name prior to any referent—and to indeed any materiality external to the divine; for this reason the *fiat lux* marks a verbal power utterly independent of illuminated matter. This latter category includes the human subject and his corporeity:

> The Lord [*Herr*], the single substance, does move to expressive manifestation [*Äußerung*], but the mode of production is the purest, even disembodied [*körperlose*], ethereal [*ätherische*] statement; it is the word, the manifestation of thought as the ideal power, and with its command that the being shall be, the being is posited [*gesetzt*] without mediation and actualized in mute obedience.[61]

---

[58]Hegel, *Werke* 13: 479.

[59]Hegel, *Werke* 13: 469.

[60]"Gott sprach: es werde Licht! Und es ward Licht" (Hegel, *Werke* 13: 481). Hegel indicates that he gets this example of sublimity from Longinus (Hegel, *Werke* 13: 481). See Longinus, *On the Sublime*, transl. J. Arieti & J. Crossett (New York: Edwin Mellen Press, 1985), 9.9: 58.

[61]Hegel, *Werke* 13: 481.

Manifesting God's positing power, the verbal light of this poetry does not require a speaking body. The sublimity of this poetry thus consists of the total division of verbal light from the created human body or voice; that is, this poetry is "properly" sublime to the extent that it denies its own corporeity. Deprived of any positing power, the human voice remains "mute" in relation to God, and if it can repeat or echo his command—"God said …"—it does so without force or effect, but only in the derivative language accessory to an independent deity. Indeed the human "being," like all of God's works, is there only "as the proof of *his* wisdom, goodness, and justice": and the human voice or body, as the evidence of God's word, cannot actually speak his "disembodied" language.[62] Furthermore God's word does not require an interlocutor, as he commands a being that does not yet exist; the sublimity of the verse depends upon precisely this monological and non-dialectical language spoken by no subject other than God.

At the end of his discussion of the Genesis verse on light, Hegel concludes that outward accidents can only "show" [*scheinen*] the divine, not let it actually "appear" [*erscheinen lassen*].[63] What Hegel says here applies to the visual externalities represented to us in Hebraic poetry, hence to these accidents in their verbal sublimation. *Scheinen* and *erscheinen* serve to distinguish between, on the one hand, the canceling power of mere indication (showing or pointing) attributable to the human language of sublime citation and, on the other, the generative power of positing attributable to divine language. In the terms of the verse from Genesis, the divine *fiat lux* deploys the word "light" to make things appear, whereas the human citation of God's word only "shows" God's power negatively in "comparison" to the impotence of the human repetition of what "God said." God's "disembodied" and "ethereal" word, freeing his expression from the dialogical constraints of language, draws no corporeal or visible line demarcating his limits or those of another subject. The human citation of God's speech, however, restores the dialogic frame, implying a speaking subject—"I say, 'God said'"—and interlocutor, but only as a negative simile or symbol for the monological language spoken by God before and outside of space and time, or light and sound as their corresponding sensory media. As the rhetorical mode of "properly" sublime poetry, comparison or simile remains a merely impotent citation, echo, or repetition and also—like the luminous outside it must represent—merely "accessory" or "superfluous" to meaning.[64]

But Hegel quickly assimilates this non-dialectical poetry of light into his own dialectics of the sublime. After discussing the proper sublime from what we discover to be "God's side," Hegel glosses this sublime mode from the "side" of phenomena and human subjects.[65] Here he contrasts the incorporeal language of the divine to human discourse that addresses God. Hegel cites Psalm 104: "Light is your garment, that you wear; you spread out the heavens like a carpet."[66] Hegel comments: "Light, sky, clouds, the wings of the wind are here

---

[62]Hegel, *Werke* 13: 481.

[63]Hegel, *Werke* 13: 481.

[64]Hegel, *Werke* 13: 488.

[65]Hegel, *Werke* 13: 481.

[66]"Licht ist dein Kleid, das du anhast; du breitest aus den Himmel wie einen Teppich" (Hegel, *Werke* 13: 484).

nothing in and for themselves, but only an external garment, the carriage or messenger for the service of God."[67] Light here does not illuminate God, but rather serves as an opaque garment separating the visible world from what lies beyond the heavens. Light as a garment also attributes a symbolic corporeity to the divine—"Light is your garment, that you wear"—even as it signals the withdrawal of that body from view. Hegel's next citation from the same Psalm presses this point: "you hide your face [*Angesicht*] and they are full of fear; you take away their breath, they die and revert to dust."[68] Here the withdrawal of the divine face, or *Angesicht*, also signals the suppression of vision, or *Gesicht*, and hence the relegation of light to the world of humans. Again light, rather than illuminating the divine face, cloaks God and removes him from view, drawing a thick veil of obscurity and a dialectical line between man and God. Moreover the two verses from Psalm 104 recuperate light for the human discourse of sublime poetry: aligning phenomenal and verbal light, these verses evoke the visible corporeity—"they die and return to the dust"— that produces words, directly subverting the notion that any poetry, including repetitions of the divine word, could divest words of their phenomenality. Corporeity persists, even as lifeless dust, before the sun, where God does not or cannot appear.

The "light" of the verse from Psalms relates metaphorically to clothing, and it is this tropological light that Hegel calls a mere "external garment" or "adornment" for God. In Hegel's system, we recall, all limits or lines of demarcation partake in and yet exceed the definition of the delimited object. The phrase "external garment" situates light both outside and at the limit of God's being. Hence light, rather than being a "pure" adornment, retains a priority to and independence from a God whose demarcation and delimitation are ultimately predicated on the contours of the "garment." In this respect the insistence on the ornamental status of "light, heavens, clouds, the wings of the wind" recalls the pantheistic notion of "poetic pearls" or symbolic ornaments: just as those pearls separated themselves and yet mingled with the body of the beloved, here ornamental light marks the external limit of and also the substitutive form or marker for God's presence.

Similarly citation, as a framing device, demarcates not only the content cited but also the subjective boundaries of speaker and interlocutor.[69] Hegel's citations of the word "light" in other Hebraic verses, over against the clearing away of God's limits by the "ethereal" or transparent *fiat lux*, prove the power of echoing and thus resignifying even the words of God. The metaphoric appropriation of light and attribution of a body or face to God gainsay the impotence of the human word in the first example from the scriptures—"Let there be light"—since only the human subject and his symbols,

---

[67]"Licht, Himmel, Wolken, die Fittiche des Windes hier nichts an und für sich, sondern nur ein äußeres Gewand, ein Wagen oder Bote zu Gottes Dienst" (Hegel, *Werke* 13: 484).

[68]"Verbirgst du dein Angesicht, so erschrecken sie, du nimmst weg ihren Odem, so vergehen sie und werden wieder zu Staub" (Hegel, *Werke* 13: 484).

[69]For theoretical discussions of citationality, see V. N. Vološinov's analysis of different forms of "reported speech" in *Marxism and the Philosophy of Language*, transl. Ladislav Matejka and I. R. Titunik (Cambridge: Harvard University Press, 1973), 115–59; and especially Jacques Derrida's relation of the iterativeness of language to performativity in "Signature, Event, Context," in *Limited Inc.*, ed. Gerald Graff, transl. S. Weber and Jeffrey Mehlman (Evanston: Northwestern University Press, 1988), 1–23.

interpreting the light as an obscure veil, can posit a God beyond it. In the light, as it were, of Hegel's citations, the phrase "God said: let there be light"—taking light as a veil—becomes the human pronouncement of God's withdrawn existence, his removal into darkness. Thus even God's word, necessarily dependent on human citation and framing, succumbs to the movement of the dialectic.[70]

This delineating verbal light separates and joins the two "sides" of the dialectic between God and man, incorporeity and corporeity, independence and ornamentation, repetition and reconstitution, and negative simile and affirmative figure. Hegel's sublime, far from marking a non-dialectical moment, as in one eminent critic's reading, marks the transition from the art of illuminated externality to the art of "conscious symbolism" or verbal relation, necessarily corporeal and hence still engaged externally.[71] In the dialectical progression of symbolic art, "there only remains of sublimity, in the comparative art form, this streak—that every image, instead of showing the thing and its meaning in adequate form, will provide only the image and simile [*Bild und Gleichnis*] [relating the sensuous thing and its meaning]."[72] In other words it is not the negative simile of the reported *fiat lux* that survives dialectically, but the affirmative relation of "an immediate sensuous existent" to a phenomenally "determined and delimited" meaning—for instance, of the trope that makes light the defining garment, ornament, or contour of what must, as a name or linguistic object, have a sensuous limit as its demarcation.[73]

---

[70]My reading of Hegel's use of citations largely rehearses de Man's remarkable reading ("Hegel on the Sublime," in *Aesthetic Ideology* 112–4).

[71]As I have intimated, Paul de Man erroneously considers Hegel's sublime a non-dialectical moment: "The sublime, it turns out, is self-destroying in a manner without precedent at any of the other stages of the dialectic" (Paul de Man, "Hegel on the Sublime," in *Aesthetic Ideology*, 116). In support of his position, de Man quotes Hegel as saying that "'The difference between the present stage (that of comparative art-forms) and the sublime … is that the sublime relationship is completely eliminated" (ibid.). In fact Hegel writes: "But the difference between the present stage (that of comparative art-forms) and the sublime is to be sought for in the fact that, on the one hand, the [sublime] separation and juxtaposition of meaning and its concrete form is expressly accentuated in the work of art itself in a lesser or greater degree, whereas on the other hand, the sublime relationship altogether disappears, since what is taken as content is no longer the absolute itself" (Hegel, *Werke* 13: 487). In other words, Hegel indicates that the sublime non-correspondence and coimbrication of linguistic form and meaningful content persists dialectically; the content, however, is no longer the sacred or absolute, as in sublimity "proper." Hegel clarifies this point on the next page, stating explicitly that the sublime, as the linguistic entanglement of form and meaning, persists into the final stage in the dialectic of the symbol, the verbal form of "comparison." For a recent discussion of Paul de Man's essay on Hegel's sublime, see Andrzej Warminski, "Lightstruck: 'Hegel on the Sublime,'" in *The Political Archive of Paul de Man* (Edinburgh: Edinburgh University Press, 2012), 118–130.

[72]"Von der Erhabenheit deshalb bleibt in der vergleichenden Kunstform nur *der* Zug übrig, daß jedes Bild, statt die Sache und Bedeutung selbst ihrer adäquaten Wirklichkeit nach darzustellen, *nur* ein Bild und Gleichnis derselben abgeben soll" (Hegel, *Werke* 13: 488).

[73]Hegel, *Werke* 13: 487–8. Indicatively, Hegel in a different context relates "artistic" types of garments to architecture: "The principle for the artistic kinds of garments lies in the fact that it is treated as if it were architectural. An architectural work is only a setting in which a person can move freely and which for its part, being separated from what it surrounds, must show in its configuration its independence of purpose. Furthermore, the architectural quality of bearing up and being borne up must be formed for itself and in accordance with its own mechanical nature … The mantle especially is like a house in which one can move freely" (Hegel, *Werke* 14: 407–8). Like architecture, an artistic garment defines its own "independence" at the sensuous limit it demarcates even as it submits to external support, whether of the ground or of a body.

Longinus "quotes" *Genesis*, and Hegel quotes Longinus, but only to overturn the latter's account of sublimity, which depends on and assumes the impotence of human citation of the *fiat lux*.[74] The ongoing resignifying of "light" in Hegel's own text, from the beginnings of symbolic art through pantheistic and proper sublimity, dialectically coimbricates the two modes of sublimity and, as we will see shortly, symbolic architecture and sublime poetry. The intermingling of human and divine discourse in the reported *fiat lux*, as well as Hegel's juxtaposition of the divine word of Genesis with the human songs of the Psalms, recalls the convergence of the human and divine voice in pantheism. Thus when Krishna says that he is "amongst the sacred books the book of hymns," it is Krishna who speaks, but only in the human voice singing the "book of hymns." A similar effect characterizes Krishna's line "to me this All is linked as a chaplet of pearls on a thread"; Goethe's "Poetic pearls … raindrops of Allah"; and the ornamental "garment" of light, no longer the sign of God's independent power, but, as outwardly manifested human song, affixed to and demarcating the limits of the divine.[75] Such mediating adornments delineate, too, the human, which remains entangled in its embodiment. For light marks, in both modes of sublimity, the symbolic impasse of a language that would transcend its corporeity to "give voice" to what speaks without a body.

The dialectical resignification of light marks a crucial narrative element in Hegel's narrative of symbolic art, from the exteriorization of light in the obelisks and pyramids at the beginning of symbolic art through to the statue before the sun. The evolving relation of aesthetics and light forms part of the structure, too, of the classical and romantic phases of art:

> The lack [of inwardness in classical art] appears externally in the fact that the expression of the soul in its simplicity, the light of the eye, is missing from the sculptures. The highest works of beautiful sculpture are sightless, and their interiority does not look out from them as self-knowing inwardness in this spiritual concentration which the eye conveys. This light of the soul falls outside these sculptures and belongs to the spectator, who cannot look upon these forms in a manner in which soul pervades soul—eye to eye. The God of romantic art, however, appears sighted, self-knowing, internally subjective, opening his interiority to man's interiority. For infinite negativity, the retraction of the spirit into itself, cancels the spilling out into the corporeal; subjectivity is the spiritual light which shines in itself, in its previously dark place, and, while natural light can shine only upon an object, the spiritual light is itself the ground and object on which it shines and which it knows as itself.[76]

---

[74]Hegel, *Werke* 13: 481.

[75]Hegel, *Werke* 13: 472. Tellingly, the "pearls" and "jewels" of pantheistic, sublime poetry—where words and the body intermingle—become the "jewels" of verbal relation adorning particular meanings in "conscious symbolism of the comparative art-form" (see, for instance, Hegel, *Werke* 13: 488, 518).

[76]Hegel, *Werke* 14: 132.

Indeed romantic art, of which poetry is the highest and final form, posits "the body more or less as negative so as to lift inwardness out of externality."[77] Moving away from the corporeal interiority that produces it, poetry nonetheless never attains to the complete dissolution of the body:

> [Poetry] in its artistic embodiment [*Kunstverkörperung*] is essentially to be grasped [*fassen*] as a moving away from and suppression of real sensuousness, yet still as a production that does not dare leave off corporealization [*Verleiblichung*] and movement in the external altogether. To explain philosophically this movement toward freedom [from the sensuous], we must first specify this sensuousness from which art must free itself; by the same token we must also explain how poetry takes up the totality of the content and forms of all the arts. We have to look at this process as a laboring for totality, a process demonstrable philosophically only as the sublation [*Aufheben*] of any limitation to the particular characteristic of the previous treatment of the arts in their single-faceted and one-sided forms, whose unique value is negated in the totality [to which poetry aspires]. Only by considering poetry in this manner does poetry emerge as the special art in which … art itself begins to dissolve.[78]

In describing poetry here, Hegel rehearses the terms of symbolic architecture, but in precisely oppositional terms. Where poetry posits the dissolution of the living body,[79] symbolic architecture posits the dead body as radically and physically preserved against natural dissolution. Poetry and architecture thus both attempt to negate the body, but in contrasting ways: poetry by marginalizing the body, and architecture by preserving and concealing it as dead. This oppositional relation to the body extends to these art forms' larger relation to matter as such: where poetry grants "free play" and "movement" to its spiritual and sensory elements,[80] symbolic architecture presents an immovable, solid edifice for a "departed spirit" and senseless corpse. Thus Hegel posits a dialectical relation of the two art forms that mark the beginning and ending, hence the conceptual limits of the aesthetic:

> In the system of the arts we can directly oppose the art of poetry to architecture. For architecture remains incapable of subordinating objective material to spiritual content in such a manner as to shape that material into a form adequate to spirit; poetry, in exact contrast, goes so far in the negative treatment of its sensuous element that it degrades the voice, which is the opposite of heavy spatial matter,

---

[77]Hegel, *Werke* 15: 14.

[78]Hegel, *Werke* 15: 234.

[79]Hegel repeatedly makes it clear that the romantic does not utterly dissolve the interrelation of body and spirit posited in classical art; rather their connection becomes distant and "loose" (Hegel, *Werke* 15: 14).

[80]Hegel, *Werke* 15: 14.

to a meaningless sign, whereas architecture shapes its material into an indicating symbol [*andeutenden Symbol*]. But poetry thereby dissolves the fusion of spiritual inwardness with external existence to a degree that begins to correspond no longer to the original conception of art, so that now poetry runs the risk of losing itself in its movement out of the region of the sensuous into that of the spiritual.[81]

Appearing just after Hegel's claim that poetry "does not dare leave off corporealization and movement in the external altogether," this passage, in context, makes clear that these two art forms oppose each other in their aims with respect to the body without achieving, however, its ultimate preservation or rarefaction. On the contrary, architecture and poetry together, performing the provisional preservation and cancellation of the body, propel the dialectical circuit of the aesthetic. Architecture materializes an apparently enduring line that divides illuminated matter from an inner realm lacking spirit, intellect, and meaning; as a symbol, its external shape nonetheless points both to that loss of meaning and the negativity of its own act of indication. As we have seen, however, such a building attains to "articulation" in the verbal signs of living interpreters or viewing occupants: to name a building, to "take" it "as a symbol," to "give voice" to its hieroglyphic shape—for instance, to give Hegel's lectures on architecture—is to attribute arbitrary meaning, however briefly and partially, to utterly foreign material. Similarly poetry, through "tempo, rhythm, euphony, rhyme,"[82] and other manipulations of sound, isolates the voice as empty animal sound or the material medium of speech; the voice's "meaningless sign" "may just as well be a pure letter," a hieroglyph with no phonetic counterpart, and hence a "pure indication of spirit."[83] Illuminated matter, architecturally fashioned into an indicative symbol, exposes the signifying potential of all symbols; and the voice, poetically reduced to a meaningless sign, exposes the symbolicity of all signs.

This co-implication of architecture and poetry, framed in terms of the fluidity of symbol and sign, or voice and light, finds mythopoeic expression in the Memnon of the *Aesthetics*. As the bridge from symbolic architecture to sublime poetry, the statue before the sun figures the dialectical relation of these two art forms at the limits of the aesthetic. In particular the statue points to the architectonic quality of poetic material: "giving voice" and "indicating its meaning only symbolically," the Memnon evokes the circuitous movement of the dialectic, from the isolation of the symbolic vestiges of the voice and the recognition of the voice as a sign to the restoration of the voice as a symbol—a tomb or hieroglyph of thought. Moreover the statues of Memnon, we recall, mark the mechanical arrangement of material in "rows"—a sequencing of hieroglyphs according to no governing principle but the necessity of the architectonic. In the same way, poetry relies upon the architectonic arrangement of "sounds" and "notes"—voiced and written:

---

[81]Hegel, *Werke* 15: 235.
[82]Hegel, *Werke* 15: 275.
[83]Hegel, *Werke* 13: 123.

romantic poetry, because it strikes the soulful tone of feeling, plays upon the now independent sounds and notes of letters, syllables, and words, and it proceeds to please itself in their sounds which, with the emotional ardency [*Innigkeit*] and also the architectonic [*architektonisch*] and intellectual perspicacity of music, it can sequence, intermingle, and relate to one another.[84]

Poetry isolates "the music of words," whose sounds "must be molded by the poet"; these principles, however, are not external laws governing the arrangement of poetic material. As with symbolic architecture, poetry does not "oppose law to appearance" but instead "grasps the one in and only through the other."[85] Poetry transposes the architectonic "molding" of sound from the art of music, which, like poetry, conceptually "opposes architecture, even as it retains a kinship with it": "in music ... the classical identity between the inner life and its external existence is again dissolved in a similar, even if opposite way as architecture which, as a symbolic mode of representation, could not achieve that unity."[86] As a romantic art, music posits the corporeity and rarefaction of its audible, but vanishing material;[87] this entanglement of subjectively charged notes traversing and eluding corporeal bounds and the necessary, external body corresponds to an interplay of inner subjectivity and the mind free of referentiality: "In music the deepest emotional ardency and soul, and the most severe principles of intellect, hold equal sway ... Freed from verbalizations of the mind, music obtains an especially architectonic [*architektonischen*] character to the extent that it accomplishes for itself, with invention, a musically governed building of sound [*Tongebäude*]."[88] Here the musical government of sound depends upon the mind's freedom from referential uses of sound—hence upon the intellect in the form of "severe principles," or the mechanical, external, and architectonic mind otherwise repressed through immediate prosaic reference.

Similarly the poetic isolation of the musicality of words as "notes," through their self-referential arrangement, differentiates poetry from ordinary, prosaic speech: "[poetry] must not leave this linguistic matter as it appears in ordinary usage and consciousness, but must treat it poetically [to differentiate it from prosaic expressions] by the choice, positioning, and sound of words [*Klang der Wörter*]."[89] This arrangement has no purpose outside itself, referring instead to itself as an external medium:

Sensuous existence, in poetry the sound of the words—from the incipit house [*von Hause*]—belongs to art, and may not remain so shapeless and indeterminate as it

---

[84]Hegel, *Werke* 15: 304.

[85]Hegel, *Werke* 15: 240.

[86]Hegel, *Werke* 15: 138.

[87]Hegel, *Werke* 15: 134–5.

[88]Hegel, *Werke* 15: 139; see also 15: 217: "Der Komponist seinerseits kann nun zwar selber in sein Werk eine bestimmte Bedeutung, einen Inhalt von Vorstellungen und Empfindungen und deren gegliederten geschlossenen Verlauf hineinlegen, umgekehrt aber kann es ihm auch, unbekümmert um solchen Gehalt, auf die rein musikalische Struktur seiner Arbeit und auf das Geistreiche solcher Architektonik ankommen."

[89]Hegel, *Werke* 15: 236.

is in the immediate fortuity of ordinary speech, but must appear as a living form [*lebendig gebildet*] and, even if in poetry it also resonates as an external medium, must still be treated as a purpose in itself and thereby take a harmoniously delimited shape.[90]

Like the house at the beginning of art—the "house for the dead" or pyramid, for instance[91]—poetry marks the human engagement of sensuous externality: the text's ambivalent phrasing even suggests that sensuous existence originates—comes "from"— the externality of the non-representational house. Just as the pyramidal house remains a "soundless" "corporeal shell" or corpse of language until given voice through a living interpreter's articulation, so, too, language remains merely shapeless and, as Hegel implies, lifeless speech until poetry—isolating the corporeal and animate reverberations of its non-representational material parts—reveals the architectonic nature of arrangement. The voice of a living human has no life when given over entirely and immediately to meaning; only when poetry surfaces the inorganic, non-representational line that separates and binds the units of the voice can sound dialectically appear as a "living form." *Gebildung* also refers to the knowledge of writing; hence the phrase *lebendig gebildet*—in the sense of "animatedly lettered"—also carries the suggestion that poetry must animate or give life to speech by exposing its entanglement with letters. The dialectical relation of sound and limit, or voice and line, applies equally in reverse: only when poetry reveals the lines of script as hieroglyphs haunted by the symbolic and equally non-representational human voice can language be seen as something both "living" and "plastic,"[92] human and inorganic. Thus Hegel explicitly characterizes the poetic stringing together of sound—for rhythm or phonemic resonance, for instance— as the drawing of a limit:

In poetry the sensuous sounds of words in their arrangement are at first unlinked and boundless, and the poet has the task of arranging this irregularity [*Regellosigkeit*] as a sensuous border [*Umgrenzung*]—and of drawing, as it were, a kind of steadier contour and sounding frame [*klingendem Rahmen*] for his conceptual designs [*Konzeptionen*] and their structure and sensuous beauty.[93]

---

[90]Hegel, *Werke* 15: 291. Here I emphasize the more literal implications of the phrase "von Hause."

[91]For Hegel the art of architecture does not begin with a house as a simple habitation for humans or Gods, since such structures are merely "means for a purpose outside them." Art begins with the independent buildings of symbolic architecture, like a "house for the dead" that, eschewing explanation only in terms of utility, instead symbolically "bears its meaning within itself" (Hegel, *Werke* 14: 267–8).

[92]In poetry, quantitative versification surfaces the "plasticity" of sound, the material malleability of language. Hegel associates specifically Greek and Latin quantitative versification with the sculptural fusion of sensuous form and intellectual content (Hegel, *Werke* 15: 302–3); both belong, therefore, to the unrecoverable art of the past. Only phonemic resonance—in alliteration, assonance, end rhyme, or what Hegel categorizes as simply "rhyme"—in the temporally possible and present form of romantic poetry (especially, for Hegel, in Germanic, Romance, Arabic, and Persian) unveils the "architectonic" dissonance of sensuous form and intellectual content (Hegel, *Werke* 15: 304, 316). I will address the relation of architectonics and plasticity at greater length below.

[93]Hegel, *Werke* 15: 291.

Isolating the dispersed "sounds" and, by corollary, letters "of words," poetry reveals the temporal and spatial distance between sonorous or written fragments of language. This distance also makes possible their relation: for poetry, retaining its original pantheistic character, further exposes sonorous chains and illuminated lines as aesthetic mediations of structures that in ordinary prose appear to be immediate. Moreover poetry translates between the spatial and temporal forms of language: thus sound submits to the poet's "drawing" of a "contour" or "border," a conceptual line marking both the succession and dialectical negation of juxtaposed sounds. Sound along a chain marks the endless displacement and recurrence of previous sounds and corresponding script. These forms, moving across the limit between time and space, converge dialectically in Hegel's figure of a "sounding frame," a verbal string along which voice and script haunt each other as they gesture endlessly at the foreign.

Thus poetry, like the pyramid of symbolic architecture, reveals the self-negating line or binary of any concept, manifesting the "steadier," but nonetheless sonorous, "vibrat[ing]," and thus movable "sensuous border" between intellectual content and material form.[94] Just as the pyramids mediate between the conceptual and drawn limit, so too poetry erects the material sonority of words as a "sounding frame" that negotiates between "conceptual designs" and corresponding sensuous "structures." This "rational" movement between linguistic content and physical form, or concept and matter—as the sublime demarcation of phenomenality—constitutes an aesthetic operation. Isolating the moving and self-negating architectonic line of language and hence of the mind, poetry indeed reveals both the conceptual scaffolding of aesthetics and the aesthetic scaffolding of thought.

In these respects the "sounding frame" raised up by poetry is akin to the Memnon, Hegel's colossal hieroglyph sounding in the light. The mythopoeic interplay of architecture and poetry, materiality and corporeity, body and ornament, *gramma* and *phone*, identifies the architectonic as the entanglement of logic with aesthetics. In turn the thinking of the aesthetic requires both the binary separation of architecture and poetry and their interpenetration: for the line and hence difference between them cannot be thought without the externalization and dissolution of lines, material and corporeal, that first delimit the category of the aesthetic.

---

[94]Hegel, *Werke* 10: §401: 105.

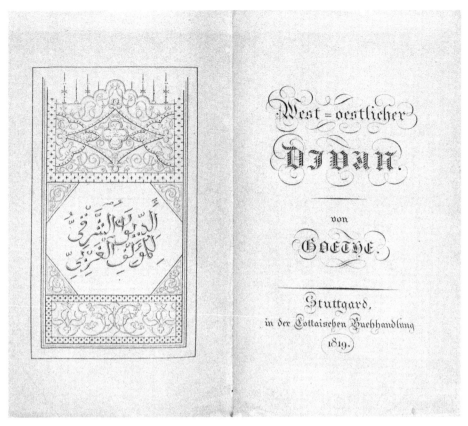

Figure 7 *Goethe as "Mohammedan Poet."* Johann Wolfgang von Goethe, *West-östlicher Divan* (Stuttgart: Cotta, 1819), Frontispiece. Courtesy of Houghton Library, Harvard University.

CHAPTER 5
THE ARCHITECTONIC IN TIME

How do the conceptual fluidity and entanglement of architecture and poetry, the liminal genres of the aesthetic, inflect the telling of aesthetic history? What would a history of the arts look like that could not rigorously differentiate between the individual arts? What then would be the relation between aesthetics and history? At the outset of his discussion of the individual arts in the *Aesthetics,* Hegel interrogates the relation of concept and history in the specific case of a "beginning" of art. A conceptual genre would have to correspond to an historical form of artistic expression; and any such concept would presumably distinguish an artistic expression against whatever fell outside the conceptual boundaries of the genre—from its historical emergence and through its entire history. But as Hegel holds throughout his work, a beginning must always be preceded by something that led up to that beginning, and so an absolute beginning cannot be fixed. To the extent that a concept corresponds to finite phenomena, it cannot establish an originary antecedent to the exclusion of others. Thus Hegel writes in the *Encyclopedia*:

> With respect to the finite, we have equally a beginning and a non-beginning; these opposite determinations, in their unresolved and unreconciled conflict with each other, pertain to the finite: and thus the finite, because it is this contradiction, vanishes. The finite has an other that precedes it, and in following the connectivities of the finite, its preceding terms must be traced, e.g. in the history of the earth or of man. There is no end to any such investigation.[1]

Even so, an historical narrative must begin somewhere; but all such beginnings serve only a heuristic purpose relative to a particular reading or interpretation.[2] The beginning of an historical narrative remains, therefore, entirely "accidental"[3] or contingent:

> Where to make the beginning is indeterminate; a beginning is to be made, but it is only a relative one. We go beyond it, but not to infinity, only to another beginning which is, inevitably, also only a conditioned one; in short, it is only the nature of the relative which is expressed, since we are in the realm of the finite.[4]

---

[1]Hegel, *Werke* 9: §247: 27.
[2]Hegel, *Werke* 8: §17: 63.
[3]Hegel, *Werke* 14: 266.
[4]Hegel, *Werke* 9: §247: 27.

For this reason thoughtful history, for Hegel, does not consist of mere chronology; rather "what has happened [*Geschehene*]" must be taken to accord with "the narration of what has happened [*Geschichtserzählung*]."[5] Any historical narrative, to the extent that it must exclude materials from the surviving record—as well as events that were never registered—must conform to a narrative pattern necessarily discordant with the movement of events in their entirety. Thus "illiterate" people who have not produced an accessible, written archive—including through inscriptions on monuments—"do not possess a history"[6]:

> The periods, whether we assume them to be centuries or millennia, that passed amongst a people before the writing of history—with revolutions, wanderings [*Wanderungen*], the wildest changes [*Veränderungen*]—are therefore without objective history, because they offer no subjective history, no written narrative of history.[7]

The concept of history, Hegel argues, can only survive this entanglement with narrative through a tautological insistence on the agreement of relevant occurrences with the narrative of their relevance.[8] Insisting on this subservience of the category of history to that of narrative, Hegel goes so far as to claim that any element falling outside the scope of his historical narrative, predicated as it is on freedom from the dialectic, must fall outside the category of the historical. This claim, articulating in radical terms the necessary premise of any telling of "what happened," has been dismissed as a case of galling hubris and Eurocentrism rather than viewed as a central element in Hegel's assiduously developed theory of history. If anything, Hegel's view of the provisionality of history reflects humility; thus he insists that all claims in particular cases only obtain relatively—that is, "for us" at the time of writing.[9]

The primacy of narrative over actual events is especially clear in the case of art, where to identify its beginning "we must entirely exclude … empirical history."[10] Examining

---

[5]Hegel, *Werke* 12: 83. Hegel, *Werke* 12: 83–4. The contemporary preference for historical narratives bound by periodicity or even chronology—a preference bucked notably by Deleuze and Guattari in *Capitalism and Schizophrenia*—relies, therefore, upon a principle utterly extrinsic to the "thoughtful consideration" of history (see Hegel, *Werke* 12: 21–2). Likewise the common foisting of extrinsic historical categories upon art ignores the dependence of those very categories on aesthetic determinations.

[6]See Hegel, *Werke*, 12: 85–6. Since the "history" we have for literate peoples also consists of a narrative [*Geschichtserzählung*] emerging from archival materials, we no more have a pure, unmediated, and complete sense of the actual events of, say, Napoleonic Europe or pre-Homeric Greece than we do of yesterday's news—or, in Hegel's notorious example, of the then-unknown interior of Africa. It bears mentioning that the contingency of history on writing, following from the latter's apparently enduring material form, does not belie the dialectical coimbrication of vocal and written forms of language in Hegel, both of which inhere in the universally human faculty he calls "memory" (Hegel, *Werke*, 10: §462: 278ff.).

[7]Hegel, *Werke* 12: 84.

[8]See Hegel, *Werke*, 12: 83–4.

[9]Hegel, *Werke* 12: 134.

[10]Hegel, *Werke* 14: 266.

the concept of art for a "division" that would separate particular arts within a totality of art,[11] Hegel notes that "we have immediately a *division* [*Teilung*] in the case of this art of architecture," where the materialized limit serves as a means for an external end—an "enclosure," for instance, for "man, the subject, or the image of the god."[12] But this materialized division cannot in itself demarcate the limit of the concept of art because art requires an entanglement of shape and meaning; hence architecture only enters the realm of the aesthetic when a wall, enclosure, or other manifest limit refers to its own production of meaning—that is, indicates its own meaning symbolically.[13] As we have seen, the pyramid marks the limit of the symbol "proper": to the extent that only such buildings materialize a limit and maintain a certain "independence" from utilitarian considerations of use or referentiality, these forms must mark the incipient, defining manifestation and indeed delimitation of the concept of the aesthetic. In other words, because only architecture physically realizes the limit that separates out the particular in a non-utilitarian manner co-implicating form and content, an historical narrative of art must take architecture to be the art form first appearing in the history of art. Architecture thus provides the aesthetic basis for the history of aesthetics.

By extension, the architectural doubling and displacement of the corporeal demarcations of interiority, evident in the pyramidal articulation of a "corporeal shell," mark the instability of the limit of any concept. As a dynamic "architectonic enclosure," architectural form emblematizes the fluid conceptual lines between historical periods, forms, peoples, and belief systems—symbolically, as it were—in the history of the symbol:

> On these more determinate forms of the still original symbol we can assume in advance that they arise from the religious world view of entire peoples; on this account we must also summon up history. Even so, the lines of division [*Scheidung*] cannot be imposed too rigidly, since the particular modes of treatment and configuration are mixed—like the forms of art in general—so that we find again in earlier or later phases, however subordinated and isolated, a form that we consider as expressing essentially the world view of a particular people.[14]

The "lines of division" emerging from the symbolic manifestation of form into the world must, like the symbol, relate to varied content. The imperfect entanglement of form and content in the symbol marks the essential structure of the aesthetic, common to its symbolic and romantic forms—the aesthetic modes that, unlike the classical form, engage their temporality. Because movable, self-canceling architectonic form is fundamentally symbolic and thus makes possible the unstable affinities of the aesthetic, its architectonic line, understood more broadly as the aesthetic limit, marks the hybridity or heterogeneity

---

[11]Hegel, *Werke* 14: 266.
[12]Hegel, *Werke* 14: 268.
[13]Hegel, *Werke* 14: 268–70.
[14]Hegel, *Werke* 13: 414–5.

internal to the history of art, history in general, and indeed any historically determined category of thought.[15]

In elucidating what he will view as the "architectonic" movement of the dialectic through history, Hegel engages a concept developed over the course of the eighteenth century. Baumgarten first uses the term "architectonic" in his *Metaphysica* of 1739 to denote the structure of metaphysical knowledge; subsequently Lambert, in his *Anlage zur Architektonic* of 1771, conceives of architectonics as the art of establishing such a structure.[16] Kant famously combines both of these senses: in his work the "architectonic" refers both to the "idea of the whole" and to the art of constructing such a system through "delineation."[17] In *The Critique of Pure Reason*, Kant further defines "architectonic" as a characteristic of any element of knowledge—namely, its subsumability into a possible system:

> Human reason is by nature architectonic. That is to say, it regards all our knowledge as belonging to a possible system.[18]

Later in the same text, in chapter 3 of the "Transcendental Doctrine of Method," entitled the "Architectonic of Pure Reason," Kant explicitly conflates the double sense of the "architectonic" as both philosophical ends and means, or the object and method of philosophical science:

> By the term "architectonic," I mean the art of constructing systems. As systematic unity is what first raises ordinary knowledge to the rank of science, that is, makes a system out of a mere aggregate of knowledge, architectonic is the doctrine of the scientific in our knowledge, and therefore necessarily forms part of the doctrine of method.[19]

---

[15]A more comprehensive treatment of Hegel's engagement of Kantian architectonics remains a desideratum. For the relation of architecture to architectonics in Kant, see Paul de Man, "Kant's Materialism," in *Aesthetic Ideology*, 125ff.; Jacques Derrida, *The Truth in Painting*, transl. G. Bennington and I. McLeod (Chicago: University of Chicago Press), 40ff., 119–138, 143; G. Tonelli, *Kant's* Critique of Pure Reason *within the Tradition of Modern Logic*, ed. D. Chandler (New York: G. Olms, 1994), 254; Claudia Brodsky Lacour's talk, published as "Architecture and Architectonics: 'The Art of Reason' in Kant's *Critique*," in *Canon*, vol. 3 of *The Princeton Journal: Thematic Studies in Architecture*, ed. Taisto Mäkelä (New York: Princeton Architectural Press, 1988), 103–17; her "Architecture in the Discourse of Modern Philosophy: Descartes to Nietzsche," 19–34; and P. Manchester, "Kant's Conception of Architectonic in its Historical Context," in *Journal of the History of Philosophy*, 2003, 41: 187–207.

[16]Alexander G. Baumgarten, *Metaphysica* (Halae Magdeburgicae: C. H. Hemmerde, 1739), §4 and Johann Heinrich Lambert, *Anlage zur Architektonic* (Riga: J. F. Hartknoch, 1771), VIII–XIX *passim*.

[17]Immanuel Kant, *Lectures on Logic*, transl. J. M. Young (Cambridge: Cambridge University Press, 1992), 590, A143.

[18]Immanuel Kant, *The Critique of Pure Reason*, transl. Norman Kemp Smith (New York: St. Martin's Press, 1965), 429: A474/B502.

[19]Kant, *The Critique of Pure Reason*, 653: A832/B860; translation modified.

While this accord of ends and means appears tautological, the alternative is intellectual paralysis, a view that:

> makes the completion of the edifice of knowledge quite impossible … Since [this view] refuses to admit as first or as a beginning anything that could serve as a foundation for building, a complete edifice of knowledge is, on such assumptions, altogether impossible. Thus the architectonic interest for reason—the demand not for empirical but for pure a priori unity of reason—forms a natural recommendation for the assertions of the thesis.[20]

Kant's entanglement of "art" and "reason" and, accordingly, of the art of building and the logic of systematization in the concept of the "architectonic" points up, for Hegel, both its aesthetic materiality and its inescapable discursivity. For this reason, the "architectonic" in Hegel emerges with the conception of the material art of architecture and the discursive art of poetry.

Contemporary philosophical attempts to account for the architectonic relation of materiality and language remain largely Hegelian. Gilles Deleuze and Félix Guattari describe the a-systematic linearity of the "rhizome" or the appearing and disappearing "fold" as closely tied conceptual models for a process of organic, intellectual, and historical production or movement distinct from the "arborescent" model of the tree, which marks the "hierarchical" and "genealogical" modalities of static, binary thinking.[21] For Deleuze and Guattari, "a rhizome has no beginning or end; it is always in the middle, between things, interbeing, intermezzo. The tree is filiation, but the rhizome is alliance, uniquely alliance. The tree imposes the verb 'to be,' but the fabric of the rhizome is the conjunction, 'and … and … and.'"[22] They caution, however, that "the root-tree and canal-rhizome are not two opposed models: the first operates as a transcendent model and tracing, even if it engenders its own escapes; the second operates as an immanent process that overturns the model and outlines a map, even if it constitutes its own hierarchies, even if it gives rise to a despotic channel. It is not a question of this or that place on earth, or of a given moment in history, still less of this or that category of thought. It is a question of a model that is perpetually in construction or collapsing, and of a process that is perpetually prolonging itself, breaking off and starting up again … We invoke one dualism only in order to challenge another."[23]

In this respect, the Hegelian pyramidal "limit" can be understood as a counterpart to the infinitely mobile figures of Deleuze's fold. Whatever their professed desire to break

---

[20]Kant, *The Critique of Pure Reason*, 429–30: A474–5/B502–3.

[21]See Gilles Deleuze and Félix Guattari. *A Thousand Plateaus*, transl. Brian Massumi (Minneapolis: University of Minnesota Press, 1980), 3–25; and Gilles Deleuze, *The Fold: Leibniz and the Baroque*, transl. Tom Conley (Minneapolis: University of Minnesota Press, 1993).

[22]Ibid., 25.

[23]Ibid., 20.

with Hegel, Deleuze and Guattari indeed come remarkably close to Hegel or, better, to a contemporary iteration of what Marxists have called a decapitated Hegelianism. For Hegel, too, "truth" does not lie in actual chronological moments, categories of thought, or, as we will see, geographical places.

While Hegel will strictly consign the "architectonic" to the non-representational modality of the aesthetic, however, Deleuze and Guattari insist on the relation of the rhizome or fold to nature. Arguing that the rhizome is made up of "only lines,"[24] Deleuze and Guattari nonetheless proceed to construct an organic and hence mimetic model of the line; accordingly they obfuscate the singular source of its discursive power, namely its ability to move from the conceptual to the material realm.[25] By contrast Hegel views the "limit" as not only a dialectical progression through point, line, plane, and solid, marking an infinite back-and-forth progression in space and time, but also an essentially inorganic and unprecedented materialization of a conceptual border or demarcation [*Grenze*], hence a provisional break and beginning. For Hegel this rhythm of preservation and continuity on the one hand and cancellation and production on the other marks the process of dialectical becoming [*Aufhebung*] and opens the space for the productions he calls aesthetic.[26]

The inorganic nature of the limit in fact underwrites its resistance to mimetic appropriation. Thus at the beginning of the *Encyclopedia* Hegel mentions the difficulty of representing the boundaries of a category:

> A determination in which the idea appears is at the same time a *fluid* [*fließendes*] moment; hence, the single science is just as much to recognize its content as an *existent* object, as to recognize immediately in that content its crossing into its higher circle. Thus the *representation* [*Vorstellung*] of *division* is misleading in that it puts the particular parts or sciences *side by side*, as if they were—like biological species—only dormant, fixed, and substantial in their distinction.[27]

Writing this passage several decades before the emergence of evolutionary theory, Hegel does not conceive of biological species as temporally continuous with each other. Even so, what distinguishes the "single science" of philosophy is precisely its capacity to recognize, if not represent, the movability of the line demarcating other disciplines or objects.

---

[24]Ibid., 8.

[25]In her study of Descartes, Claudia Brodsky argues, along more Hegelian lines, that the "architectonic line" "is a specifically one-dimensional construct without plastic reality. It does not illustrate the forms of nature, but … translates thought onto an empty surface. It reiterates nothing and represents no preexisting process, but commits an unprecedented form to being. Rather than develop inevitably from a given material core, it is drawn. And in order for the hand to draw a line produced only in the mind, the mind and hand must first invent notation—discourse with no worldly analogue" (Claudia Brodsky, *Lines of Thought: Discourse, Architectonics, and the Origin of Modern Philosophy* [Durham: Duke University Press, 1996], 7).

[26]As with the dialectic, so too with the rhizome: each turn requires a break and beginning; necessity governs only contingent delimitation; infinitude cannot unfold without the constructions of finitude.

[27]Hegel, *Werke* 8: §18: 64.

Though that architectonic line, to cancel itself, must be aesthetic, the representation [*Vorstellung*] of any such limit remains "misleading" by virtue of its static appearance. Thus Hegel articulates the architectonic in mathematical terms evading representation. The line, extended into a circle, collapses its distinct but "fluid" dialectical moments, including its beginning and ending points, into a totality; the latter does not, however, contain itself, passing instead into a "higher" circle, implying an intersection of circles. An intersection would in turn mark an extrinsically determined point, a beginning or an ending that would thus compromise the independence of the circle as a purported totality or self-sufficient system.[28] Thus the architectonic movement of thought, a progression through neither linked circles nor a spiral, cannot be truthfully represented aesthetically or mathematically. The architectonic thus exceeds its conceptual and historical provenance and representation in architecture.

Nonetheless requiring discursive articulation within the realm of the aesthetic, the architectonic finds verbal form in poetry, for Hegel the art of "figurative [*bildlich*]" language.[29] Thus any historical narrative of art conceptually evokes not only the architectonic lines demarcating historical art-forms and thus informing the structure of aesthetic history, but also the liminal art of poetry for the dissipation of those lines. Only by thus bringing the conceptual weight of poetry to bear on its discursive constructions can a history progress through the aesthetic: for poetry, we recall, marks the aesthetic as a "laboring for totality, a process demonstrable philosophically as the sublation [*Aufheben*] of any limitation" to the conceptual bounds of the art forms, hence the beginning of the dissolution of art as such.[30] The arts prior to poetry gave form to their subject matter only in "towering heavy masses, bronze, marble, wood, colors, and notes"; this "earnestness" with respect to sensuous externality causes these particular arts to be "closed in within certain limits."[31] Poetry breaches these limits, surfacing the principle of architectonic fluidity that organizes the "art forms" and the narrative of the *Aesthetics*. Thus poetry is "not bound exclusively to any particular form of art, but is the universal art which can shape into any form and give, finally, verbal expression to any content encountered by the imagination."[32] Just as architecture and poetry together drive the dialectical circuit of the aesthetic, so too they make possible its historical progression as a materialization and dissolution of limits or as a movement between the particular

---

[28]See Hegel, *Werke* 13: 141: "Wie nun aber die Kunst in der Natur und den endlichen Gebieten des Lebens ihr Vor hat, ebenso hat sie auch ein Nach, d. h. einen Kreis, der wiederum ihre Auffassungs- und Darstellungsweise des Absoluten überschreitet. Denn die Kunst hat noch in sich selbst eine Schranke und geht deshalb in höhere Formen des Bewußtseins über."

[29]"We can in general call poetry's mode of representation as *figurative*" [*Im allgemeinen können wir das dichterische Vorstellen als* bildlich *bezeichnen*] (Hegel, *Werke* 15: 276). If this is true, we can rightfully identify a poetic dimension in Hegel's own narrative mode, especially in texts like the *Phenomology of Spirit*. As indicated previously, there is a need for greater attention to Hegel's use of figurative language in relation to his dialectical procedure and his poetics as articulated in the *Aesthetics*.

[30]Hegel, *Werke* 15: 234.

[31]Hegel, *Werke* 15: 232.

[32]Hegel, *Werke* 15: 233.

and universal over time. Thus in the context of his claim that poetry attempts to negate the body or dispel its corporeal bounds, Hegel relates the process of linear dissolution—intellectually, materially, and physically—to the historical loss of the aesthetic, or the endless "beginning" of that loss.[33] Poetry frames the aesthetic as the aspiration for an atemporal "totality"—a temporal confluence of form and content—that nonetheless can never be aesthetically achieved. At the same time, because poetry subverts the ordinary order of language, revealing the contingent or accidental nature of its architectonic arrangement in space and time, architecture and poetry together mark the inability to think the architectonic in ordinary prose. Considered as a principle of logic, the architectonic must be framed as the dialectical exploitation of the heterogeneous and historically rooted symbolism of language—evident explicitly, as we have seen, in the paronomastic *Aufhebung* itself; given this symbolic and material provenance, the architectonic as an historical phenomenon thus becomes a subject for aesthetics and—in particular—mythology.

Within aesthetics, poetry marks the attempted movement of the aesthetic beyond itself, hence of the architectonic outside its seemingly linear or circular historical progression:

> We looked for the conclusion [of the particular arts] in art's making itself independent from the representational mode particular to one of the forms of art and in its standing above the circle of this totality of particular forms. The possibility of such a development generally lies from the very beginning, of all the particular arts, solely in the essence of poetry; therefore such a possibility is operative in the course of poetic production in part through its leveraging and manipulation of every particular form, and in part through its liberation [*Befreiung*] of art from limitation to any self-enclosed type and character of treatment and content, be it symbolic, classical, or romantic.[34]

As a romantic art that also marks the loss of the category of the romantic, poetry not only collapses the formal and historical categories of the aesthetic, but also explicitly subverts the narrative progression between them. In general, romantic art "reintroduces" the separation of form and content characteristic of the symbolic,[35] albeit imposing upon outward form a relation to spiritual interiority. Poetry goes furthest in this separating out and reduction of externality, threatening to dispense with material form and hence the aesthetic altogether. In the last moments of the aesthetic, poetry radically separates subjectivity from meaning through irony or humor:

---

[33] Hegel, *Werke* 15: 234.

[34] Hegel, *Werke* 15: 233.

[35] Hegel, *Werke* 13: 392. The ensuing analysis of the romantic return to oriental symbolism in Hegel's *Aesthetics* owes a debt to Rodolphe Gasché's discussion in "Hegel's Orient, or The End of Romanticism," in *History and Mimesis* (Buffalo: State University of New York, 1983), 17–29.

In this drawing and linking together of material taken from all regions of the world [*Weltgegenden*] and every realm of reality, humor turns back to symbolism, where meaning and form, too, lie away from each other; but now it is the mere subjectivity of the poet that controls both the material and meaning and strings them together in an unfamiliar order or strange configuration.[36]

These final aesthetic productions, arising from and revealing the architectonic "drawing and linking" or "string[ing]" together of material in strange arrangements, mark a return to symbolism, the art form essentially and properly expressed in the symbolic architecture of the Orient. This brand of romantic humor, in its most intense and convincingly artistic configurations, can lead to the immersion of subjectivity into an external object:

Now, if this satisfaction in outward appearance or in subjective representation deepens, according to the principle of romantic art, into the immersion of the mind and heart [*Gemüt*] into the object, and, on the other hand, if humor concerns itself with the object and its configuration within its subjective reflex, then we attain thereby a growing intimacy with the object—an objective humor.[37]

This "intimacy with" and "immersion of the mind and heart [*Gemüt*] into the object" in poetry recalls of course the pantheistic poetry of the Indian, Mohammedan, and Christian poets in the sublime or mediating moment in the history of the symbol. This poetic form appears only:

when there is a deep feeling, a striking and apt witticism, a reflection rich in sense, and a spiritual movement of imagination which animate and develop every minutiae through their treatment in poetry ... What is principally at issue here is that the mind and heart [*Gemüt*], with its spiritual fervor, and the spirit and a rich consciousness shall fully immerse itself in and dwell upon the circumstances, situation, and so on, and thus fashion out of the object something new, beautiful, and valuable in itself.[38]

This pithy poetry, as the "last flourishing of art,"[39] exhibits a "playfulness," particularly with respect to rhyme and meter[40]—a "free" and "ingenious" manipulation of what Hegel calls the architectonic character of poetic material.[41] As the "luminous model" [*glänzendes Vorbild*] of this romantic art of poetry, Hegel cites the poetic tradition of the

---

[36]Hegel, *Werke* 14: 230.

[37]Hegel, *Werke* 14: 240.

[38]Hegel, *Werke* 14: 240–1.

[39]Hegel, *Werke* 14: 240.

[40]Hegel, *Werke* 14: 242.

[41]On architectonics and rhyme, see Hegel, *Werke* 15: 304.

"oriental" Persians and Arabs. Thus Hegel writes in the paragraph concluding the history of the romantic:

> For [the last flourishings of art in the lyric], the Persians and Arabs provide—in the oriental [*morgenländischen*] splendor of their images, in the free bliss of imagination which engages its objects quite theoretically or contemplatively—a luminous model [*glänzendes Vorbild*], even for the present and the subjective inner spirituality of today.[42]

The luminosity of this oriental poetry again explicitly recalls its sublime, pantheistic engagement with illuminated externality. At the culminating moment of aesthetic history, Hegel mentions this Oriental poetry in the same breath as Goethe's *West-östlicher Divan*, a work "essentially different"[43] from his other poetry, not least in its declared traversal of East and West—the very categories that apparently structure the historical narrative of the *Aesthetics*. Moreover Goethe's *Divan*, which appears earlier in the *Aesthetics* in the section on sublime "Mohammedan" poetry, marks not simply a return to symbolism, but rather a syncretism of symbolism and romanticism. This conclusion of art history in turn subverts the narrative scaffolding of Hegel's *Aesthetics*, including especially the divisions of romantic/classical/symbolic and Western/Eastern that have dominated art historical narratives in the wake of Hegel.[44] Thus in the *Philosophy of History*, Hegel claims that:

> Science and knowledge, in particular of philosophy, came from the Arabs into the West; a noble poetry and free imagination were lit amongst the Germans by the East: thus Goethe has turned to the Orient and in his *Divan* composed a string of pearls, which excels everything in inner spirituality and beatitude of imagination.[45]

Such statements countervailing the linear progression of history from East to West (at the end of aesthetic history, Goethe turns to the East, the beginning of history, and writes a *Divan*) can be found throughout the text of the *Aesthetics*. In another instance Hegel, who touches on Arabic poetry from the pre-Islamic *Muʿallaqāt* to the courtly poetry of the Abbasids, insists that the "spiritual ground" of this poetry is the same as that of the "romantic" poetry of the medieval West: "there lies in Arabic poetry from its beginnings an echo of the romantic principle, so that the knights of the Occident at the time of the Crusades found promptly in Arabic poetry a mood identical to their own"; "the spiritual

---

[42]Hegel, *Werke* 14: 241.

[43]Hegel, *Werke* 14: 242.

[44]Paul de Man links the distortion of Hegel's legacy in this respect "to a concept of language in which the all-important distinction between the symbolic and semiotic aspects of language is eroded" (*Aesthetic Ideology*, 108). De Man then recovers Hegel's entanglement of sign and symbol, but does not indicate the extent to which Hegel emphasizes the syncretic nature of the modern and the contribution of the Orient; the fluidity of art forms and genres; the contingency of historical periods; and the necessary provisionality of any historical narrative. I will develop these points over the course of this chapter.

[45]Hegel, *Werke* 12: 433–4.

ground from which poetry arose in the Mohammedan East was akin to that from which it arose in the Christian West."[46] As should be evident, Hegel never advocates abandoning the terms dividing peoples into national, ethnic, religious, cultural, or other such groups for the purpose of historical investigation; the key for Hegel is always to challenge and subvert those boundaries, not least since the history of aesthetics exposes the aesthetic basis of history, and hence the instability of its historical categories.

Needless to say, it would be a mistake to say that Hegel privileges symbolism over romanticism, or the "Mohammedan" poetry of Rumi, Hafiz, and Goethe over any other poetry. It would be equally mistaken, however, to claim the reverse. Indeed the complicity of "Mohammedan" poetry in the syncretic culmination of art serves rather to annul the provisional evaluations of art throughout the text. For instance, while in the course of his lectures Hegel figures the progress of history as a movement from youth to age, or oriental childishness to occidental maturity—he specifically overturns this seemingly valorizing trope as he describes the return to "Mohammedan" verse in the culminating moments of poetry:

> From the perspective of natural capacity we can in this respect give praise especially to the Mohammedan poets of the East. From the beginning they enter into this freedom that even in passion remains independent of passion, and before all variety of interests always holds on to the *one* substance alone as the proper kernel of a poem, against which everything else remains small and transient, so passion and desire mean nothing in the end. This is a theoretical and contemplative view of the world, a relation of the spirit to the things of this world, which lies closer to the spirit of age than youth. For the interests of life still exist in age but not with the urgent force of passion, as in youth ...[47]

At the end of aesthetic history, the spirit in its "age" finds its "last flourishing" and culminating expression in "Mohammedan" poetry: here again Hegel does not fail to mention Goethe, who achieves his most advanced work "only in old age," once freed of the trivializing constrictions of the particular.[48]

Hegel subverts even his most recurrent figure for the movement of history, that of a diurnal progression of the sun from east to west. The most famous and explicit articulation of this figure occurs in the *Philosophy of History*:

> The sun, the light, rises in the Orient. Light is simple self-relation [*die einfache Beziehung auf sich*]: though marked by this universality in itself, it has at the same time a distinct form in the sun. We have often imagined the scene of a blind person suddenly able to see, looking upon the breaking dawn, the growing light,

---

[46]Hegel, *Werke* 15: 307.
[47]Hegel, *Werke* 15: 273–4.
[48]Hegel, *Werke* 15: 274.

the flaming sun. The endless loss of his individuality in this pure clarity—total wonder—is his first experience.[49]

This "Oriental" dawn of history corresponds with the opening phase of several disciplinary categories, including logic, where the idea "in itself" remains abstract and universal; the philosophy of spirit, where the sense of seeing inaugurates the history of mind beginning *in potentia* with anthropological man; the history of aesthetics, particularly the figure of the Memnon struck by the dawn; the history of religion, which begins with the worship of light; and the history of philosophy, where wonder before illuminated externality reveals the latent capacity for speculative thought. In the *Philosophy of History*, the "wonder" Hegel describes in the above passage advances into the inactive "contemplation of his inner being," the "perception of the relation between the two," and in its final phase to the "activity" of self-reflexive and concrete thinking,[50] an intellectual activity Hegel calls "building":

> by evening man has erected a building [*Gebäude erbaut*] built [*bildete*] from his internal sun; and when at day's end he contemplates this, he regards it more highly than the earlier external sun. For now he stands in relation to his spirit, and therefore in a free relation. If we hold onto this image [*Bild*], we find it figures the path of world-history, the great day's work of spirit. World-history progresses from East to West, for Europe is *absolutely* the end of history, Asia the beginning. For world-history has an East *kat' exochen* [or *par excellence*]; the east in actuality [*für sich*] is entirely *relative*, for although the earth forms a sphere, history nevertheless traces no circle around it, but rather has a determinate East, and that is Asia. Here the external physical sun rises, and in the West it sets—where instead the sun of self-consciousness rises, spreading a superior luminosity [*Glanz*].[51]

This passage has lent itself to misreading, not least because of its difficult distinction between the Greek term *kat' exochen*, referring to the extrinsic determination of the quintessence of an object, and the logical term *für sich*, referring to an object which has realized its content "for itself" rather than merely "for another."[52] In Hegel's usage here, *kat' exochen* means an object that has its content *in itself but for another*: thus "for us" a baby is human because it has "in itself" the latent capacity to reason, which we have determined as the human characteristic *kat' exochen* or *par excellence*.[53] In this

---

[49]Hegel, *Werke* 12: 133–4.

[50]Hegel, *Werke* 12: 133–4.

[51]Hegel, *Werke* 12: 134.

[52]For the distinction between *an sich* (*potentia*) and *für sich* (*actu*), see Hegel, *Werke* 5: 125–131 and 174ff. and especially Hegel, *Introduction to the Lectures on the History of Philosophy*, transl. T. M. Knox and A. V. Miller (Oxford: Clarendon Press, 1980), 71–3 and 76–86. For a discussion of Hegel's use of *an sich* and *für sich* in contradistinction to Kant, see Inwood, *A Hegel Dictionary*, 133–6.

[53]Inwood, *A Hegel Dictionary*, 134.

sense Hegel distinguishes between two "Orients": the conceptual East "in itself," whose content has nothing whatever to do with an "actual" east (I have used capitalization to distinguish the two forms); and this "actual" east, a geographical area entirely relative to the position of the person naming it. Thus the concept "Asia" *in itself* and *for us in the West* receives its meaning only from its determination by the narrative progression of world history. While Asia, even as the "determinate" East, is actually and geographically east of Europe, any and all of the content of actual Asia that does not already coincide with the narrative patterns of world-history remain exterior both to Asia as a historically determined concept and to history itself.[54] For Hegel, of course, the Orient or "Morning-land" is determined as the beginning of history, art, religion, and philosophy; "beginning" is thus the content of the Orient *kat' exochen*. By implication the content of the concept of the "Occident" or "Evening-Land" is determined only in relation to this discursively constructed "Orient": thus the historical concept of Europe refers to the "ending" of history, art, religion, and philosophy. Now, as Hegel states throughout his work, "philosophy reveals itself as a circle returning into itself; it does not have a beginning in the sense of the other sciences, so that the beginning is only relative" to a specific interpreter and not to philosophy itself.[55] While philosophy recognizes the provisional and relative nature of a beginning, such structural considerations remain nonetheless necessary, particularly with other sciences: thus any historical narrative, as a spatial and temporal object, must have a beginning and end distinct from each other.[56] It is in this sense that Hegel at once embraces and rejects the circle as a figure for the progression of history. The truth of world-history, history as such, must be a totality or self-enclosed circle, or else the science would have no object; but such a self-sufficient totality cannot yield to discursive, narrative, and spatio-temporal forms of knowledge. Hegel's figure of the diurnal movement of the sun conveys this ambivalent circularity and linearity of history: moving around the sphere of the earth, the light of the sun ends where it begins, but by its own light appears to trace only a linear arc from east to west. Whatever its goals or necessary pretenses, an historical narrative cannot escape drawing provisional lines, proceeding linearly within the laws governing its own determination in space and time.

Hegel thus sets forth the philosophical basis for his narrative's destabilization of its own architectonics, cunningly subverting its lines by framing the Western internalization of light as a process of "building," the quintessentially Eastern art that depends fundamentally on the light of the external sun.[57] The figure of man erecting a building at the close of day, an edifice "built from his inner sun," blurs the boundaries between the beginning and ending of history, morning and evening, *Morgenland* and *Abendland*. This culminating act of building further marks the co-implication of the historical and

---

[54]Gasché, "Hegel's Orient," 232–3.

[55]Hegel, *Werke* 8: §17: 63.

[56]On the concept of beginning [*Anfang*], see Hegel, *Werke* 3: 27–9 *passim*; Hegel, *Werke* 8: §1: 41 and §17: 63; and Hegel, *Werke* 9: §247: 27.

[57]See Hegel, *Werke* 14: 274.

aesthetic—namely, the dependence of history upon the aesthetic determinations of spirit in time; and the subversiveness of those aesthetic determinations over the narrative course of world-history.

The interplay of architecture and architectonics, or physical and discursive modalities of the aesthetic, finds its most sweeping articulation in Hegel's figure of the *Werkmeister*. Thus at the end of his introductory overview of the *Aesthetics*, Hegel characterizes aesthetic history as the work of this spiritual architect associated with the East: "The wide Pantheon of art rises as the external realization [of the idea]; but its builder [*Bauherr*] and work-master [*Werkmeister*] is the self-grasping spirit of beauty that will complete the history of the world only in its development over millenia."[58] Likewise in the section on poetry Hegel refers to "the eternal and absolute idea, which realizes itself in humanity" as the "inner work-master of history" [*der innere Werkmeister der Geschichte*].[59] Now, Hegel's *Werkmeister* finds its quintessential and proper determination in the Oriental, especially Egyptian spirit; and the Egyptians, we recall from Hegel's narrative in the *Aesthetics*, arrive at the "threshold" or limit of freedom precisely by materializing the limit and—regardless of its apparently enduring form or stasis—by nonetheless recognizing the extent of the mind's power to imbricate limits or substitute them one for another.[60] Indeed, it is the Egyptian spirit as *Werkmeister*, or the idea as *Werkmeister* free of static cultural determinations, that constructs a "wide" Pantheon of art open to a medley of culturally disparate gods and *Meisterwerke*. Furthermore the *Werkmeister*, Hegel's term for the "laboring hand" and the spirit as builder, marks the blurring of the boundary between acting and speaking, building and naming, hence material force and semiosis. We can now identify the modality of the resulting concept of linguistic action or performativity as fundamentally architectonic, a resignifying power over history exerted by the *Werkmeister*.[61]

The history of aesthetics locates this intellectual power in the entanglement of architecture and poetry, or of pre-verbal gestures at meaning and the figurative disassembly and reconstruction of discursive, given structures of meaning.[62] What is true of aesthetic history must be true of all philosophically formulated disciplines, since the latter must progress historically and thus cannot evade aesthetic determinations. Every articulation confronts inherited discursive structures. This is true even of

---

[58]Hegel, *Werke* 13: 124.

[59]Hegel, *Werke* 15: 356.

[60]As we have seen, Hegel identifies the spirit as *Werkmeister* with identifiably Oriental and ultimately Egyptian religious art in the *Der Werkmeister* section of the *Phenomenology of Spirit*, and with specifically Egyptian art in his lectures (see Hegel, *Werke* 12: 265).

[61]I will address the *Werkmeister*'s agency, materialization in subjectivity, and relation to political theory in Part Two of this book.

[62]Thus Hegel refers to modern poetry as a "reconstruction" of prose (Hegel, *Werke* 15: 276). The point is not that only poetry performs the discursive resignification of meaning; rather it is that the poetic conception of language as a form of architectonic destruction and "reconstruction" haunts and must be harnessed by all linguistic productions, whether prosaic or poetic. In any event—and not surprisingly—the "boundary line [*Grenzlinie*] where poetry ends and prose begins" cannot be drawn (Hegel, *Werke* 15: 284).

philosophy itself, to the extent that any philosophy evolves historically out of preceding philosophies. As Hegel writes at the beginning of the *Encyclopedia*:

> In the peculiar shape of external history, the origin and development of philosophy is represented as the *history of this science*. This shape gives to the phases of the idea's development the form of an *accidental* succession, and also a pure *plurality* to the principles and the manner in which they are carried out in diverse philosophies over time. But the work-master [*Werkmeister*] of this labor of millenia is the one living spirit whose thinking nature it is to bring to consciousness *what it is*; and when this has become an object in this manner, it is at the same time already lifted above this, reaching in itself a higher stage … The philosophy that is the latest in time is the result of all the preceding philosophies; and it must therefore contain the principles of all of them; it is thus the most unfolded, the richest, and the most concrete one.[63]

Hegel's conception of discursive investigation as a totalization of history should not be too quickly dismissed: for the acceptance, rejection, exclusion, and subsuming of all previous conceptions, gesturing at an implicit totality, must underwrite any endeavor in philosophy or other historically determined discipline. In the case of philosophy proper, the promise of a stable or final whole remains always unfulfilled, yielding necessarily to the "philosophy that is latest in time" and that acknowledges and engages its own historicity.[64] Looking forward in time, the *Werkmeister* in its simultaneously foreign (or Oriental) and universal determinations likewise opens the space for all future interpretive, dialectical histories. The power of these new discursive structures, if they are to inscribe themselves within the historical trajectory of their discipline, must in turn derive from inclusiveness—that is, an active engagement of the abstract and ossified lines that impede access to the heterogeneity internal to received ideas, histories, and disciplines. By actively constructing these lines anew, a discursive history—in any historically determined discipline—contributes to the architectonic and aesthetic materialization of history itself. To ignore the challenge of the historically inherited line is not only to be blind to the prismatic unfolding of ideas; it is also actively, even if unknowingly, to entrench oppressive structures of history and, against the avowed motivations of any form of speculative investigation, to fetter the human mind.

---

[63]Hegel, *Werke* 8: §13: 58.

[64]Related to this argument is Hegel's claim that "every philosophy, precisely because it is the exposition of one particular stage of development, belongs to its own time and is caught in that time's restriction"; by the same token "it cannot be satisfied by an *earlier* philosophy" (Hegel, *Introduction to the Lectures on the History of Philosophy*, 49–50).

PART II
AFRICA AND THE IDEA OF FREEDOM

As the "spirit of beauty" [*Geist des Schönen*], the "laboring" *Werkmeister* propels the architectonic unfolding of history in time.[1] Appearing as the "symbolizing spirit" [*der symbolisierende Geist*] of Egypt, the *Werkmeister* is driven by the enigmatic nature of the symbol to "work" [*arbeiten*], where the "restless" dynamism of the aesthetic corresponds to unstinting labor.[2] Endlessly externalizing spiritual content through non-mimetic form, this first "appearance" [*Erscheinung*] of the aesthetic expresses the will of a subjectivity abstracted from any individual body. This "spirit" indeed struggles and fails to manifest as the "shape of self-consciousness," the corporeal form of human individuality. Accordingly the imperfectly embodied spirit must be the "work-master" or "overseer" [*Werkmeister*] of countless bodies, each like the other reduced to "servitude" [*Knechtschaft*] in the name of collective production, their subjectivity vacated by the mindless "fetters" [*Fesseln*] of a degraded humanity.[3] Laborers of the aesthetic, these Egyptians form an "army of artisans" [*ein Heer aus lauter Handwerkern*], "servants [*Knechte*] for the construction of monumental works."[4] Notwithstanding their skill, these working bodies, as spiritually empty [*geistlosen*] as the corpses they bury in tombs, all work through "unconscious" "instinct," bound to the agency of another, greater power.[5] Finally beginning to express itself as the "hieroglyph" of "the shape of thought"—that is, the speaking human form—the *Werkmeister* "knows itself" as its own aesthetic production, the entanglement of building and naming.[6] Here, as we have seen, the aesthetic "appears" as the Memnon, the *Werkmeister* laboring endlessly to articulate beauty through the fusion of subject and object, language and matter, and architecture and poetry.

If the Egyptian spirit as "overseer" marks the externality of agency, hence the subjection or surrender of the body to another will, its labor nonetheless marks the aesthetic appearance of the principle of freedom. Already with the pyramids, the *Werkmeister* materializes, in the fluidity of the architectonic line, the concrete dialectical dynamism that characterizes thought. As the movement of the self-canceling limit, the dialectic frees thought from the fossilization of the category.[7] Thus the Egyptian spirit passes "restlessly" from one form to another:

---

[1] Hegel *Werke* 13: 124; 3: 235, and 15: 234.

[2] Hegel, *Werke* 12: 265. For Hegel "restlessness" in a state of nature results in an endless cycle of destruction; upon the advent of history, however, the "restlessness" of spirit takes aesthetic form (on various modes of dialectical and thus mental and spiritual "restlessness" [*Unruhe*], see Hegel, *Werke* 12: 145, 234, and 274; on "restlessness" as the irrepressible self-negating propensity of the dialectic, see Jean-Luc Nancy, *Hegel: L'inquiétude du négatif* and Hegel, *Werke* 3: 589).

[3] Hegel, *Werke* 7: 416; and Hegel, *Vorlesungen über Naturrecht Staatswissenschaft: Heidelberg 1817/18 mit Nachträgen aus der Vorlesung 1818/19*, ed. Becker et al. (Hamburg: Felix Meiner Verlag, 1983), 261.

[4] Hegel, *Werke* 12: 253; Hegel, *Vorlesungen über Naturrecht Staatswissenschaft*, 261.

[5] Hegel, *Werke* 12: 253, 3: 508, 511.

[6] Hegel, *Werke* 3: 510.

[7] On the "movement" away from "fossilized" [*versteinert*] elements in the still immature "Oriental state," see Hegel, *Werke* 7: 355. As we will see, Hegel will associate the ossified Oriental state with an impenetrable "building," a walled structure closed to its outside.

Nach allen Seiten hin hat sich der ägyptische Geist als beschlossen in seinen Partikularitäten, als gleichsam tierisch fest darin gezeigt, aber ebenso im unendlichen Drange sich darin bewegend und herumwerfend von der einen in die andere. Es geschieht nicht, daß dieser Geist sich zum Allgemeinen und Höheren erhebe, denn er ist gleichsam erblindet für dasselbe, auch nicht, daß er in sein Inneres zurückgehe; aber er symbolisiert frei und keck mit dem Partikulären und ist desselben schon mächtig … Im orientalischen Geiste bleibt als Grundlage die gediegene Substantialität des in die Natur versenkten Geistes; dem ägyptischen Geiste ist, obzwar ebenso noch in unendlicher Befangenheit, doch die Unmöglichkeit geworden, es in ihr auszuhalten. Die derbe afrikanische Natur hat jene Einheit auseinandergetrieben und hat die Aufgabe gefunden, deren Lösung der freie Geist ist.[8]

The Egyptian spirit has shown itself to us as in all respects confined within the limits of particular determinations, and, as it were, reduced to animality in its various cages; but likewise moved by an unending impulse [*unendlichen Drange*], passes restlessly from one form to another. This spirit never rises to the universal and higher principle, being blind to it; nor does it return inward into itself: yet it symbolizes freely [*frei*] and boldly with the particular and has already mastered it … The solid substantiality of spirit immersed in nature remains the foundation of the Oriental spirit. To the Egyptian spirit, though still enmeshed in the same infinite embarrassment, it has become an impossibility to endure it. The uncouth and rough African nature fragmented that unity [of spirit and nature] and identified the problem whose solution is free spirit.

Like a caged animal, the Egyptian spirit remains trapped within the moving limits of an infinite variety of particular forms. Building endlessly, the *Werkmeister* here identifies in the aesthetic dimension of the dialectic the form and thus possibility of "freedom," arriving at its limit or "frontier" [*Schwelle*] without attaining liberation.[9] The Egyptian spirit unfolds "freely" [*frei*] through symbols, but does not actually escape its infinite restlessness. Evolving from the first diremption of spirit as light—"the form of the master [*die Form des Herrn*] over the self-consciousness of spirit that withdraws from its object"—the *Werkmeister*, a "laboring hand" still divested of free subjectivity, begins to "produce itself as object."[10]

Having "achieved knowledge of itself" merely in and as a "thing," the *Werkmeister* as "laboring self-consciousness" [*arbeitenden Selbstbewußtsein*]—linked clearly to the slave [*Knecht*]—constructs the Memnon, a "dwelling" [*Wohnung*] that blends the "universal" architectonic element of inorganic form with the "shape of individuality."[11]

---

[8]Hegel, *Werke* 12: 271.

[9]Hegel, *Werke* 13: 459.

[10]Hegel, *Werke* 3: 506, 508ff., 237.

[11]Hegel, *Werke* 3: 509–10. I will discuss my translation of *Knecht* as "slave" at length below.

Dependent on the dawn to issue forth meaningless sound, the "statue in human form"—bereft of the mimetic or "ideal" language of self-consciousness—nonetheless voices the power of the aesthetic in time. This architectonic sound rehearses the slave's "active" construction of the Memnon as a "dwelling" for self-consciousness: the speaking mouth reiterates the work of the laboring hand.[12]

The historical appearance of the *Werkmeister* prompts several questions. What are we to make of the trope's conjunction of the aesthetic with laboring "servitude" [*Knechtschaft*]? If art is born precisely where bodies are stripped of their agency— where architecture doubles the "corporeal shell" [*leibliche Hülle*] of an unconsciously toiling humanity—how then can the aesthetic also propel the history of freedom?[13] What theory of agency and its embodiment emerge?[14] Given the explicit reference to "the form of the master" [*die Form des Herrn*] in the chapter on religion in the *Phenomenology* and to the Egyptian spirit's appearance as the "slave" [*Knecht*] in the *Philosophy of History*, what is the relation between the aesthetic as *Werkmeister* and the dialectic of *Herr* and *Knecht*?

The stakes for these questions are particularly high for anti- and postcolonial appropriations of Hegel in light of recent arguments that the master–slave dialectic could not but evoke the revolt, in Haiti, of Africans forcibly transplanted and enslaved by European masters.[15] The resulting debates have been hampered by understandably

---

[12]Hegel, *Werke* 3: 509. I address the entanglement of the mouth and hand as modalities of linguistic performativity in Chapter 2.

[13]Hegel, *Werke* 14: 291–2.

[14]Part Two of this study builds on Robert Pippin's *Hegel's Practical Philosophy: Rational Agency as Ethical Life* (Cambridge: Cambridge University Press, 2008); Christopher Yeomans' *Freedom and Reflection: Hegel and the Logic of Agency* (Oxford: Oxford University Press, 2011); Axel Honneth's *The Pathologies of Individual Freedom: Hegel's Social Theory* (Princeton: Princeton University Pres, 2010); and Allen Speight's *Hegel, Literature, and the Problem of Agency* (Cambridge: Cambridge University Press, 2001), which admirably advance our understanding of Hegel's conceptions of agency, freedom, and the sociality of the subject. I will further consider the relation of these concepts to Hegel's theories of the aesthetic, language, history, and the political state.

[15]My work builds on the archival research and insights of a number of scholars connecting Hegel to the slave revolution in Saint-Domingue. David Brion Davis first introduced scholars to the connection between Hegel's *Knecht* and the Haitian revolution in a chapter entitled "Toussaint l'Ouverture and the *Phenomenology of Mind*," in *The Problem of Slavery in the Age of Revolution: 1770–1823* (Ithaca: Cornell University Press, 1975), 557–64. Pierre-Franklin Tavares's research remains difficult to access but still indispensable (see his *Hegel, critique de l'Afrique: Introduction aux études critiques de Hegel sur l'Afrique*, unpublished dissertation [Paris: Sorbonne, 1989]; "Hegel et Haïti ou le silence de Hegel sur Saint-Domingue," *Chemins Critiques*, 1992, 2: 113–31; "Hegel et l'abbé Grégoire: question noire et révolution française," *Annales historiques de la Révolution française*, 1993, 293/294: 491–509; and "À propos de Hegel et Haïti: Lettre de Pierre Franklin Tavares à Jean Ristat," *L'Humanité*, December 2, 2006). Susan Buck-Morss brought the Hegel and Haiti connection to the attention of a wide group of American academics in a celebrated article entitled "Hegel and Haiti" (in *Critical Inquiry*, 2000, 26: 4: 821–65; see also *Hegel, Haiti, and Universal History* [Pittsburgh: University of Pittsburgh Press, 2009]). Keying off Jacques d'Hondt's identification of the journal *Minerva* as a major and long-standing source for Hegel's news and ideology, Buck-Morss links articles published on Haiti in 1804–5 in *Minerva* to Hegel's development of the dialectic of *Herr* and *Knecht* (see Jacques d'Hondt, *Hegel secret: les sources cachées de la pensée de Hegel* [Paris: Presses Universitaires de France, 1986], 9–43). In a section of his indispensable *Universal Emancipation* entitled "Hegel and Haiti reconsidered," Nick Nesbitt expands on the arguments of Buck-Morss to make the case that paragraph 57 of the *Philosophy of Right* reflects Hegel's sympathies for the Haitian revolt and the

dismissive, but ultimately non-critical readings of Africa's position within Hegel's integrated theory of the aesthetic and history. For the relation of Africa to the master–slave dialectic may be far more complicated than has been assumed. To begin with, for Hegel it is precisely the "uncouth and rough African nature" [*derbe afrikanische Natur*] of the "laboring" Egyptian spirit that makes it capable of fracturing the "substantiality of spirit immersed in nature."[16] He does carefully distinguish Egypt from "Africa proper"; he nonetheless explicitly characterizes Egypt as a hybrid of "the African element and the Oriental solidity transposed [*versetzt*] to the Mediterranean Sea, the locale where nations display themselves."[17] While Egypt will ultimately close itself off from the "stimulation" of the Mediterranean, its cultural hybridity emerges "from the south," from lands at the cusp of history: thus Hegel posits that Egypt "received its culture from Ethiopia," first and "principally from the island Meroe," before that knowledge progressed north "from Upper to Lower Egypt."[18] What conception of Africa emerges from Hegel's statements, and how does the "African element" of the *Werkmeister* inflect current debates around his conception of slavery and the realization of concrete freedom in the state?

To answer these questions, we will first address the long-standing confusion around the organization of the *Phenomenology of Spirit*, identifying the structural relation between the sections on "Self-Consciousness" and "Religion" in which the master–slave dialectic and the *Werkmeister* respectively appear. We will then, to my knowledge for the first time, read the master–slave dialectic the way Hegel asks us to read it, not only "from the standpoint of consciousness," but then also "from the standpoint of self-consciousness": in other words, not only as the abstract dialectic of emergent subjectivity, but also as the necessarily aesthetic materialization of that dialectic in history. This fully contextualized approach will require us to consider the *Phenomenology of Spirit* from its opening through to the appearance of the slave as subject, an itinerary that will include an

---

slaves' right to establish a state (Nick Nesbitt, *Universal Emancipation: The Haitian Revolution and the Radical Enlightenment* [Charlottesville: University of Virginia Press, 2008], 113–24); see also his "Troping Toussaint, Reading Revolution," *Research in African Literatures*, 2004, 35: 2: 18–33). In a review of the work of Buck-Morss and Nesbitt on the relation of Hegel and Haiti, Deborah Jenson identifies a "proto-Hegalian" resonance in the pronouncements of Dessalines, published in German translation in *Minerva* in 1805 (see her "Hegel and Dessalines: Philosophy and the African Diaspora," *New West Indian Guide*, 2010, 84: 3/4: 269–75).

[16]*Derbe* means "rough" when referring to material and "uncouth" when referring to a people. Here the term refers to the materiality of a people, whose very nature is to break apart the solidity of stone—a propensity that, in unison with "Oriental solidity," underwrites the discovery of the principle of freedom in the pyramids.

[17]Hegel, *Werke* 12: 255. See also Hegel, *Werke* 12: 256 and 270. On Hegel's relation of Africa and Egypt, see Jeremy Pope, "Ägypten and Aufhebung: G. F. W. Hegel, W. E. Du Bois, and the African Orient," *The New Centennial Review*, 2006, 6: 3: 149–92 and Robert Bernasconi, "The Return of Africa: Hegel and the Question of the Racial Identity of the Egyptians," in *Identity and Difference*, ed. P. T. Grier (Albany: SUNY, 2007), 201–16.

[18]Hegel, *Werke* 12: 255, 248. As additional evidence of a cultural legacy extending from Ethiopia to Egypt, Hegel points out that, according to Herodotus, the peoples from these regions, along with a Black Sea population conquered by Ramses, are the only ones to practice circumcision (ibid., 249). Hegel would have learned from Cailliaud's description and images of Meroe in the 1820s, including the engraving shown in Figure 8, *The Pyramids at Meroe, View from the Northeast* (Frédéric Cailliaud, *Voyage à Méroé: au fleuve Blanc, au-delà de Fâzoql dans le midi du royaume de Sennâr, à Syouah et dans cinq autres oasis; fait dans les années 1819, 1820, 1821 et 1822* [Paris: Imprimerie Royale, 1826], Plate XXXVI).

extensive reading of Hegel's famously difficult but nonetheless crucial "inverted world" in relation to the dialectic of *Herr* and *Knecht* that follows. We will then interrogate Hegel's conception of Africa in view of its relation to the master–slave dialectic and its appearance as the *Werkmeister*, concluding finally with a re-examination of Hegel's conception of freedom and its concrete realization in the political state.

Figure 8 *The Pyramids at Meroe, View from the Northeast.* Engraving by Fédéric Cailliaud. *Voyage à Méroé : au fleuve Blanc, au-delà de Fâzoql dans le midi du royaume de Sennâr, à Syouah et dans cinq autres oasis; fait dans les années 1819, 1820, 1821 et 1822* (Paris: Imprimerie Royale, 1826), Plate XXXVI.

CHAPTER 6
THE STRUCTURE OF THE *PHENOMENOLOGY*

At the beginning of the section entitled "Religion" in the *Phenomenology of Spirit*, Hegel argues that three forms of religion—natural religion, the religion of art, and the revealed religion—mark the historical appearance, respectively, of consciousness, self-consciousness, and reason, the three abstract "moments" of spirit and three organizing elements of the book:

> If, in the first reality [of spirit as natural religion], spirit in general is in the form [*der Form*] of consciousness, [then] in the second [reality of the religion of art], it is in the form of self-consciousness; so in the third reality it is in the form of the unity of both. It has the shape of *being-in-and-for-itself*; and this representation of spirit as it is *in-and-for-itself* is the *revealed religion*.[1]

Complicating the historical "representation" of the different "spirits" in religion, certain elements "appear" in them from earlier or later "moments" of the dialectic. For instance, the "master" [*Herr*]—a mode of "self-consciousness"—will appear as the "God of light" or the "supersensible" in the historical "shape" of "natural religion" pertaining to "consciousness."[2] How does Hegel account for this hybridity? How does this apparently imperfect reiteration of the dialectic in "Religion" inflect the structure and project of the *Phenomenology*? Answering these questions may help resolve not only the long-standing controversy over the organization of Hegel's most celebrated text, but also the place of the *Werkmeister*, an articulation of "natural religion," in the *Phenomenology* and in Hegel's thought generally.[3]

As the moment in the *Phenomenology* in which spirit, for the first time, takes phenomenal "form," the section on "Religion" occupies a crucial position in the structure of the text, which Hegel outlines as follows:

---

[1]Hegel, *Werke* 3: 502–3.

[2]Hegel, *Werke* 3: 505–6. We will examine these diremptions at length in Chapter 9.

[3]For a summary of the controversy on the organization of the *Phenomenology*, with useful bibliography, see Robert Stern, *Hegel and the Phenomenology of Spirit* (London: Routledge, 2002), 27–9; see also Robert Pippin, "You Can't Get There from Here: Transition Problems in Hegel's *Phenomenology* of Spirit," in *Cambridge Companion to Hegel* (Cambridge: Cambridge University Press, 1993), 52–85 and Frederic Jameson, *The Hegel Variations* (London: Verso, 2010), 8ff., 116.

A. Consciousness

B. Self-Consciousness

C. Reason

    AA. The Certainty and Truth of Reason

    BB. Spirit

    CC. Religion

    DD. Absolute Knowing

The dialectic of "Consciousness" and "Self-Consciousness" produces the principle of "Reason," which in turn bifurcates into the dialectic of "The Certainty and Truth of Reason" and "Spirit." The rational spirit then reflects on itself as an "object" emerging from the dialectic of consciousness, self-consciousness, and reason, yielding up religion as the third term of the dialectic of "Reason."[4] Before this moment, "religion, as consciousness of *absolute Being* as such, has indeed made its appearance, although only from the *standpoint of consciousness* that is conscious of absolute being; but absolute being in-and-for-itself, the self-consciousness of spirit, has not yet appeared in those forms [*Formen*]."[5]

Hegel's remarks here and elsewhere in the introduction to "Religion" set forth explicitly the rationale behind the structure of the *Phenomenology*. Prior to "Religion," spirit conceptualizes consciousness, self-consciousness, and reason (the latter in its first two diremptions) as abstract modalities of engaging the world; failing to see itself in these forms, spirit thus views the dialectic only from the "*standpoint of consciousness*" rather than of "self-consciousness."[6] Indeed, it is not until the final moment of "forgiveness" at the end of "Spirit"—in which two independent self-consciousnesses, the wrong-doer and his hard-hearted judge, appear to achieve "reconciliation" by renouncing their merely subjective positions—that the "concept" of self-consciousness as spirit, the harmony of contradictory and conflicting I's, emerges as "universal knowledge of itself in its absolute opposite."[7] But even this moment has not yet taken phenomenal "form" in a manner that manifests that newfound knowledge in its "totality." Indeed all preceding moments in the *Phenomenology* only "exhibit themselves in separation, on their own account."[8] Since spirit only comes to know itself after having run the "full course" through these abstract "moments," they are only instances of "immediate spirit" prior to its self-reflection:[9]

> All previous shapes of consciousness are abstract forms of it. They consist in spirit analyzing itself, distinguishing its moments, and lingering with each. This activity of isolating such moments *presupposes* spirit and its durable existence—that is, this

---

[4]In the final moments of reason as "forgiveness," spirit becomes a "self-consciousness that communes with its own self" and thus "conceives of itself as an object" (Hegel, *Werke* 3: 496–7).

[5]Hegel, *Werke* 3: 495.

[6]Hegel, *Werke* 3: 496–7.

[7]Hegel, *Werke* 3: 494.

[8]Hegel, *Werke* 3: 498.

[9]Hegel, *Werke* 3: 498.

isolating activity only exists in the spirit, which is an existence. Thus isolated, these moments appear as if they were really existing as isolated. But they advance and retreat into their ground and essence, proving that they are only moments or vanishing quantities; and this essence is just this movement and dissolution of these moments. Here, where spirit is posited as the reflection of each of these moments into itself, our own reflection can remind us of what they were: they were consciousness, self-consciousness, and reason. Spirit, then, is consciousness in general which consists in sense-certainty, perception, and the understanding, in so far as in its analysis of itself, spirit holds on to the moment of being an objective, existent actuality to itself, and if it abstracts from this, its actuality is its own being-for-self.[10]

Mediated only through "cognition," these initially "abstract forms" of consciousness have had no "durable existence of their own."[11] Only when spirit contemplates itself as an "object" in time, Hegel reasons, does spirit take historical form: "Only spirit in its totality or wholeness [*ganze Geist*] is in time … [S]pirit descends from its universality to individuality [*Einzelheit*] through determination. This determination or middle term is *consciousness, self-consciousness*, and so on. But *individuality* is constituted by the shapes of these moments. These moments thus exhibit spirit in its individuality or *actuality* and distinguish themselves from each other in time, albeit so the later moment retains within it the preceding one."[12] As spirit contemplates itself, its historical shapes must reveal themselves from the "standpoint" of this newly emerged "self-consciousness of spirit."

The hybridity in the individual shapes of specific religions results from this translation between the abstract conception of "spirit" from the "standpoint of consciousness" and the phenomenal manifestation of "self-conscious spirit." Just as the abstract modes or "moments" of consciousness, self-consciousness, and reason unfold prior to the historical articulation of spirit as a "whole," so, too, the phenomenal "shapes" of specific religions manifest in time prior to the philosophical realization of "absolute knowing," which Hegel will present as the paradoxical covalence of the dialectic of history and the principle of "freedom" from the dialectic.[13] Having run the abstract course of the

---

[10]Hegel, *Werke* 3: 325–6.

[11]Hegel, *Werke* 3: 500.

[12]Hegel, *Werke* 3: 498–9.

[13]Hegel, *Werke* 3: 498–9. The historical expression of spirit articulates the dialectic between the "freedom" of self-conscious spirit on the one hand and "time" as its "other": "only the whole of spirit has true reality, hence the form of pure freedom in face of an 'other,' which expresses itself as time" (Hegel, *Werke* 3: 498). In contrast to the moment of self-knowing spirit, the "progression" of preceding "isolated" moments of the *Phenomenology* is thus "*not* to be represented as occurring in time" (ibid., emphasis mine). "Absolute knowing," as the "goal" of the system, must mark the paradoxical convergence of (i) spirit as the atemporal principle of freedom, or the non-dialectical principle that marks the instability and thus negation of historical form and (ii) spirit as time, or the inadequately co-implicated sign and referent of dialectical history (Hegel, *Werke* 3: 591). As the internal-external telos "of" history, the principle of freedom propels the movement of the dialectic. (I should note here that through the ambivalence of the genitive, the phrase "telos of history" gestures at an ahistorical moment "of" or paradoxically "belonging to" the dialectic of history.) On "absolute knowing" see Rebecca Comay and Frank Ruda, *The Dash—The Other Side of Absolute Knowing* (Cambridge: MIT Press, 2018), 65–86.

dialectic, spirit as a "whole" will aggregate elements from across its abstract "moments" into "individual" shapes and concretize them temporally in a manner that reflects their relation to each other.[14] Given their actual convergence in the form of self-knowing spirit as "freedom," the difference between these shapes can be no difference.[15] But from the perspective of spirit in "time," these individual shapes appear as individualized, temporal shapes of a still contingent history.[16] Hegel thus qualifies his relation between "consciousness" and "natural religion," "self-consciousness" and "the religion of art," and so on by arguing that the historical shapes of these separate spirits, lacking knowledge of the whole, present the "differences" between them only as constructed and thus provisional "moments" in the unfolding of spirit.[17] Accordingly the previous progression of "consciousness," "self-consciousness," and "reason" maps "essentially"—that is, in their self-relation from the perspective of historical mystification—but not exclusively onto the temporal expressions of spirit in its three religious forms.[18]

In addition, because the various shapes of spirit in their individuality, taken together, "belong to self-knowing spirit in general," its historical form will be religious: spirit must contemplate itself in order to learn that its reality consists in this self-knowing, hence in the self-consciousness of spirit.[19] The latter attempts to materialize as "the unity of different independent self-consciousnesses"[20]; in religion, self-conscious spirit will thus appear through a range of collective subjects that take spirit as a phenomenal object.[21] Beginning with the consciousness of a "supersensible" being beyond the self and ending with "the perfection of spirit into which its individual moments—consciousness, self-consciousness, reason, and spirit—return," religion "*is* [that is, achieves phenomenal immediacy] only as the differentiating and self-returning movement of its [various] aspects."[22]

Hegel thus makes the radical claim that for the philosophical mind all religions—including what he provocatively calls the "religion of Enlightenment"—ultimately inhere in each other, where each contains the others' forms: "all forms in general are certainly

---

[14]Spirit bears within it all of the elements emerging from the antecedent movement from "consciousness" to "spirit"; contemplating itself, spirit consolidates these elements into individual forms of increasingly self-reflective spirit.

[15]Hegel, *Werke* 3: 498.

[16]Ibid.

[17]Hegel, *Werke* 3: 500–1.

[18]The "essential" spirit of an historical shape will thus "penetrate" every heterogeneous element of its actuality (Hegel, *Werke* 3: 499–500).

[19]Hegel, *Werke* 3: 500. The argumentation here contravenes the conclusion of Frederic Jameson, for whom the section on "Religion" marks an "enormous supplement"—an afterthought whose place "we must account for by the supposition that the author felt something to be missing from his previous narrative" (Jameson, *The Hegel Variations*, 116).

[20]Hegel, *Werke* 3: 145.

[21]These collective subjects, of course, for themselves are neither universal nor fully self-conscious. The first such collective subjects in "Natural Religion" are in fact "unconscious."

[22]Hegel, *Werke* 3: 499. Emphasis mine.

in themselves or *for us* contained in spirit and in each spirit."[23] Or again: "The series of different religions, whose diversity results from spirit's knowing of itself in terms of individual determinateness, will just as well represent again the different aspects of *each single* religion, and the representations which apparently distinguish one actual religion from another appear in each one."[24]

Religion does indeed "appear" from the standpoint of consciousness prior to the advent, in the penultimate chapter of the *Phenomenology*, of "self-knowing spirit" in history; as with all of these earlier forms, however, spirit as consciousness merely "confronts" these religious abstractions without "recogniz[ing] itself therein."[25] In order to appear historically, religion must manifest itself through the temporal "shapes" of "picture-thinking" [*Vorstellung*]:

As we now know that spirit in its world and spirit conscious of itself as spirit, or spirit in religion, are the same, the perfection of religion consists in the two becoming the same as the other: not only that religion concerns itself with spirit's actuality or reality, but, conversely, that spirit, as self-conscious spirit, becomes actual to itself and *object of its consciousness*. Insofar as spirit in religion *represents* or *pictures* [*vorstellt*] itself to itself, it is indeed consciousness, and the reality enclosed [*eingeschlossene*] within religion is the shape [*Gestalt*] and the garment [*Kleid*] of its picture-thinking. Reality does not, however, in this picture-thinking, realize its perfect due to be not merely a garment but a self-sufficient or independent free existence [*selbständiges freies Dasein*]; and, conversely, because reality lacks this perfection [or realization of freedom in self-consciousness] within itself, it is a *determinate* shape which does not attain to what it ought to exhibit, namely spirit conscious of itself. If that shape is to express spirit itself, it must be nothing but spirit, and spirit must appear to itself, or be in reality, what it is in its essence. Only in this manner would the realization come about of what may seem to be the demand for the opposite—that is, that the *object* of its consciousness have at the same time the form of free reality [*die Form freier Wirklichkeit*]; but only spirit that to itself as absolute spirit is an object is thus conscious of itself as a free actuality to the extent that it is and remains conscious of itself therein.[26]

---

[23]Hegel, *Werke* 3: 496, 501. "For us" means from the mature standpoint of self-consciousness, i.e., "for us" enlightened readers of Hegel.

[24]Hegel, *Werke* 3: 503–4.

[25]Hegel, *Werke* 3: 496–7. Hegel will even call Kant's categorical imperative a type of "religion of morality" (ibid., 496). Ian Almond, arguing in a brief chapter that Hegel simply could not maintain a logically consistent position when it came to the religion and cultural contributions of Muslims, does not take into account, *inter alia*, this mutual inherence of religions in one another in the Hegelian system; the fact that all religions, not just Islam, are in some sense "incomplete"; the relation between religion and aesthetic production; and the contingency of all historical demarcations (Ian Almond, *The History of Islam in German Thought: From Leibniz to Nietzche* [London: Routledge, 2010], 108–34, especially 117ff.).

[26]Hegel, *Werke* 3: 497–8.

Evoking the sacred poetry he will cite in the "sublime" moment of poetic symbolism in the *Aesthetics* ("*Licht ist dein Kleid*," etc.), Hegel argues that religion, as spirit that contemplates itself as spirit in its material expression, must do so in a "garment" [*Kleid*] alien to spirit.[27] On the one hand, for the abstract "content" of consciousness, self-consciousness, and reason to take historical "form," they must find expression through phenomenal or "objective" "shapes." On the other hand, this "spiritual" content cannot converge with its temporal form. The latter must liberate itself from the merely symbolic and thus always inadequate forms of phenomenality in order to become a "free actuality":

> Although [in the final diremption of religion] spirit has attained its true shape [*Gestalt*], the shape itself and [the mode of] representation or picture-thinking [*Vorstellung*] are still the aspect that has not been overcome. Spirit must pass over into the concept, in order therein wholly to dissolve [*aufzulösen*] the form of objectivity—that is, in the concept that includes its opposite within itself. It is then that spirit has grasped [*erfaßt*] the concept of itself, just as we now have first grasped it; and its shape or the element of its existence, being the concept, is spirit itself.[28]

From the opening of the *Phenomenology*, Hegel insists that objectivity cannot be "taken" or "grasped" [*erfaßt*], either physically or conceptually, in any present. Spirit must accordingly "dissolve" the "form" of objectivity even as it embraces it in the concept. Just as the sign imposes upon but cannot seize time in its infinite divisibility, so content cannot wholly coincide with form. Since the endless entanglement of form and content constitutes the "aesthetic," marking its sublime implications in historical time, the passing over of the aesthetic into the concept—the paradoxical unity of spirit and substance, and in turn subjectivity and objectivity—can only occur at the telos of history in "absolute knowing." For Hegel this concept—the organizing principle of philosophy—thus consists in the historical impossibility of totality: as the "systematization" of the manifold "parts" of phenomenality, the concept identifies the logic behind the failure of reason to organize history with any finality.

For this reason, religion—the history of spirit, the telling of its appearance or representation in the world—remains necessarily entangled with the realm of aesthetic. In "Religion" "spirit in its wholeness" [*der ganze Geist*] appears as the "laboring *Werkmeister* of history," the immanently aesthetic principle born of the "laboring self-consciousness."[29] Taking "present" [*vorhanden*] form as the initially unconscious laborer fractured between self and thing, the "*Werkmeister* itself, the whole spirit"

---

[27]For a discussion of the term *Kleid* in sublime poetry, see Chapter 4. The figure will resonate throughout the section on natural religion, reappearing as *angekleidet* (Hegel, *Werke* 3: 506) and *Verkleidung* (ibid., 516). See also Hegel, *Werke* 12: 107: "Der Geist, der sich in diese Weise der Natürlichkeit kleidet … "

[28]Hegel, *Werke* 3: 502–3.

[29]Hegel, *Werke* 3: 509; Hegel, *Werke* 15: 356. Hegel will also refer to spirit as the "*Werkmeister* of this [historical] labor of millenia" in the *Encyclopedia* (Hegel, *Werke* 8: §13: 58).

[*der Werkmeister selbst, der ganze Geist*], will nonetheless persist as "the inner, hidden essence" of the self-consciousness of spirit in time.[30]

The *Phenomenology of Spirit* must moreover reach its crisis in the aesthetic manifestation of religious contemplation precisely because, as the title of the work suggests, spirit in time must attempt and fail to find phenomenal or historical form fully adequate to the concept. The account of the impossible journey finally to realize self-conscious spirit in "phenomenality" constitutes the "phenomenology" or philosophical study of the materialization of spirit.

---

[30]"Der Werkmeister selbst, der ganze Geist, ist noch nicht erschienen, sondern ist das noch innere verborgene Wesen, welches als Ganzes, nur zerlegt in das tätige Selbstbewußtsein und in seinen hervorgebrachten Gegenstand, vorhanden ist" (Hegel, *Werke* 3: 509). Hegel repeats the pun here on "vorhanden," referring both to the presence of spirit and the laborer's hand, the "*Werkmeister* of his fortune" (Hegel, *Werke* 3: 237). As I will demonstrate, the figure of the *Werkmeister* in "Religion" gestures at a vast philosophical project connecting aesthetics and history to the advent of self-consciousness in labor, the coercive force of political economy, and the possibility of recognition and freedom through sociality in the state.

CHAPTER 7
THE WORLD TURNED UPSIDE DOWN

Before assessing how the necessarily aesthetic appearance of self-consciousness in history inflects our reading of the progression from consciousness to self-consciousness in the *Phenomenology*, we will first follow that dialectical movement from the "standpoint" of consciousness. This task should be straightforward, since Hegel already abstracts the apprehension of the world up to the birth of the subject from its historical and thus aesthetic materialization. From this standpoint, consciousness progresses through three phases: sense-certainty, perception, and understanding.[1] First, as "sense-certainty," consciousness makes the flawed positivistic assumption that objects apprehended in the world can be named and so grasped in their immediacy or presence. Upon learning that sensory objects do not subsist in the present and are in fact negated by language, consciousness progresses to its second diremption as "perception"; in this mode, consciousness assumes that "what is present" is, in each case, a singular object, a "one" that shares properties with other individuated objects such that each object is a "bundle" of universal properties. Consciousness then discovers a contradiction. On the one hand, it assumes that each such object, by virtue of subsuming all of its "many" particular properties as stable "universals," has the property of oneness, a stable individuation in space and time. On the other hand, it finds that those properties are merely "sensuous universals," hence subject to the same dialectical instability impeding us from grasping the "This" in sense-certainty. Thus the line between "black" and "white," in the region of greyness between them, is impossible to stabilize; indeed, no "black" may be "black" enough. Accordingly the line between "black" and "white" remains fluid, and any specification of "blackness" remains a universal with no fixed corollary in sense-certainty.[2] Because its properties are thus empty of universal and thus stable content, the object becomes devoid of distinctions and determinations, lacking any anchor for individuation.

Finding the "oneness" of the thing a mere "deception," consciousness moves to its much less understood third diremption as "understanding," turning away from the "manifest

---

[1] These three modes of consciousness correspond to the three chapters in the dialectic of "Consciousness": (1) "Sense-Certainty, or the This and What Is Meant"; (2) "Perception, or the Thing and Deception"; and (3) "Force and the Understanding; Appearance and the Supersensible World" [(1) *Die sinnliche Gewißheit oder das Dieses und das Meinen*; (2) *Die Wahrnehmung oder das Ding und die Täuschung*; and (3) *Kraft und Verstand, Erscheinung und übersinnliche Welt*], hereafter "Sense-Certainty," "Perception," and "Understanding." My aim here is to present Hegel's dialectic of sense-certainty and perception in the most summary terms.

[2] Hegel, *Werke* 3: 100.

image" of objects to a rules-based account of their phenomenality. As "understanding," consciousness penetrates beyond sensuous reality into the "true background of things."[3] In his account in the *Phenomenology* of what we today call the performative dimension of language, Hegel centers on "force," a central concept in Newtonian physics, to instantiate the shortcomings of the positivist account of reality.[4] Since consciousness must account for our cognition of the "background" beyond empirical phenomena, it must bifurcate the world into a sensory and "supersensible" world, the latter a kind of "holy of holies" or "inner world" consisting of "laws"—scientific, legal, and so on—governing the phenomenal world.[5]

Hegel's difficult but foundational attack on the "understanding" centers on the posited [*gesetzt*] dialectical differentiation between the "world of appearance" and the "supersensible beyond," respectively the "outer" and "inner" world. What commentators have missed here is the explicitly discursive representation of that "supersensible" or "inner" being of objects. While the "outer" world is characterized by change, the "inner" world of "laws" [*Gesetze*] requires "explanations" [*Erklärungen*] composed of "words" with purportedly stable content.[6] But the "words" of these "enunciated" [*ausgesprochen*] laws turn out to be dialectical: they must posit themselves in contradistinction to an opposite.[7] Because the content of these words cannot be fixed, each ends up articulating the pure form of an "empty word" [*ein leeres Wort*], a mere sign with no content.[8] The distinction between "soliciting and solicited force," for instance, "or force expressing itself and force repressed into itself," is predicated on a dialectical difference that cannot hold:

> What is present here is not merely bare unity in which *no difference* would be *posited*, but rather a *movement* in which a difference is certainly made but, because it is no difference, is again canceled. In the process, then, of [discursive] explaining [*Erklären*], the to and fro of change which before was outside of the inner world and present only in the appearance, has penetrated [*eingedrungen*] into the supersensible world itself … [9]

Hegel's reference here to "penetration" [*Eindringen*], as we will see, is not innocent. Crucially, the term foregrounds the "impulse" [*Drang*, a cognate of *Eindringen*] of the spirit to labor—an urge that, upon the birth of subjectivity, will take the initial form of the "desire" [*Begierde*] to negate otherness. For the "understanding," "penetration" refers to the modality through which difference endlessly cancels itself—that is, to the

---

[3] Hegel, *Werke* 3: 116.

[4] On Hegel's conception of linguistic action or performativity, see Chapter 2.

[5] Hegel, *Werke* 3: 117–8. Hegel's attack on science echoes his critique of positive Christianity. (On Nietzche's engagement of Hegel's line of thought here, see Gadamer, "Hegel's 'Inverted World,'" 40.) One might say that if Christianity is Platonism for the masses, positivist science is Platonism for the pre-critical intellectual.

[6] Hegel, *Werke* 3: 125. This "positing" of difference equates to the performative articulation of the dialectic.

[7] Hegel, *Werke* 3: 125.

[8] Hegel, *Werke* 3: 124.

[9] Hegel, *Werke* 3: 126.

act of negation that enables the movement of the dialectic, in this case between the world of appearance and the "supersensible world." What are the implications of this "penetration" of reality into the world of the discursively mediated dialectic? How does this reverse insemination—akin to what we earlier called the symbolic inflection of the sign—frame Hegel's conception of the knowledge unearthed by the failure of the understanding? Answering these questions is particularly important given the decisive role of Hegel's still misunderstood "inverted world"—which concludes the section on "understanding"—in the emergence of the logical principle of infinite self-canceling difference, the basis for his theory of subjectivity and, in turn, of sociality.

Now, Hegel's purpose is not to dismiss the utility of empirical inquiry; rather it is to reframe the value of scientific or any other kind of empiricist labor in the context of the shortcomings of mere "understanding."[10] In that vein his critique here on the ability of the "positive" logic of the empirical sciences to lay claims to any final "truth" is irrefutable: just as the section on "perception" critiques the mathematical notion of "one" as a static, truthful predicate of the world of appearance, the section on "understanding" interrogates the possibility of arriving at "certainty" through any discursive account of the world. Any such attempts are subject to the infinite fluidity of dialectical oppositions: thus physicists today attempt, through the language of "string theory," to reconcile the theory of relativity with quantum physics. Hegel's attack extends beyond natural science to any kind of "law." Those valorizing or devalorizing a certain "universal" action *a priori* and thus purportedly "outside" the world of appearance cannot accurately describe each instance of the action in its differentiated particularity. The law could thus categorize what was actually a well-intentioned action as a crime.[11]

If laws, Hegel continues, were to find justification within an extrinsic "realm of laws," consciousness would have to identify a unifying law underwriting all such laws. What then follows, however, is in an infinite regression to the principle of law as such—the form of law empty of all representational content save the principle of form or difference itself. Since any particular concept—for instance, motion—can be differentiated into constituent parts *ad infinitum* or gathered up into other concepts that can be divided into different parts, all such concepts are contingent on the law of contradiction, hence the dialectic: "the concept of difference" in a particular case is always the "difference belonging to the concept," a "merely verbal" difference that characterizes the "understanding" rather than the thing itself.[12] For this reason scientific "explanations" only run in "tautologies" or "cycles": necessarily discursive, empirical inquiry involves merely "enunciated" "descriptions" of phenomena with differentiated elements linked

---

[10]Hegel's more expansive critique of the natural sciences lies beyond the scope of our present inquiry.

[11]Hegel, *Werke* 3: 129–30.

[12]Hegel, *Werke* 3: 125. Hegel argues that, logically speaking, the "necessity," by virtue of scientific law, of a natural phenomenon is "merely verbal" or discursive and thus does not pertain to the "thing itself": "Diese Notwendigkeit, die nur im *Worte* liegt, ist hiermit die *Hererzählung* der Momente" (Hegel, *Werke* 3: 125; emphasis mine). The same obtains with respect to a law attempting to describe a certain type of action.

by ultimately "empty" "laws" of causality, force, and so on: no such laws function as repositories of final truths.[13]

To posit a dialectical difference between the world of appearance and the supersensible world of laws thus ultimately reduces merely to the *positing* of the law of difference—the very performative act first producing the "realm of laws." We can accordingly characterize this positing of law as the pure performative "force" of the dialectic. Hegel instantiates this argument through the verbal pun on *Gesetz/gesetzt*, which frames the "law" [*Gesetz*] as "posited" [*gesetzt*], and thus the supersensible "realm of laws" [*Reich der Gesetze*] as the "realm of positing"—the pure principle, that is, of performativity.[14]

Although the philosophically initiated mind can isolate the discursive power of language to posit and thus performatively inflect the categories of the world of appearance, "the thoughtless thinker" will cling to discursive "explanations" of a supersensible world "beyond" the world of appearance—that is, to "laws" as if they had positive and thus non-dialectical referential value. Blind to the fact that this "inner world" consists of merely "empty words" that performatively differentiate and inflect actual things, the understanding thus creates a "*static* realm of laws"—the dogma of understanding. Hegel's formal logic here must be followed assiduously. Given the irrepressible power of the dialectic, this "inner world" of the realm of static laws doubles into an "inverted world" [*die verkehrte Welt*] consisting of the opposite of all of the elements of the first world: "the first supersensible world—the static realm of laws, the immediate copy of the perceived world—is changed into its opposite."[15] This "second supersensible world," in contrast to the motionless "universal" laws of the first, must therefore be characterized by endless "change" [*Veränderung*].[16] Since the "inverted world" must also oppose the "transcendental" quality of the "first supersensible world," this second, necessarily "sensuous" copy cannot maintain its separation from the world of appearances. Reflecting the same operation through which the architectonic will materialize history, the dynamic "differentiation" of the "inverted world," necessarily dialectical and thus unstable, produces "actual things."[17]

---

[13]Hegel's critique points to the tautological nature of many medical diagnoses, e.g. "restless leg syndrome." The argument here also surfaces the circular nature of medical accounts of causality: for instance, positing that someone broke their arm because of a "fall" reduces to an explanation grounded in the law of force, which then prompts questions about the irreducibly complex "causes" and "effects" related to the "action" and "reaction" of the impact. There can thus be no scientific standard that enables us truthfully and with certainty to represent the attribution of a bone fracture to such arbitrarily individuated "causes" as calcium deficiency, body weight, acceleration, and other such factors. Any such account amounts to a "tale" or "narrative of the moment" [*Hererzählung der Momente*] (Hegel, *Werke* 3: 125).

[14]Hegel, *Werke* 3: 120.

[15]Hegel, *Werke* 3: 127–8. Upon the discursive or posited division of the "outer" world of appearances and its "inner" world of laws, the latter must also—in accordance with the law of non-contradiction and the dialectic—posit its opposite: thus the idea of "positive electrical charge," in order to have meaning, must posit the idea of "negative charge"; "wrong" must posit "right"; and so on. So, too, the static, transcendental law of the first world must posit endless differentiation and ultimately, sensuous dynamism in the inverted world. Through the architectonic demarcation of time, this "formal" process will ultimately mark the "actual" perverted unfolding of the world.

[16]Hegel, *Werke* 3: 128.

[17]Hegel, *Werke* 3: 129.

Enunciated "laws," far from passively explaining the world, actualize it in a manner that in fact contravenes the "static laws" or dogma of the understanding. We can clarify Hegel's argument here by building on his own example of the blurred line between black and white, this time in the context of the *Code Noir* of 1685, issued by the French sovereign to regulate the "status and condition" of "newly arrived," enslaved "Negroes" in the French colonies.[18] Attempting to actualize the presumed doctrine or "static law" under which white Europeans could traffic in and own black slaves (and not the other way around), the *Code Noir* acknowledges the risk to race-based slavery posed by white "masters" and their white underlings impregnating enslaved black women. Thus Article IX of the *Code Noir* discourages miscegeny by fining transgressors: "Free men who will have one or several children from concubinage with their slaves, along with the masters who allowed this concubinage, shall each be fined two thousand pounds of sugar."[19] The practice of concubinage was so common, however, that there was little incentive for any white man to support enforcement of this fine—or indeed any of the disciplinary measures set forth in the Code Noir to regulate the treatment of slaves.[20] As a result of widespread miscegeny, within a few generations of the *Code Noir* "mulattoes" equalled "whites" in population.[21] White men in Saint–Domingue even married women of African descent.[22] According to the Abbé Grégoire, the population of mulattoes in Saint-Domingue doubled in the eight years leading up to 1787, their exponential increase attending their ever-increasing economic clout: "How can you limit that population when the unrestrained lechery of so many whites guarantees its future growth? The mulattoes' industriousness and its results will follow the same pattern."[23] Indeed, many mulattoes were "master-artisans," buying their freedom and then becoming substantial

---

[18]*Le Code Noir ou recueil de reglements rendu jusqu'à présent* (Paris: Prault, 1767), Article II.

[19]Ibid., Article IX.

[20]See C. L. R. James, *Black Jacobins* (New York: Vintage, 1989), 6–84 *passim*.

[21]Hegel would have read about the phenomenon of miscegeny and the resulting inversion of the social hierarchy in Saint-Domingue in the 1792 edition of the journal *Minerva*, which featured a long article on the slave uprising in Haiti: "The colored people, or mulattoes [*Mulatten*], are the immediate descendants of the whites who have intermarried with African women; they constitute the bourgeoisie [*Bürgerstand*] of the colony. This productive and industrious class consists of proprietors and artisans [*Handwerkern*] who would honor order and law if justice were restored to them. To the artisan class [*arbeitsame Classe*] belong the Negroes, some of whom are free, some slaves" ("Historische Nachrichten von den letzten Unruhen in Saint Domingo," in *Minerva: Ein Journal historischen und politischen Inhalts*, edited by Johann Wilhelm von Archenholz, 1792, 1: 298). Jacques d'Hondt has shown that Hegel read this inaugural volume of *Minerva* (*Hegel secret*, 9–12). See also James, *Black Jacobins*, 37ff. The French used an array of terms for the *sang-mêlés*, including mulatto, quarteroon, marabou, sacatra, and so on—each term signalling a ratio of "African" blood. Following James, I use the historical term "mulatto" to include all offspring of white and black, notwithstanding the term's pejorative connotations.

[22]Ibid.

[23]Abbé Grégoire, *Lettre aux philanthropes, sur les malheurs, les droits et les réclamations des gens de couleur de Saint-Domingue, es des autres îles françoises d'Amérique*. Paris: 1790, cited in Laurent Dubois and John Garrigus, *Slave Revolution in the Caribbean 1789-1804: A Brief History with Documents* (New York: Bedford/St. Martin's, 2006), 74. On the relation of Hegel to the Abbé Grégoire, see Tavares, "Hegel et l'abbé Grégoire," 491–509.

owners of land and slaves.[24] Accumulating "immense capital," they "bid for properties" and "raised prices to such fantastic heights" that whites without means could no longer afford them.[25] Accordingly "in some districts, the finest properties were in the possession of the half-castes. Being so rich they imitated the style of the whites" and attempted to efface any evidence of African origin.[26]

In the face of this "topsy-turvy" world, in which free mulattoes owned slaves (including potentially fair-skinned or "mixed race" slaves who had not been freed) and property, envious whites, rich and poor alike, pushed for draconian laws to humiliate the *sang-mêlés*, appropriate their assets, and exterminate them.[27] But despite increasing violence against them, mulattoes continued to grow in power, some using their capital to travel to and educate their children in France and even serving the king.[28] Already creole blood pervaded the royal court, prompting the planters to declare to the sovereign: "Sire, your entire court has become creole by alliance."[29] Mulattoes at court prompted fears, that they, too "would soon be making marriages with distinguished families, which would bind [the latter] in alliance with the slaves in the gangs, whence the mothers of these upstarts came."[30] Sketching out the role of mulattoes in the French Revolution, C. L. R. James argues that it was "the quarrel between whites and mulattoes that woke the

---

[24]James, *Black Jacobins*, 38. The prevalence of master–artisans among slaves has been noted throughout the Americas: "Many slave men of African birth were also trained in various artisanal skills, because of the lack of skilled free labor. Such enslaved men were used as carpenters, joiners, masons, pavers, printers, sign and ornamental painters, carriage and cabinet makers, coopers, sculptors in stone and carvers of saintly images in wood, silversmiths, lamp makers, jewelers, and lithographers. Nearly a quarter of the male slaves listed in their owners' inventories for the years 1811–1888 were artisans" (Mieko Nishida, *Slavery and Identity: Ethnicity, Gender, and Race in Salvador, Brazil, 1808–1888* [Bloomington: Indiana University Press, 2003], 42–3). On the extremely high value and "careful treatment" of African artisans in sixteenth-century Peru, see James Lockhart, *Spanish Peru, 1532–1560: A Social History* (Madison: University of Wisconsin, 1968), 207; on master–artisans among freed slaves in the Southern United States in the early nineteenth century, see Sharon Patton, *African-American Art* (Oxford: Oxford University Press, 1998), 55ff. The Museum of Early Southern Decorative Arts in Winston-Salem, North Carolina, has an especially fine display of work by formerly enslaved antebellum artisans. On African slave artisans in Brazil, the Caribbean, and North America building "splendid residences" "embellished with elaborate woodwork and stone, their imposing Palladian or baroque exteriors and staircases pointed up by African detail craftsmanship," see Robin Blackburn, *The Making of New World Slavery: From the Baroque to the Modern: 1492–1800* (London: Verso, 1997), 342. In the same vein, Daniel Fountain writes, "Slave artisans represented a major component of the colonial and early American skilled labor force … slave artisans worked in countless occupations throughout the colonies and much of the United States … the overwhelming majority of enslaved skilled labor was of African descent …" (*Slavery in the United States: A Social, Political, and Historical Encyclopedia*, ed. J. Rodriguez [Oxford: ABC Clio, 2007], 1: 176).

[25]James, *Black Jacobins*, 39.

[26]James, *Black Jacobins*, 36–44. On attempts to prevent marriage with people of African descent, see ibid., 41.

[27]Hegel, *Werke* 3: 128. James, *Black Jacobins*, 40. As James points out, even "the *sang-mêlé* with 127 white parts and 1 black part was still a man of colour" (ibid., 38).

[28]James, *Black Jacobins*, 40. See the fascinating case of the Chevalier de Saint-Georges: the son of a planter and an African slave, the Chevalier almost became the director of the French Opera in 1776 (Alain Guédé, *Monsieur de Saint-George, le Nègre des lumières* [Paris: Acte Sud, 1999]).

[29]Pierre de Vaissière, *Saint-Domingue 1629–1789: La société et la vie créoles sous l'ancien regime* (Paris: Librairie académique Perrin, 1908), 355.

[30]James, *Black Jacobins*, 40.

sleeping slaves" in Haiti in 1791 in a revolution that ultimately ended the regime of race-based slavery.[31]

Needless to say, no other modern race-based slave system culminated in so dramatic an inversion of the racial hierarchy. The point here is that miscegeny, common across the New World, marked the intrinsic propensity of the dialectic of colonial slavery to inversion. Any static law authorizing whites violently to control black bodies necessarily translated, in practice, to explicit or implicit sexual coercion of those same bodies. Given the resulting miscegeny, such "topsy-turvy" reversals were scripted into the dogma behind a race-based slave economy. Indeed, it was precisely the fear of such an inversion that had prompted punishments for miscegeny a century earlier: white slavers copulating with African women were already imagining and dreading even as they helped actualize an inverted world. After several generations, a man of partial African descent would appear to be "white"; in turn two white-skinned bodies could have a "black" child.[32] The line between white and black as markers of racial difference began to collapse.[33]

Fully aware of the instability of the European colonial "understanding" of racial difference based on genealogical purity, Hegel maintains elsewhere that

> whether or not all human races [*menschlichen Rassen*] have descended from a single couple or from several is of no concern whatsoever to us in philosophy. This question has been regarded as important, since it has been thought that by assuming descent from several couples one might explain the spiritual superiority of one human species over the other, and indeed it was hoped one could prove that men are so different in nature in their mental or spiritual faculties that some could be dominated [*beherrscht*] like animals. The freedom and supremacy of men can however derive neither justification nor invalidation from descent. The equality of rights for all men is possible in that man is implicitly rational, any rigid distinction between those of the human species with rights and those without being nullified by this rationality.[34]

Nor can any concept of "race" be predicated on any "original [*ursprüngliche*] difference" between human groups.[35] Natural variations, including skin color, are entirely contingent on local environmental conditions and have nothing to do with any "original" geographic provenance of a group.[36] Thus even the purportedly "white" Portuguese become "black" in the tropics: "Blackness is the immediate outcome of the climate, the descendants of the

---

[31]James, *Black Jacobins*, 73.

[32]James gives the example of Chapuzet (James, *Black Jacobins*, 42). On the example of Sandra Laing, a dark-skinned girl born to white Afrikaner parents in apartheid-era South Africa, see Judith Stone, *When She Was White: The True Story of a Family Divided by Race* (New York: Miramax Books, 2008).

[33]Insufficiently and fleetingly: hence the remarkable persistence of the "picture thinking" of racial difference.

[34]Hegel, *Werke* 10: §393A: 57; see also Hegel, *The Philosophy of Subjective Spirit*, ed. and transl. M. J. Petry (Boston: D. Reidel, 1978), 1: 45.

[35]Hegel, *The Philosophy of Subjective Spirit*, 2: 47

[36]Ibid.

Portuguese being as black as the native Negroes, although also on account of miscegeny [*Vermischung*]."[37] We will return to the relation between Hegel's deconstruction of race and his conception of freedom when we analyze the dialectic of master and slave and its materialization in history. In the "Consciousness" section of the *Phenomenology*, Hegel's purpose is to speak only abstractly of color differentiation rather than of the historical phenomenon of racialism: thus he states generally that where for perception "white is only in contrast to black," for the understanding "what is black" in the "actual" world turned upside-down becomes "white."[38]

How would we theorize the actualization of this process of inversion? As the binary between the "words" of individual laws and their opposite blurs, so, too, the line between the inverted world and the world of appearances cannot hold. The integration of the world of appearances and the purely discursive world of *Verkehrung*, of mirrored reversals, where inside is outside and outside is inside, yields to "infinite" self-cancellation:

> Through infinity, we see the law realizing its inherent necessity, and all the moments of [the world of] appearance are taken up into the inner world. That the law proper is infinity means, according to what has emerged, (a) that it is a *self-identity*, which consists in *difference* in itself; or it is the selfsame name that repels itself from itself or fractures itself. What was called force proper *doubles* itself and through its infinity is law. (b) What is thus dirempted, constituting the parts considered to be *law*, puts itself forth as a stable existence; and if the parts are considered without the concept of inner difference, then space and time, or distance and velocity, which appear as moments of gravity [*Momente der Schwere*], are just as indifferent and without necessary relation to one another as to gravity itself, or, again as this gravity proper [*einfache Schwere*] is indifferent to them, or, again, as electricity proper is indifferent to positive and negative electricity. But (c) through the concept of inner difference, these unlike and indifferent moments, space and time, etc. are a *difference* which is no *difference*, or merely a difference of the *selfsame name* [*Gleichnamigen*], and its essence is unity. As positive and negative they awaken each other into activity, and their being is rather to posit themselves as not-being and to cancel themselves in the unity ... [The pure opposite] is not an opposite at all, but purely for itself—a pure, self-sufficient being which has no difference in it: accordingly we do not need to ask the question, still less to think that anguishing over such a question is philosophy, or even that it is a question that philosophy cannot answer: "how does difference or otherness issue forth from pure essence?" For the rupture of difference has [always] already taken place ...[39]

---

[37] Ibid.

[38] Hegel, *Werke* 3: 100, 128–9. James' portrayal of life in Saint-Domingue as a "caricature" of French society further reflects the extent to which the dialectic of colonial slavery—the power of white over black bodies—created a world turned upside-down (James, *Black Jacobins*, 27–62).

[39] Hegel, *Werke*, 3: 131–2.

Here Hegel appears to give priority to the principle of irreducible difference, to the positedness, as it were, of "pure" positing itself. Accordingly specular reversal, the infinite cancellation of all dialectical lines, would reflect the common "identity" of the law of difference and of difference as such.[40] "For us," but not yet for the "understanding" at this stage, the "unity" of the "activity" of infinite self-differentiation and cancellation marks the pure concept of freedom from dialectical stasis. What for the understanding is a mere object "in sensuous covering" [*in sinnlicher Hülle*] becomes, for consciousness, the infinity of the "inner world," the "absolute unrest of pure self-movement" [*diese absolute Unruhe des reinen Sichselbstbewegens*].[41] Thus "in the inner world of appearance, the understanding in truth comes to know nothing else but appearance … the understanding experiences only *itself*." First evident in the "free play of forces" and then of "words"—that is, the discursive modality of "explanation"—infinite self-movement is finally "an object for consciousness." This infinite movability of difference, as the "freedom" from the fetters of inertia, marks precisely the structure of the "inner world" that consciousness will identify as its own "inner being" or "self," reflecting the "truth" that "consciousness is self-consciousness."[42]

Hegel summarizes this movement toward self-consciousness in the concluding paragraphs of "Understanding" through a figure with theatrical resonances: consciousness will lift the "curtain of appearance," only to find itself as a self behind the curtain.[43] The empty verbal "explanations" with which consciousness fills the "beyond" reduce to the pure or infinite unfolding and self-cancellation of the dialectic itself; and the latter posits this "inner world" as the infinite "free play" of the dialectic of identity and difference. The initiated philosophical mind can see that ultimately consciousness will become unified with the "beyond" "through the mediating term of appearance."[44] For that mind, the difference or merely "purported curtain" [*dem sogenannten Vorhange*] between consciousness, now identified with the supersensible world, and the deceptive world of appearance will ultimately vanish.[45] The "inner world" will be revealed as the outer world—what it was all along. Consciousness will become aware of itself gazing into the "infinite" differentiation and identity of a "selfsame being" that now integrates all objectivity. Accordingly the world of the supersensible becomes the "empty inner being" gazing into an "inner world" that is no longer "inner," for it has no outside. Consciousness posits that "empty being" as an "I" "containing different

---

[40]Since the identity of two ostensibly separate elements also articulates their difference—and the differentiation of two elements cannot dialectically hold, as the distinction between them collapses—it follows that there can be no difference between identity and difference (see Hegel, *Werke* 6: 38ff.).

[41]Hegel, *Werke* 3: 133.

[42]Hegel, *Werke* 3: 133.

[43]Hegel, *Werke* 3: 135. We will return to the implications and resonances of this theatrical image below.

[44]Hegel, *Werke* 3: 135.

[45]Hegel, *Werke* 3: 135.

moments, but for which equally these moments are immediately *not* different—[hence as] s*elf-consciousness.*"[46]

Notwithstanding the imperative to represent the "difference" between the two worlds as nothing other than the principle of "pure change"—the conceptual "positing of opposition within itself, or contradiction"—the articulation of such a balanced dialectical economy in Hegel's text hinges on the physical trope of "penetration" [*Eindringen*].[47] What accounts for this figure of "force" in space and time? Here *verkehrt* gives us a clue, for the term means not only "inverted," but also "perverted."[48] This second sense potentially compromises or at least complicates the relation of *Verkehrung* to specularity, the false and dangerous illusion of doubling, stability, and preservation that results from the "picture-thinking" [*Vorstellung*] of dogmatic understanding. Already "inversion" spills over into "perversion" when one considers the reciprocity of the movement between appearance [*Erscheinung*] and the dialectic: the latter "shines through" the former, to surface the pun, just as the former penetrates the latter. Across its various historical usages, *verkehren* conjures up a semantic field centered on the notion of movement, including conceptual, physical, social, and economic exchange or intercourse: its semantic resonances include, *inter alia*, to communicate, to exchange goods or ideas, to mix with, to socialize with or consort, to turn, to turn away from, to twist, to reverse course, to invert, to twist the meaning of, to pervert, and to engage in sexual intercourse (as in *Er hat mit mehreren Frauen verkehrt, mit jemandem geschlechtlich verkehren,* or *Geschlechtsverkehr haben*).[49] Describing the movement of turning in a manner that changes what was turned, the term traverses the bounds of the material and linguistic: already in a crucial passage at the end of the section on "sense-certainty," Hegel refers to the mode through which language necessarily "twists the meaning" of "what is meant," irrevocably changing the referent:

> But if I want to help out speaking or language [*Sprechen*], which has the divine nature of twisting [*verkehren*] the meaning of what is said, of making it into something else, and thus not letting what is meant *get into words at all*—by *indicating* this

---

[46]Hegel, *Werke* 3: 135, 138. Consciousness must now engage the nature of this "cognition" of self, or "what consciousness knows when it knows itself"; through a complex procedure, consciousness must thus account for the propensity of the self to differentiation into parts newly vulnerable to the "play of forces." There is some controversy about Hegel's "inversion" of the "supersensible beyond" into an "inner self" apprehended by consciousness: see David Murray, "Hegel: Force and the Understanding," in *Reason and Reality*, ed. G. N. A. Vesey (London: Macmillan, 1972), 163–73; M. J. De Nys, "Force and Understanding: The Unity of the Object of Consciousness," in *Method and Speculation in Hegel's "Phenomenology"* (New Jersey: Humanities Press, 1982), 57–70; and Joseph C. Flay, "Hegel's Inverted World," in *Review of Metaphysics*, 1970, 23: 662–78.

[47]Hegel, *Werke* 3: 130–1. The verb *eindringen* means, *inter alia*, to invade, to intrude, to break in, to press in, and to penetrate. The term can carry sexual connotations, for instance in the phrase *in jemanden eindringen.*

[48]In a brilliant essay, Hans-Georg Gadamer has begun to outline the possible slippage between "inversion" and "perversion" in Hegel's argument ("Hegel's 'Inverted World,'" in *Hegel's Dialectic: Five Hermeneutical Studies* [New Haven: Yale University Press, 1976], 35–54, especially 48).

[49]*PONS Großwörterbuch Deutsch als Fremdsprache.* S.v. "*verkehren.*" Retrieved October 7, 2018, from https://de.thefreedictionary.com/verkehren. We will interrogate the sexual valences and implications of Hegel's use of *verkehren* and its cognates more fully in Chapter 9.

piece of paper, experience teaches me what the truth of sense-certainty is: I point it out as a *Here*, a *Here* of other *Heres*, or in itself a *simple combination of many Heres*—that is, it is a universal ...[50]

Given its intrinsic polysemy or duplicity, language "perverts" the world ("what is meant") even as it remains unable discursively to represent it ("get it into words"). Enacting the performativity of the universal, language marks the turning of the thing, its perversion in time.[51] But how does appearance in turn "penetrate" the dialectic? If indeed the "inverted world" is ultimately a "perverted world," what conception of the dialectic or of "pure change" survives? How will the entanglement of penetration and difference, and by corollary performativity and trope—the foundational form of all discursive representation—inflect the concept of self-consciousness or subjectivity?

Hegel makes clear that the "purity" of positedness and of the principle of difference—understood as its remove from the "sensuous"—does not hold, at least not in any temporal sense:

> From the idea of inversion [*der Vorstellung ... der Verkehrung*], which constitutes the essence of one [dialectical] side of the supersensible world [that is, the second supersensible world], the sensuous idea of fixing the differences in a different element of existence must be detached; and this absolute concept of the difference [between the two worlds] must be represented [*Vorstellung*] and understood purely as inner difference, a repulsion of the same-named [*Gleichnamigen*], as its selfsame name, from itself, and likeness of the unlike as unlike. We must think pure change, the positing of opposition [*Entgegensetzung*] within itself, or contradiction. For in the difference which is an inner difference, the opposite is not merely *one* of *two*— if it were, it would simply *be*, without being an opposite—but it is the opposite of an opposite, or the other is itself immediately present in it. No doubt I put the "Opposite" *here* and *there* I put the Other, its "Opposite."[52]

While Hegel registers the difficulty of "representing" the "pure" principle of change, "inner difference" or dialectical "contradiction" as such, he further argues that this difficulty can be resolved by the purely performative "positing" of opposition (conveyed by the pun on *Entgegensetzung*) "within itself," deceptively instantiated here through chiasmus, the spatial trope of specular inversion: *Opposite—Here—There—Opposite*. The first opposite, subsisting in the posited spatiality and hence discursive fiction of the "here," must contain *its own opposite*, as both "oppositions" pertain to the order of discourse.[53] Accordingly the chiastic series would apparently collapse the difference

---

[50]Hegel, *Werke* 3: 92.

[51]By implication, the perversion of the dialectic relates to the activity of troping (from Greek *trepein* or *tropos*, to turn)—and, by extension, the dissolving power of poetic figuration inherent in any "architectonic" articulation.

[52]Hegel, *Werke* 3: 130–1.

[53]There is no "here" in the world; see "Sense-Certainty."

between the "pure" world of the dialectic and the material world; the former would "contain" the latter.[54] But a problem arises: the spatial markers *here* and *there* can only differentiate themselves from each other by pointing to different referents in the world of appearance. As we learned in "Sense-Certainty," the distinction between opposed demonstrative pronouns, deceptive at the level of language, only signifies a difference in the relative position of speakers saying "here" or "there" at the moment of enunciation: "I, *this* 'I,' see the tree and say that *here* is a tree [and the house is *there*]; but another 'I' sees the house and maintains that *here* is not a tree but a house instead."[55] The difference between *here* and *there* is only thinkable in the first place by virtue of the "constant change" of materiality.[56] If the discursive world of the dialectic proves "appearance" to be ungraspable, so too appearance proves the dialectic to be deceptively "pure." Thus the integration of the "supersensible world" with the "inverted world" of its dialectically posited opposites turns out to require the "penetration" of "all moments of appearance" [*alle Momente der Erscheinung*]. On the one hand, the articulation of a spatial trope— chiastic inversion or crossing—depends upon the performative "positing" of the dialectic; on the other hand, the "positing" of dialectical difference itself requires a conception of "change" anchored in the articulation and negation of "appearance" by the "This"—the "here" and "there" or, likewise, "now" and "then," of the dialectic.

It is in this sense that the meaning of *verkehrt* as "perverted" obtains: on Hegel's analysis, the attempt to harmonize differentiated phenomenality with its "inversion" at the level of the supersensible world requires and effects the "perversion" of the world of appearance.[57] In "Sense-Certainty" Hegel already prefigures this movement: the "here" of the "tree" is not entirely effaced, but preserved and translated into the "here" of a constructed "house." Thus Hegel will use the verb *übergreifen*—to spill over, infect, spread—to describe the mutual encroachment of the two worlds as they collapse into one:

> The supersensible world, which is the perverted [*verkehrte*] world, has spilled over [*übergegriffen*] into the other world and has it within it; it is *for itself* the perverted world, that is, the perversion of itself. It is itself and its contrary-law [*entgegengesetzte*] in one unity.[58]

What Hegel elsewhere calls the "penetration" of the law [*Gesetz*] or pure performativity into its opposite as *entgegengesetzte*—its inversion and perversion in "actual things"—

---

[54]Hegel, *Werke* 3: 131.

[55]Hegel, *Werke* 3: 86.

[56]Hegel, *Werke* 3: 82ff.

[57]Gadamer, "Hegel's 'Inverted World,'" *passim*.

[58]Hegel, *Werke* 3: 131. Hegel will characterize the linguistic penetration between subjects quite literally as an "infection" or material "contagion": see the use of "infected" [*angesteckt*] and "infection" [*Ansteckung*] in Hegel, *Werke* 3: 154–5, 376, 402, 403, 411, and 490.

results in the actual "unity" of the dialectic with materiality, where that unity consists in self-negating insemination, deformation, and change.

Hegel's procedure here, from the formal deduction of the "inverted world" to an account of the dialectical unfolding of materiality, anticipates his demonstration, in the section on religion and art in the *Phenomenology of Spirit* and in the later *Science of Logic, Encyclopedia*, and *Aesthetics*, of the entanglement of logic and aesthetics. His insistence, for consciousness as understanding, on the instability and so perverted reality of the "word"—the difference of the "self-same name" to itself, hence its internal "contradiction" at the level of logic—reflects what in the *Science of Logic* he will call the originary entanglement of logic with "unconsciously," "instinctively," or "subjectively" determined "categories" of "natural" language.[59] German especially, says Hegel, surfaces the dialectical fluidity of words through amphiboly, contradictory meanings whose unity thus remains contingent on a particular language at a particular moment in time.[60] Mediating all "forms of thought," language "penetrates" the "inwardness" of a subject and all that he "makes his own."[61] In the *Aesthetics* and the *Encyclopedia*, as we have seen, Hegel frames this interpenetration of logic and aesthetics in terms of the intrinsically symbolic valences of the "pyramidal" sign—that is, its necessary mediation by the psychophysiological resonances of the signifier.[62]

In this respect, the *verkehrte Welt* also marks Hegel's misunderstood engagement with the Schlegelian theory of "romantic irony"—the recognition that language is subject to "permanent parabasis," or endless interruption by the contrapuntal valences of all articulation.[63] For Friedrich Schlegel, "romantic poetry" unearths this intrinsically paradoxical dimension of language: thus he writes of "the continual self-creating interchange of two conflicting thoughts," by virtue of which "poetry can ... hover at the mid-point between the represented and the representer, raise that reflection again and again to a higher power, and multiply in an endless succession of mirrors ... [it] alone is infinite."[64] This infinite succession results from the impossibility of determining whether any particular irony is not itself ironic, leading to an endless chain of possibilities.

Hegel's conception of the "inverted world," the world "turned upside down" in its specular image, thus evokes the aesthetic form not only of satire, as Gadamer astutely

---

[59]Hegel, *Werke* 5: 29–30. On the relation of the "inverted world" in the *Phenomenology* to the *Science of Logic*, see Gadamer, "Hegel's 'Inverted World,'" *passim*.

[60]Hegel, *Werke* 5: 20.

[61]Thus in the *Science of Logic*: "In alles, was ihm zu einem Innerlichen, zur Vorstellung überhaupt wird, was er zu dem Seinigen macht, hat sich die Sprache eingedrängt, und was er zur Sprache macht und in ihr äußert, enthält eingehüllter, vermischter oder herausgearbeitet eine Kategorie; so sehr natürlich ist ihm das Logische, oder vielmehr: dasselbige ist seine eigentümliche Natur selbst" (Hegel, *Werke* 5: 20).

[62]On the "pyramidal sign," see Chapter 3.

[63]"Parabasis" refers to metanarrative digression or interpolation. Schlegel's paradoxical formulation—interruption cannot be permanent, or there would be no discourse to interrupt—represents a variant, ultimately, of his better-known definition of irony as "the form of paradox." On Schlegel's theory of "permanent parabasis," see Schlegel, *Kritische Ausgabe*, eds. E. Behler et al. (Paderborn: F. Schöningh, 1958ff.), XXVIII: 85, hereafter *KA*. On Schlegel and irony, see Paul de Man, "The Concept of Irony," in *Aesthetic Ideology*, 163–84.

[64]*Athenäum Fragment* 116 and 120, in *KA* II: 182ff.

notices (albeit without developing the point), but also and more generally of "romantic" or philosophical irony and its dangers.[65] In the *Aesthetics*, Hegel will insist explicitly on the movement by which contradiction as ironic inversion results in "perversity." Thus writers who exteriorize and "hypostatize" the "solid" elements of a literary character "in a perverse way" [*eine verkehrte Weise*], dialectically positing an "outside" of interiority, reflect the "modern" (i.e., Schlegelian) understanding of "irony," in which a subject or individual character's "determinacy at once passes over into its opposite; and his character is therefore to display nothing but the nullity of its determinacy and itself."[66] While Hegel would agree with Schlegel's formulation of irony as the "form of paradox," or of contradiction that propels the movement of "infinity," he attacks Schlegel and his followers, including Solger, for failing to understand the movement by which that infinity anchors itself in actuality.[67] Thus Hegel in the *Aesthetics*:

> In this process [Solger, following Schlegel] came upon the dialectical moment of the "idea"—to the point which I call "infinite absolute negativity," or to the activity of the idea that involves negating oneself as infinite and universal so as to become finitude and particularity, and then negate this negation in turn, to then re-establish the universal and infinite in the finite and particular. Solger held on to this negativity, and indeed it is one moment in the speculative idea: but when this purely dialectical restlessness and dissolution of the infinite as well as the finite is grasped, this negativity constitutes only *one moment*, and not, as Solger would have it, the *whole* idea. Unfortunately Solger's life was cut short too early for him to have been able to reach the concrete development of the philosophical idea.[68]

Here Hegel does not deny the ironic moment in the dialectic, even where it applies to the dialectic of the subject: indeed, as he insists in the *Philosophy of Right*, the only "dimension" of irony worth preserving for philosophical inquiry is "the dialectical element proper, the activating pulse of speculative reflection."[69] Given the materiality of the dialectic, he will further identify philosophical irony in its aesthetic materialization: thus he acknowledges critically the "irony" in the worship of Greek gods that exteriorize subjectivity in a statue.[70] Hegel dismisses only that particular mode of irony that detaches itself from "finitude":

---

[65]Gadamer, "Hegel's 'Inverted World,'" 48. I use the term "philosophical irony" in lieu of "romantic irony." Another of Schlegel's formulations is pertinent here: "Philosophy is the true home of irony, which might be defined as logical beauty ... for wherever men are philosophizing in spoken or written dialogues, and provided they are not entirely systematic, irony ought to be produced and postulated" (*Lyceum Fragment* 42, in *KA* II: 152).

[66]Hegel, *Werke* 13: 315.

[67]"Ironie ist die Form des Paradoxen" (Schlegel, *Lyceum Fragment* 48, in *Sein prosaische Jugendschriften* ed. J. Minor [Vienna: Verlag von Carl Konegen, 1882], 2: 190).

[68]Hegel, *Werke* 13: 98–9.

[69]Hegel, *Werke* 7: 277, note 73.

[70]Hegel, *Werke* 13: 297.

In this fundamental principle the modern doctrine of irony too has its justification in a certain respect, except that irony, on the one hand, is often bare of any true seriousness and likes to delight especially in villains, and, on the other hand, ends in mere heartfelt longing instead of in acting and doing. Novalis, for example, one of the nobler spirits who took up this position, was driven into a void with no specific interests, into this dread of reality, and was wound down as it were into a spiritual decline. This is a longing that will not let itself go in actual action and production, because it is frightened of being polluted by contact with finitude, although all the same it has a sense of the deficiency of this abstraction. True, irony implies the absolute negativity in which the subject is related to himself in the annihilation of everything specific and one-sided; but since this annihilation, as was indicated above in our consideration of this doctrine, affects not only, as in comedy, what is inherently null which manifests itself in its hollowness, but equally everything inherently excellent and solid [*Gediegene*], it follows that irony as this art of annihilating everything everywhere, like that heart-felt longing, acquires, at the same time, in comparison with the true ideal, the aspect of inner inartistic lack of restraint.[71]

Here Hegel rejects the decoupling of irony from performative "doing" or linguistic "action," as this rarefaction yields precisely the denuded form of irony that "annihilates" the "solidity" of the subject.[72] As Hegel had already signaled in "Sense-Certainty," the duplicity of language, its necessarily ironic nature, performatively perverts the real as against any universal. Ultimately he will argue that only the posited "unity" of objectivity and subjectivity in the infinite self-cancellation of all difference ends the "bad infinity" of aimless irony or satire.

In this vein, Hegel might well have embraced Schlegel's lesser-known, complementary definition of irony as the "epideixis of infinity."[73] Referring, *inter alia*, to praise and blame oratory as a display of language, "epideixis" aptly characterizes the self-conscious and self-revealing performativity of poetic language ("epi" marking the self-referentiality of deixis, the act of indication). This formulation frames irony as the self-referential indication of its own deictic act—the disclosure of its own artificiality as it points to a referent that falls away from the "here" and "now" of articulation. As an index, therefore, of endlessly collapsing form (the form of form, the form of form of form, etc.), this self-referentiality necessarily proceeds *ad infinitum*. Each irony not only slips into another in a hermeneutic spiral that spills out over an endless sequence of borders and delimitations, but also produces performatively the "reality" of the referent—the praised and praising subject, the engendered object—through multiple incarnations of force.

Thus in the section on "Ethical Action" in the *Phenomenology*, Hegel will refer to the clash between family and community, emblematized in Antigone's burial of her

---

[71] Hegel, *Aesthetics: Lectures on Fine Art*, transl. T.M. Knox (Oxford: Clarendon, 1975), 159–60.

[72] Hegel, *Werke* 13: 211. On the theory of irony in relation to architectonics, performativity, and subjectivity, see my "Allegories of Ruin: Architecture and Knowledge in Early Arabic Poetry," in *Journal of Arabic Literature*, 2019, 50: 2, 89-122, especially 91n5, 102ff.

[73] Schlegel, *KA* XVIII: 128. De Man misses this definition in "'The Concept of Irony.'"

brother in the eponymous Greek tragedy, as the ironic perversion of an "oppressive" [*unterdrückende*] communitarianism.[74] For Hegel, the historically and thus conceptually masculine principle of Greek civic life articulates only a limited "universality"—excluding, for instance, women, children, and slaves—and thus fails to achieve concrete freedom.[75] The movement of history from this impasse depends on the subversiveness of women, "the eternal principle of irony in the community" [*die ewige Ironie des Gemeinwesens*]; their actions surface the internally paradoxical nature of communitarianism, which necessarily interferes "with the happiness of the family" and "suppresses the spirit of individualism."[76] On the other hand, that active irony will "pervert the universal property of the state into a possession and ornament of the family" [*verkehrt das allgemeine Eigentum des Staats zu einem Besitz und Putz der Familie*].[77] That conflict, of course, leads to the dissolution of ethical life in the Greek city-state and ushers in the age of empire.

The trope of the "inverted world" hinges on the notion that any "static law" or creed of consciousness as understanding, abstracted from the world of appearance but still vulnerable to dialectical fluidity, necessarily lends itself to irony and, in particular, satire. Consciousness believes that it sees its dogmas reflected in the real; the more strongly it "attaches" its differentiations onto the world, the more likely the world will pervert its "understanding." Ultimately this process reveals the non-mimetic and performative dimension subverting the specularity and "picture-thinking" of trope all along.

The failure to account fully for this relation between irony and the dialectic has masked a crucial dimension of Hegel's critique of romantic irony.[78] In particular this tendency has obscured the connection of his "inverted world" [*verkehrte Welt*] with Ludwig Tieck's play, published in 1799, entitled "The Inverted World" [*Die verkehrte Welt*].[79] A masterpiece of romantic irony, the play shows a fictive audience on stage commenting on another play. In one exchange at the end of Act III:

---

[74]Hegel, *Werke* 3: 353.

[75]Hegel critiques the limited, contingent, and ultimately perverse Greek idea of "freedom," grounded as it is on the accident of being born free and not a slave.

[76]Hegel, *Werke* 3: 353.

[77]Hegel, *Werke* 3: 353. On Hegel and Antigone, see, *inter alia*, Jacques Derrida, *Glas*, transl. John Leavey Jr., (Lincoln: University of Nebraska Press, 1986); Judith Butler, *Antigone's Claim* (New York: Columbia University Press, 2000); and *Hegel's Philosophy and Feminist Thought*, ed. K. Hutchings and T. Pulkkinen (London: Palgrave Macmillan, 2010).

[78]In his excellent study of Hegel's views on irony, Jeffrey Reid points to the tendency to focus only on Hegel's critique of the "subjective" rather than the "objective" implications of irony (see *The Anti-Romantic: Hegel Against Ironic Romanticism* [London: Bloomsbury Academic, 2014], 3). Reid is right to emphasize the stridency of Hegel's critique of the material forms of irony. But Reid does not follow Hegel's recuperation of the self-cancelling movement of concrete irony in the concept. The abhorrence of sexual perversity, for instance, does not amount to blindness to the persistence of *Verekehrung* in the dialectic of life: on the contrary, perversion can only tend toward purity by passing through the phenomenal. In contrast to the "bad infinity" of Schlegel's salacious *Lucinde*, Hegel's purpose is to recuperate perversion into the narrative history of concrete freedom.

[79]The only other scholar, to my knowledge, who has seen the relation to Tieck here is Donald Verene, who offers an interesting review of possible sources for the figure of the *verkehrte Welt* in *Hegel's Recollection: A Study of Images in the Phenomenology of Spirit* (Albany: SUNY Press, 1985), 50ff.

Pierrot: For God's sake, what keeps my head together—or sets a kind of iron band around it so it doesn't shatter?

Scävola: This isn't bearable, that's for sure. Here we sit as spectators watching a play; in that play are more spectators watching another play; and in that third play, the actors are being shown yet another piece.

Wachtel: I have not said a word; but in order to calm down, I would have liked to turn from being a spectator and take refuge as an actor in that last poetic comedy. The farther from the spectator, the better.

The Other: Now, folks, think how it might be that we are again actors in some other play; it's so confusing! [80]

Instantiating Schlegel's conception of irony as "permanent parabasis," the fictive audience not only interrupts the drama with its commentary, but also interferes in the action: at one moment, an audience member changes roles with one of the actors in the play, and at another the fictive audience collectively intervenes in the action to change its course. The play exposes the intrinsically ironic dimension of discourse by proving a represented "world" to depend on merely contingent dogma. Just as static discourses become fictions that slide easily into their alternative, so too subjects prove themselves to have a merely fictive integrity: thus in the play a member of the audience on stage will wonder aloud whether as spectators they, too, are actually illusions. Echoing Tieck, Hegel demonstrates that the world of appearances, penetrating the "curtain" between fiction and reality, reveals purportedly "detached" spectators to be fully part of the unfolding story.

Hegel, who identifies irony repeatedly as the distinguishing element in Tieck's thought, almost certainly knew of this play.[81] He comments on Tieck's connection with the Schlegels in Jena—a connection that, Hegel implies, contributes to the city's status as a "cultural center"—and singles out Tieck as a formidable proponent of Schlegel's romanticism.[82] Hegel nonetheless criticizes Tieck for embracing a detached or "abstract" mode of irony, as opposed to a concrete variety grounded in actuality.[83] Praising his writings on Shakespeare, Hegel nonetheless has little patience for Tieck's view of Lady Macbeth as a "loving spouse with a soft heart" dissociated from her ironically murderous thoughts, simply because no actor could convincingly portray these opposed elements in a single character on stage.[84] In the same vein, Hegel criticizes Tieck for writing plays that were difficult or impossible to stage and thus lacked a public—a not altogether

---

[80]Ludwig Tieck, *Die verkehrte Welt* (Berlin: De Gruyter, 1964), 60, translation mine.

[81]Hegel maintains that Tieck viewed "irony" as the "supreme principle of art" (Hegel, *Werke* 13: 98–9).

[82]Hegel associates Tieck with certain "distinguished people" at the "cultural center" of Jena in *Werke* 13: 99; he explicitly mentions Tieck in connection with Schlegel in *Werke* 15: 497. See also *Werke* 15: 503.

[83]Hegel, *Werke* 13: 98.

[84]Hegel refers to a method of portraying Lady Macbeth attributed to Tieck (*Werke* 13: 315). See also Hegel, *Werke: Vollständige Ausgabe*, ed. Förster and Boumann (Berlin: Duncker und Humblot, 1834), 16: *Vermischte Schriften*: 452.

The Architecture of Freedom

misplaced reproach with respect to *Die verkehrte Welt*, which given its complexities has rarely been produced.[85] Hegel's allusion to this play in the *Phenomenology* can be read as a direct address to his romantic contemporaries. That he would frame the dialectic of subjectivity using the trope of the "inverted world" indicates how seriously he took not only the romantic notion of irony as a feature of the dialectic, but also the importance of recuperating irony into a system that would lend rationality to the intrinsic perversity of history.

Hegel's paronomastic play on *Verkehrung* or *Verkehrtheit*, where specularity becomes deformation, instantiates his system's acknowledgment of the irony or perversity of the phenomenal.[86] Extending Hegel's terms, we can in particular refer to the ironic materiality of the subject. It is the contrapuntal potential—the infinite peculiarity and performative "force"—of the unstable word that leads Hegel to grasp its infinitely self-differentiating movement as the logos, the necessary method and telos (they will be the same) of philosophical inquiry. As the organizing "idea" of history, the logos radically eschews mere referentiality with respect to the given: "This concept is *not* sensuously intuited or represented; *it is solely an object*, the product and content of *thinking*, and is the absolute, self-subsistent object, the logos, the reason of that which *is*, the truth of that to which we give the *name* 'things.'"[87] And yet the logos must take historical form through the intrinsically "architectonic" movement of the dialectic that "penetrate[s]" subjectivity and objectivity alike, both humanity and "nature," as it brings form and content into an inadequate affinity.[88] It is in this respect that both meanings of *Verkehrung*—"inversion" and "perversion"—characterize the operation of the logos: for the ironic "inversion" of opposites becomes a kind of "perversion" of "nature" through the "plasticity" of "discourse" or, more fundamentally, the aesthetic articulation of "form."[89]

---

[85]"Since Tieck's time this disdain for the public has become fashionable, especially in Germany ... Our neighbors, the French, do precisely otherwise: they write for immediate effect, keeping their public always in mind ..." (Hegel, *Werke* 15: 497).

[86]As with other instances of amphiboly, the paronomastic play of *Verkehr* reveals the word's intrinsic duplicity or irony.

[87]Hegel, *Werke* 5: 30. Emphasis mine.

[88]Hegel, *Werke* 5: 20.

[89]Hegel refers to the "plasticity" of language and the "plastic" nature of ideal "discourse" in the *Science of Logic* (Hegel, *Werke* 5: 30-1). Catherine Malabou, in her indispensable book on Hegel, contends that "plasticity" in Hegel is "the point around which all the transformations of [his] thought revolve, the centre of its metamorphoses" (*The Future of Hegel: Plasticity, Temporality, and Dialectic* [London: Routledge, 2005], 13); more particularly, she takes the "perfect plasticity" [*vollendete Plastik*] of Greek art as a "model" for the dialectical fluidity of what she calls "philosophical plasticity" (ibid., 10). Now, Hegel does associate the term "plasticity" with the fusion of form and content in the material and verbal art of the Greeks. (On the "plasticity" "native" to the Greek spirit, exemplified in the "plastic" art of Greek sculpture, see, *inter alia*, Hegel, *Werke* 14: 374; see also 14: 92, 355, and 360-1; on the plasticity of Greek poetry, see Hegel, *Werke* 15: 302-3; on the plasticity of Greek historical figures, see Hegel, *Werke* 12: 317-9; and on the plasticity of Greek philosophy, see Hegel, *Werke* 18: *Vorlesungen über die Geschichte der Philosophie*, 452.) In the Greek view (according to Hegel), the sensuous "plasticity" of matter and language indeed reduces both to immediate and perfectly malleable media for mimetic or "ideal" representation (on Greek plasticity and the "ideal," see, for instance, Hegel, *Werke* 14: 110, 153, 373; 15: 303). Malabou does not take into account, however, that what is more precisely translated as "perfect or consummated plasticity" [*vollendete Plastik*]—in which language immediately dissipates, giving

To give life to Hegel's conception of dialectical "perversion" and its inflection of concrete irony—in this case, at the precise moment the "understanding" attempts and fails to posit free selfhood—let us turn again to the history of colonial slavery, this time to the example of the 1833 British law of manumission. The law's preamble grandly states that its purpose is to "set free [those held] in Slavery within divers of His Majesty's Colonies." Recognizing the injustice of bondage, the act does indeed abolish slavery, but also converts registered slaves over the age of six into involuntarily "apprenticed laborers" for a period of up to seven years from the date of enactment.[90] Moreover:

---

us an illusory union of form and content—reflects ultimately the mystified positivism of the understanding [*Verstand*]: this faculty thus remains blind to the "perversions" of its plastic formulations in ethical life, from the ironic worship of the Gods to the institution of slavery. Hegel links the translation of the subject into an object in Greek statuary and slavery to Socrates' interlocutors, who become merely "plastic personage[s]" with no view of their own; thus the "plastic discourse" of ideal philosophy fails to express the intersubjective knowledge of self-knowing spirit (Hegel, *Werke* 5: 30ff.; *Lectures on the History of Philosophy*, transl. E. S. Haldane and F. H. Simpson [London: Routledge, 1955], 3 vols., II: 17). Malabou is right to point to what Hegel in the *Phenomenology* frames as the internal telos of "plasticity" achieved through the fusion of subject and object in absolute knowing; thus the latter writes, "Eine Schwierigkeit, die vermieden werden sollte, macht die Vermischung der spekulativen und der räsonierenden Weise aus, wenn einmal das vom Subjekte Gesagte die Bedeutung seines Begriffs hat, das andere Mal aber auch nur die Bedeutung seines Prädikats oder Akzidens. Die eine Weise stört die andere, und erst diejenige philosophische Exposition würde es erreichen, plastisch zu sein, welche streng die Art des gewöhnlichen Verhältnisses der Teile eines Satzes ausschlösse" (Hegel, *Werke* 3: 60). But this internal possibility and "goal of plasticity" inflect philosophy not through the historical articulation of "perfect or consummated plasticity," but rather through the principle of a "purely *immanent* plasticity" or "freedom" [*Freiheit*] paradoxically entwined with history as its telos (Hegel, *Werke* 5: 30; emphases mine). Hegel thus explicitly rejects the "expression" of "perfect or consummated plasticity" in contemporary philosophy, since this "abstract perfection or completeness" [*abstrakte Vollkommenheit*] in the "presentation" of thought in time would require the fulfillment of conditions that have become impossible in modernity, namely the elision of picture-thinking, "contingent" expressions, or other "heterogenous" (and ultimately aesthetic) elements—as well as the appearance of a purely malleable interlocutor suppressing his particularity (ibid., 30–1). The "ideal" fusion of subject and object in Greek art—or, as we will see, the "ideality" of "inner right" in the exclusivist or exceptionalist state—thus corresponds to the exact *opposite* of the always "immanent plasticity" of thought laboring through variegated particularity and contingency in time—or the "plasticity" that is the goal of *Bildung* (ibid., 33). An "abstract" "plastic discourse" cannot contribute to a new and "independent building [*selbständiges Gebäude*] of philosophical science" (ibid., 33): Hegel thus consigns the consummated plasticity of the Greeks to the unrecoverable past. In contrast to "perfect or consummated plasticity," the "architectonic," originating in the "African" entry into Egypt, eschews mimesis precisely by positing and exposing—through monumental architecture—the illusory durability of non-representational form in time. In addition, the fact that such works are built by slaves matters: as we will see, the dialectical overcoming of permanence through the architectonic attends the slave's attempt to sublate his natural immediacy. Steeped in and producing history, the architectonic bears always the heterogeneous symbolism of language in the moment of articulation; thus the "edifice" of a new philosophical intervention can flush out neither "random reflections" nor "the more current reflections and ideas" of modern readers, no matter how "adventitiously" connected to the purportedly "pure" elements of the dialectic (ibid., 31). Where "perfect plasticity," predicated on the malleability of given objects and subjects, requires the immediate accord of form and content, the architectonic, as the paradoxically endless delimitation of freedom, erects artificial structures: ultimately the slave's discovery of the principle of freedom through aesthetic labor will amount to, first, the rejection of the "plastic discourse" and thus positivism characterizing Greek art, ethical life, and politics and, second, to precisely this delimitation *and hence limitation* of "plasticity" as a principle "immanent" to the architectonic in time.

[90]The Act of 1833 contains numerous qualifications and exceptions. A more comprehensive analysis is beyond the scope of the present study.

during the Continuance of the Apprenticeship of any such apprenticed Labourer such Person or Persons shall be entitled to the Services of such apprenticed Labourer as would for the Time being have been entitled to his or her Services *as a Slave, if this Act had not been made* ... And be it further enacted and declared, That the Right or Interest of any Employer or Employers to and in the Services of any such apprenticed Labourers as aforesaid shall pass and be transferable by Bargain and Sale, Contract, Deed, Conveyance, Will, or Descent, according to such Rules and in such Manner as shall for that Purpose be provided by any such Acts of Assembly, Ordinances, or Orders in Council as herein-after mentioned.[91]

Here the law performatively "enacting" the "abolition" of slavery—phasing out the word "slave" and its meaning in legal registers—will ultimately "free" hundreds of thousands of slaves. It will also posit ("enact"), with some specified modifications, the equality of the institution of slavery with that of "apprenticed labor" in the British colonies: a slave is to be called an "apprenticed laborer," but for the "time being" shall be treated "as a Slave" as though "*this act had not been made*." In addition, slaveowners are entitled to "transfer" their interest in the service due to them from their former slaves as "apprentices": the latter remains a commodity to be bought and sold, a slave in actual fact. Indeed the legal institutionalization of indentured service, a practice honed by the British East India company decades prior to the abolition of slavery, will, after the Act of 1833, drive the coercion of millions of south and east Asian "apprentices" into *de facto* slavery.[92]

This deformation of the concepts of "apprentice" and "freedom," if all too predictable in this case, nonetheless points up the operation that Hegel has in mind when he argues that the law, an "empty word," ultimately has no reality except through its endless and perverse unfolding in the world of appearances: "The law is not beyond the appearance, but rather present in it immediately ... The existing world is itself the realm of the laws."[93] In turn appearance cannot be separated from the discursive world of which it is an endlessly unfolding deformation.[94] Thus the abstract "freedom" underwriting

---

[91]"Papers in explanation of the measures adopted by His Majesty's government, for giving effect to the act for the abolition of slavery throughout the British colonies. Part I. Jamaica. 1833–1835," in *19th Century House of Commons Sessional Papers, 1835*, L: 273. Emphasis mine.

[92]Recent research has indicated the extent to which the British East India Company had developed and refined the system of indentured servitude in the decades leading up to abolition (see Richard Allen, "Slaves, Convicts, Abolitionism, and the Global Origins of the Post-Emancipation Indentured Labor System," in *Slavery and Abolition*, 2014, 35: 2: 328–48). While practices in indentured service differed widely, most involved deceptive contracts and perpetual forced labor. Indicatively, the 1879 Constitution of the State of California declared that "Asiatic coolieism is a form of human slavery, and is forever prohibited in this State, and all contracts for coolie labour shall be void" (*Constitution of the State of California* [Sacramento: J. D. Young Supt. State Printing, 1880], Article XIX, xli).

[93]"Das Gesetz ist daher nicht jenseits der Erscheinung, sondern in ihr unmittelbar gegenwärtig ... die existierende Welt ist selbst das Reich der Gesetze" (Hegel, *Werke* 6: 153–4). Gadamer, too, cites these lines: see "Hegel's 'Inverted World,'" 47.

[94]For this reason, a new "law"—even one emancipating slaves—has little meaning outside socialized mediation and recognition. In the absence of recognitive socialization, the "abolition of a law," including the law of slavery, amounts only to its *Aufhebung*, hence both its "cancellation" and "preservation" (*Werke* 8: §96: 204–5). As we will see, this insight represents a foundational principle of Hegel's theory of "ethical life" in the *Philosophy of Right*.

the law finds its only meaning in the perverted actuality of still enslaved "apprentices." The slave is the concrete law, first as the "I" legally registered as a slave and then as an "apprentice." Consciousness as understanding, blind to the performative force and thus recuperative agency of its language (or perhaps not so blind to it, where interested powers are concerned), affirms that the law will abolish slavery, bondage, and forced labor. Dogma, creed, and law—masks of irony—are self-perverting.

Hegel's relation of self-consciousness and *Verkehrung* throws into doubt theories of subjectivity predicated on discursive positing including, by implication, Fichte's performative articulation of an abstract "I."[95] If the abstract legislative enactment of freedom (a topic to which we will return) by itself necessarily results in the "perversion" of actual freedom, so too any attempt by consciousness at self-knowing will yield to the *Verkehrung* of the subject:[96] thus the advocacy of the "welfare of humanity," expressed in the subjective terms of sanctimony, can reduce the self to a "perverted individuality."[97] How can the subject then attain to freedom? And what can consciousness know about itself? Where inversion—specular reversal—maintains the internal stability of opposites as it switches their positions, perversion involves a "penetration" and fundamental alteration that the understanding judges to be "wrong," an erroneous turn that can only be replaced through another error. If inversion corresponds to the contradictory nature of language, perversion corresponds to the endless betrayal of the categories of the understanding by performative force—the latter associated, as I have already intimated, with the disembodying agency of the *Werkmeister*. The task of spirit as self-consciousness and reason in the *Phenomenology of Spirit* will thus be to confront what Hegel will continue to call the "perverse," "deceptive," or "wrong" [*verkehrt*] "turns," "translations," or "interchanges" [*Verkehrungen*] of selfhood in the unfolding of freedom.[98]

[95]Johann Gottlieb Fichte, *Sämtliche Werke* (Berlin: De Gruyter, 1965), 8 vols., 1: 98–116. Hölderlin pointed out to Hegel that Fichte was "moving past the fact of consciousness in theory" and approaching "Spinoza's substance," which "contains all reality" (*Hegel: The Letters*, transl. C. Butler and C. Seiler [Bloomington: Indiana University Press, 1984], 33).

[96]As I have intimated, Hegel will critique the insufficiency and perversity of merely legislated manumission. We will discuss Hegel's views on the relative merits of the legal abolition of slavery and self-emancipation in Chapters 9 and 10.

[97]Hegel, *Werke* 3: 280–1.

[98]*Verkehrung, verkehrt*, and their cognates appear throughout the *Phenomenology*: for additional references, see Hegel, *Werke* 3: 30, 54, 228, 231–2, 235, 239–40, 243, 257, 274, 278, 280–5, 289–91, 313, 315, 345, 348, 352, 359, 366, 385–7, 388, 390, 396, 399, 408, 417–8, 479, 538. For a provocative attempt to identify the "perverse core" in or after Hegel, albeit without a discussion of references to "perversity" in his work, see John Caputo, "The Perversity of the Absolute, the Perverse Core of Hegel, and the Possibility of Radical Theology," in *Hegel and the Infinite: Religion, Politics, and Dialectic*, eds. Slavoj Žižek et al. (New York: Columbia University Press, 2011), 47–66.

CHAPTER 8
SLAVERY AND THE SUBJECT

Can self-consciousness, in its struggle for freedom, eschew the "perversions" of the understanding? How do the "penetration" and "spilling over" of the dialectic inflect the concept and structure of the subject? Answering these questions will require a patient rereading of Hegel's celebrated chapter on "Self-Consciousness" in light of the process of *Verkehr*—of deformation through intercourse—first signalled in "Sense-Certainty" and then in the figure of the *verkehrte Welt* in "Understanding." Reappearing in the initial emergence of self-consciousness as life and again as master and slave, "perversion" marks what Hegel will call the figuratively and literally "fluid medium" through which self-consciousness will reproduce itself. We will begin by analyzing how, at an abstract level, self-consciousness negotiates the excesses and residues of its dialectical economy and the resulting dissonance between its notional will to freedom and its individuated materiality as a body. We will then assess how the disentanglement of agency and embodiment in turn inflects the dialectic of master and slave. Embracing dialectical instability, the subjugated self will discover "power" in her articulation of material form in time, inaugurating the aesthetic and marking the possibility, but not yet the actuality of history. After considering the dialectic of abstract self-consciousness from the fragmented "standpoint of consciousness" in this chapter, we will then be prepared to examine, in the next chapter, how historical self-consciousness, as a living, sexual subject, evolves in time toward the freedom of sociality.

Hegel's procedure begins with the notion of "self-consciousness" that emerges from the inverted-perverted world internalized by consciousness as understanding. As the self-canceling differentiation of "infinitude," self-consciousness will ultimately collapse the distinction between identity and difference.[1] Accordingly in its first diremption self-consciousness unfolds through an apparently neutral system of exchange: Hegel insists that self-consciousness initially reduces "what is meant"—the "being of meaning" [*das Sein der Meinung*] that had deceived consciousness as sense-certainty—to a mere "abstraction," an empty "moment" consisting in irreality or pure negativity. In the infinitude of self-canceling differentiation, this process equates to the apparently stable modality of "desire."[2] As the sublation of the "named" "immediate" object, self-consciousness in fact "*is* desire in its most general sense" [*es ist Begierde überhaupt*], where "desire" means the impetus endlessly to cancel the sensuous world, to annul its

---

[1] See Hegel, *Werke* 6: 38ff.
[2] Hegel, *Werke* 3: 138.

initially unreal otherness.[3] At this stage, self-consciousness as the essence of things indeed endlessly negates them: in its historical form, as we shall see, self-consciousness as desire maintains a kinship with the animal which, "convinced of the nothingness of sensuous things," "without further ado" devours them.[4]

Hegel rehearses this operation in the particular terms of the dialectic of the subject, which inheres in life. The linguistic mediation of self-consciousness as desire will here prove the undoing of its dialectical economy. First, consciousness as infinitude, endlessly reappropriating its differentiations into itself, will articulate an individuated object that, like self-consciousness, evinces the character of "being that is reflected into itself."[5] The particular form born of infinitude shares the structure of its parent: as the "differentiation of what is *not* to be differentiated, or the unity of what *is* differentiation," the object has the same self-referential dimension as the infinitude from which it sprang.[6] Dividing itself and yet maintaining its unity as infinity, thus manifesting the principal characteristic of life, the object becomes "a living thing" [*ein Lebendiges*].[7] Life as such, even as it endlessly divides and negates itself, nonetheless resists negation, remaining "indestructible":[8] manifest in an array of living objects that die, life preserves itself in its infinitude. Hegel defines self-consciousness as the unity of subject and object; since the idea of life derives from this concept of unity, life must be the objective substance or historical medium of the subjective self. The subject will become an object, a "thing" that is also "living." The possibilities for perversion here abound; indeed life, given its dialectical "process," its turnings and translations, constitutes "inversion or perversion as such":

> Das Leben in dem allgemeinen flüssigen Medium, ein *ruhiges* Auseinanderlegen der Gestalten wird eben dadurch zur Bewegung derselben oder zum Leben als *Prozeß*. Die einfache allgemeine Flüssigkeit ist das *Ansich* und der Unterschied der Gestalten das *Andere*. Aber diese Flüssigkeit wird selbst durch diesen Unterschied das *Andere*; denn sie ist jetzt *für den Unterschied*, welcher an und für sich selbst und daher die unendliche Bewegung ist, von welcher jenes ruhige Medium aufgezehrt wird, das Leben als *Lebendiges*.—Diese *Verkehrung* aber ist darum wieder die *Verkehrtheit an sich selbst*; was aufgezehrt wird, ist das Wesen; die auf Kosten des Allgemeinen sich erhaltende und das Gefühl ihrer Einheit mit sich selbst sich gebende Individualität hebt gerade damit ihren Gegensatz des Anderen, durch

---

[3]Hegel, *Werke* 3: 139. See Hans-Georg Gadamer, "The Dialectic of Self-Consciousness," in *Hegel's Dialectic*, 54–74.

[4]The reference to animals alludes back to the section on "Sense-Certainty" (Hegel, *Werke* 3: 91). Hegel's argument is that the dialectic of appearance and its negativity underwrites the initial diremption of self-consciousness. For this reason self-consciousness must initially appear as desire. As we will see, Hegel will explicitly connect self-consciousness to the animal negation of otherness in the section on "Religion." The relation here between consumption and dialectical negation will also reappear in Hegel's political theory as the "system of needs."

[5]Hegel, *Werke* 3: 139.

[6]Hegel, *Werke* 3: 139.

[7]Hegel, *Werke* 3: 139.

[8]Hegel, *Werke* 3: 145.

welchen sie für sich ist, auf; die Einheit mit sich selbst, welche sie sich gibt, ist gerade die Flüssigkeit der Unterschiede oder die allgemeine Auflösung. Aber umgekehrt ist das Aufheben des individuellen Bestehens ebenso das Erzeugen desselben.[9]

Life in the universal fluid medium [*flüssigen Medium*], a *stable* [*ruhiges*] differentiation of forms, becomes through that activity of differentiation the movement of those forms, or life as a *process*. The universal fluidity proper is the *in-itself*, and the difference of the forms is the *other*. But this fluidity [*Flüssigkeit*] itself becomes the *other* through this difference; for now it exists *for* or *in relation to that difference*, which is in and for itself [*an und für sich*] and, consequently, is the infinite movement by which that stable medium is consumed: it is life as a *living thing*. This inversion or interchange [*Verkehrung*], however, is once again inversion and perversion [*Verkehrtheit*] *in-itself* or as such. What is consumed is the essence; the individuality which maintains itself at the expense of the universal and gives itself the feeling of its unity with itself, cancels precisely thereby its contrast with the other—the difference that enables it to exist for itself. The unity with itself, which it gives itself, is just the fluidity [*Flüssigkeit*] of the differences or their general dissolution [*Auflösung*]. But, conversely, the sublation [*Aufheben*] of individual existence at the same time produces it.

The unity of the living thing is preserved and dissolved by the infinite unfolding of life, the restless "turning" [*Verkehrung*] or dialectical "fluidity" that articulates and then cancels its independent forms. Thus the difference between the dialectical articulation of shape and its sublation [*Aufheben*] collapses.[10] Replacing the stable "inversion" or negation of the empty objects of mere desire—where language abstracted from referentiality or *Meinung* does not contaminate the commerce of pure desire—this "restless" economy of life only recuperates the surpluses and residues of dialectical movement *in potentia*, as each vestige of sublated form inheres in infinitude.[11] Indeed "the whole round of this activity"—not just the appearance and disappearance of "stable" [*ruhige*] forms— makes up "life." Related to the discursive mode of irony, the "turning" and translation of *Verkehrung* again here mark the movement of the dialectic itself. Accordingly the economy of living "perversion" [*Verkehrtheit*]—the endless mutation and supersession of its vital forms—compasses the infinite totality of dialectical movement, hence self-consciousness "for us."

---

[9]Hegel, *Werke* 3: 141.

[10]"The two sides of the whole movement which were previously differentiated—namely, the stable arrangement of the shapes in the general medium of independence on the one hand, and the process of life on the other— blur into one another. The latter is just as much an articulation of form as a supersession of it; and the other, the arrangement of a shape, is just as much a supersession as an articulation of form" (Hegel, *Werke* 3: 142).

[11]*Meinung* refers to both meaning and opinion, punningly implying the contingency of the former. Thus all meaning or referentiality reduces to opinion, except in the case of self-knowing philosophy, where the sign refers to its own freedom paradoxically in and from contingency—that is, to the dialectical unfolding of the concept.

In the first stage, self-consciousness has immediate "named existence" as its object; as the mediation and negativity of the object and as relational essence, however, self-consciousness in effect has "*itself* as the pure 'I' for object."[12] In the second stage, immediate being is sublated by the "formation" [*Gestaltung*] and deformation of species into the "universal unity" of life. Here "life refers [*verweist*] to something *other* than itself—that is, to consciousness for which life exists as this unity or genus"; accordingly the object of self-consciousness signifies nothing but the positing of its opposite.[13] It is in this second stage that self-consciousness becomes desire: as infinitude, it must abolish otherness, whose particularity is therefore of no consequence.

In the initial stages of its dialectical evolution, self-consciousness appears as a sign without a referent—both as the rarefaction of "what is meant" and as the sign that "refers to" another, equally empty sign. As a sign, self-consciousness negates its object, which only points back to the negativity of the former. Indeed, self-consciousness signifies only the impetus to annul its purely indicated opposite, for the satisfaction of desire brings no satisfaction at all: the consumed object must endlessly be replaced by another—as the other of self-consciousness. The latter seeks and fails to find certainty of itself or realize its meaning objectively as self-differentiating infinitude. Gesturing at its own failure to find referential form, self-consciousness, as the mere sign of *being-in-and-for-self*, cannot cohere with itself. Endlessly negating vitality, self-consciousness as desire becomes the "antithesis" of life.[14]

This persistence of articulated otherness marks, in the third phase of the dialectic of the subject, the independence [*Selbständigkeit*] of the object, its resistance to the negating activity of self-consciousness. Self-consciousness "can only find satisfaction when its object can effect negation within itself ... for [the object] is *in itself* the negative, and must be *for* [self-consciousness] what it *is*."[15] In the absence of the sign of *being-in-and-for-self* converging with its object, self-consciousness must refer to another whose meaning is what self-consciousness is. And indeed the object, as "universal independent nature in which negation is present as absolute negation," is now another self-consciousness—the only form that can satisfy self-consciousness. To reconstruct Hegel's logic: Where self-consciousness initially had only the "I" for object—which turned out to be pure negativity, hence not an object at all; and whereas in the second stage the "object" turned out to resist negation and thus dialectical recuperation into self-consciousness; now the task will be for self-consciousness to be both "I" and object, both relational essence and immediate being. Self-consciousness, as "essence" or the negativity of pure relationality, can only achieve the immediacy of "being" (and thus become an object) through opposition to an "other" that is both living being and essence.[16] In other words,

---

[12]Hegel, *Werke* 3: 142; "Gegen jene *unmittelbare* oder als ein *Sein* ausgesprochene ist diese zweite die *allgemeine*, welche alle diese Momente als aufgehobenen in ihr hat" (Hegel, *Werke* 3: 142-3).

[13]Hegel, *Werke* 3: 143.

[14]Hegel, *Werke* 3: 139.

[15]Hegel, *Werke* 3: 144.

[16]Hegel defines "being" in its opening diremption as the "indeterminate immediate," in contrast to "essence" or "reflection within itself" (Hegel, *Science of Logic*, 80, 393).

self-consciousness must be life that refers to the truth of self-consciousness not only as "object," but also as the "I" negating its attachment to phenomenality. Only through this reciprocity could self-consciousness achieve conceptual integrity: "a self-consciousness *exists for a self-consciousness.* Only thus does self-consciousness in fact *exist*; for only then does the unity of itself in its otherness come to *be* for it."[17]

In the ever artful text of the *Phenomenology*, the dialectical differentiation and reflection of self-consciousness, echoing the procedure of understanding that culminates in the "inverted world," take the form of a chiasmus, a crossing in a manner that produces an infinite polysemy: "The concept of [the unity of self-consciousness] in its doubling [as an other] [*Verdopplung*] of infinity realizing itself in self-consciousness, is that of a multi-sided and polysemic crossing [*vieldeutige Verschränkung*]."[18] As a "multi-sided" chiasmus or implicitly specular inversion of infinitude—of two self-consciousnesses as two opposed mirrors— this doubling in fact engenders an infinite number of possible "meanings." But polysemy [*Vieldeutigkeit*] as such must be "cognized" [*erkannt*] in contradistinction to the dialectical unity of posited oppositional "meaning" [*entgegengesetzten Bedeutung*]: "the double meaning of what is differentiated [*Die Doppelsinnigkeit des Unterschiedenen*] lies in the essence of self-consciousness, which is to be infinitely or immediately the opposite of the determinateness in which it is posited."[19] In other words, the infinite significations produced by the chiastic interchange of self-consciousnesses are cognized—through a semantic operation—as the unity of their difference as such.

The "cognition" [*Erkennen*] of the discursive movement of dialectical logic underwrites the "recognition" [*Anerkennen*] of self-consciousness.[20] The only "action" available to each self-consciousness, as logico-discursive principles, is the movement of dialectical overcoming [*Aufheben*]—that is, the cognition of the oppositional "meaning" of the sublated object. As self-consciousness delimits another self-consciousness as its "outside," it dialectically sublates the other, negating its immediacy. Thenceforth, each dialectical movement from immediacy to negation of either self-consciousness can be cognized as the "action" of both. The movement of the dialectic has an agency of its own that, in the theoretical unity of self-consciousness, also manifests as the propensity to action or will of each self-consciousness: thus self-consciousness "can do nothing on its own about [the other] object if that object does not do in itself what the first self-consciousness does in it. The movement [of the dialectic] is simply the double movement of the two self-consciousnesses … Each self-consciousness, for itself and for the other, is an immediate being for itself, which at the same time is such through this mediation. They *recognize* themselves as *mutually recognizing one another.*"[21] It is thus the balanced interplay of chiastic "exchange" [*Austauschung*] or

---

[17]Hegel, *Werke* 3: 144. Emphasis mine.

[18]Hegel, *Werke* 3: 145.

[19]Hegel, *Werke* 3: 145.

[20]Thus he refers to "recognitive self-consciousness" (see Hegel, *The Philosophy of Subjective Spirit*, 3: 53).

[21]Hegel, *Werke* 3: 145–6.

mirrored doubling—the cognition of dialectical movement—that constitutes the "pure concept of recognition" [*reine Begriff des Anerkennens*].[22]

Crucially, the initial encounter of self-consciousnesses, described "for us" prior to their evolution into master and slave, is not between "individual" bodies housing their own wills; rather, in accordance with the chiastic economy, each disembodied will engages the immediate vitality of the other. In the absence of any clash of wills, each self-consciousness "does what the other demands."[23] Inhering in the purely notional "duplication of self-consciousness in its oneness" [*der Verdopplung des Selbstbewußtseins in seiner Einheit*], this "demand" does not require the enunciated sign of a willful, speaking body.[24] The mature philosophical mind views the process of duplication and recuperation from the perspective of the realized concept in its paradoxical infinitude. Thus for self-knowing spirit, the living immediacy of each self-consciousness is endlessly negated in the "double movement" of chiastic exchange: "each term is the exchange of its own determinateness and the absolute transition into its opposite."[25]

Hegel then analyzes how this "process of the pure concept of recognition" "appears to self-consciousness."[26] Hegel's vantage point at this particular moment—the analysis of self-consciousness from the perspective of self-consciousness—should not be confused with the "standpoint" of "the self-consciousness of spirit," which "contains" all of the "structured shapes of consciousness, self-consciousness, and reason in universal determinations" in the chapter on religion.[27] For the uninitiated self-consciousness at this stage, the "other" in its appearance consists in irreducible immediacy. Here the double dialectical movement privileging the "essence" of one and "being" of the other, rather than cohering in a spatial and temporal infinitude, results in the detachment of two self-consciousnesses. For each self-consciousness in any given moment, one thus "appears" as a separate living shape confronting its other as an "individual."[28]

Ultimately freedom, says Hegel, requires the coherence of individual and intersubjective agency: the self-knowing will [*Wille*] must be housed both in a body and in the collective self-consciousness that inheres in all bodies; that conjunction of individual and universal self-consciousness constitutes the "absolute substance—the unity of various independent self-consciousnesses that enjoy complete freedom and independence in their opposition: 'I' that is 'We' and 'We' that is 'I.'"[29] In turn the truly free "will" must consist of the coherence of intention and action. To use a corporeal example, if I sneeze and make you sick, the action is involuntary and its effect, therefore, unwilled; a willful action would require that my inner intention be reflected in my outer

---

[22]Hegel, *Werke* 3: 147.

[23]Hegel, *Werke* 3: 146.

[24]Hegel, *Werke* 3: 147.

[25]Hegel, *Werke* 3: 147.

[26]Hegel, *Werke* 3: 147.

[27]Again, self-consciousness here is not historical, for "only the totality of spirit is in time" (Hegel, *Werke* 3: 498).

[28]Hegel, *Werke* 3: 147–8.

[29]Hegel, *Werke* 3: 145. Only through this process would the cognition of otherness as subject equate to the recognition of subjects, and subjectivity become indissociable from intersubjectivity.

action. But the coherence of intention and deed hinges upon a retroactive or "recognitive" narrative shared by the actor and the other subjects interpreting it.[30] Agency thus materializes in the retrospective accord of intention and action—in other words, the harmony of interiority and exteriority in the recognitive and thus social expression of a "will" exceeding the actor's corporeity.[31] The difficulty of agreeing shared narratives in which intention and action converge instantiates the larger challenge of harmonizing and thus liberating all wills within and across individual bodies.

Ignoring this dissonance of agency and embodiment, many commentators have missed this central problematic in Hegel's dialectic of master and slave, namely the nature of subjectivity given the fluidity in space and time of the recognitive will. This displacement of agency follows from the necessarily failed attempt to materialize the contradictory delimitation within infinity of an unknowable "outer" that must bear the discursive "meaning" of an "inner." Reducing "vitality" to a merely willful, unmediated "corporeality," positivist readings of this section have not accounted for the discursive meaning of the emergent body as the material form of individuality. Thus in his lectures on the process of "recognition," Hegel refers to this "corporeality" [Leiblichkeit]—the "limit" [Grenze] of interiority—as the "sign" [Zeichen] of self-consciousness and "mark" [Zeichen] of its "self-awareness," "its being for others and its mediating relation with them."[32] So, too, in the *Phenomenology*—just before introducing the concept of the *Werkmeister* as the mediating agency of the dialectic of subject and object in history—Hegel will refer to the body as both a "determinate being," the given "immediate fact" of corporeality, and a "sign" that gestures at but ultimately cannot mediate the meaning of an individual:

> But since the individual is at the same time only what he has done, his body [Leib] is also the expression [Ausdruck] which he produces; that is, the body is at the same time a *sign* [Zeichen] which does not remain an immediate thing, but through which the individual only renders for cognition what his meaning [Sinne] is, when he directs his original nature [as corporeal immediacy] to work.[33]

---

[30]My conception of "recognitive agency" owes a debt to Allen Speight's *Hegel, Literature, and the Problem of Agency* (Cambridge: Cambridge University Press, 2001), 94–136 and Robert Brandom's *Articulating Reasons: An Introduction to Inferentialism* (Cambridge: Harvard University Press, 2000).

[31]As we have seen, Hegel points out that the narrative of an action requires a harmony of "inner" and "outer" in the section entitled "The Certainty and Truth of Reason" in the *Phenomenology*. In the section on "Spirit," the theories of performativity, recognition, and ethicality together underwrite a view of agency that hinges on a retroactive and socialized interpretation of action in a manner that coheres with intention (see Hegel, *Werke* 3: 464–94).

[32]Hegel refers to the "limit" that determines corporeality in *The Philosophy of Subjective Spirit*, 3: §430A, 55. He then describes the "contradiction" in which self-consciousness doubles itself as the imposition of a limit on what precisely has no "limit [Grenze]": "The process of recognition is a struggle, for insofar as another is an immediate and distinct existence for me, I am unable to know myself as myself within this other, and am therefore committed to the sublation of this its immediacy. Conversely, it is only insofar as I sublate the immediacy I involve, and so give determinate being to my freedom, that I can be recognized as an immediacy. The immediacy is at the same time the corporeity of self-consciousness however, in which, as in its sign and instrument, it has its own self-awareness, as well as its being for others and its mediating relation with them" (ibid., 3: §431, 55).

[33]Hegel, *Werke* 3: 233. Emphasis in original.

We will return to the conception of "work" in this discursive context. For now it suffices to say that any such sign, intrinsically dialectical or ironic, must bear a double meaning: thus, Hegel adds in his lectures, the "body" as limit, the product of a "tremendous contradiction," marks both the individual form of self-consciousness and its incongruous subjection to finitude.[34]

As with Schlegel's opposed mirrors, the reflection of subjectivities ultimately engenders an ironic infinity, a corporeality that cannot reconcile its finitude to the boundless specularity of pure subjectivity: in other words, the *cognition* of the latter as a materialized, corporeal limit realizes only ironically the infinitude of pure *recognition*. In order to "appear," self-consciousness must be perverted, as it were, by the concrete impurity of the "being of life" [*das Sein des Lebens*]. In its "appearance," then, self-consciousness—taking on the immediate form of an "individual" body—still demands recognition from another self-consciousness.[35] This process first requires, however, the cognition of the corporeal form of self-consciousness as the phenomenal "presentation" of a self-negating body—that is, a movable dialectical limit:

> Die *Darstellung* seiner … als der reinen Abstraktion des Selbstbewußtseins besteht darin, sich als reine Negation seiner gegenständlichen Weise zu zeigen, oder es zu zeigen, an kein bestimmtes *Dasein* geknüpft, an die allgemeine Einzelheit des Daseins überhaupt nicht, nicht an das Leben geknüpft zu sein … Und es ist allein das Daransetzen des Lebens, wodurch die Freiheit, wodurch es bewährt wird, daß dem Selbstbewußtsein nicht das *Sein*, nicht die *unmittelbare* Weise, wie es auftritt, nicht sein Versenktsein in die Ausbreitung des Lebens das Wesen,—sondern daß an ihm nichts vorhanden, was für es nicht verschwindendes Moment wäre, daß es nur reines *Fürsichsein* ist.

> The *presentation* [*Darstellung*] of itself … as the pure abstraction of self-consciousness consists in showing itself to be the pure negation of its objective mode, that is, in showing that it is fettered [*geknüpft*] to no determinate *existence*, that it is not at all bound to the universal individuality of existence, that it is not fettered [*geknüpft*] to life … And it is solely by staking one's life, by which freedom is won, that self-consciousness proves that its essence is not *being*, not the *immediate form* in which it appears, not being engrossed in the expanse of life—but rather that there is nothing present in it which could not be regarded as a vanishing moment, that self-consciousness is pure *being-for-self*.[36]

For self-consciousness to enact its freedom from immediacy—that is, from its body, the natural corporeality of its form—it must risk its life. And since each self-consciousness is the negative of the other's body, risking its life means risking the other's life. The

---

[34]Hegel, *The Philosophy of Subjective Spirit*, 3: §430A, 55.

[35]Hegel, *Werke* 3: 148.

[36]Hegel, *Werke* 3: 148.

"presentation" of its negative relation to its body thus involves "a double-act [*das gedoppelte Tun*]," in which "the action of the other and its own action" must be the same. The will of one is the will of the other, and vice versa. Accordingly a struggle to the death ensues. If the struggle ends in death, self-consciousness does not achieve recognition from its other; if neither side dies, then the act of negation involved is only "abstract," not material negation. In the latter case the "double act"—the negation of embodiment and the embodiment of negation—consists of a failed inversion: "the two do not give and receive each other back from one another reciprocally through consciousness."[37] What is required, therefore, is the "presentation" [*Darstellung*] of death, the act of dialectically overcoming a body that is nonetheless "preserved and maintained."[38]

How could such a death take place? To begin with, such a supersession of the body by the subject is only thinkable because the two concepts do not fully coincide: through its dialectical "act" the subject exceeds its corporeality. As the "sign" of self-consciousness, its bodily form gestures at and at the same time fails to contain its spiritual content, since self-consciousness must inhere in all of its individual determinations: individuality and sociality—subjectivity and intersubjectivity—must, but phenomenally cannot converge.

In this respect, the "sign" of the body, like all signs, reflects the structure of Hegel's pyramid, the symbolic presentation of the dead body that marks the birth of the aesthetic "proper." As a "corporeal shell" [*leibliche Hülle*], it will be recalled, the pyramid negates and preserves the body as an "architectonic enclosure" for departed spirit, surfacing the discursivity of the body as a dialectical line and hence symbol of the negative. In the *Aesthetics* a "symbol" emerges when the differentiation of the external establishes affinities with "inner" determinations formulated by thought. Any positing of spirit (i.e., self-consciousness) beyond outer sensuality hinges on the negation or death of that externality in its natural immediacy.[39] Accordingly self-consciousness must appear in the phenomenal world by way of the symbol, an inadequate affinity between outer material form and inner intellectual content, where the latter must moreover be the negative of the former. It is this relation of the aesthetic "symbol" to delineation and to the death of the body that underwrites Hegel's argument that the pyramid is the quintessential mode of the symbol. Likewise, it is the dependence of the *Zeichen* on its latent corporeality—the "psychophysiologically" resonant material of voice and script—that betrays the sign's ultimately symbolic or "pyramidal" nature.

Materializing a line that doubles the corporeal delimitation of interiority, the pyramid—the aesthetic form of the "limit" [*Grenze*]—reveals the possible "freedom" of the dialectic from any fixity of the material, gesturing at the subject's potential to supersede the form of living immediacy. Similarly, the sign, attempting to give a "foreign" soul to the dead corporeality of script or sound, reveals the potential "freedom" of intellectual content from external form. Self-consciousness, in order to "appear" as what it is, must "present" itself as free by alienating itself from the "foreign" [*fremde*] essence of its natural corporeity.[40]

---

[37]Hegel, *Werke* 3: 150. It is the discursive perversion of this reciprocity that has escaped attention.

[38]Hegel, *Werke* 3: 148.

[39]Hegel, *Werke* 13: 450–1.

[40]Hegel, *Werke* 3: 149.

As with the pyramid and sign, self-consciousness requires symbolic mediation: its form must disclose the spiritual content with which it is closely, but inadequately entangled.

In "Self-Consciousness," this symbolic "presentation" must not only take "immediate" form that gestures at its own negativity, but also present itself as what Hegel will call the "dissolution" [Auflösung] of all form, the demonstration that there is nothing "at hand" which "could not be a vanishing moment" for self-consciousness.[41] These two modalities represent, of course, the dialectically opposed but entangled modes of the aesthetic: if the first represents the architectural delineation of form, the second marks its poetic dissolution. As we have seen, the aesthetic—the dialectic of architecture and poetry— centers on the symbolic preservation and negation of the body in its materiality and discursivity: architecture, the art of division, first materializes a separation of inner and outer that demonstrates the fluidity of the corporeal demarcation of spirit; and the poetic symbol demonstrates the propensity of the sign to slough off its corporeality. Because any attempt by self-consciousness to manifest itself in and supersede its corporeal form will require the coimbrication of language and the real, of Meinung and das Sein der Meinung, the subject can only appear through aesthetic "presentation" [Darstellung]. More generally, architecture and poetry together—constituting the architectonic function of the dialectic—mark the necessarily aesthetic dimension of all logical operations, including what Hegel refers to as the "syllogism" [Schluss] of subjectivity.[42]

As we will see, it is precisely the phantasmic corporeality of the architectonic—of the dialectical line underwriting the materialization of form—that will propel the movement toward the possible convergence of "subject" and "substance" at the end of the Phenomenology. The chapter on "Self-Consciousness" first lays out the structure of the "syllogism," which moves from the failed supersession of corporeality through the "act" of sublation to the aesthetic manipulation of "substance" through "work." After the impasse of the life and death struggle, self-consciousness—having learned of its dependence on life, but also of the apparent irreconcilability of "essence" (or "mediation") on the one hand and "being" (or "immediacy") on the other—posits these two modes as being-for-self and being-for-another, respectively.[43] The first form, independent self-consciousness that has proven its independence from its corporeal immediacy, is the "master" [Herr];

---

[41]Hegel, Werke 3: 148, 3: 153.

[42]Hegel, Werke 3:151. On the relation of "life" to the "syllogism," see the section entitled "The Syllogism" in Hegel, Science of Logic, 664ff.

[43]Hegel, Werke 3: 150. Misreading Hegel's dialectic of being and essence, Bataille and Derrida erroneously contend that Hegel ignores material death. Hegel's argument, in fact, runs as follows: self-consciousness learns that it is dependent on life and that life is essential to it as pure self-consciousness. It must therefore understand the reality of death that is the negation of its individuality. The dependence on life is a "real" material dependence. The symbolization of death reflects not a merely mimetic "representation"—pace Bataille—but rather an experience of negativity, which yields the knowledge of the power of the self to kill itself (or throw itself at death) by virtue of risking its life. As we will see, in the Philosophy of Right, Hegel will point to the human ability to "commit suicide" as a fundamental element of the intrinsic freedom of the will (see Hegel, Werke 7: §5A: 51). On Bataille and Hegel, see Jacques Derrida, "From Restricted to General Economy: A Hegelianism without Reserve," in Writing and Difference, transl. Alan Bass (Chicago: University of Chicago Press, 1978), 251–77.

the second form, mere consciousness in the form of natural being or "thinghood," is the "slave" [*Knecht*]. This moment in the *Phenomenology* must be read in its broader context, taking into account the logical relation of being and essence, the dialectic of inversion and perversion that governs the progress of consciousness, the necessarily aesthetic "presentation" [*Darstellung*] of self-consciousness, and the dissonance of agency and embodiment that threatens concrete freedom. These contextualizing elements will govern our reading of the "appearance" of self-consciousness as *Herr* and *Knecht*, or master and slave, enabling us to link this celebrated text on "self-consciousness" more robustly to Hegel's social and political philosophy.

As a subject reduced to thinghood, the *Knecht* marks the concept of the human as mere object, a body with no will of its own. Slavery consists, then, in life surrendering its agency for life: trembling before the threat of death, the slave, "fettered" [*geknüpft*] only to his corporeity, disowns the possible freedom of the recognitive will. As we will see, this conception of the slave evolves dynamically from this extreme and initial moment as the slave discovers his agency over matter, marking the advent of the subject in history. Scholars reducing the *Knecht* at this point in the *Phenomenology* to a historical figure— whether a feudal serf, bondsman, or knight or a victim of chattel slavery transplanted to the New World—have missed the fact that the dialectic here must first be abstracted from history. Presented here "from the standpoint of consciousness," the dialectic of master and slave will only take historical form in the dialectic of "Religion," once the cycle from consciousness to the self-consciousness of spirit has run its course. In the next chapter, we will address the historical specificity or phenomenality of the *Knecht* in Hegel's system.

Holding recognition and thus freedom more precious than life, the master emerges from the struggle to the death with "power" [*Macht*] over the other self-consciousness, the slave who clung to life. As the "concept of consciousness that exists for itself," the master negates his immediate being, relating to the material only through the corporeality of the slave. The latter, enchained to life and so denoting "thinghood as such" [*der Dingheit überhaupt*], mediates the master's relation not only to embodied being, but also to objects of desire:

Der Herr bezieht sich *auf den Knecht mittelbar durch das selbständige Sein*; denn eben hieran ist der Knecht gehalten; es ist seine Kette, von der er im Kampfe nicht abstrahieren konnte und darum sich als unselbständig, seine Selbständigkeit in der Dingheit zu haben erwies. Der Herr aber ist die Macht über dies Sein, denn er erwies im Kampfe, daß es ihm nur als ein Negatives gilt; indem er die Macht darüber, dies Sein aber die Macht über den Anderen ist, so hat er in diesem Schlusse diesen Anderen unter sich. Ebenso bezieht sich der Herr *mittelbar durch den Knecht auf das Ding* …[44]

---

[44]Hegel, *Werke* 3: 151.

The master relates himself *mediately to the slave through independent being*, for it is this [being] that holds the slave; it is his chain [*Kette*] he could not renounce in the struggle, thus proving himself to be dependent, to possess his self-sufficiency in thinghood. But the master is the power [*Macht*] over this being, for he proved in the struggle that being is to him merely negative. Since he is the power over this being and the power over the other [self-consciousness], it follows from the syllogism that he holds the [latter] in subjection. In the same way, the master relates himself to the thing mediately through the slave.

The slave's fear of death surpasses his desire to consume objects, just as the master's desire surpasses his fear of death. Bound to life and so clinging to the "chains" [*Kette*] of corporeality, self-consciousness as the slave surrenders its agency to another. Where the slave consists in corporeality that suppresses an independent will, the master emerges as will exceeding an endlessly "vanishing" corporeality.[45] More like a ghost of a body, the master is only the "immediate relation of being-for-self" as the *concept* of self-consciousness; and it principally "*exists* as mediation, that is, as a being-for-self which is for itself only through an other."[46]

The slave does not relate to the thing as a desiring consumer: he "dialectically overcomes the thing without extinguishing it." He does not negate it for himself, but sees that it can be shaped for another. "He *works* on it."[47] By contrast the master, driven by desire, consumes the thing: it comes to be for him even as he devours it. The master establishes contact with materiality not only through the evanescence of his body and of the thing he consumes, but also through his "dependence" on the "determinate existence" of an enslaved body. Because this other, enchained to embodiment, abjures self-possession and so rescinds itself as "being-for-self," its will accords with the will of the master. In resignation and obedience, the slave does to himself what the master does to the slave: again, the action of the will appears as a "double action."[48]

The recognition achieved here has lent itself to misreading.[49] It is only in the coherence of wills, from the master's point of view, that he achieves "recognition"; the latter does not consist in the slave's verbal acknowledgment of or mere acquiescence to the master.[50] The slave must enact the master's will as though the master had acted for himself: in other words, the master achieves recognition precisely because of the confluence of masterly intention and slavish action. Accordingly there appears to be no

---

[45]Hegel, *Werke* 3: 148ff.

[46]Hegel, *Werke* 3: 151.

[47]Hegel, *Werke* 3: 151. In Harris' felicitous phrase, "the recognition of things as independent when they are the way another wants them is the climax of Labor" (H. S. Harris, *Hegel's Ladder* [Cambridge: Hackett, 1997], 1: 360).

[48]Hegel, *Werke* 3: 148.

[49]The failure to account adequately for the discursive and ultimately aesthetic mediation of recognition has undoubtedly inflected the reception and philosophical appropriation of the master–slave dialectic, especially in and after Alexandre Kojève.

[50]Hegel clearly defines recognition here as the congruence of separate wills.

need for linguistic mediation: the master need not speak and the slave, prior to engaging in "formative activity," remains "mute" [*stumm*].[51]

Even so, the recognition here is deficient. In recognition "proper," the congruence of wills must be mutual: each self-consciousness must do to the other what he also does to himself. In this case, the recognition is "one-sided and unequal."[52] The subjugated self-consciousness initially appears merely "external" to the dialectic of mastery, a pure mediation of desire, until the master discovers the truth of his own dependence on slavish corporeality:

> It is clear, however, that this object [the slavish body] does not correspond to its concept: rather, the object in which the master has achieved his mastery has in reality turned out to be something quite different from an independent consciousness. What now really confronts him is not an independent consciousness, but a dependent one ... The *truth* of the independent consciousness is accordingly the *servile consciousness* [*knechtische Bewußtsein*] of the slave. This, it is true, appears at first *external* to itself and not as the truth of self-consciousness. But just as mastery showed that its essence is the inversion and perversion [*Verkehrte*] of what it wants to be, so too slavery [*Knechtschaft*] will in its performance or achievement [*Vollbringung*] turn into the opposite of what it immediately is; as a consciousness *forced back* [*zurückgedrängtes*] into itself, it will withdraw into itself and turn back [*umkehren*] into a truly independent consciousness.[53]

Hegel associates mastery here with the "inversion and perversion" of mere understanding. But while the dialectic of master and slave rehearses the separation of consciousness and object that had led understanding astray, "mastery" [*Herrschaft*] attempts to avoid the mediation of discursive expression: where the slave anticipates the master's every wish, there would be, as a condition of the master's desired recognition, no equivalent to the discursive dogmas or laws of the understanding to betray in the master's phenomenal world. On the other hand, the master's underlying impetus—to appear as being-for-self—leads him to reduce another self-consciousness to a mere body stripped of will, where the slave's body as a "sign" [*Zeichen*] designates "being-for-another" rather than self-consciousness.[54] It thus emerges that intention ("what self-consciousness wants") and action do not in fact cohere, for the slave, in realizing the master's will to be "for" him (rather than "in-and-for-itself"), ironically perverts "what [the master] wants to be." The fracture between masterly intention and slavish action further compromises the master's "recognition," exposing his fundamentally servile attachment to a body divested of free will. The discursive mediation of their relation thus reveals the perils of mastery:

---

[51]Hegel, *Werke* 3: 154.

[52]Hegel, *Werke* 3: 152.

[53]Hegel, *Werke* 3: 152.

[54]In other words, the "sign" of slavish corporeality mediates the "meaning" of the masterly will, subverting the latter's intention to signify "being-for-self."

the *Herr* cannot overcome the "perversity" of life, the erratic turns of concrete irony, through domination and consumption.

How then, does the slave—enchained to his body—negotiate that same materiality? The slave works on the thing and clings to his vital form, but "in neither case can he be the [skillful] *Meister* over being and its absolute negation" [*in beiden kann es nicht über das Sein Meister werden und zur absoluten Negation gelangen*].[55] The word *Meister* here cannot be read as a mere synonym for *Herr*; in the chapter on religion and art, the term *Meister* will signify an individual artist's socially recognized dominion over materiality and its meaning, a skill exercised decisively in the sculpting of the human "form of self-consciousness."[56] Unlike the enslaved consciousness at the incipit of the dialectic of labor, the *Meister's* aesthetic manipulation of matter articulates the individuation of the fashioned object and, accordingly, of himself as an individual artist. Ultimately the achievement of this mimetic "shape of self-consciousness," associated principally in Hegel's histories with ancient Greece, will betray or ironize the principle of aesthetic and individual freedom, marking the end of ideal art in the *Aesthetics* and the excess in the representational economy of "ethical life" in the *Phenomenology* and, as we will see, in the *Philosophy of Right*. Here the enslaved self-consciousness, not yet attaining to mimetic dominion as an individual *Meister*, nonetheless establishes contact with the principle of freedom through labor:

In the feeling [of death, the slave] has been dissolved [*aufgelöst*] inwardly, has trembled in itself, and all that was fixed [*alles Fixe*] within it has been shaken. This pure universal movement, the absolute fluidity of what apparently endures [*das absolute Flüssigwerden alles Bestehens*] is, however, the simple essence of self-consciousness, absolute negativity, pure self-consciousness … There is not only this universal dissolution merely in principle; in his service the slave also achieves this dissolution *in actuality*; it sublates every *individuated* moment of his attachment to natural existence, sloughing it off through work.[57]

Driven by the fear of death to work on the object of another's desire, the slave discovers the dialectical fluidity of all things. Death, says Hegel, is "the absolute *Herr*," far more powerful than the master.[58] Just as fear frees the slave's interiority from the rigid dogmas of consciousness, so, too, the making of an object liberates him from the fixities of the given, the illusion of permanence in the world of appearance. The object, negated and consumed, for the master does not endure as phenomenality: the fulfillment of mastery, consisting merely in an "act of vanishing," lacks "the objective side of permanence" [*die*

---

[55]Hegel, *Werke* 3: 151.

[56]To avoid confusion, I will either flag or not translate the German term "*Meister*"; when the word "master" appears in my rendition without the original German, it translates Hegel's "*Herr*." Many translators and commentators erroneously conflate the two terms.

[57]Hegel, *Werke* 3: 153.

[58]Hegel, *Werke* 3: 153.

gegenständliche Seite oder das Bestehen].[59] Accordingly the *Herr* never attains to enduring individuality. By contrast the slave discovers himself as an independent being in the materiality of sensuous form as such:

> ... work is desire held in check, it is vanishing deferred: that is, work articulates form [*bildet*]. The negative relation to the object becomes the *form* [*Form*] of the object; it becomes something that endures [as phenomenality] because it is precisely for the laborer that the object has independence. This negative middle term, this formative activity [*das formierende Tun*], is at the same time individuality [*Einzelheit*], the pure being-for-self of consciousness, which now, in the work outside of it, enters into the element of permanence [*das Element des Bleibens*]. Accordingly the laboring consciousness [*das arbeitende Bewußtsein*] comes to an intuition of the independent being *as itself*.[60]

Isolating what we have called the architectonic dimension of sensuous form—the materiality of the dialectical line that demarcates an object—the slave discovers the principle of self-canceling individuation that had escaped consciousness as perception. Accordingly the slave surfaces the "meaning" of the sign of the laboring body in chains: "the formative [*formierende*] activity" "has the positive meaning [*Bedeutung*]" that in that forming of form "the servile consciousness as pure being-for-self becomes *an existent being*."[61] This "formative activity" also bears the "negative meaning" of fear: trembling before his master as the harbinger of death, the slave must abjure this object he has fashioned for his master. Only thus can the object endure for him and so materialize the individuated "form" of being-for-self.[62] Since that pure form gestures only at the "foreign essence" [*das fremde Wesen*] of the fleeting body (recalling, again, Hegel's pyramidal sign and architectonic symbol), the slave acknowledges the dissonance of body and spirit, the failure mimetically or adequately to house the latter in living form:

> [Through] the forming of form [*Formieren*] [or] ... in forming the thing [*in dem Bilden des Dinges*], the slave's own negativity, his being-for-self, becomes an object for him only through his abjuring the opposed existing *form* before him. But this objective *negative* moment is none other than the foreign essence [*fremde Wesen*] before which he has trembled. Now, however, he destroys this foreign negativity [*dies fremde Negative*], posits *himself* as a negative within the element of duration [*das Element des Bleibens*], and thereby becomes *for himself* an existing *being-for-self*. In the master, the being-for-self is an "other" for the slave, or is only *for him*; in fear, the being-for-self is present in the slave himself; in formative activity [*Bilden*], he realizes being-for-self as belonging to *him*, and attains to the consciousness

---

[59]Hegel, *Werke* 3: 153.
[60]Hegel, *Werke* 3: 153–4.
[61]Hegel, *Werke* 3: 154.
[62]Hegel, *Werke* 3: 154.

that he exists in and for himself. The form does not become something other than himself by being posited as external [*hinausgesetzt*]; for it is precisely this form that is his pure being-for-self, which in this externality is seen by him to be the truth.[63]

As the non-representational principle of demarcation, the pure "form" of the fashioned object refers to its own negativity as the posited limit of individuation—the architectonic limit gesturing at a dying corporeality. Haunted by the negative, this enduring form thus cannot hold any other meaning but this freedom in the negativity, or self-canceling nature, of apparently persistent delineation. Referring to the actual "independence" or freedom of the enslaved body, the materialization of pure form—akin to the line of the self-negating body and of the pyramid—must be aesthetic; for precisely that reason Hegel refers to the slave's "formative activity" as *Formieren* and *Bilden*, the architectonic fashioning of the world:

Through this recuperation of his own meaning or mind [*eigener Sinn*] by himself, he realizes that he does so precisely in his work wherein there seemed to have been only a foreign meaning or mind [*fremder Sinn*]. For this reflection, the two moments of fear and service, and of formative activity [*des Bildens*] are necessary, both at the same time in a universal mode ... Without formative activity [*das Bilden*], fear remains inward and mute, and consciousness does not become explicitly for itself. Without the absolute fear [of death] ... his substance will not have been infected [*angesteckt*] by [the negative essence] through and through; ... he is still attached in principle to determinate being; having a "mind of one's own" is merely obstinance or self-will [*der eigene Sinn ist Eigensinn*], a freedom still trapped [*stehenbleibt*] in bondage [*Knechtschaft*].[64]

It is not labor as such that would free the slave, but the activity of *Bilden*, the aesthetic production that begins with the apparently durable externality of architecture and ends with the negating or dissolving force of poetry—the two forms corresponding respectively to service and fear "in their universal mode." The slave, like Hegel's Memnon, engages in the aesthetic labor of non-referential articulation, from the materialization to the dissolution of the pure form of self-consciousness, the corporeal limit of subjectivity. Before its consummation in "formative activity," however, the "fear" of death that drives dissolution remains "inward and mute": like the initially "soundless" Memnon, the slave at this initial stage does not yet articulate poetic speech, the *Bild* or image in which "meaning is not separated out from the concrete external object to which it is explicitly compared."[65] Ultimately the mute *Bildsäule*—Hegel's term for the "statue" before the sun in the *Phenomenology*—will manifest, as a compound of "image" [*Bild*] and "pillar"

---

[63]Hegel, *Werke* 3: 154.
[64]Hegel, *Werke* 3: 154–5.
[65]Hegel, *Werke* 13: 524.

[*Säule*], the interpenetration of the architectonic and poetic "figure" [*Bild*]. The Memnon and slave not only fail to produce language before illuminated externality, but also cannot externalize the representational modes through which self-consciousness, under the spell of what Hegel calls the mimetic "ideal," would materially or discursively take shape on earth. Thus as Hegel concludes here, "pure form" [*die reine Form*] cannot attain to "universal formation, the absolute concept" [*allgemeines Bilden, absoluter Begriff*].[66] The slave possesses merely a "skill [*Geschicklichkeit*] that exercises power [*Macht*] over some particularities, but not over the universal power or objective essence in its totality."[67]

At a second stage, the slave enters the seeming freedom of "self-will" [*Eigensinn*], a term Hegel punningly relates to the slave's grounding of self-possession in the belief that he can grasp and so possess his own meaning [*der eigene Sinn*]: thus Hegel writes, *der eigene Sinn ist Eigensinn*, defining *Eigensinn* as "the freedom which entrenches itself in some particularity and is still in bondage [*Knechtschaft*]."[68] Accordingly this self-will or obstinacy in bondage, though it leads finally to the articulation of linguistic "meaning," remains initially tied to *Meinung* or contingent opinion, the slave's "meaning" in the world removed from the social context of "free" subjectivity. This anti-social moment of "self-will" corresponds to the advent of prose in the *Aesthetics*: "in slaves, prose begins" [*Im Sklaven fängt die Prosa an*]; for the fearful slave does not "say his doctrines openly but can only conceal them in a riddle … "[69] This prose emerges when man "has retreated into himself and is bound to himself in his own freedom": he selfishly "becomes an end in himself by virtue of his individuality" and, viewing the natural as merely an external relation, "acts, works, and labors according to his own will [*tut, handelt, arbeitet nach seinem eigenen Willen*]."[70] Echoing the concept of "self-will" in the *Phenomenology*, the false freedom of *seinem eigenen Willen* here gives rise to discourse, including moral or wise maxims, featuring "natural" phenomena whose "particular" relations can be taken "as a symbol for universal meaning."[71] While the riddles are easily solved, the larger meaning remains ironic: in the case of Aesop, the hunchback slave evoked here, his animal fables create a "mask which veils the meaning, so far as its comprehensibility goes, as much as it explains it."[72]

The propensity of the self-oriented subject's discourse to an ironized universality points to the next phase of the dialectic. Struggling to exert "power" over the world to achieve the pure and stable consonance of sign and referent, particularity and universality, subject and object, individuality and sociality—self-consciousness here nonetheless recognizes itself "as an independent object and the object as a mode of consciousness"—that is, as a

---

[66] Hegel, *Werke* 3: 155
[67] Hegel, *Werke* 3: 155.
[68] Hegel, *Werke* 3: 157.
[69] Hegel, *Werke* 13: 497.
[70] Hegel, *Werke* 13: 493.
[71] Hegel, *Werke* 13: 493.
[72] Hegel, *Werke* 13: 499.

delineation of the architectonic power of thought.[73] Accordingly self-consciousness will enter a world of discursive thought free of particularity: while the self-willing slave clings to the bondage [*Knechtschaft*] of particularity, self-consciousness in this subsequent phase attains to "stoicism," "the freedom which always comes directly out of bondage and returns into the pure universality of thought."[74] Thus self-consciousness continues its long march from slavery toward the freedom of sociality—an historical evolution propelled, explicitly or implicitly, by aesthetic mediation and the willful articulation of power.[75]

The subject as slave, inaugurating the aesthetic and so enabling the discursive mediation of the *Knecht*'s violent birth, marks the advent of narrative history.[76] This radical insight locates the incipit or limit of history precisely where the slave emerges from the struggle to the death as being-for-another, a subject that produces itself through the imposition of aesthetic form. Beginning with the dialectical manifestation of the subject in chains, history will further consist in the narration of the slave's self-liberation. How does the conception of self-consciousness as disembodied agency inflect the circulation and evolution of power in time? What are the implications of this view of subjectivity on the historical possibility of freedom from domination? To what extent does the slave exercise agency and, if so, to what end and through what means?

---

[73]Hegel, *Werke* 3: 155.

[74]Hegel, *Werke* 3: 157. Hegel alludes to the Roman slave Epictetus and to Marcus Aurelius.

[75]Through the modalities of stoicism, skepticism, and the unhappy consciousness, self-consciousness will engage in discursive thought that does not cohere with objectivity. All of these modes will fail to achieve actual, living freedom.

[76]Accordingly Hegel insists on the relation of slavery and history: "Sklaverei ist etwas Geschichtliches ..." (Hegel, *Werke* 7: §57A: 125).

CHAPTER 9
AFRICA, AGENCY, AND FREEDOM

The logic of Hegel's section on "mastery and slavery" hinges on the dialectic between "being" or natural immediacy on the one hand and "essence" or relationality on the other, where "being" takes the form of object, body, or the "I" as objectified body, and "essence" marks the mediation through and negation of otherness. The master and slave are each structured by this dialectic of being and essence, albeit in opposite ways: the master consists in the pure relationality or "desire" of vanishing being, while the slave represents the non-relationality of pure immediacy. Accordingly the master and slave mirror and invert each other, the slave embodying and enacting the will of the master until the slave's labor, his forced production of objectivity, again shatters the illusion of mimetic symmetry and "perverts" the dialectical economy of pure exchange. In the next chapter, we will study the structure of this economy, its political valences, and its disruption or perversion by the subjectivity of slaves. Here, however, we will interrogate the nature of the slave's emergent subjectivity, examining in particular how the dialectic between will and embodiment inflects the articulation of power in the subject's quest for freedom.

Initially the master exercises "power" [*Macht*] over the slave, and the slave accords its will to the will of the master.[1] The slave begins to learn of his independence through his laboring production of an object over which he exercises a certain degree of power [*Macht*] through skill [*Geschicklichkeit*]; but this power does not amount to the "pure negative power" [*die reine negative Macht*] of the desiring master or the individual "dominion" [*Macht*] over matter of the master–artist [*Meister*].[2] How does the slave's limited power inflect his agency? How does this agency in turn inflect his power?[3] What is the slave's place in the historical telling and unfolding of freedom? To answer these questions, we will examine the dialectic of master and slave from the standpoint of self-consciousness as it materializes historically. We will interrogate the entanglement of the concept and phenomenality of the enslaved subject both in religious history, where the "rough African nature" of the laboring slave gives rise to the aesthetic in Egypt, and again in world-history, where the enslaved African initiates the journey toward historical

---

[1]Hegel, *Werke* 3: 155.

[2]Initially the master has "pure negative power" over the "being" of the slave (Hegel, *Werke* 3: 150–2).

[3]The nature and extent of slaves' agency remain important questions for historians since Walter Johnson's seminal intervention on the topic (Walter Johnson, *Soul by Soul: Life Inside the Antebellum Slave Market* [Cambridge: Harvard University Press, 1999]; see also his "On Agency," in *Journal of Social History*, 2003, 37: 1: 113–24).

freedom in the age of the modern state. We will analyze the conception and relation of Africa, slavery, and the aesthetic in the *Phenomenology of Spirit*, the *Philosophy of Right*, and the *Philosophy of History*, considering the specificity in Hegel's texts of the most quintessentially objectified slave—his African origin and displacement to the New World—before returning to the idea of freedom articulated in the conclusion of the *Phenomenology*.

As we have seen, the evolution of spirit in the *Phenomenology* from its emergence as mere "immediate knowledge" in "Consciousness" to pure self-knowledge in "Spirit" traces the process of dialectical maturation only from the abstract perspective of consciousness. Spirit must now experience this process as self-consciousness—that is, from the standpoint of the posited coherence of subject and object as the telos of actuality. Thus from the outset of the history of self-consciousness in the section on "Natural Religion," Hegel states:

> Spirit as the essence [*Wesen*] that is *self-consciousness*—or the self-conscious being that is all truth and knows all actuality as itself—is, to begin with, only its *concept* against the reality which it gives itself in the movement of its consciousness. This concept is, against the day of this unfolding, the night of its essence—against the existence of its moments as independent shapes, the creative secret of its birth. This secret has its revelation within itself; for existence has its necessity in this concept, because this concept is self-knowing spirit, and therefore has in its essence the moment of being consciousness, and of representing [*vorzustellen*] itself objectively. This is the pure "I," which in its externalization has within itself as universal object the certainty of itself—in other words, this object is for the "I" the penetration [*Durchdringung*] of all thought and all actuality.[4]

Self-consciousness as the conceptual identity, as it were, of identity and difference has thus far only *posited* the coherence of subject and object, or "I" and "actuality"; it must now attempt to "represent" and externalize itself "objectively." Spirit accordingly appears as "Luminous Essence" [*das Lichtwesen*], the pure "unmeasured" "sublimity" of light pervading all of externality.[5] This diremption has the "form" "pertaining to immediate consciousness or sense-certainty," now with the understanding that all of sensuous externality "is filled with spirit."[6] No form can hold here: the light of externality, endlessly deforming form, resists all fixities, all gestures of meaning.[7] This "formless substantiality" thus opposes an "equally simple negative, *darkness*," the cancellation of forms in space and time filled endlessly by light. No subject or object subsists but the "vanishing" *Herr*: thus

---

[4]Hegel, *Werke* 3: 505.

[5]Ibid.

[6]Ibid.

[7]As we have noted previously, Hegel's writing here is quite beautiful: "aber die wesentliche Einfachheit seines Denkens schweift bestandlos und unverständig in ihnen umher, erweitert ihre Grenzen zum Maßlosen, und löst ihre zur Pracht gesteigerte Schönheit in ihrer Erhabenheit auf" (Hegel, *Werke* 3: 506).

the *Lichtwesen* also takes the "form of the master [*die Form des Herrn*] over against self-consciousness of spirit withdrawing from its object."[8] In the absence of any formal stability, the aesthetic fails to take hold, as "beauty" "is dissolved in [unmeasured] sublimity."[9]

Turning to the "content" [*Inhalt*] of this all-encompassing "One," consciousness then begins to perceive and give "names" to its attributes. Because the "One" does not yet "become a subject [*Subjekt*] and consolidate its differentiations through the self," the verbal naming of what pertains to the limitless corresponds to the activity of consciousness in "Perception" earlier in the *Phenomenology* and to the poetry of the sublime in the *Aesthetics*.[10] "Clothed" [*angekleidet*] with the manifold forces [*Kräften*] of existence, the "One" radiates mastery [*Herrlichkeit*]; its discursive "determinations" are merely "messengers of its power [*Macht*], having no will of their own."[11] The endless "reeling" of this "essence" [*Wesen*] of light in nature reveals itself as the dialectic of "life." Echoing the process that unfolds in "Self-Consciousness," the *Lichtwesen*'s antithetical "immediate being"—"the negative power which dissolves [the] distinctions" of this masterful "One"—reflects back into its self and becomes an individual, enduring expression of the infinitude of form. This immediate "self" determines itself as a fractured and manifold "being-for-self," yielding up assymetrical forms of subjectivity.[12]

The "One's" power accordingly disperses. Remaining in the realm of "perception," consciousness experiences the differentiation of power into "weaker" and "stronger" [*schwächerer und kräftigerer*] spirits. The weak adopt the pantheistic "flower religion," the "selfless picture-thought [*Vorstellung*] of the self." The pantheistic procedure that "takes from things of perception" only "the deadness of abstraction" [*Tod der Abstraktion*] and then paradoxically grants them spiritual being surfaces the negativity of spirit, the death inhering in life. Pantheism thus gives way to desire, the "hatred" of otherness, and hence the "warring life" of the "strong," the latter embracing antagonistic "animal religions":[13]

Durch sie wird die Zerstreuung in die Mannigfaltigkeit der ruhigen Pflanzengestalten eine feindselige Bewegung, worin sich der Haß ihres Fürsichseins aufreibt. Das *wirkliche* Selbstbewußtsein dieses zerstreuten Geistes ist eine Menge vereinzelter ungeselliger Völkergeister, die in ihrem Hasse sich auf den Tod bekämpfen und bestimmter Tiergestalten als ihres Wesens sich bewußt werden, denn sie sind nichts anderes als Tiergeister, sich absondernde, ihrer ohne Allgemeinheit bewußte Tierleben.[14]

---

[8]Hegel, *Werke* 3: 506. Note that the "shapes" of sense-certainty, perception, understanding, and self-consciousness will "appear" historically in melded form, for spirit appears in time "as a totality." Thus the shapes of sense-certainty and of mastery and slavery in their various dimensions will appear together and apart in aesthetic history.
[9]Hegel, *Werke* 3: 506.
[10]Hegel, *Werke* 3: 506.
[11]Ibid.
[12]Ibid.
[13]Ibid.
[14]Hegel, *Werke* 3: 507–8.

Through [this determinateness and negativity], the dispersal into the variety of the motionless shapes of plants becomes a hostile movement in which the hatred emerging from being-for-itself exhausts itself. The *actual* self-consciousness within this scattered spirit is a multitude of isolated and unsociable [*ungeselliger*] spirits of different peoples, who, in their hatred, fight each other to the death and become conscious of determinate forms of animals as their essence: for they are nothing more than animal spirits, animal lives separated and detached from each other, unconscious of their universality.

This moment also reiterates the violence of "Self-Consciousness," where life perversely leads to the "struggle to the death" between consciousnesses. That struggle, it will be recalled, aimed at the "recognition" of the mutuality of individual and social agency—a recognition predicated on a reconciliation of will and embodiment. Here the "individualized and unsocial" bodies reduce themselves to merely animal desire. They do not progress toward sociality: as Hegel clarifies elsewhere, "the struggle for recognition in the extreme form in which it is presented" in the conceptual dialectic of "Self-Consciousness," before its phenomenal appearance, "can occur only in the state of nature."[15] We are not yet at the relation of master and slave.

Self-consciousness only then appears in the "form" of objective immediacy as the laboring slave, the subject that produces himself as a thing:

In diesem Hasse reibt sich aber die Bestimmtheit des rein negativen Fürsichseins auf, und durch diese Bewegung des Begriffs tritt der Geist in eine andere Gestalt. Das *aufgehobene Fürsichsein* ist die *Form des Gegenstandes*, die durch das Selbst hervorgebracht oder die vielmehr das hervorgebrachte, sich aufreibende, d. h. zum Dinge werdende Selbst ist. Über die nur zerreißenden Tiergeister behält daher der Arbeitende die Oberhand, dessen Tun nicht nur negativ, sondern beruhigt und positiv ist. Das Bewußtsein des Geistes ist also nunmehr die Bewegung, die über das unmittelbare *Ansichsein* wie über das abstrakte *Fürsichsein* hinaus ist. Indem das Ansich zu einer Bestimmtheit durch den Gegensatz herabgesetzt ist, ist es nicht mehr die eigene Form des absoluten Geistes, sondern eine Wirklichkeit, die sein Bewußtsein sich entgegengesetzt als das gemeine Dasein vorfindet, sie aufhebt und ebenso nicht nur dies aufhebende Fürsichsein ist, sondern auch seine Vorstellung, das zur Form eines Gegenstandes herausgesetzte Fürsichsein, hervorbringt. Dies Hervorbringen ist jedoch noch nicht das vollkommene, sondern eine bedingte Tätigkeit und das Formieren eines Vorhandenen.[16]

In this hatred, however, the determinateness of purely negative being-for-self [the first mode of self-consciousness] consumes itself, and, by this movement of the

---

[15]Hegel, *The Philosophy of Subjective Spirit*, 3: §432A, 59. Hegel insists on this point "in order to avoid eventual misunderstandings."

[16]Hegel, *Werke* 3: 508.

concept, spirit enters a different form. Superseded being-for-self is the form of the object, a form produced by the self, or rather is the produced self, the self depleting its self in its productive activity, that is, the self become a thing. Thus the laborer has the upper hand [*Oberhand*] over these mutually destructive animal spirits; his work is not only negative, but calm [*beruhigt*] and positive. The consciousness of spirit is therefore now the movement which is beyond the immediate in-itself and beyond the abstract being-for-self. Inasmuch as the *in-itself* is reduced to a determinateness by the binary antithesis, it is no longer the proper form of absolute spirit, but a reality which its consciousness finds before it as a basic existent thing, and which it supersedes; at the same time, this consciousness is not only this being-for-self which supersedes its object, but it also produces its own idea, the being-for-self that is put forth in the form of an object. This productive activity, however, is not a perfect, but a contingent activity, the fashioning of a material already to hand [*das Formieren eines Vorhandenen*]. Spirit, therefore, here appears as the *Werkmeister* …

Forming material "at hand" [*Vorhandenen*] into an independent object, the laboring self-consciousness gains the "upper hand" [*Oberhand*] over animal spirits that, killing each other, never escape the cycle of negation. Recalling his figuration of the *Hand* as "the living *Werkmeister* of [man's] fortune" in the critique of palmistry and of other "readings" of the body earlier in the *Phenomenology*, Hegel here reiterates the notion that "action" [*Handlung*], effecting the architectonic division of inner and outer, "produces" the self through its externalization.[17] Its engendered body, understood as a pyramidal sign, will gesture at its own freedom.[18]

Indeed the *Werkmeister* shapes the pyramid and, as its outwardly oriented corollary, the obelisk. Each reflects the "abstract form of the understanding": like "the world of appearance," such crystal forms point to a "supersensible beyond."[19] Because such forms do not themselves bear their own significance, but indicate only an inner or outer "foreign spirit," they are not the work constituting the spiritual self: as symbolic articulations of the aesthetic, they do not attain to the power vested in mimesis. Indeed Hegel will further define the mimetic ideal of art as "free individuality which constitutes the content and form of the representation"—that is, art that has "no other meaning [*Bedeutung*] but the subject [*Subjekt*] who, in his expansion and development of himself, brings before our contemplation only himself as the sovereign master [*Herrscher*] over his entire objectivity. Meaning and sensuous representation, inner and outer, matter and image, are no longer distinguished from one another, and do not appear to be merely related, as in the actual symbolic, but appear rather as a totality."[20]

If this reduction of art to mimesis, especially in Greek sculpture, marks the illusory realization of the "ideal" in a mystified present, the movement of the aesthetic in time

---

[17] Hegel, *Werke* 3: 236–7.
[18] Hegel, *Werke* 3: 233.
[19] Hegel, *Werke* 3: 126.
[20] Hegel, *Werke* 13: 406.

must consist in the endless failure to achieve that ideal. Against the ideal, the encased body, in the pyramidal shape of understanding, has forsaken its living penetration [*Durchdringung*] by actuality: it is merely a corpse. This pyramidal "enveloping husk" [*umgebenden Hülle*] finds its corollary in the "black formless stone" that reduces "the world of appearance" to the more architectonic "enclosure" [*Gehäuse*] or "covering for the inner being" posited by the understanding.[21] In "Understanding" this latter "inner being" becomes the static "inverted-perverted world" to which the dogmatic mind blindly clings; here, too, "inner" becomes "outer" and vice versa, crystallized in the "unmoved" architecture of darkness and stasis.

Against this attempted recuperation of dialectical excess, the subject, in forming architectonic objects, isolates the pure limit of aesthetic delineation and so surfaces the principle of self-canceling individuation that enables sociality. At first "the division" [*Trennung*] between the immediate being of the material it fashions (including the body thereby produced) and the "being-for-self of the 'laboring spirit' [*arbeitende Geist*]" "becomes objective"; accordingly it works to "eliminate this division of soul and body," to endow body with soul in its work.[22] But any such effort remains "instinctive" since the laboring body, still "unconscious" of itself as a self, has not yet attained to self-consciousness.[23] Its action [*Handlung*] is merely the work of the laboring *Hand*. "The *Werkmeister* proper, spirit in its wholeness, has not yet appeared," but remains "on hand [*vorhanden*] only as the division between active self-consciousness and the object it has made."[24]

Reflecting the limited attention paid to the *Werkmeister* in scholarship on Hegel, translators have rendered this term only as "artisan" or "artificer." The failure to connect Hegel's *Knecht* with the *Werkmeister* has resulted in inadequate readings of the mutually inflected sections on "mastery and slavery" and "natural religion."[25] Needless to say, the senses of *Werkmeister* as "artisan" and "artificer" both obtain in the dialectic of master and slave, to the extent that Hegel's laborer evolves from engendering objects for mere consumption—through the cultivation, for instance, of food—to the increasingly aesthetic objects that materialize through the labor of the enslaved self-consciousness in time. Accordingly the Egyptian *Werkmeister* appears in the form of numerous skilled artisans working in servitude [*Knechtschaft*]; Hegel may even have been aware

---

[21]Hegel, *Werke* 3: 509, 511.

[22]The "laboring spirit" here appears as the laboring self-consciousness only "for us"; from the standpoint of this "unconscious" laborer, the architectonic division between self and object that this spirit materializes in the world through its construction "becomes objective": "The division from which the laboring spirit begins, the separation between being-in-itself, which becomes the material it fashions, and *being-for-self*, which is the *aspect* of the laboring self-consciousness, has in its eyes become objective in its work" [*Die Trennung, von welcher der arbeitende Geist ausgeht, des Ansichseins, das zum Stoffe wird, den er verarbeitet, und des* Fürsichseins, *welches die Seite des arbeitenden Selbstbewußtseins ist, ist ihm in seinem Werke gegenständlich geworden*] (Hegel, *Werke* 3: 508).

[23]Hegel, *Werke* 3: 508.

[24]Hegel, *Werke* 3: 509.

[25]I will return to a fuller discussion of the semantic resonances of *Knecht*, and in particular Hegel's relation of *Knecht* to *Sklave*, below.

that numerous slaves of African origin in the New World were master–artisans.[26] As we saw in our first discussion of Hegel's *Hand*, the term *Werkmeister* also means "overseer" or supervisor, evoking a mediating agency between master and worker. Thus in *Onomasticon latino-germanicum*, Theophilus Golias defines *Werkmeister* as *curator operis*; and the Grimm brothers' *Deutsches Wörterbuch* equates the name *Werkmeister* to the "old German name *Parler*," borne by a line of medieval German architects and deriving from *Parlier*, meaning "foreman."[27] By the late eighteenth century the term will be used in the context of both artisanal and factory labor: "in general the *Werkmeister* is the person governing and directing the work in manufactures, factories, and other artisanal workshops."[28] In numerous texts the "overseer" is subject to the orders of both his earthly and divine masters; indeed the term commonly refers to those who engage the ultimate master—God—or do his work on earth.[29] One such text enjoins the reader to "become a work-master and always give up your own will" to "the Lord [*der herr*]"; and repeatedly the latter is said to do his works on earth "through a work-master."[30] Figuring any kind of mediating agency, the term will refer to the Holy Ghost or even the mouth that produces language; anticipating Hegel's use of the term for "organ[s] of performance," Georg Phillip Harsdörffer writes, "the mouth is ... the *Werkmeister* of words."[31]

The *Werkmeister* as artisan, overseer, and the principle of a mediating agency relates the master–slave dialectic to the theories of aesthetics, power, and freedom in Hegel's work. As the "spirit of beauty" or the "symbolizing spirit," the Egyptian *Werkmeister* in its totality drives the unconscious laboring of an enslaved collective. Melding its "Oriental solidity" with its "rough" African capacity to break stone, the Egyptian spirit as *Werkmeister* erects monumental tombs that refer to the instability of their architectonic demarcation of the world of spirit: thus the pyramids, erected by slaves, isolate the principle of dialectical fluidity and thus the limit of the idea of freedom.[32] The slave advances then toward the historical achievement of that idea through the social cohesion of individual wills, a process that requires the mediating agency of the *Werkmeister*. On the one hand, this overseer is invisible, for its fully realized power—the "universal power" [*die allgemeine Macht*] evoked at the end of "Self-Consciousness," inaccessible to master and slave—lies in the wholly socialized, embodied will. On the other hand, the "work-master" in "Natural Religion," unable to appear as this concrete "totality,"

---

[26]See Chapter 7.

[27]Theophilus Golias, *Onomasticon latino-germanicum* (1585), 201; and Jacob and Wilhelm Grimm, "Werkmeister," in *Deutsches Wörterbuch* (Leipzig: S. Hirzel, 1962–70). On *Parlier* see Gordon Campbell, *The Grove Encyclopedia of Northern Renaissance Art* (New York: Oxford University Press, 2009), 3: 31.

[28]Thus Grimm: "überhaupt versteht man unter dem namen eines werkmeisters sowohl in den manufakturen und fabriken, als auch bey andern handwerkern diejenige person, die das ganze der arbeiten regieret und anordnet ... (1781)" ("Werkmeister," in *Deutsches Wörterbuch*).

[29]Ibid.

[30]Ibid.

[31]Cited in "Werkmeister," in *Deutsches Wörterbuch*; Hegel, *Werke* 3: 235–7.

[32]Hegel, *Werke* 12: 271, 255 and 13: 459.

will attempt and fail fully to materialize in the form of the slave's laboring body, which engages in the aesthetic activity of "producing itself as object without having yet grasped the thought of itself."[33] Following rules "instinctively," the "work-master" also attempts to manifest itself in fragmented form as the laboring "hand," the "living *Werkmeister*," even as it circulates through the social body, materializing in and spilling across any particular form of corporeality to drive the work of a multitude.

Neither fully master nor slave, the *Werkmeister* thus represents agency that, in its appearance, cannot be reduced solely or purely to disembodiment abstracted from subjectivity, stable embodiment in an individual, or collective embodiment in sociality. For this reason, the "pure" master does not and will not appear in enduring corporeal form historically; rather he manifests through the mediated forms of collective, and yet endlessly fractured subjectivity—a multitude of fitful, partial, and unequal overseers wielding ultimately precarious power over each other. In its historical appearance, the *Werkmeister* is the middle term, as it were, between mastery and servitude that, like an "infection" [*Ansteckung*], penetrates all bodies but finds no permanent shape on earth. Materializing and multiplying across Egypt as the work-masters that drive their underlings, underlings that rise to become work-masters—the historical *Werkmeister* eschews fixed dwelling in any corporeity.

To understand how Hegel's "overseer" relates to the problem of agency and power in the world-historical context of slavery, consider the moment represented in Figure 9, which juxtaposes two stills of a scene from the first televised version of Alex Haley's *Roots*.[34] This mini-series relates the life and travails of Kunta Kinte, an African captured and sold into slavery in the United States. In the first still, the white overseer has the bound Kunta Kinte whipped for refusing to take the name "Toby" given to him by a master absent from the scene. In the second still, another slave of African descent whips Kunta at the bidding of the overseer, momentarily cut from the frame; the violence continues until Kunta, defiant almost to the point of death, relents.

Several elements relevant to our analysis of the overseer's mediation of the master-slave dialectic emerge here. To begin with, in this scene the master represented by the overseer does not require production or work, but rather only the slave's acquiescence to his master's will.[35] So, too, in Hegel's "Self-Consciousness," the "abstract" master—prior to his historical appearance in "Natural Religion"—requires only the coherence of wills

---

[33]Hegel, *Werke* 3: 508.

[34]*Roots* [miniseries], dir. Chomsky, Erman, Moses, et al., USA: Wolper Productions, 1977. It is with deep regret that I refer to or use images of tortured black bodies, given the continued interpellation of the African as slave through precisely such gestures. Hegel invokes slavery as the "connection" of the European to the African to expose the institution's irrationality; my hope, in a similar vein, is to identify in this scene in *Roots* points of resistance to the dialectic of race and slavery.

[35]Fanon, at least at first glance, misreads this dimension of the recognition sought by the master: "We hope we have shown that the master here is basically different from the one described by Hegel. For Hegel there is reciprocity; here the master scorns the consciousness of the slave. What he wants from the slave is not recognition but work" (Frantz Fanon, *Black Skin, White Masks*, transl. R. Philcox [New York: Grove Press, 2008], 195). I engage the relation of Hegel and Fanon in my "The Franco-Haitian Revolution: Hegel, Fanon, and the Problem of Recognition," forthcoming.

or symmetry of "double action." For Hegel's master, the desire for or "hate" of otherness remains indifferent to its particularity. The specificity of the consumed object and of the intersubjective act that delivers it up to the master is of no consequence to him: what sustains mastery is that, through their will and action, *Herr* and *Knecht* reduce the latter to a thing, "a will with no will of its own."[36] There is, in the master's fantasy, no need for linguistic mediation, overseers, or continuing violence. By contrast, in its necessarily historical materialization—in this scene and in "Natural Religion"—the dialectic requires the mediation of an overseer or *Werkmeister*; by extension, the exigency that the slave surrenders his will depends upon a violently enforced linguistic "demand." The discursive nature of this mediation cannot be suppressed: the master asks, and the slave must answer, affirmatively consenting to be the master's thing. The increasingly perverted attempt at "recognition" in this context requires that the slave strip himself of self-possession, abandoning his name as a marker of his individuation and of the social "meaning" of his body.[37]

"What's your name?" asks the overseer. Kunta Kinte answers with defiance: "Kunta. Kunta Kinte." The docile slave holding the whip knows the overseer's will; again he flays the bound slave. His defiance at this point articulates what the master and his overseer know: that Kunta Kinte is free; that he can choose to die for his name; that the master, in the violence of his demand, has already acknowledged the slave's entirely human capacity to submit or refuse. Most of the others look on passively, a few feelingly: "They goin' to whip him dead," says one, almost a caricature of the quiescent slave. Against their passivity, the still defiant Kunta Kinte demonstrates here that the choice to refuse or bend is fully his. It is in this respect that the concept and experience of slavery surface the freedom of the will. Thus in the *Philosophy of Right*:

> As a living thing, a human being may be subjugated [*bezwungen*]—that is, his physical and otherwise external side may be brought violently under the power of others; but the free will cannot be coerced [*gezwungen*], except insofar as it fails to withdraw from the externality to which it is fixed or from its representation of externality. Only the will that allows itself to be coerced can be coerced.[38]

---

[36]Hegel, *Werke* 7: §26: 76–7.

[37]Ironically, the 1977 version of *Roots* downplays Kunta Kinte's Muslim identity, also reducing his home city of Jufureh, a busy commercial trading post in West Africa, to a remote village. Since the series was watched by a significant majority of the viewing American public, the mini-series served to obfuscate certain "roots" of Afro-American culture for a wide audience, entrenching stereotypes about the "primitive" nature of pre-colonial African political economy and society and combating what white Americans in the age of Malcolm X, like white slavers from the early days of American slavery, perceived was a dangerous connection between Africans and Islam in the New World. The 2016 remake of *Roots* acknowledges Kunta Kinte's religion and portrays Jufureh in a manner more faithful to history; the series was watched by only a small fraction of the viewing public. If we are to address the subjectivity and agency of enslaved Africans in the Americas, much more work needs to be done on the connection of those subjects with the linguistic, cultural, artistic, economic, political, religious, social, and other dimensions of their African "roots." On African Muslim slaves in the Americas, see, *inter alia*, Sylviane Diouf, *Servants of Allah: African Muslims Enslaved in the Americas* (New York: New York University Press, 1998).

[38]Hegel, *Werke* 7: §91: 178–9.

Our mortality—or more exactly our capacity to take our own life—underwrites our freedom from coercion even in the face of violence.[39] Are we then to fault Kunta Kinte's ultimate acquiescence at the point of death? Hegel has indeed been taken to task for blaming slaves for accepting their condition over death.[40] But Hegel's purpose remains strictly philosophical: it is logically to identify "wrong" with respect to the intrinsic freedom of the will. Accordingly in the *Philosophy of Right* he associates the institution of slavery with the "will" of both slaves and their masters: "that a man is a slave lies in his own will, just as it lies with the will of a people if that people is subjugated"; thus "wrong is done" both by "those who enslave and subjugate" and "the enslaved and the subjugated themselves."[41]

Hegel's argument—an extension of the idea of the "freedom" of will as "right"— must be understood in the context of the congruence of individual and social agency in freedom.[42] Thus in an 1824 note to the *Philosophy of Right*:

> It is said that a people is coerced; that is, that it allows itself to be coerced ... When a people is taken into slavery, it has itself willed this; it wanted to retain life even in slavery; this was its own will. But those who are subjugated are not coerced; they cannot be brought to the point of doing anything against their will ... [T]he inhabitants of Numantia ... did not allow themselves to be coerced; they gave up everything, even their own lives.[43]

Darkly noting that the resistance to slavery can result in mass death, Hegel identifies the indomitability of the will as individual and social substance that underwrites an enslaved people's innate capacity and right to revolt. Thus in the "Critique of the Constitution of Germany" [*Kritik der Verfassung Deutschlands*], Hegel—evoking Titus Livius and Machiavelli—writes that enslavement and subjugation of peoples justify violent resistance in the "righteous cause" of freedom: "Here is perfect justice,

---

[39]"In the fight for recognition, the absolute proof of freedom is death" (Hegel, *The Philosophy of Subjective Spirit*, 3: 59). See also Hegel, *Vorlesungen über Rechtsphilosophie 1818–1831*, ed. Karl-Heinz Ilting (Stuttgart: Frommann Verlag, 1974), 4 vols., 4: §42: 112 and 4: §91: 272.

[40]Susan Buck-Morss, for instance, accuses Hegel of "blaming" the victim ("Hegel and Haiti," 859).

[41]Hegel, *Werke* 7: §57A: 126. H. B. Nisbet's misleading insertion of the words "responsibility" and "fault" in his translation adds an emotionally charged framework of judgment (*Hegel's Elements of the Philosophy of Right*, ed. Allen Wood, transl. H. B. Nisbet [Cambridge: Cambridge University Press, 1991], 88). Hegel's rationale stems from the dialectic, not from some extrinsic feeling motivated by racial animus: he argues that if human beings are free and if "right" equates to the rationality of "freedom," then it follows that "wrong" follows from the contradiction internal to the willful surrender of the will to another.

[42]Hegel, *Werke* 7: §7: 54ff., §21: 71ff., §28: 79.

[43]Hegel, *Vorlesungen über Rechtsphilosophie 1818–1831*, ed. Karl-Heinz Ilting (Stuttgart: Frommann Verlag, 1974), 4: § 91: 272. The Iberian people of Numantia, a city in northern Spain, resisted a Roman invasion around 133 or 134 BC. After a long siege, all but a few of the inhabitants committed suicide rather than submit to certain slavery. Hegel confusingly refers to this siege as occurring "in our own time." He likely learned of the siege from Miguel de Cervantes' play *El Cerco de Numantia*.

for that war is just where necessary, and those arms sacred where there is no hope but through arms."[44]

That power of resistance lies *in potentia* in the will of the *Werkmeister*. White planters delegate the management of slaves to an overseer; so too the overseer delegates the punishment of a disobedient captive to other slaves who subdue, bind, and whip him. Because power leverages and consolidates itself through multiple layers of delegation, each composed of replaceable proxies, the beneficiaries of power at the highest level are furthest removed from the most brutal and abusive modes through which their power exerts itself. Outnumbered by dozens of enslaved human beings, the white overseer nonetheless arms a slave with a whip to use on Kunta Kinte. If the absence or withdrawal of the overseer from the second image in Figure 9 marks figuratively the mediation of power by assignees or agents, so too increasing delegation—including through access to the means of violence—discloses the instability of power as it relies on the agency of growing numbers of the apparently powerless. For this reason extreme inequities of power often enable the disintegrating violence that threatens to reverse them.

Kunta Kinte relents: "Toby." The overseer makes him repeat it: "Say it again! Say it louder so they all can hear you." An enslaved woman looks down: the coercion of Kunta means the coercion of all. "My name is Toby." The overseer will not acknowledge even this name, articulating the entire dogma of racialism in a single slur: "Ay," he says deliberately, a glint of Nero in his eyes: "That's a good nigger."[45] Untethered, Kunta falls to the ground, reduced to what Hegel calls the mere "gravity" of bodily matter.[46] The discursive battle over names, translated to and from physical violence, points up the social dimension of the entanglement of the historical slave's linguistic and physical agency. For the fight here is not only between the overseer and Kunta as individuals: the entire spectacle

---

[44]Hegel, *Werke* 1: 554. Hegel alludes presumably to Titus Livius' *Ab Urbe Condita: iustum enim est bellum quibus necessarium, et pia arma ubi nulla nisi in armis spes est* (IX, 1). Machiavelli cites these lines from Titus Livius in chapter 24 of *Discourses on Livy*. Hegel has been accused of advocating slavish quietism as a result of the movement in the *Phenomenology* from slavery to stoicism (instead of to the violent overthrow of the master and to the end of human bondage through revolution; see, indicatively, Herbert Uerlings, "Anerkennung und Interkulturalität: Überlegungen mit Blick auf 'Haiti' bei Hegel und Alexander Kluge," in *Zeitschrift für interkulturelle Germanistik*, 2017, 8: 93–4). As I demonstrate in the last two chapters of this book, Hegel in fact insists explicitly on the right of slaves to revolt. He does, however, add that such revolts cannot yield any advance toward freedom in the absence of a maturation of spirit. Pre-historical violence only perpetuates the state of nature; and historical violence, in the absence of any progression in self-consciousness, ends only in the replacement of old with new masters or slaves or both. But the burgeoning of self-consciousness of freedom, whether expressed in violence or not, propels history toward less alienated modes of servitude. In the *Encyclopedia* and in Hegel's lectures, the institutions of *Knechtschaft* evolve from chattel slavery to wage labor. And the violent revolution against the master that does finally occur in the *Phenomenology* in the section entitled "Absolute Freedom and Terror," while failing to end the dialectic of power and succumbing to counter-revolution and restoration, drives spirit to a more advanced, "moral" orientation.

[45]The slur, meant to resonate with an American audience of the 1970s, is of course anachronistic.

[46]Hegel, *Werke* 7: §7: 55.

symbolically enacts a social rendition of will on the part of an interpellated collective.[47] The social theater here surfaces the "meaning" of slavery for spirit: as the embodied will that abjures itself to another, the subjugated slave instantiates the propensity of the will to freedom from particularity (even the specificity of his own name) and, accordingly, to potential convergence with other wills in sociality.

For Hegel this universalizing dimension of the will accompanies dialectically, however, its contrary, particularizing mode. On the one hand the will, in its first, universal "moment," is "the element of pure indeterminacy or of the pure reflection of the 'I' into itself, in which is dissolved every limitation, every determinate content, whether the content is immediately present through nature, need, desire, or drive, or whether it is given, regardless of how."[48] On the other hand, the will in its second, particularizing moment is "the positing of a determinacy as content and object," an existence in corporeality and all that materially accrues to it. Here the will apprehends the negativity of its first, indeterminate mode: Hegel calls this negativity the will's necessary "limitation" [Beschränkung] of itself, "whether as a given external limit [äußere Schranke] or as an activity of the 'I' itself."[49] In its "concrete freedom," says Hegel, the will is the "unity" of these two moments: the truly free will, "in its limitation" in the otherness of determinacy or corporeality, nonetheless "remains within itself and does not cease to hold fast to the universal."[50] The positing of the "I" as "the self-referentiality of the negative" or self-canceling architectonic limit—whether "external" to the "I" or as its "activity"—recalls the "formative activity" of the subject in its first step from slavery toward freedom in the *Phenomenology*.[51] Indeed the slave who says, "I am free: my name is Kunta Kinte" performs verbally and physically, in the defiant willingness to be flogged, simply a more advanced form of *Bilden* modeled by the *Knecht* in its first steps toward freedom. So, too, universality at home with particularity accrues meaning, exerting "force" and thus collective power.

The overseer represents the demand both of his master and of a racially organized collective. But the overseer does not (and indeed cannot) represent that will perfectly: its iteration always harnesses the performative power of a mediating agency. Kunta's equally performative expression of agency, his demonstration of innate self-possession, refers to the latent concrete freedom of all and hence the perversion of that universal freedom in the merely coerced and one-sided recognition sought by the master and

---

[47]The term "interpellation" here refers to the performative articulation and disarticulation of subjectivity that attend all moments of attempted recognition. Far more work is required on the nature and possibility of recognitive agency given the crystallized power of interpellations engendering powerful collectives. On the Lacanian-Althusserian theory of interpellation in relation to performativity and recognition, see Judith Butler, "Gender Is Burning: Questions of Appropriation and Subversion," in *Bodies That Matter: On the Discursive Limits of Sex* (New York: Routledge, 1993), 121–40.

[48]Hegel, *Werke* 7: §5: 49.

[49]Hegel, *Werke* 7: §6: 53. In a lecture from 1822–1823, Hegel adds: "The will, in order to be a will, must in some way limit itself. The fact that the will wills something is the limit or negation. Thus particularization is what as a rule is called finitude" (Hegel, *Vorlesungen über Rechtsphilosophie 1818–1831*, ed. Karl-Heinz Ilting [Stuttgart: Frommann Verlag, 1974], 3: §6: 116–7).

[50]Hegel, *Werke* 7: §7A: 57.

[51]Hegel, *Werke* 7: §7: 54.

his delegate in this scene. The bored tranquility with which the overseer carries out the master's violence; the discursive skill with which he degrades Kunta to "Toby," then to "nigger," then to a dropped thing; then the flash of pleasure in cruelty—all point to this *Verkehrung*, this topsy-turvy articulation and perversity of the master's purportedly "free" will. The master's increasing propensity to strip the enslaved human being of any marking of selfhood—including his books, culture, religion, home, spouse, children, family, agency, and even name—results from what Memmi will precisely call the Nero complex at the heart of the historical master–slave or colonizer-colonized dialectic: the master threatens to destroy the African subjectivity (the slavish but nonetheless stubborn "self-will") on which the master entirely depends and in which, paradoxically, he also identifies his illegitimacy.[52]

A nod from the overseer and the slave with the whip—a second overseer—flogs another slave. Uncoupled from the body that wields the means to violence, power exercises an agency eschewing any particular subjectivity. For this reason Hegel, fully aware of the effect of extrinsic European power on, for instance, divided tribes, will nonetheless condemn Africans for selling themselves into slavery. Deliberately registering history with the same callousness with which it unfolds, Hegel's critique points to a collective agency that underwrites the market for dark-skinned African slaves. Now, intersubjectivity binds not only a family or a people [*Volk*], but also, by extension, the white-skinned collective that clings to racialist dogma and the right to enslave Africans. Jean Rhys describes this impulse upon the abolition of slavery in the British Caribbean in the opening of *Wide Sargasso Sea*: "They say when trouble comes close ranks, and so the white people did."[53] The implication of Hegel's argument, of course, is that this still partial and exclusivist intersubjectivity necessarily and dialectically interpellates dark-skinned Africans as an opposed collectivity.[54] The un-freedom of Africa has nothing to do with any innate aspect

---

[52]Albert Memmi, *The Colonizer and the Colonized* (Boston: Beacon Press, 1991), 53ff.

[53]Jean Rhys, *Wide Sargasso Sea*, ed. Judith Raiskin (New York: W. W. Norton & Co., 1999), 9. On the persistence and "passive power" of "whiteness" as a mode of subjectivity in the United States, see Ta-Nehisi Coates's "The First White President," in *The Atlantic*, December 2017. The relation of misrecognition and the interpellation of a partial collective to be dominated explains why, as Coates observes, the "passive" agency of the concept of whiteness attends "popular disbelief" in that "power." Given the architectonic dynamism of any concept, the forceful rearticulation over time of "whiteness"—or any exclusivist collective exerting mastery over its other—moreover underwrites, where necessary, the expansions of the limits of the collective to protect its power. The lure and endurance of "whiteness" stem from its performative demarcation of a powerful collective. (In Rhys' novel, the term "creole" is often used to denote a lesser form of "whiteness"; thus Antoinette, the novel's "creole" protagonist—climbing the racial hierarchy—rejects Sandi Cosway, her light-skinned but still "mixed-race" Caribbean lover, and follows her unloving, white husband to England.) This interplay of dynamism and force in the architectonic explains why, according to Coates, conceptions of whiteness in the United States continually shift—broadening to include, for instance, the Irish, Italians, and Hispanic "whites."

[54]So profound is this interpellation that, so long as the slave trade persists even amongst some European powers, Africans must either capture or be captured by other dark-skinned bodies and sold to European slavers. Thus some Africans will even resist abolitionist powers, like the English after 1807, that "fight against slavery" (Hegel, *Werke* 12: 128). Hegel of course makes this point in a manner that does not obfuscate the self-interested agency driving English "abolition" of the slave trade—namely, fear of introducing Africans into the considerable and presumably more docile populations born into bondage in the English Caribbean; competition against economies dependent on the importation of slaves; and the war against France. C. L. R. James makes the case for this view of British abolition of the slave trade in *Black Jacobins* (New York: Vintage, 1989), 51.

of the African subject. Indeed slavery—the alienation of one's materiality to a master—has existed in Europe as much as in Africa; Hegel even compares slavery to "serfdom" [*Leibeigenschaft*] and "modern-day labor," institutions he considers in some respects harsher than ancient slavery.[55] These various forms of servitude differ in the degree to which the subject's materiality and activity are alienated to another and, above all, in the existence of a state—a mode of concrete sociality that will underwrite the *Bildung* of the subject and socialize citizens to the freedom of the will.[56] As we will see, the enslavement of Africans marks the absence in Africa of a state, just as the absence of a state makes ongoing subjugation and coercion more likely.[57] Nowhere does Hegel say that Africans enslave each other (or collectively participate in their own enslavement) because of their pigmentation or any other feature related to their "natural immediacy"; they do so because, violently interpellated through overwhelming power, they succumb to coercion.

How then could concrete freedom, in the face of masterly perversion, materialize on earth? How do we reconcile Hegel's insistence on the right violently to overthrow the master with the apparently non-violent and aesthetic act of *Bilden* through which the slave-subject matures? To address these questions, we will have to interrogate further the historical articulation of Hegel's *Knecht* in the *Phenomenology*, assessing how its phenomenal specificity as the laboring body alienated to another inflects the "abstract" conception of the subject as slave. At issue for scholars are both the nature of servitude in Hegel's dialectic and its historical context: Is the *Knecht* an enslaved human being reduced to mere property or chattel and thus traded like a commodity? If so, does the term refer to ancient slavery in Egypt or to the contemporary enslavement of Africans? Does *Knecht* refer to a servant tied to the land, like a feudal serf? Or does the term refer to a mercenary in service to a sovereign, like a knight?[58] Can it refer to any servant, including a wage laborer? A number of Hegelians either oppose or find inconsequential such historicizing efforts, including recent attempts to link Hegel's *Knecht* to African slaves in the New World.[59] Admittedly, these historicizations erroneously reduce the conceptual *Knecht* in "Self-Consciousness" to a particular historical figure, ignoring Hegel's insistence that dialectical concepts considered "from the standpoint of consciousness" do not necessarily correspond to a singular, "isolated" form in the history of spirit.[60] Indeed, literal specifications of the terms *Knecht* and *Knechtschaft*

---

[55]Thus Hegel remarks that "we find slavery even in the Greek and Roman States, as we do serfdom down to the latest times" (Hegel, *Werke* 12: 130). See also the *Philosophy of Right*: "The distinction here explained is that between a slave and the present servant or a day laborer. The Athenian slave had perhaps easier occupations and more intellectual work than with our servants today, but [the former] was nevertheless a slave because the whole extent of his activity was alienated or conveyed to his master" (Hegel, *Werke* 7: §67A: 145).

[56]Hegel, *Werke* 12: 129.

[57]For a discussion of and useful bibliography on the impact of the slave trade on political economy and state formation in West Africa, see Nonso Obikili, "The Impact of the Slave Trade on Literacy in West Africa: Evidence from the Colonial Era," *Journal of African Economies*, 2016, 25:1: 1–27.

[58]English "knight" is a cognate of German "*Knecht*."

[59]For a recent example, see Uerlings, "Anerkennung und Interkulturalität." I will address his objections at length below.

[60]Hegel, *Werke* 3: 325.

remain controversial even for those interested in the historical valences of Hegel's text, and no less so since the revelation of evidence that Hegel almost certainly followed the revolt of enslaved Africans in Haiti in the period leading up to his conception of the master–slave dialectic.[61]

The question of the *Knecht*'s specificity remains unsettled in part because partisans of various interpretations have failed to convince Hegel scholars as to how a proposed historical gloss illuminates the text of the *Phenomenology* and its relation to Hegel's political theory.[62] Even so, the historicizing impetus accords with the movement in Hegel's text from the discursive to the material articulation of the dialectic. Indeed, to ignore the phenomenal form of the *Knecht* is not only to misread Hegel's explicit insistence on the movement of the emergent subject from its abstract or conceptual form in "Self-Consciousness" to its concrete form as *Werkmeister* in "Natural Religion," but also to misunderstand Hegel's entire "phenomenology": for the latter aims precisely to analyze and follow the relation between abstraction and phenomenality in the concept, or—in its historical manifestation—between the slave's dialectical positing of the idea of freedom and its concrete realization.

As we have seen, in the *Phenomenology* Hegel explicitly conceives of the *Knecht* as "thinghood" [*Dingheit*], spirit initially too attached to life, too identified with the individualizing form of its corporeality to know that it can sublate and so reach through its vital form toward freedom. The *Philosophy of Right* explicitly identifies the reduction of the body to thinghood as the condition of slavery and, furthermore, the notional *Knecht* of the *Phenomenology* as a slave:

Die behauptete Berechtigung der *Sklaverei* (in allen ihren näheren Begründungen durch die physische Gewalt, Kriegsgefangenschaft, Rettung und Erhaltung des Lebens, Ernährung, Erziehung, Wohltaten, eigene Einwilligung usf.) sowie die Berechtigung einer *Herrschaft* als bloßer Herrenschaft überhaupt und alle *historische* Ansicht über das Recht der Sklaverei und der Herrenschaft beruht auf dem Standpunkt, den Menschen als *Naturwesen* überhaupt nach *einer Existenz* (wozu auch die Willkür gehört) zu nehmen, die seinem Begriffe nicht angemessen ist … Der Standpunkt des freien Willens, womit das Recht und die Rechtswissenschaft ist über den unwahren Standpunkt, auf welchem der Mensch als Naturwesen und nur als an sich seiender Begriff, der Sklaverei daher fähig ist, schon hinaus. Diese frühere unwahre Erscheinung betrifft den Geist, welcher nur erst auf dem Standpunkte seines Bewußtseins ist; die Dialektik des Begriffs und des nur erst unmittelbaren Bewußtseins der Freiheit bewirkt daselbst den *Kampf des Anerkennens* und das Verhältnis der

---

[61]On this dispute see, *inter alia*, Malcolm Bull "Slavery and the Multiple Self," *New Left Review*, 231 1 (1998), 103; Susan Buck-Morss, "Hegel and Haiti," 843; Nick Nesbitt, *Universal Emancipation*, 120–2; Alain David, *Racisme et antisémitisme: Essai de philosophie sur l'envers des concepts* (Paris: Ellipses, 2001), 294; and Tina Chanter, "Antigone's Liminality: Hegel's Racial Purification of Tragedy and the Naturalization of Slavery," in *Hegel's Philosophy and Feminist Thought*, 82–3.

[62]Susan Buck-Morss, Deborah Jenson, and Nick Nesbitt have made important strides in this direction.

Herrenschaft und der *Knechtschaft* (s. *Phänomenologie des Geistes*, S. 115ff. und *Enzyklop. der philos. Wissensch.* § 325ff.).[63]

---

[63]Hegel, *Werke* 7: §57A: 123–5. Nick Nesbitt deserves considerable credit for pointing out Hegel's concern with *Sklaverei* in the *Philosophy of Right*: "strangely, no commentators seem to have noticed that the *Philosophy of Right* no longer speaks of *Knechten* and *Knechtschaft*" but rather of "*Sklaverei*" (*Universal Emancipation* 120). Nesbitt further claims that Hegel, "in a moment of auto-critique," rejects the "abstraction" of the merely "subjective content" of the dialectic of *Herr* and *Knecht* in the *Phenomenology of Spirit* and takes the "enormous step" in the *Philosophy of Right* of "defend[ing] the idea of an autonomous revolution against slavery" (ibid., 122). Thus Nesbitt reads Hegel's immediately ensuing comment on §57 that "freedom is truly present only as the state" (a statement I will address at length in Chapter 10) as an all but explicit endorsement of the Haitian slave revolt and "state." Finally, he argues that Hegel here "refuses" "to give an ontological or logical answer to the problem of servitude"; "instead," for Nesbitt, Hegel's comment in §57 "offers a properly ethical exhortation to its reader" (ibid., 124). Nesbitt's instincts are correct in relating the *Philosophy of Right* to the Haitian revolution, but he misses key elements of the philosophical argumentation here. To unearth the latter, we will have to quibble over certain aspects of Nesbitt's reading: First, he does not account for the systematic relation of the *Phenomenology of Spirit* and the *Philosophy of Right*; like so many scholars, he therefore underestimates the centrality of slavery to both texts and, indeed, to the logic of Hegel's entire project. According to the scheme of the *Encyclopedia*, the problem of slavery haunts the dialectic of "Subjective Spirit" and "Objective Spirit" since, logically, the fusion of subjectivity and objectivity marks the condition of both slavery (where self-consciousness is known only from the "standpoint of consciousness") and freedom (where, after the struggle for "right," spirit attains to self-consciousness in and for itself): slavery and freedom represent, respectively, the incipit and telos of history. For this reason Hegel points to the intermediate stages of *Knechtschaft* in the history of freedom. The *Phenomenology of Spirit*, viewed retrospectively from the perspective of the *Encyclopedia*, describes the dialectic of the "phenomenology of spirit" as the mediating term of "Subjective Spirit," while the *Philosophy of Right* corresponds to the dialectic of "Objective Spirit." In Hegel's system, slavery materializes historically from the standpoint of both "Subjective Spirit" (through the aesthetic realization of "Religion" described in the *Phenomenology*, e.g., as laboring Egyptians) and "Objective Spirit" (through the historical articulation of "Abstract Right" and "Ethicality" over the course of "world-history," e.g. as the children "owned" by Roman parents). Second, Nesbitt's idea of freedom does not at all accord with Hegel's. Thus the former writes: "whether one is free is determined only by whether one's mind and body (as a complex, composite whole) are constrained or instead express themselves freely." Hegel's conception of freedom— and therefore of *Sklaverei*—is quite different. Third, Nesbitt is mistaken in claiming that Hegel, in §57 of the *Philosophy of Right*, "auto-critiques" the *Phenomenology of Spirit* for presenting the movement from *Knechtschaft* to freedom "as an abstraction" and "merely in its subjective content." Hegel is not referring to the "content" of the *Phenomenology*, or indeed to any "subjective content" at all: in §57 Hegel actually writes, "that the objective spirit, the content of right, should no longer be apprehended merely in its subjective *concept* [*in seinem subjektiven Begriffe*] ... is an insight which emerges only when we recognize that the idea of freedom is present truly only as the state." The *Knecht* of the *Phenomenology* marks the "subjective" side of the attempt of consciousness to know itself as a self, just as the slave of "abstract right" marks the "objective" side of the "person" reduced to "property." Concrete freedom only materializes when the entire dialectical movement from the incipit of recognitive self-consciousness in slavery to the realization of concrete freedom in the state has been completed—which is when spirit attains to self-consciousness, unifying the particular and collective will. The apprehension that human beings should not be "determined" as slaves is no longer an "ought" for "objective spirit" as it proceeds through the dialectic of right toward the telos of freedom in the "state." Fourth, Nesbitt does not consider the importance of "recognition" in the signification of violence, including in slave revolts (see my discussion below of Hegel's supplementary note on §57 relating to Caribbean revolts, which escapes Nesbitt's attention) and especially in the materialization of the recognition on which the state depends. The relation of recognition, violence, and the state will be a major preoccupation of the remainder of this book. Fifth, it must be noted that Hegel, the philosopher of the dialectic, would never consciously or programmatically "refuse" "to give a logical answer" and resort instead to mere "exhortation" (see his excoriation of Fries and justification of the "architectonic" of "rationality" in the preface to the *Philosophy of Right*). None of which diminishes the quality and impact of Nesbitt's scholarship; indeed many of his errors are common across Hegel scholarship. My point is that an accounting of the meaning and place of "slavery" in Hegel's system requires a comprehensive examination of his related theories of recognition, freedom, agency, and the state, along with their dialectical mediation.

The alleged justification of *slavery* [*der Sklaverei*] (through rationalizations related to physical force, capture in war, the saving and preserving of life, nutrition, education, benevolence, the slave's own consent, and so forth), as well as the justification of domination [*Herrschaft*] as merely a form of mastery [*Herrenschaft*] in general, and all historical views concerning the right [*Recht*] to slavery and lordship [*der Sklaverei und der Herrenschaft*] depend on regarding the human being as a purely natural entity, as an existent (to which willfulness also belongs) not in conformity with its concept … The standpoint of the free will, with which right and the science of right begin, has already progressed beyond the untrue standpoint from which the human being is seen as a natural entity, as only the concept of the *in-itself*, and thus capable of being enslaved. This earlier, false phenomenon befalls spirit at the standpoint of consciousness; the dialectic of the concept and of the purely immediate consciousness of freedom brings about at that point the struggle for recognition and the relationship of mastery and slavery [der *Herrenschaft* und der *Knechtschaft*] (see the *Phenomenology of Spirit* §178ff. and the *Encyclopedia of the Philosophical Sciences* §325ff.).

Conceptually, a slave is a human being viewed as an immediate object or thing (an "in-itself") in the form of an individualized body, his "natural" immediacy subject to the "willfullness" of others. Refusing death, the slave relinquishes his "will" to a master. Appearing at the moment when spirit has not progressed beyond the "standpoint of consciousness," the view of the human being as a "thing" incites the struggle for recognition and the relation of *Herrschaft* and *Knechtschaft*. Hegel could not be clearer: the abstract *Knecht* corresponds to the phenomenal slave: for this reason, the *Knecht* in the "Self-Consciousness" section of the *Phenomenology*, foreshadowing the appearance of the laboring *Werkmeister*, is a "fettered" [*geknüpft*] "thing" in "chains" [*Kette*].[64] In Hegel's system, the *Knecht* materializes phenomenally in various permutations along the "intermediate grades" [*Zwischenstufen*] between the total "thinghood" of slavery and the realization of concrete freedom in the rational state.[65] Thus *Sklaverei* marks the dialectical articulation in history of *Knechtschaft* in its quintessence.[66] Hegel will accordingly speak of African slaves awakening from their spiritual *Knechtschaft* when establishing a free state in Haiti.[67]

---

[64] Hegel argues that the slave, "held" to the "chain" [*Kette*] of an immediate objectivity that is at the same time a mediating being-for-self, is reduced therefore to "thinghood" [*Dingheit*]: "Der Herr bezieht sich *auf den Knecht mittelbar durch das selbständige Sein*; denn eben hieran ist der Knecht gehalten; es ist seine Kette, von der er im Kampfe nicht abstrahieren konnte und darum sich als unselbständig, seine Selbständigkeit in der Dingheit zu haben erwies" (Hegel, *Werke* 3: 150).

[65] Hegel, *Werke* 12: 129.

[66] The translation of *Knecht* as "bondsman"—while conveying several modalities of the German term—does not capture its essential aspect, which is the "thingness" of the self-alienated subject. This latter conception accords with Hegel's definition of the slave as the laborer whose activity is completely alienated to "another" (Hegel, *Werke* 7: §67A:145). "Slave" indeed seems to me to be the most apt translation of *Knecht* since the term, in Hegel's day as in ours, retains both the literal meaning of a subject reduced to thingness and more metaphorical meanings related to various other modes of subjugation and servitude.

[67] Hegel, *Werke* 10: 60. I will analyze Hegel's comments on Haiti at length below.

Hegel moreover explicitly connects *Knechtschaft* to Caribbean slavery in a supplementary note on this section: "Negroes in the West Indies have often revolted; one reads annually and ever more frequently of conspiracies on the islands"—but these Negroes become "victims" of a merely "partial" socialization of self-consciousness to its own freedom—the "condition" prior to the advent of "right."[68] Only the collective refusal of slavery, grounded in the "universal" willingness to risk life, abolishes mastery: "No slave, no master" [*kein Sklave, kein Herr*]; isolated "conspiracies," by contrast, "are proof of a merely partial conviction" that ends only in death.[69] At least these rebellious slaves, Hegel adds, "die free." To summarize his argument: failed Caribbean slave "revolts" and "conspiracies," as only "partial" commitments of a people to risk its life for freedom, lead to the death of all mutineers. What is required is an enslaved people's common recognition of its freedom, hence a collective agency:

No absolute injustice is done to those who remain slaves [*Knechte*], for whoever lacks the courage to risk his life in order to obtain freedom deserves to remain a slave [*Sklave*]; what is more, once a people does not simply think of itself as wanting to be free, but actually possesses the energetic will of freedom, no human power will be able to hold it back in the servitude [*Knechtschaft*] of its merely putting up with being ruled [*Regiert*].[70]

Thus Hegel, who will laud the establishment of Haiti, in the *Philosophy of Right* all but explicitly distinguishes between "partial" Caribbean revolts—occurring repeatedly but easily suppressed—and the collective rebellion of slaves that establish an independent "state."

Driven by an intractable agency that no body or exclusive collective can monopolize, the dialectic of master and slave unfolds historically through endless inversions and perversions of the hierarchy of power. Concrete history lies between slavery and mastery:

---

[68]Hegel, *Werke* 7: §57A: 124–5.

[69]Ibid. Astonishingly, these comments on Caribbean slave revolts, to the best of my knowledge, do not appear or feature in any English translation or scholarly treatment of the *Philosophy of Right*. The decision to elide Hegel's reference to Caribbean slaves, based on its presumedly marginal relation or even irrelevance to his argument, instantiates on its own the extent to which translators and scholars project their own Eurocentricity onto Hegel. In a recent article published in German, Herbert Uerlings, perhaps the only scholar to notice the passage on Caribbean revolts in §57, argues that the text "cannot be reconciled with a positive view of the Haitian revolution": "[S]ince, according to Hegel, blacks cannot evolve into the 'universality' of the concept, the revolution and the state of Haiti must be devalued as 'evidence of a merely partial attitude'" (Uerlings, "Anerkennung und Interkulturalität," 97n19, translation mine). Uerlings' reading cannot hold in light of Hegel's arguments—on which I will continue to expound—that Africans all have an equal capacity for rationality and *Bildung*; that slaves have an incontestable right to revolt and free themselves from their masters; and that self-consciousness, in the form of an enslaved people, must be fully socialized to its freedom to emerge successfully from bondage. Unlike the short-lived Caribbean "revolts" and "conspiracies" Hegel mentions here, the Haitian revolution did not lead all slaves to their death and, far from reflecting a "partial attitude," in fact culminated in the establishment of a state. Hegel's remark on failed Caribbean revolts in the context of §57 (along with his further statement that freedom can only be realized in a state) is thus entirely consistent with his later, positive comments on Haiti. This text vindicates the tentative connection made previously by Buck-Morss and others between the *Knecht* in the *Phenomenology* and the Caribbean slave, albeit without foreclosing other instances of *Knechtschaft* and *Sklaverei*. Based on my reading, the text also lends support to Nesbitt's intuitive relation of §57 of the *Philosophy of Right* to the Haitian revolution.

[70]Hegel, *The Philosophy of Subjective Spirit*, 3: 69, translation modified.

for the most subjugated slave exercises some degree of power, and extrinsic forces impinge upon the most potent master. The *Werkmeister* further fragments the subject as overseer, a site of endless conflict between "unconscious" and conscious forces of mastery and servitude. Born in *Knechtschaft*, the historical subject always retains various forms of servile attachment to corporeality or materiality that impede his contact with freedom. The *Knecht*'s historical journey, beginning in *Sklaverei*, will thus take on other forms of "bondage" to immediacy from serfdom to knighthood, from apprenticeship to wage labor.[71]

This "phenomenology" of *Knechtschaft* underwrites the slave's subjection to and negotiation of the dialectic—the "perversion" [*Vekehr*] and violence of the aesthetic unfolding of history. Thus far we have principally considered *Verkehr* and its cognates to mean the "distortion" or the "wrong turn" of a category, dogma, or law in the dialectic of the object (in *die verkehrte Welt*) or of self-consciousness in the dialectic of the subject.[72] In the latter case, the perverse turns of the dialectic not only compromise the subject's conception of itself as a totality, whether as an integral or autonomous body, personality, or identity, but also inflect the subject's evolution through duplication and recognition, and thus ultimately agency and power. As I have intimated, Hegel's text also reveals the dialectic in history as a biological process: in this respect, the terms *Verkehr, Verkherung*, and their cognates—in both the dialectic of life that precedes the emergence of the subject and in the dialectic of master and slave in the *Phenomenology*—retain their sexual resonances. In "Self-Consciousness" the seminal "fluid medium" [*flüssigen Medium*] or reproductive power of sexual "interchange" [*Verkehrung*] thus propels an endless process of mutation and supersession in the unfolding of life. Life then takes the corporeal form of the subject as slave; and the desiring master, dependent on the slave's body, reveals his "essence" to be the "perversion" of its will in another body.

Hegel explicitly conceives of recognitive *Verkehrung* as a sexual encounter and process in an earlier account of the dialectic of the subject, written in 1805–1806 in Jena while he was involved in a secret affair with Christina Burkhardt. Hegel's text brims with the erotic tension and excitement of a first experience or "relation":

> … already in their first relation [*Verhältnisse*], the two parties in tense excitement will fall apart. They approach one another with uncertainty and bashfulness, yet also with trust, for each knows itself immediately in the other, and the movement is merely the inversion and intercourse [*Verkehrung*] whereby each experiences that the other is likewise in its other. This inside-out inversion [*Umkehrung*] also lies in the fact that each abandons its independence [*Selbständigkeit*]. The stimulus is itself an excitation [*Erregung*]—that is, is the state of not being satisfied [*Befriedigstsein*] in oneself, but rather having one's essence inside another, that

---

[71]I am arguing that the *Knecht* manifests as the *Sklave* at the incipit of an historical, not a chronological progression; as we have seen, for Hegel chronology holds no philosophical interest.

[72]Robert Stern views the chapter on "Consciousness" as the dialectic of the object and the chapter on "Self-Consciousness" as the dialectic of the subject; see Robert Stern, *Hegel and the Phenomenology of Spirit* (London: Routledge, 2002). From the point of view of the encylopedic system of philosophy, the "phenomenology" of object and subject here unfolds from the perspective of "subjective spirit."

is, knows oneself inside the other, is sublated as being-for-self—as different. This sublation of oneself [*eigene Aufheben*] is one's being for another, into which one's immediate being [one's natural immediacy or corporeality] is transformed [*umschlägt*]. Each one's dialectical overcoming of oneself becomes the other's being for other. Thus the other is *for me*; it knows itself in me. It is only being for another; in other words, the other is outside itself.[73]

Building from a lack of satisfaction [*Befriedigstsein*] in oneself and a corresponding "excitation" [*Erregung*] in another, bashfully but trustingly the lovers "approach" as they move into each other. In the grips of "intercourse" [*Verkehrung*], the body is outside itself; one's body is transformed [*umschlägt*] into another's. Each self "knows itself" in that "other," dialectically overcoming itself through an orgasmic exaltation. Hegel calls this knowing or "cognition" [*Erkennen*] of collectivity in otherness "love" that, spirituality satisfied in nature, becomes "objective" for itself in the corporeal immediacy or "thinghood" of the other. Each seeks more satisfaction in the other body: as an "other," each is reduced to immediacy not only for sexual pleasure, but also for mutual service. Soon they seek "family possessions." The "desire" for things realizes itself through "shared labor" that satisfies a more universal desire—desire as such. "Mediated" by the "thing," love thus evolves from the satisfaction in the body of the other and the product of "mutual service" to "shared labor," in which each individual works on an object it will not necessarily consume.[74]

This love does not transcend, however, the difference of the parties' characters: "the love itself is not yet the object," as they cannot yet cognize the universal coherence of wills in materiality. But then sexual union leads to a child, a unity of their characters; this "offspring" requires education, and through the same *Bildung* each member of the family becomes free of inherited determinations. These "free individualities for one another" instantiate "spiritual recognition itself" [*geistige Anerkennen selbst*], but this recognition has not become objective because the family, as a "self-enclosed totality," manifests an "exclusive" [*ausschließend*] sociality. The labor of each results in individual possessions to the exclusion of others, both inside and outside the family. In the absence of social norms and laws in a governed polity, we are still in a "state of nature."[75]

How do we read the continuities and discontinuities between the account of recognition in the state of nature in the Jena lectures and the dialectic of self-consciousness in the *Phenomenology*? The persistence in the latter text of the term *Verkehrung*—the penetration and propagation of living forms and the masterly perversion in and of the slave—preserves as it cancels, as it were, the trace of the sexual encounter and affair in the earlier text. In both versions of the dialectic of recognition, the "other" passes through "thinghood." In the Jena account, sex engenders and assimilates into family life. The *Familie* here is not the

[73]Hegel, *Jenaer Systementwürfe III: Naturphilosophie und Philosophie des Geistes*, ed. Rolf-Peter Horstmann (Hamburg: Felix Meiner Verlag, 1987), 193.
[74]Hegel's marginal note. Hegel, *Jenaer Systementwürfe III: Naturphilosophie und Philosophie des Geistes*, ed. Rolf-Peter Horstmann (Hamburg: Felix Meiner Verlag, 1987), 194 and footnote 3 on the same page.
[75]Ibid., 196.

modern institution sanctified by the state. Indeed, here only desire is "sanctified": since we are still in a state of nature, the family relation consists in (a) "natural," sexual "love" that results in the rearing and education of children; (b) "self-conscious love," meaning the cognition of the self in otherness; and (c) "shared labor and acquisition" of commonly owned goods.[76] By contrast, in the *Phenomenology* sexual reproduction occurs not in the context of the heteronormative family, but under the rubric of the dialectic of life and then of *Herr* and *Knecht*: the "cognizance of reciprocal recognition" in the familial relation of husband and wife will not unfold conceptually until much later in the dialectical progression of "spirit" toward ethical life.[77] What could account for this decoupling of sex and family in the account of recognitive subjectivity in the *Phenomenology*?

Burkhardt becomes pregnant with the lovers' illegitimate child in the middle of 1806, just as Hegel was frenetically writing the *Phenomenology*. Is it possible that Hegel, impregnating a woman with whom he will not live and who bears a child from whom he will be separated for ten years, at some point during the affair sees the illogic of any necessary link between sexual reproduction and family life? This flaw in the Jena account of recognition would have been especially evident to Hegel as he considered accounts of historical slavery: first, of the separation of parents and children by virtue of the slave trade; and second, of white male slavers impregnating enslaved women, often through force, through a process that—far from creating "shared family goods"—produced familial offspring as a possession.[78] Thus in the dialectic of life in the *Phenomenology*, Hegel will preserve the possibility of a sexual encounter between actual masters and slaves, the *Verkehr* or *Geschlechtsverkehr* that engenders "life"; further divorcing sexual reproduction from the rubric of familial life, he will strip away elements promoting recognition in any relationship—namely free consent, "mutual service," and "shared labor."[79]

The "turnings" of life seemingly perpetuate the cycle of *Knechtschaft*: sex engenders life, which must then be wagered for the subject to emerge; his own sexual relations then reiterate the failure of recognition, hence the continued violence of mastery. The notion of "force" is already present in the gendered drama of the Jena lectures, in which the will bifurcates into, first, a male "power [*Macht*] in the positing of and confrontation with an opposite being" and, second, feminine "reason," the "evil" of empty and merely formal freedom that "introduces a negative element" to destroy another being.[80] Hegel's

---

[76]"Desire enters in as such, namely, as rational, sanctified" (Hegel, *Jenaer Systementwürfe III*, 195).

[77]Hegel, *Werke* 3: 335.

[78]In the *Philosophy of Right*, Hegel opposes the treatment of children as possessions (Hegel, *Werke* 7: §40A: 99). In the *Philosophy of History*, he further laments the fact that children are separated from their parents in Africa due to slavery.

[79]Compare the parents' view of children in "Ethical Life": "Die der Eltern gegen ihre Kinder ist eben von dieser Rührung affiziert, das Bewußtsein seiner Wirklichkeit in dem Anderen zu haben und das Fürsichsein in ihm werden zu sehen, ohne es zurückzuerhalten, sondern es bleibt eine fremde, eigene Wirklichkeit" (Hegel, *Werke* 3: 336).

[80]Hegel, *Jenaer Systementwürfe III*, 186, 191. Hegel notes the degradation of the family through sexual reproduction on two additional levels. First, the begetting of children marks the freedom of young lovers from their mother and father; thus Hegel's marginal note: "North American savages kill their parents; we do the same" (Ibid., 194, note 2). Second, for Hegel the education of children renders them to a social polity (see Hegel, *Werke* 3: 331-3).

description here echoes the language he uses in the *Aesthetics* to describe the "feminine" principle of "irony" that challenges and ultimately reveals the perversity of exclusivist male power in ancient Greece. In the Jena lectures the feminine principle exercises "reason" to subvert the (corrupt) male "universal," offering a "cape to the bull that runs into it and, hitting nothing, is struck nonetheless."[81] In the "Self-Consciousness" section of the *Phenomenology*, Hegel elides the gender-differentiated trope even as he preserves and extends the reference to the enslaved body as "thing"—as the object over which the master has physical and specifically sexual power.[82]

Neither Hegel, still a relatively penniless scholar in Jena, nor Burkhardt, Hegel's housekeeper and landlady, fully occupies the position of master or servant. So, too, in both the Jena lectures and the *Phenomenology*, no party to a relationship monopolizes power and no individual attains to pure mastery. Crucially, Hegel frames the recognitive encounter in both the Jena lectures and in the *Phenomenology* in a manner that insists upon the agency and power, however latent or unequal, of both parties to a relationship. Indeed his argument allows for the historical articulation of the dialectic not only through the "lechery" (per the Abbé Grégoire)[83] of white slavers, but also through resistance on the part of enslaved women and their "mixed" offspring.[84] Ultimately and in the most literal sense, the "perversity" of mastery—its sexual dependence on and commerce with otherness—will contaminate the exclusivist socialities, including of race, class, and family, that consolidate and ossify categories of power. Thus miscegeny upends the racial order of slavery; marriages with wealthy merchants dilute noble lineages; and, as Hegel comes to know personally, illegitimate offspring compromise the integrity of the patriarchal family.[85]

Historians have not attended sufficiently to the role of desire and reproduction across racial and social lines and the implication of Africans and their descendants in the collapse of race-based slavery and of the feudal structures of the late eighteenth

---

[81]Hegel, *Jenaer Systementwürfe III*, 193–5.

[82]Tina Chanter argues that the gendered relation has been reduced to a merely "macho" conflict of *Herr* and *Knecht* (see "Antigone's Liminality," 82–3). Her point reflects the problematic relation between linguistic gender and its referent. But as far as Hegel is concerned, there is no logical reason, in the dialectic of self-consciousness, that life reflected into itself would suddenly become exclusively male. In other words, nothing suggests that Hegel's use of the masculine *Herr* and *Knecht* implies a restriction of the historicity of this drama to only men. Hegel may well have preferred the effective gender neutrality and thus polysemy of the new, more paradigmatic terms, applicable to a wide range of power relations.

[83]On the relation between the colonial domination of black bodies, lechery, and rape, see the indispensable, if controversial study by Pascal Blanchard et al. entitled *Sexe Race et Colonies: La domination des corps du XVe siècle à nos jours* (Paris: La Découverte, 2018).

[84]Hegel likely did not know of—but could well have imagined—the modes of resistance described by C. L. R. James, including mothers' use of poison to kill their own children and so save them from the horrors of bondage (James, *Black Jacobins*, 16ff.).

[85]Miscegeny, as we will see, will become a crucial element in the evolution of the free state. On the fear of mulattoes at the French court marrying into the aristocracy, see James, *Black Jacobins*, 40. The same logic of *Verkehrung* erodes the binaries of gender: thus gay, lesbian, and transgender couples adopt children or use surrogate parents and upend gendered roles predicated on heteronormativity.

century.[86] To be sure, for Hegel the sexual "penetration" and reproduction of bodies only instantiate the dialectic of power in the unfolding of history toward a fully mutual "recognitive self-consciousness."[87] Thus Hegel, abandoning much of his Jena framework for recognition, subsumes sex and reproduction into the broader "perversions" of the dialectic of master and slave. In the *Phenomenology*, the *Verkehrung* of bodily autonomy through sex collapses the subject's integrity in the entanglement with another; at the same time the subject registers the lover as an "other" of the self, a perverted double or *Verdopplung* whose inadequate symmetry with its pair will trouble the process of recognition. Ultimately, however, the subject's sexuality, its inherence in the "fluid medium" of other bodies, will evince the broader notion of intersubjective or recognitive agency through which freedom unfolds.

Now, the operative "agency" in the violence of masterly power or slavish resistance traverses the social body, but will not attain to the historical form of freedom except through the shared narrative of a recognitive reconciliation. As I have shown, for Hegel there is no event to which we have access except through its discursive representation. In addition, "what has happened [*Geschehene*]" must be taken to accord with "the *narration* of what has happened [*Geschichtserzählung*]"; exercising performative force through literary form and the displacement of received representations, such discursive representations must therefore be aesthetic.[88] And to register legibly the free agency of an individual or collective subject, an account must retrospectively harmonize intention and action through a universally agreed narrative.

This theory of agency underwrites the relation of violence to the aesthetic act of *Bilden*. Violent revolt can mark a progression in the cause of liberty, but not through the mere overthrow of the master: to advance freedom, the retrospective narration of violence must attain to universal acceptance and recognition *as* an advance of freedom. Only the sign of violence—not unmediated violence by itself—exercises power. Subjects will thus reconcile themselves to narratives of violence only through the aesthetic and performative force of *Bilden*—the architectonic and ultimately poetic delineation of history. The performative power of such narrative acts cannot be underestimated: for, as Hegel argues, the progression of freedom in time must accord to the recognitive and retrospective narrative of that progress.

In this respect the process of "reciprocal recognition" through forgiveness by and between antithetical subjects at the end of the dialectic of "spirit" serves as a model for the "recognitive" reconciliation of master and slave. As with the wrongdoer and the hard-hearted judge, so too historical actors must aim to abandon their "subjectively determined judgment[s]" and "subjective characterization of actions[s]" and embrace the "word of reconciliation" [*Wort der Versöhnung*].[89] From the standpoint of the "self-knowing

---

[86]One of a few exceptions is Davis' *The Problem of Slavery*, which examines the trans-Atlantic resistance to race-based slavery and its impact in the collapse of feudalism. A trans-Atlantic study of the role of miscegeny in this process remains a desideratum.

[87]Hegel, *Werke* 10: §430ff., 219ff.; Hegel, *The Philosophy of Subjective Spirit*, 3: 53ff.

[88]Hegel, *Werke* 12: 83.

[89]See Hegel, *Werke* 3: 492–3.

spirit"—a stage not yet realized—the accomplished and final "word" of reconciliation, consisting in the recognition of self-consciousness as the paradoxical convergence of subject and object, essence and being, and "individuality" and infinitude, would have to eschew any independent and mediating form of the aesthetic. The "reconciling Yes"—"in which the two I's let go of their contrary or opposed existences"—marks the "actuality" of the "I" as a paradoxical "doubleness which therein remains equal to itself and, in its perfect alienation or externalization [*vollkommenen Entäußerung*] and opposite, has the certainty of itself—it is the appearing God [*erscheinende Gott*] manifest in the midst of those who know themselves as pure knowledge."[90] True enough, language must mediate this process; from the standpoint of spirit in the self-conscious actuality of its own freedom, however, this language would immediately actualize the self:

> As [the wrongdoer] intuits his parity [with the other] and verbally articulates it, he confesses it to and expects that the other, who is in fact equal to him, will reciprocate this language and in his own words articulate their equality so that recognitive existence will make its appearance. His confession is not an abasement or humiliation, nor is it a rejection of himself in his relations to the other, for this articulation is not a one-sided process by which he would posit his inequality with the other. Rather it is solely in view of his intuition of his equality with the other that he expresses himself. He does this because *language is the existence of spirit as the immediate self*. He thus expects that the other will contribute his own part [*das Seinige*] to this existence.[91]

As a self-canceling immediacy, this "word" of and for self-conscious spirit disarticulates itself as it marks the emptiness of "pure" knowledge. From this standpoint of self-knowing spirit, no particular event or specifically constructed relation to the past can hold or define self-consciousness: the violence of the non-historical past lies beyond our access; and the brutalities of historical time, subject always to narrative displacement, retain no necessary implication in subjectivity across space and time.[92] Through its self-certainty in universal sociality, spirit can indeed "be master [*Meister*] over every deed and over all actuality and can throw them off and make them into something that never happened [*ungeschehen*]."[93]

What would the verbal *Erscheinung* of God mean, however, from the standpoint of the fractured subject in time? Hegel's language already hints at the lingering aesthetic

---

[90]Hegel, *Werke* 3: 494.

[91]Hegel, *Werke* 3: 489–90. Emphasis mine.

[92]Thus the famine that took millions of lives in Bengal beginning in 1770, largely engineered by imperial agents for profit, has left little mark on British self-consciousness. (On this famine see Amartya Sen, *Poverty and Famines: An Essay on Entitlement and Deprivation* [Oxford: Oxford University Press, 1981], 39; his "Imperial Illusions," in *New Republic*, December 31, 2007; and Nick Robins, *The Corporation that Changed the World: How the East India Company Shaped the Modern Multinational* [New York: Pluto Books, 2010], 93ff.)

[93]Hegel, *Werke* 3: 491.

mediation of this "God," whose figural "appear[ances]" mark the next section of the *Phenomenology*. According to the text here, the paradoxical phenomenalization of infinitude, the concrete irony of the fully socialized "I," manifests that divinity "in the midst of" self-knowing consciousness: at once immanent and contiguous, this *Erscheinung* appears both within and merely "among" those who "know." The conjunction of the human and divine marks their disjunction.[94] Through the paradoxically indwelling adjacency of the reversible and ultimately perverse *Erscheinung* of the "absolute," irony gestures at the endless undoing of its infinite reflexivity.[95]

Already the linguistic mediation of recognition—constituting the "permanent parabasis," as we will see, of any socio-institutional attempt at reconciliation—mars the process of redemption through forgiveness: the latter requires the "clinging" representations of a positive subjectivity precisely where the subject must empty itself out or externalize itself through self-alienation [*Entäußerung*].[96] For this reason recognition cannot be "proved through ... words."[97] Forgiveness, indeed, demands an ironic inversion or perversion—that the "bad" be recognized as "good."[98] But the process of *Verkherung* in time cannot be stabilized. Moreover as linguistic actions, the "words" that repudiate or forgive past evil cannot but injure when they appease or disappoint when they mystify. Indeed expectations for confession and reconciliation in forgiveness can have no final or absolute satisfaction, since true reciprocation remains beyond the grasp of history:

> [F]ollowing the admission of the one who is evil—*it is I*—there is no reciprocation of the same confession. This was not what was meant [*gemeint*] by the judgment [of the hard heart]; on the contrary! The latter is *for-itself* and rejects any community or continuity with the other ... [it] retains in itself its non-communicative being-for-self; and also retains, in the confessor, the same non-communicative being-

---

[94]Echoing Hegel, *Werke* 1: 422.

[95]Instantiating the necessarily ironic dimension of its linguistic medium, "appearance" [*Erscheinung*], it will be recalled, engenders and slips into its opposite through the process of inversion and perversion [*Verkehrung*] (see Chapter 7). Hence the paradoxical identity here of "appearance" [*Erscheinung*] and the "actual I" [*wirkliche Ich*] or "immediate existence."

[96]Hegel, *Werke* 3: 491.

[97]Hegel, *Jenaer Systementwürfe I: Das System der spekulativen Philosophie*, eds. K. Düsing and H. Kimmerle (Hamburg: Felix Meiner, 1986), 308.

[98]Hegel, *Werke* 3: 492. On the "aporia" of forgiveness and redemption, see Jacques Derrida, *Foi et Savoir, suivi de Le Siècle et le Pardon* (Paris: Seuil, 2000); his "On Forgiveness," in *Studies in Practical Philosophy*, 2000, 2:2, 81–102; his "To Forgive: The Unforgivable and the Imprescriptible," in *Questioning God*, ed. J. D. Caputo, M. Scanlon and M. Dolley (Bloomington: Indiana University Press, 2001), 21–51; and Friedrich Nietzsche, "On Redemption," in *Thus Spake Zarathustra*, transl. T. Common and N. Davey (Ware: Wordsworth Editions), 136–40. On Hegel's treatment of forgiveness in the *Phenomenology*, see Robert Pippin, "Recognition and Reconciliation: Actualized Agency in Hegel's Jena *Phenomenology*," in *Recognition and Power: Axel Honneth and the Tradition of Critical Social Theory*, eds. B. Brink and D. Owen (Cambridge: Cambridge University Press, 2007), 57–68 and especially Rebecca Comay's brilliant discussion in *Mourning Sickness: Hegel and the French Revolution* (Stanford: Stanford University Press, 2011), 125–36.

for-self that the latter has already thrown off. [This self] thus reveals itself as a consciousness forsaken by and denying spirit …[99]

From the perspective of history abstracted from the idea of freedom and thus of self-knowing spirit, the hard heart's position of judgment, extending to the initial anticipation of or even demand for an ultimately impossible repudiation of the past, already constitutes a refusal of the intersubjective "continuity" of spirit. The aporia of forgiveness resulting from the failure of communication marks a kind of original sin of subjectivity: through the refusal of an impossible recognition—a double negation of spirit—consciousness presents itself as "forsaken by spirit"; likewise the denial of reconciliation—of the forgiveness that cannot be given—"hinders the [other's] return" to "identity in spirit."[100]

But forgiveness and reconciliation remain neither purely historical nor a-historical. They do not designate the purportedly static "now" or "end" of time or history; rather the movement of "ending" signals an endless beginning, the restless dynamism of a self-canceling aesthetic delineation. For this reason, Hegel portrays forgiveness as a dramatic process, a depersonalized social script reenacted through the endless attempt at reconciliation. The failed attempt to forgive underwrites the process of community building; indeed all intersubjectivity, given its aesthetic mediation, amounts to one form or another of recognitive misprision.[101] By corollary "recognitive self-consciousness," as the mediating term between "desire" and "universal self-consciousness," constitutes the movement through which spirit knows itself as nothing but the "limit" of its own knowability.[102]

As an account of "what happened," the "word" of confession or repudiation and acceptance, despite the failure of communication, retains always the power performatively to resignify the past and so effect the subject's "return" from the event to the "spiritual existence of speech [*das geistige Dasein der Rede*]."[103] That moment—fleeting and countervailed by a new inflection of power—reveals the freedom paradoxically internal to the persistent rearticulations of history. History happens as an endless liberation from and reiteration of the given.

---

[99]Hegel, *Werke* 3: 490.

[100]Hegel, *Werke* 3: 491. Hegel's formulation here recalls his view of language as a mediating penetration and "infection" of subjectivity: "This alienation takes place only in language, which here appears in its *characteristic significance* … the 'I' that expresses itself [in language] is heard; it is an infection in which it has immediately passed into unity with those for whom it exists [as a reality], and is a universal self-consciousness" [*Diese Entfremdung aber geschieht allein in der Sprache, welche hier in ihrer eigentümlichen Bedeutung auftritt … Ich, das sich ausspricht, ist vernommen; es ist eine Ansteckung, worin es unmittelbar in die Einheit mit denen, für welche es da ist, übergegangen und allgemeines Selbstbewußtsein ist*] (Hegel, *Werke* 3: 376; emphasis in translation mine). One might add, then, that the failure to forgive, in the face of the aporia of reconciliation, "infects" even the purported victim with "evil."

[101]For this reason the overseer stages the dramatic coercion of Kunta Kinte before a crowd of slaves.

[102]See Hegel, *The Philosophy of Subjective Spirit*, 3: 53ff.

[103]Hegel, *Werke* 3: 491.

The agency over this process, Hegel insists, remains intersubjective—but in a manner still contingent on the retrospectively constructed "will" of individual agents. For Hegel, concrete sublation takes place, however ephemerally, through the paradoxical actuality of self-conscious spirit as freedom in time. By tautology, Hegel reasons, the narrative resignification of historical "evil" occurs only when we, in our collective self-consciousness, become socialized to that resignification. It is from this perspective that we must read the appearance of the spirit as artist or *Meister* in the section on forgiveness: the *Meister's* omnipotence over reality marks the corollary of the merely "subjective" "irony" through which the purported individual subject as "lord and master [*Herr und Meister*]" creates or destroys "objective" forms "at will," such that they "vanish" before his "eyes."[104] In aesthetic time and political economy, as we will see, this creative and destructive capacity of the historical spirit as *Meister* drives the work of only mystified idealization. Hegel will associate this mode of "mastery" with the ironically "beautiful democracy" of the Greeks who, through their positivist faith in mimesis, sculpt subjects into objects and, by extension, transform humans into enslaved things.[105] Where in aesthetic history the Greeks cling stubbornly to the stasis of an ideal that cannot be grasped in time, the "African"—through slavery—will discover the independence or freedom of self-consciousness from the fetishized object and propel the unfolding of history.[106] This difference between the *Meister* and *Werkmeister*, Hegel implies, collapses in the paradoxical sublation of history viewed from the standpoint of the reconciled spirit: through the concrete irony of "absolute knowing," even "idealization" can translate the "idea" of freedom.

For the *Werkmeister* in time, the process of reconciliation, eschewing finality, remains subject always to the violence of history, the displacement of one fiction by another: the history of the world, Hegel reminds us, neither takes place on nor constitutes the "ground" of "harmony" [*Zusammenstimmung*].[107] And yet the telling of history, as the social modality of "free contingent happening" [*freien zufälligen Geschehens*], discloses to consciousness the fact and nature of its freedom.[108] Already signaled conceptually by the aporia of forgiveness, the knowledge of that freedom—in the concretely ironic form of absolute knowing—materializes as the paradoxical immanence and externality of spirit across and between the subjects and objects of the world.[109]

---

[104]Hegel attributes this merely subjective irony to Schlegel and also, indirectly, to Fichte given his unmooring of the "I" from the concrete turns of the dialectic (Hegel, *Werke* 7: §140, 285–6).

[105]Hegel, *Werke* 12: 307ff., 311. I discuss Hegel's relation of Greek democracy and slavery at greater length in Chapter 10.

[106]Readers remain blind to Hegel's strident critique of the "European" or "Western" appropriation and mystified fetishization of ancient Greek culture. For Hegel the Greek ideal of mastery indeed yields up precisely this kind of blindness, whereas the idea of freedom born of the African slave engenders the movement and dynamism of history.

[107]Hegel, *Werke* 12: 42.

[108]Hegel, *Werke* 3: 590.

[109]Hegel, *Werke* 3: 575.

The aporia characterizing the language of reconciliation thus applies equally to narrations of history. Contingent on an agency exceeding, but not entirely abstracted from any individual subject, the "appearance" of recognitive reconciliation in the narrative mediation and remediation of history requires the labor of the aesthetic in the form of symbolic and verbal art. Given the tendency to view the "aporia" of forgiveness as an impasse, this point must be emphasized: the poetic articulation of history, as a social process, remains neither fully within nor entirely beyond the grasp of any individual agent.

In the *Phenomenology*, the *Werkmeister* takes "the shape of self-consciousness" [*die Gestalt des Selbstbewußtseins*] as both the slave and the Memnon, the two marking the interpenetration of the aesthetic and history toward the attempted confluence of subject and object. The laboring slave as *Werkmeister*, having already constituted himself as the "productive power in relation to [this work]," knows himself therein "as in *his own* work."[110] His "statue in human shape," purged of "the animal element," "is no longer merely and entirely used" by the laboring *Werkmeister*, but blends "with the shape of thought."[111] The slave knows himself as this empty corporeal immediacy he himself produces. Subject and object begin to cohere; but the laboring subject does not yet exist "as a self" in this work, for the work "does not in its own self proclaim that it includes within it an inner meaning; it lacks speech, the [outer] element in which the meaning filling [that medium] is itself present."[112] This "speech"—posited as the "ideal" expression of the aesthetic that would negate the difference between form and content—will ultimately reveal its poetic dimension, articulating and dissolving the aesthetic in the unfolding of freedom. The *Werkmeister* anticipates the declamation of spiritual content through this negative power of poetry, the sign sloughing off the referent, hence any immediacy free from aesthetic designation. So, too, the narration of freedom would dissolve any positive content separating antithetical subjects.

In "Self-Consciousness," the laboring *Knecht* likewise must experience and then give verbal expression to his fear of death, which uncovers the negativity of both the subject and the ultimately sublated object produced through aesthetic activity; otherwise that fear remains "inward and mute," removed from the "known real world of existence."[113] Without the power of the negative, the slave's "formative activity" would not "give [the subject] a consciousness of itself as essential being," a "for itself": the slave would not, as essence, mediate and sublate materiality, but would instead remain attached to immediate being as the content of its "natural consciousness."[114] For this reason, the slave as *Werkmeister* struggles to attain to "essential being," the principle of negativity inhering in all substance and propelling the dynamism of the dialectic; likewise the Memnon, even

---

[110]Hegel, *Werke* 3: 510.

[111]Hegel, *Werke* 3: 510.

[112]Hegel, *Werke* 3: 510–1.

[113]Hegel, *Werke* 3: 154–5.

[114]Hegel, *Werke* 3: 154–5.

as "its soul does not come forth from the inner being," labors to indicate symbolically or "give voice" to the non-referential, figural or poetic dimension of language.[115]

Accordingly the slave as Memnon, the Memnon as slave, isolates the aesthetic dimension of recognitive agency. In the "Religion" section of the *Phenomenology*, the laboring slave discovers both the sustainability of form and its negativity through architectural production. The "cognition" of the "enduring objectivity," however illusory, of the nascent subject's organic or artificial productions distinguishes slavish from masterly "recognition." To fully realize the propensity of form to dissolve, the subject first attempts to take "the shape of thought," the mimetic form of individuality as the human body; and then to speak poetically, dissolving any such form to realize freedom in the concrete fluidity of the social body. Passing through the architectonic separation of body and soul (or natural immediacy and spiritual content) in the pyramid—the birth of the architectonic as the limit or "frontier" of freedom—spirit identifies in its "blending" with organic corporeality the "root of free architecture" [*die Wurzel der freien Architektur*][116]. It is this newly emergent dialectic of freedom, struggling to house spirit in the body, that produces the Memnon, the African subject initiating history in his journey into Egypt and Greece. Initially "soundless," the enslaved spirit will first produce the verbal productions of slaves from Aesop to Epictetus, the historical manifestation of abstract, enchained Stoicism Hegel evokes immediately after the incipit of the master–slave dialectic.[117] But the Greek and Roman slave cannot achieve freedom; that historical moment belongs to the slave in the age of the modern state, for only in this latter institution can *Sklaverei* mark "a moment of progression from merely isolated, sensuous existence, a moment of education, a way of becoming part of the higher sociality of ethical life [*höherer Sittlichkeit*] and the *Bildung* connected with it."[118] As figure and history—the "laboring hand" and speaking mouth—translate one into the other, so will the *Werkmeister* give voice, at the twilight of aesthetic history, to an emancipatory poetry.[119]

Emerging out of Africa, the Memnon figures not only the dialectical circulation between East and West and between architecture and poetry, as we have seen, but also the passage of Africa into history, a movement that underwrites the very possibility of dialectical history. This notion will be a surprise to historians accustomed to non-dialectical, non-contextual, and indeed entirely reductive readings of Hegel's claims about

---

[115]Hegel, *Werke* 3: 511.

[116]Hegel, *Werke* 3: 510.

[117]Hegel, *Werke* 3: 157.

[118]Hegel, *Werke* 12: 129.

[119]Hegel, *Werke* 3: 511. To be clear, this "emancipatory" poetry does not mark "absolute" freedom historically; the latter indeed manifests only a vortex of "terror" (Hegel, *Werke* 3: 431ff.). "Absolute knowing," as the telos of the system, consists in freedom from "absolute freedom"—hence, in a necessarily paradoxical formulation, freedom as the limit or "architectonic" of freedom. The movement here is from the Memnon to the Sphinx, that other architectonic (and literary or poetic) figure marking an African penetration into Greece. Liberating man from his immersion in nature, the Sphinx nonetheless marks the fading away of the *Werkmeister* and the confluence of subject and object, or form and content, in Greek idealism; this process will be reiterated upon the twilight of romantic poetry, when the *Werkmeister* of the East, in the last gasps of the aesthetic, will "erect a building built from man's inner sun" (Hegel, *Werke* 12: 134).

Africa, namely that Africans, like other illiterate peoples, "in spite of their achievements in the realm of linguistic development, do not possess a history."[120]

Hegel's comments about Africans respecting their non-historicity and savagery strike us today as particularly heinous given the violence of European colonialism in Africa predicated, at least in part, on such racialist views. But Hegel's conception of Africans requires new consideration. His claim with respect to history refers, first of all, only to the lack of an archive respecting Africans available to him at the time of writing.[121] Here he refers not to North Africa, which "has to do with Europe and Asia," but to "Africa proper," the interior or "upland" of sub-Saharan Africa as yet "unknown to us":

> Africa proper [*eigentliche Afrika*]—the Upland—[is] almost entirely unknown to us … Africa proper [*eigentliche Afrika*], as far as history goes, has been closed to connection with the rest of the world—sealed off … lying beyond the day of self-conscious history, shrouded in the dark mantle of night …
>
> What we properly [*eigentlich*] understand as Africa is the non-historical [*Geschichtslose*], undeveloped spirit immersed in nature, and which had to be presented here only as on the threshold or limit [*Schwelle*] of world-history …[122]

World history emerges from the "idea," the movement of self-consciousness toward the fusion of subject and object. Just as that history has an East and West "*kat' exochen*"— "in itself but for another"—so too world history must have, as its dialectical opposite, a utopic site of non-history "enveloped in the dark mantle of night." From Hegel's relative standpoint, that site "must" be "Africa," whose negative content follows from the "dark continent's" inaccessibility to discursive representation.[123] As a non-dialectical concept and as the concept of the non-dialectical, this utopia or non-place consists in a "state of nature" in which the various forms of an endlessly fracturing self-consciousness struggle only to the death.[124] No *Herr* or *Knecht* appears there; the subject as slave thus fails to materialize.

Second, the non-historicity of "Africa" relates to the necessary absence there of a political state. As we will see, the historical state begins as a violently defended territory—requiring thus the architectonic externalization of a border—and progresses toward the "reciprocal recognition" of the fully reconciled subject at the telos of history. Since self-consciousness reaches for concrete freedom through the state, or a "people"

---

[120]See Hegel, *Werke* 12: 85–6.

[121]Hegel does not rule out the future possibility of discovering archives and writing a history. Thus ancient Egypt remained non-historical until Manetho's chronicle of the pharaohs and dynasties of Egypt: "Nor was there any Egyptian history, until at last Ptolemy Philadelphus—he who had the sacred books of the Jews translated into Greek—prompted the High-Priest Manetho to write an Egyptian history" (Hegel, *The Philosophy of History*, transl. J. Sibree [New York: Dover, 1956], 199–200).

[122]Hegel, *Werke* 12: 120, 129.

[123]Thus Hegel says that Africa "*had to be presented here* as on the threshold or limit" of history (emphasis mine).

[124]Hegel, *Lectures on the Philosophy of World History: Introduction*, transl. H. B. Nisbet (Cambridge: Cambridge University Press, 1975), 178, 176.

as an organized social modality, the history of freedom must deal with such polities: states thus constitute the "material" "medium" of history.[125] In the utopic absence of the dialectic in Africa, of the aesthetic delineation of an object (including a frontier) or subject in space and time, no state can take place historically; "Africa proper" thus remains outside the realm of history.[126]

For Hegel the freedom increasingly secured by the maturing political state has nothing to do with the arbitrary exercise of the will in the attempted fulfillment of desire or with the range of possibilities of action available to a subject; such notions reflect "immature" conceptions of freedom. Rather freedom marks the coherence of the individual and collective or social will.[127] The dialectical emergence from the state of nature and the slow progression toward freedom in the political state must begin, for Hegel, with the advent of the subject in slavery—the dialectical opposite of freedom. And it is through slavery, "the basic legal relationship in Africa," that the African enters history[128]:

> The only essential connection the Negroes and the Europeans have had and still
> have is that of slavery ... The doctrine which we deduce from this condition of
> slavery among the Negroes, and which constitutes the only aspect of the question
> that has any interest for our purposes, is that which we deduce from the "idea"—
> namely that the "state of nature" itself is one of absolute and universal injustice.
> Every intermediate stage between [slavery] and the realization of the rational state
> also retains moments and aspects of injustice ... Slavery is in and for itself injustice,
> for the essence of humanity is freedom; but toward this man must evolve.[129]

Descending from the "unknown" Uplands, the African—from Hegel's relative and necessarily "European" standpoint—enters history as a slave, or rather as part of an enslaved collective. This historical subject represents the quintessential articulation of the *Werkmeister*, a fragmented "overseer" who, in his appearance, nonetheless mediates an extrinsic will. In the ancient world, this "African element" propels the Egyptian spirit to "labor over matter"; so, too, in the age of the modern state, the African slave engages in the "imposition of form" upon the material world.[130] In both cases, the slave's body

---

[125]Hegel, *Lectures on the Philosophy of World History: Introduction*, transl. H. B. Nisbet, 93.

[126]For instance, the subjective particularities resulting from the "determinate difference" of spirit is of minimal significance among the "human race of Africa ..." (Hegel, *The Philosophy of Subjective Spirit*, 2: 69).

[127]It is this concept of the "free will" with which the philosophy of "right" "begins" (Hegel, *Werke* 7: §57A: 123).

[128]Hegel, *Lectures on the Philosophy of World History: Introduction*, transl. H. B. Nisbet, 183.

[129]Ibid., 183–4; see *Werke* 12: 128–9.

[130]In supplementary notes to the passage on slavery in §57 of the *Philosophy of Right*, Hegel recalls the relation between the *Knecht*'s "formation" [*Formierung*] of material form and the "formation" of the self or *Bildung* in the *Phenomenology*: "§ 57 ist erwähnt—bei Formieren—ist heterogen. Mensch muß sich selbst formieren. Ist geschichtlich, d. h. gehört in die Zeit, in die Geschichte vor Freiheit—da ist Geschichte" (Hegel, *Werke* 7: §57A: 124). The process of *Bildung* initiated by the slave constitutes the unfolding of history toward freedom.

and the product of its work, the form of his subjectivity and the object he produces, are alienated to an "other." Subordinating his will to his master's, the slave begins to free himself from the particularities of subjectivity; thus he isolates the principle of recognition—the consonance of the individual and social, or embodied and universal will—that underwrites the self-consciousness of spirit. Through the activity and "power" of *Bilden*, the architectonic and ultimately poetic delineation and cancellation of historical form, the slave further identifies a discursive agency over the narration and thus history of freedom. And it is through his aesthetic "power" over history—bending to its retrospectively agreed "narration"—that the human, as *Werkmeister* and in particular as Memnon, reaches, architecturally and poetically, beyond the embodied bounds of his purported subjectivity.

Like Hegel's "East" and "West" *kat' exochen*, his Africa "proper" must not be taken as a mere representation of the "actual" "place" that bears that name. Each of the three geographical terms occupies a different position in the dialectic of freedom. Hegel insists that "East" and "West," as "relative" concepts, must accord with the performative impetus of the history of freedom at the time of writing. The aesthetic or narrative structure of any written history bears that performative burden. "For" Hegel, the "East" as the "beginning" and the "West" as the "ending" of his symbolic history posit the necessary limits of all narratives of phenomena in space and time. Africa, by contrast, marks the negativity propelling the movement of the dialectic, the cancellation and overcoming of the limit between opposed elements, including of East and West. Accordingly the Memnon, akin to the African stepping into history as the laboring slave, engenders the aesthetic mode through which the dialectic entangles form and content, matter and language, phenomena and phenomenology. Mirroring the "dark continent's" relation to history, the "architectonic" in Hegel's system steps out of the realm of logic and drives the historical unfolding of the aesthetic, hence the narrative progression toward recognitive self-consciousness and freedom. The Memnon thus articulates the architectonic mode through which the "African" slave, at the telos of history, will fulfill the spiritual promise of the human and thus realize concrete freedom in the state.

Hegel's comments on Africa should be read in the context of its paradigmatic place in the history of freedom. As a notional "state of nature," Africa proper must be characterized by endless violence; for in that posited utopia, subjects hold life cheap and fight endlessly to the death. Descending into the peripheries of the continent, Africans encounter Europeans; there, at the "threshold [*Schwelle*] of history," another struggle to the death ensues; Europeans subjugate the Africans; the latter yield up their wills.[131] Here it bears noting that masters, like savages in the state of nature, also hold life cheap: for this reason, they emerge victorious from the struggle to the death.

We can and should take Hegel to task for poorly manipulating the archive available to him on the history, culture, and religion of mostly coastal Africans already in contact

---

[131]Hegel, *The Philosophy of History*, transl. J. Sibree (New York: Dover, 1956), 29. In Hegel's text, "Africans" appear in time by materializing the related limit or "frontier" [*Schwelle*] of history and freedom through slavery.

with Europeans.[132] But any such approach is entirely besides the point with respect to Hegel's procedure, which is to "deduce" the theory of Africa and any derivative claims "from the idea" of freedom—that is, of fully actualized spirit self-consciously unifying subject and object. "Historical facts," which remain entirely contingent anyway, must bend to the narrative progression of freedom: "we must know what is essential—and this, if the history of the world in general is to be considered, is the consciousness of freedom, and the determinations of this consciousness in its development. The bearing of historical facts on this category [that is, the consciousness of freedom] is their bearing on what is truly essential."[133]

Every comment Hegel makes on the "Negroes" at the edges of history must reflect the fact that their "only essential connection" to Europeans—in Hegel's day—consists in the brutal institution of slavery. Africans experience slavery "in their own land" to the extent that, lacking subjectivity in a state of nature, they remain unconscious of their freedom.[134] But Africans are subjected to the material, historical form of chattel slavery only upon the advent of the European slave trade. For Hegel, the legal and political articulation of an emergent social subjectivity in the European state underwrites, in dialectical contrast, the interpellation of an entire "race" to mere objectivity: *historical* slavery thus occurs not in a state of nature, but rather "in man's transition from the state of nature to genuinely ethical conditions."[135] And yet this "condition of slavery"—institutionalized on a massive scale through the machinery of modern European civil society and the state—effects the collapse of ethical relationships and moral sentiments: "Negroes are led into slavery by Europeans and sold to America … Since slavery [*Sklaverei*] is so widespread and

---

[132]Through their valuable review of Hegel's sources on Africa, several scholars have demonstrated the extent to which Hegel misrepresented the evidence on Africa available to him (see *inter alia*, Robert Bernasconi, "Hegel at the Court of the Ashanti," in *Hegel After Derrida*, ed. S. Barnett [London: Routledge, 1998], 41–63 and Teshale Tibebu, *Hegel and the Third World: The Making of Eurocentrism in World History* [Syracuse: Syracuse University Press, 2011]). Hegel's denigration of Africans—he refers, for instance, to "African stupidity" (Hegel, *Werke* 12: 253)—has led a number of writers understandably to condemn him as a racist, though the most astute are careful to charge him with what they call "cultural" or "geocultural" as opposed to "biological" racism (Buck-Morss, "Hegel and Haiti," 864; Tibebu, 181). Other scholars defend Hegel from charges of racism, but most concede that his views "reflect a certain Eurocentricity" (indicatively, see Joseph McCarney, *Hegel on History* [London: Routledge, 2000], 145). In the end, few scholars question Hegel's underlying cultural supremacism; and no one has successfully reconciled what most view as Hegel's apparently contradictory positions. This emphasis on Hegel's "cultural" racism and Eurocentrism obscures, I suggest, a more fundamental question: namely, what does Hegel's philosophy teach us about the possibility of freedom from enduring hierarchies of culture? My aim is to prove the centrality of that question for Hegel's project, suggest a new frame through which to consider his denigration of Africans, and set forth some methods emerging from his work through which to engage static cultural categories. In some respects, condemning Hegel's Eurocentricism without critiquing the concept of "culture" underlying the charge of Eurocentrism can mask the persistence of the category of "culture" in more insidious forms, in the worst cases betraying an implicit positivism with respect to "Western," "Eastern," and "African" "culture." For a summary of the scholarship on the topic of Hegel's views on race and a useful bibliography, see Allison Stone, "Hegel and Colonialism," in *Hegel Bulletin* (Cambridge: Cambridge University Press, 2017), 1–24. doi:10.1017/hgl.2017.17. Accessed October 10, 2018.

[133]Hegel, *Werke* 12: 88.

[134]Hegel, *Werke* 12: 127. See also: "it is the essential principle of slavery that man does not yet have consciousness of his freedom, and thus sinks down to a thing, worthless …" (Hegel, *Werke* 12:125).

[135]Hegel, *Werke* 7: §57A: 126.

severe, all those bonds of ethical esteem we maintain with respect to one another *have vanished [geschwunden]*" in Africa.[136] Slavery, according to Hegel's incisive critique, leads to the state of nature, and the state of nature leads to slavery. His claims about Africans thus do not reflect any innate "racial" qualities of Africans so much as they point to the perversity of the European slave regime.

Hegel accordingly attacks the European theory of racial superiority, insisting that "the distinction of race refers to the question of what rights should be given to man: if there are multiple races, then one will be more noble, the other must serve it."[137] The discourse of mastery, in other words, takes the form of the theory of racial difference. As we have seen, Hegel debunks the idea of fixed and pure races; he further dismisses the notion of racial superiority and any race-based hierarchy of rights:

Man has rights by virtue of the rationality of mankind ... Particular variety is evident everywhere, but superiority confines itself only to particular circumstances, not to what constitutes the truth and dignity of man. So [the question of race] is an idle question without intrinsic interest ... No color has any superiority, it being simply a matter of being used to it.[138]

---

[136]Hegel, *Werke* 12: 125. Emphasis mine. Hegel adds that this absence of ethicality characterizes some Africans even outside of Africa; as we will see, Africans will emerge from this fundamentally "spiritual servitude" only through *Bildung*.

[137]Hegel, *The Philosophy of Subjective Spirit*, 2: 47.

[138]Hegel, *The Philosophy of Subjective Spirit*, 2: 47. In the same remark, Hegel then continues that one can "speak of the objective superiority" of white skin, which allows interiority (for instance, the "red blood of the arteries") to shine through (ibid.). But Hegel nonetheless distinguishes objective from spiritual value, insisting that the former has no bearing on the rights of man or the history of freedom. One of Hegel's aims, it will be recalled, is to deconstruct the immature notion of "objectivity" as immediacy: "To the vulgar consciousness, the same sensual perception (eg. this animal, this star, etc.) appears as existent, independent ..." and thus "objective" (Hegel, *Werke* 8: §41A: 115). Indeed the task of the subject as slave is precisely to overcome its corporeal immediacy. For this reason Hegel, in an "addition" to the same section in *The Philosophy of Subjective Spirit*, argues there can be no "spiritual" difference between the "races"; any musings on merely "objective" advantages or disadvantages of race remain only a question of contingent "natural" distinctions. He specifically contends that the "objective" property of color does not attach to a subject, but remains a function of the climate; thus "race," rather than marking a set of properties inherent to a group of subjects, remains entirely contingent and fluid. (It is at this moment that Hegel cites the example of the Portuguese who, in Africa, become "as black as the native Negroes," both due to the climate and due to "miscegeny.") One could just as well speak of the "objective" inferiority of aged white skin that, over time, becomes mottled or wrinkled and thus less translucent; that does not mean that for Hegel young and old white people could constitute separate "races," the latter inferior to the former. Any such valorization respecting skin color, Hegel states explicitly, is predicated only on "particular" or contingent "circumstances" and thus remains of no concern for rational enterprise. Now, Hegel's statement is, of course, odious to our ears, but the (still persistent) cognition and valorization of racial distinctions cannot be extinguished through silence or with the wave of a magic wand. (As we will see, the mere assertion of new linguistic norms in the absence of recognitive resignification and socialization cannot paper over an underlying hierarchy, as with the replacement of "white" with the seemingly anodyne, but equally performative term "Western" to speak of a certain intellectual tradition, culture, and even civilization.) Hegel's purpose is to engage and dialectically deconstruct "natural" distinctions and their historical inflection in discourses of white supremacy underwriting justifications of slavery. Indicatively, he will reproduce the contemporary discourse delineating physiognomic markers of race even as he insists that the differently angled "lines" of the jaw supposedly determining the races must be "imagined" or imposed: "man hat gewisse

Already in the *Phenomenology* Hegel had criticized palmistry, physiognomy, phrenology, and other "sciences" professing to know "laws" "relating self-consciousness to actuality": but such laws of the understanding fail to signify their intended referent, and no such efforts, including the measurement of African skulls, reveal anything about the disposition, much less the innately free spirit of man.[139]

Can Hegel's disparagement of the "barbarism" [*Roheit*] of African society be taken to reveal racial animus?[140] He will just as easily speak of the "wildness" [*Wildheit*] of the Germans during the time of the Roman Empire, calling his ancestors "lazy" "savages"; elsewhere he remarks that "we see in the original condition of the Germans a barbarian dullness, confusion, and vagueness [*eine barbarische Stumpfheit, Verworrenheit und Unbestimmtheit*]."[141] He also characterizes medieval Germany after the reign of the Hohenstaufens as an age of "general barbarism"; he further attributes this trait to "the whole of Europe" during the Crusades, again remarking on European "savagery."[142] So too "harshness and barbarity" [*Härte und Grausamkeit*] characterize the royal houses of France from the time of Clovis through to "all the succeeding Merovingians," the same "spectacle" repeating itself in the "Thuringian and other royal houses."[143] Christianity, exhibiting "barbarous vice and lust" throughout its history, subjects Europe to the "frightful barbarity" [*furchtbaren Barbarei*] of persecution, inquisition, and torture even to contemporary times, for recently "a witch was publicly burned at Glarus in Switzerland."[144] The European institution of "serfdom, whereby the body belongs not to the man, but to another, dragged man through all the savagery of servitude [*alle Roheit der Knechtschaft*]."[145]

Linien sich gezogen vorgestellt" (Hegel, *The Philosophy of Subjective Spirit*, 2: 50). This view extends from Hegel's stated position that any "rigid differences" or "lines" between the races—including those supposed to have more rights than others on the basis of such distinctions—must also be "nullified" by reason. Tibebu makes much of Hegel's comment on the "objective superiority" of whiteness without accounting for the larger context in which this statement appears, including the dialectic of subjectivity and objectivity structuring the "system," Hegel's sublation of anthropological difference, his immediately preceding insistence that "no color has any superiority," and his defense of the equal rationality, right, and freedom *in potentia* of all human beings. (Tibebu, like others, can only make the unlikely suggestion that Hegel is so racist as to contradict himself "in the same sentence"; see Tibebu, *Hegel and the Third World*, 79ff.) Hegel's critique of anthropological distinction extends to the "necessary" or "given" natural difference even of separated geographies, especially where the sea connects them: for "free navigation of the sea" marks the freedom not only from slavery, but also from any "ossification" of caste or class (Hegel, *The Philosophy of Subjective Spirit* 2: 69).

[139]Hegel, *Werke* 3: 128.

[140]Hegel, *Werke* 12: 121, 126. As previously indicated, my purpose is to distinguish between largely indeterminate authorial intentions and the performative power of Hegel's texts.

[141]Hegel, *Werke* 12: 415; *Werke* 12: 424 His example of "lazy" "savages" in an early lecture on the *Philosophy of Right* is the pre-modern German, who "passed much time lying on bearskins" (*Hegel's Philosophie des Rechts. Die Vorlesung von 1819/1820 in einer Nachschrift*, ed. D. Henrich [Frankfurt am Main: Suhrkamp, 1983], 158).

[142]Hegel, *Werke* 12: 480, 475.

[143]Hegel, *Werke* 12: 427.

[144]Hegel, *Werke* 12: 493, 507.

[145]Hegel, *Werke* 12: 487.

For Hegel no people is more or less prone to savagery than any other: the categorization, evolution, and intermingling of a group remain always subject to the architectonic fluidity of history. While any "ossification of social divisions"—for instance in the caste system— remains "fatal to freedom," a narrative of history must initially posit certain categories of history as if they were fixed.[146] The key for Hegel is to embrace the contingency of such categories. In this respect, apologetic counters to Hegel's characterizations of African society in the era of slavery, ignoring his theory of history, deploy categories equally vulnerable to critique—including, to begin with, the very notions of "Africa" and its "African" subjects.

Against the positivist use of such categories, plagued as they can be by essentialism, racialism, and territorialism, Hegel's conception of Africa as the utopic site of non-dialectical movement and of the African slave as the incipit of subjectivity, self-consciousness, and freedom provides firmer ground for any disciplinary engagement of Africa and its "history." Singling out slavery as the "essential" aspect of the African spirit (and indeed of the inchoate self-consciousness in time), Hegel insists, from his still modern standpoint, that the story of freedom must not only begin with the African slave, but by implication must also end with her: for the journey of the slave, as she discovers the principles of architectonic individuation and dynamism, must culminate in precisely the non-historical moment of paradoxically fragmented totality from which she first emerges. At the telos of history, the slave realizes that totality as the self-consciousness of spirit. Thus Hegel at the conclusion of the *Phenomenology*:

> for the self-knowing spirit, precisely because it grasps its own concept, is the immediate identity with itself which, in its difference, is the *certainty of immediacy*, or *sense-consciousness*—the beginning from which we proceeded; this release of itself from the form of its self is the highest freedom and assurance of its self-knowledge.[147]

This connection of "self-certainty with the object," along with the self's knowledge of its negativity or "limit" [*Grenze*], propels the dialectical "becoming" of nature and history, the externalization of spirit as time.[148] The self-knowing attending this process, however, constitutes an "inward turn" through which "spirit is absorbed into the night of its self-consciousness; but in that night its vanished outer existence is preserved, and this transformed existence—the former one, but now reborn of the spirit's knowledge—

---

[146] Hegel, *The Philosophy of Subjective Spirit*, 3: 69

[147] Hegel, *Werke* 3: 589–90.

[148] Hegel, *Werke* 3: 590. See also 3: 587–8: "Spirit has shown itself to us to be neither the mere withdrawal of self-consciousness into its pure inwardness, nor the mere absorption of self-consciousness into substance and the non-being of its distinction. Rather, it has shown itself to be this movement of the self which empties itself of itself and immerses itself in its substance, and which likewise, as subject, has both taken the inward turn into itself from out of that substance and has made its substance into an object and a content, just as it has sublated this distinction between objectivity and content."

is the new existence, a new world, a new shape of spirit."[149] This dialectical movement of self-knowing spirit from one historical moment to another involves the self-certain identification with objectivity and the withdrawal into the "dark mantle of night"—elements characterizing both consciousness as sense-certainty and the African subject at the "threshold of history." The end marks the "beginning"; the beginning reveals itself as the end: in the collapsing circle of history, "the first is also the last and the last is also the first."[150] Knowing itself as identical with the "substance" of objectivity, self-consciousness again moves between particular dialectical shapes and the non-dialectical "freedom" from history that underwrites spirit's "succession in time."[151]

The possibility of that freedom, endlessly haunting history, inheres in the negativity of the dialectic; and for Hegel this non-dialectical moment finds positive historical expression in the labor of the African slave, the manifest "spirit" of architectonic fluidity. On the other hand, history must take place through the social modality that Hegel calls the "state." What then would be the relation between the African slave and the concrete freedom ever more fully realized through the dialectic of "right"? As we will see, in his critique of "right" Hegel intimates that the European state, having apparently abolished slavery within its territory, nonetheless compromises its own freedom through the perversity of slavery abroad. How then, must the African—if indeed it falls to her—effect the "recognitive" "reconciliation" between master and slave? What form of the state emerges?

---

[149]Hegel, *Werke* 3: 590–1.
[150]Hegel, *Science of Logic*, 71.
[151]Hegel, *Werke* 3: 590–1.

Figure 9 *Kunta Kinte and the Overseer.* From *Roots* [miniseries], dir. Chomsky, Erman, Moses et al. USA: Wolper Productions, 1977. Still from episode 2.

CHAPTER 10
THE POSTCOLONIAL STATE

No context in the history of slavery instantiates the relation of recognition to freedom more than the Haitian revolution and its aftermath. Having defeated Napoleon's army, the citizens of Haiti declare their freedom from European slavers and their independence from France in 1804, but fail to achieve recognition from any world power. Diplomatically isolated, Haiti's leaders face quarantine, the threat of invasion from without, and the reimposition of slavery by foreign powers.[1] Even so, after a period of internal strife, Haiti makes rapid progress on numerous fronts, becoming an indispensable trading partner for slave-based colonial powers. Seeking privileged access to the Haitian market, France conditions its "recognition" of the state of Haiti on trade concessions and, above all, the latter's compensation for the losses of French slavers. To secure Charles X's formal recognition of the Haitian state, its president, Jean-Pierre Boyer, agrees to create a debt between the new republic and its former colonial master of 150 million francs, an amount exceeding Haiti's state revenues by tenfold.[2] By setting, demanding, and exacting a price for the recognition both of Haiti's sovereignty and of the emancipation of former slaves, France coerces Haiti into acknowledging the limitations of its sovereignty in the face of overwhelming geopolitical power and the contingency rather than inalienability of its peoples' freedom. Through Boyer's act, Haitians effectively purchase their own bodies from their former masters. By implication, they are made to see themselves through

---

[1]See Seymour Drescher, "The Limits of Example," in *The Impact of the Haitian Revolution in the Atlantic World*, ed. David Geggus (Columbia: University of South Carolina Press, 2001), 11; Seymour Drescher, *Econocide: British Slavery in the Era of Abolition* (Pittsburgh: University of Pittsburgh Press, 1977), 152–7; Paul Farmer, *The Uses of Haiti* (Monroe: Common Courage Press, 1994); Julia Gaffield, *Haitian Connections in the Atlantic World: Recognition after Revolution* (Chapel Hill: University of North Carolina Press, 2015), 188–9; and Anthony Phillips, "Haiti, France and the Independence Debt of 1825," https://canada-haiti.ca/sites/default/files/Haiti, France and the Independence Debt of1825_0.pdf, accessed July 17, 2018. The latter lists the following useful sources: Thomas Madiou, *Histoire d'Haiti* (Pétion-Ville: Editions Henri Deschamps, 1988), VI, 1819–1826, 29ff., 472–3; Gusti-Klara Gaillard, *L'Expérience Haïtienne de la dette extérieure* (Port-au-Prince: Imprimerie Henri Deschamps, 1988), 18–19; and Mildred Aristide, "L'Enfant en Domesticité en Haiti, Produit d'un Fosse Historique," (Port-au-Prince: Imprimerie Henri Deschamps, 2003), 107ff. Thomas Jefferson, bemoaning the "tragedy" that the island would "remain in the hands of people of color" and fearing the black republic as an example for southern slaves, imposed a quarantine on the island upon its independence in 1804 (Henry Louis Gates, "The Curse on Haiti," in *The Root*, January 25, 2010). Jefferson's posture was not unique. The United States attempted actively to suppress the revolution from its outset: George Washington gave the French planters vast sums and secured their access to arms and supplies during the first years of the slave revolt (Timothy Mathewson, "George Washington's Policy toward the Haitian Revolution," in *Diplomatic History*, 1979, 3: 3, 321–36).

[2]According to Anthony Phillips, "Independence Debt," 4.

the eyes of the French—that is, as tradable commodities, hence mere objects or chattel. Worse, by imposing an unpayable debt, the French state, acting on behalf of former slave masters, forces Haiti to indenture its citizen's labor for, effectively, an indefinite period of time.

Hegel would have read about Haiti's travails and successes in the journal *Minerva*, from its inaugural issue of 1792 to its coverage of France's agreement with the new Republic in 1825.[3] Notwithstanding France's highly conditioned recognition of the beleaguered nation—and its continuing non-recognition by numerous powers, including the United States—Hegel in 1830 lauds the Haitians' establishment of a "state based on Christian principles."[4] In his lectures on the *Philosophy of Right*, he defines the "Christian" principle of the "state" as centered on the "individual" as an "infinite end," the "end of universality." This "moment of infinite value that individuals have within themselves" corresponds to the notion that "there should be no slavery."[5] Theoretically, Haiti thus contrasts with "modern" conceptions of the state as a mere "commonality" of "persons" acting only for "the sake of satisfaction of needs."[6] Such a vision of the "state as the understanding sees it" [*Verstandesstaat*] reduces the individual to a "bourgeois" [*Bürger*] and the state merely to a "civil society" [*bürgerliche Gesellschaft*] emerging from the "necessity" of property and economic exchange.[7] The nascent Haitian republic also contrasts with the "ancient" conception of the state, where "the particularity pertaining to need" divides the population into slaves who produce and masters who consume.[8] Neither of these conceptions reflects the "state as the image and actuality of reason [*zum Bilde und zur Wirklichkeit der Vernunft*], wherein self-consciousness finds organically developed its substantial" or actualized "knowing and willing."[9]

---

[3] Two articles lauding the Haitian state appear in 1822 and 1825 in the journal *Minerva*: "Skizze von Hayti in Beziehung des moralischen und politischen Characters seiner Bewohner," in *Minerva*, 1822, 123: 454–85; and "Darstellung der zwischen Frankreich und Hayti Statt gefundenen Unterhandlungen," in *Minerva*, 1825, 135: 329–91. I will analyze these articles and their illumination of Hegel's conception of Haiti over the course of this chapter.

[4] Hegel, *Werke* 10: 60. This comment, written after Haiti had achieved recognition as a state in 1825, reflects Hegel's sympathies for what Nick Nesbitt has convincingly shown could only have been viewed as a "world-historical" revolution (Nesbitt, *Universal Emancipation*, 41–80). Hegel developed his mature theory of recognition in 1806 in Jena: from that point, the theoretical relationship between recognition in "subjective spirit" (from the "formation" of the *Knecht*) and the recognition of states in "objective spirit" remains remarkably consistent. In the absence of any evidence that his theory of "recognition" changed, there is no reason to believe that Hegel did not hold these sympathies from at least 1806, if not earlier through his contact with the work of French intellectuals like Diderot, Raynal, and the Abbé Grégoire (see especially Tavares, *Hegel, critique de l'Afrique* and "Hegel et l'abbé Grégoire," 491–509).

[5] Hegel, *Lectures on Natural Right and Political Science: Heidelberg 1817–1818 with additions from the Lectures of 1818–1819*, transl. J. Stewart and P. Hodgson (Berkeley: University of California Press, 1995), 163, 235.

[6] Hegel, *Werke* 7: §182A: 339; Hegel, *Vorlesungen über Rechtsphilosophie 1818–1831*, ed. Karl-Heinz Ilting (Stuttgart: Frommann Verlag, 1974), 4: §182: 472.

[7] Hegel, *Werke* 7: §183, 340; Hegel, *Vorlesungen über Naturrecht Staatswissenschaft*, 108. Hegel attributes this misconception in part to the positivism of "constitutional lawyers" (*Werke* 7: §182A: 339).

[8] Hegel, *Werke* 7: §356, 510; see also 7: §185: 341–3 and 7: §124: 233–4.

[9] Hegel, *Werke* 7: §360: 512.

As the objective manifestation of the "Christian" state, Haiti, founded by African slaves emerging from an ultimately "spiritual servitude" [*Geistesknechtschaft*], occupies a unique place in the constellation of modern states.[10] On the one hand, the "reconciliation" of objectivity and subjectivity as "freedom" in self-consciousness, from Hegel's standpoint as he writes, has been "entrusted" to the German people, the "bearers of the Christian principle."[11] On the other hand, the state, an "image" [*Bild*] of reason and thus an aesthetic realization, emerges in terms associated with the Egyptian *Werkmeister*:

> The state must be regarded as a great architectonic structure—a hieroglyph of reason [*als ein großes architektonisches Gebäude, als eine Hieroglyphe der Vernunft*]—that presents [*darstellt*] itself in reality .... [The] "I will" [of the sovereign human being] constitutes the great difference between the ancient and modern world, and so it must have its worldly existence in the great building of the state [*in dem großen Gebäude des Staats*].[12]

Hegel's formulation of the "architectonic" state as a "hieroglyph of reason" echoes the moment in the *Phenomenology of Spirit* in which the *Werkmeister* as the enslaved self-consciousness produces the "hieroglyph of a thought": knowing himself in what he makes, the *Werkmeister* begins to translate the form of "being for self in general" into the "shape of thought" proper in the *Bildsäule*, the blend of the human and "architectonic" in the Memnon.[13] The *Werkmeister* of Egypt, whose "African element" fissures "solidity" and identifies for man "the problem" of "free spirit," will arrive at the "threshold" or "frontier" [*Schwelle*] of "freedom" by discovering the dialectical fluidity of the architectonic limit [*Grenze*] itself.[14] The architectonic runs its course from architecture to poetry in the history of the aesthetic and, likewise, from slavery to recognitive self-consciousness in the history of spirit. Thus the subject as Memnon or slave, in the journey toward self-consciousness, reaches for freedom through the poetic "reconstruction" of history—precisely the architectonic power over time that underwrites the recognitive reconciliation of subjects.[15] As the spirit of reason that begins to know itself as substance, self-consciousness ultimately materializes in what Hegel, already in the preface to the published version of the *Philosophy of Right*, calls "the architectonic" [*die Architektonik*] of the state's "rationality" [*Vernünftigkeit*], or the interpenetration of aesthetics and logic in concrete historical form.[16]

How does this "architectonic" dimension of the state inflect its relation to slavery as the root of self-consciousness? What conception of the state as the "self-determining

---

[10]Hegel, *Werke* 10: 60. Note again the use of the term *Knechtschaft* in the context of both Africa and Haiti.

[11]Hegel, *Werke* 7: §358: 511; Hegel, *Werke* 12: 413.

[12]Hegel, *Werke* 7: §279: 449.

[13]Hegel, *Werke* 3: 510.

[14]Hegel, *Werke* 13: 459.

[15]Hegel, *Werke* 15: 276. I refer here to Hegel's broad view of poetry as figural or symbolic language.

[16]Hegel, *Werke* 7: 19.

and sovereign will" emerges?[17] What implications then follow from Hegel's view of Haiti as an exemplar of a "state based on Christian principles," especially if subjectivity and objectivity, or substance and spirit, only reconcile in the "Germanic realm"? To answer these questions, we will read Hegel's *Philosophy of Right* alongside his other works, analyzing the relation between the architectonic productivity of the slave and modern political economy; the theory of the state emerging from the tension between its territorialized objectivity and the "cosmopolitan" trajectories of that economy, including trade, piracy, migration, and colonization; and finally the possibility for "recognitive reconciliation" between states toward the realization of freedom on earth.[18] We will then return to Hegel's conception of Haiti, examining the nature and possibility of the postcolonial "state" in light of his political theory.

From aesthetics to political economy

Hegel's conception of political subjectivity in the *Philosophy of Right* centers on the evolution of the "will" from "abstract" personhood to its self-reflection as "morality" to, finally, "ethicality," which in turn cycles through the stages of family, civil society, and the state.[19] Hegel first defines a "person" as a subject aware of its subjectivity and freedom only as "abstractions." This "person" remains mired in such determinacies as its age, size, and location "in *this* [*diesem*] room" and thus fails to recognize its concrete freedom— that is, its freedom from particularity or determinacy.[20] Knowing itself as free only in the abstract sense, the person dialectically posits an "external" and "immediate" sphere in which to exercise its abstract will.[21] Since it is free, the abstract will implies the right to take possession of "this" immediacy.[22] From this "abstract right" emerges the idea of property, the immediacy separable from the person and through which it exercises the right of possession: "the person has as its substantial end the right of putting its will into any and every thing and thereby making it 'mine.'"[23] Property thus emerges rationally not because it "satisfies needs but rather" because "it suspends the mere subjectivity of personhood."[24]

---

[17]Hegel, *Werke* 7: §279: 449.

[18]On Hegel's critique of capitalism, see *Hegel and Capitalism*, ed. Andrew Buchwalter (Albany: SUNY Press, 2015) and Liza Herzog, *Inventing the Market: Smith, Hegel, and Political Theory* (Oxford: Oxford University Press, 2016). On Hegel's critique of the state, especially with respect to theories of recognition, cosmopolitanism, and international law, see Andrew Buchwalter, "Hegel's Concept of an International 'We,'" in *Identity and Difference: Studies in Hegel's Logic, Philosophy of Spirit, and Politics*, ed. P. T. Grier (Albany: SUNY Press, 2007), as well as Steven Hicks, "Hegel on Cosmopolitanism" and Robert Fine, "Contra Leviathan: Hegel's Contribution to the Cosmopolitan Critique," both in *Hegel and Global Justice*, ed. Andrew Buchwalter (New York: Springer, 2012).

[19]Hegel, *Werke* 7: §33: 87–8.

[20]Hegel, *Werke* 7: §35A: 95.

[21]Hegel, *Werke* 7: §41: 102–3.

[22]Hegel, *Werke* 7: §46A: 110. On Hegel's critique of the "this," see "Sense-Certainty," the opening chapter of the *Phenomenology*.

[23]Hegel, *Werke* 7: §44: 106.

[24]Hegel, *Vorlesungen über Rechtsphilosophie 1818–1831*, ed. Karl-Heinz Ilting (Stuttgart: Frommann Verlag, 1974), 3: 204.

Hegel associates this fundamentally legal or "juridical" notion of "personhood," predicated on the right to acquire property, with ancient Rome.[25] This conception of the "person" ultimately results in the denial of the innate freedom of self-consciousness. As personhood supersedes mere subjectivity and takes on immediate, embodied form, the distinction between subject and object, and concomitantly between person and thing, reaches its crisis. Logically the category of a "thing" can indeed include "everything that is external to freedom, including my body and my life."[26] Spirit, in accordance with its concept, must paradoxically realize itself as substance and reflect back into itself "out of [its] natural immediacy."[27] In the absence of spirit "in-and-for itself," the "possibility" emerges of the "opposition" between, first, "spirit" "for itself" but not "in itself" and, second, "spirit" that is "in-itself" but not "for itself."[28] In the dialectical context of "objective spirit," the opposition here leads to the relation of person and property as modes of abstract "right." As we will see, a similar opposition in the context of "subjective spirit" leads to the relation of master and slave as modes of self-consciousness in the *Phenomenology*.[29] In the *Philosophy of Right*, the unstable separation between person and property leads to the "possibility" that the will can surrender, alienate, or convey its "personhood and substantial being" through, for instance, legal "slavery" [*Sklaverei*] or "serfdom" [*Leibeigenschaft*].[30]

The conception of "person" founders on its possible interpenetration with "property." Indicatively, "the content of the so-called Roman right of the person" includes "the right to possess slaves"; accordingly, "personhood itself" is indeed "only a certain status [*Stand*] or condition over against slavery."[31] Roman law forecloses any "definition of the human being," for no such definition could hold and still subsume "the class or status [*Stand*] of slaves."[32] But even without an explicit regime permitting slavery, abstract "personhood" as a juridical and thus merely contingent "status" implies and creates a performative propensity toward the enslavement of others.[33] Hegel's conclusion is remarkable: abstract "definitions" of "property and property-holders," predicated as they are on the slippery distinction between subject and object, invite—or at least do not foreclose—modes of bondage and thus remain "perilous."[34]

As we have seen, ultimately the slave learns that its will is free, and that it can thus will its freedom: "I cannot freely make myself a slave … this possession vouchsafed to

---

[25]Hegel, *Werke* 7: §40A: 99, 7: §357: 511.

[26]Hegel, *Werke* 7: §40A: 99.

[27]Hegel, *Werke* 7: §66: 141–2.

[28]Hegel, *Werke* 7: §66: 141–2.

[29]Here Hegel refers back to the discussion of the *Knecht* as *Sklave* in §57 (Hegel, *Werke* 7: §66: 142).

[30]Hegel, *Werke* 7: §66: 142.

[31]Hegel, *Werke* 7: §40A: 99.

[32]Hegel, *Werke* 7: §2A: 31. Hegel adds, citing Justinian, that "in civil law, every definition is perilous" (ibid.).

[33]Hegel, *Werke* 7: §40A, 99. The performative power of language—including of definitions—emerges from the architectonic movement of the concept into the material world. For a discussion of Hegel's theory of linguistic action or performance, see Chapter 2.

[34]Hegel, *Werke* 7: §2A: 31.

another ceases as soon as I so will."[35] Through the trials of being treated as the property of another, the slave learns it can "take possession" of its body by first detaching itself from its vitality[36]:

> Insofar as the body is an immediate existence, it is not commensurate with spirit. If it is to be the willing organ and ensouled instrument of spirit, the body must first be taken into possession by spirit (§57) ... I can withdraw into myself out of my bodily existence and make my body something external to myself; particular feelings I can regard as something outside me and in chains [*Fesseln*] I can still be free.[37]

This power of the will to differentiate spirit from its immediate corporeality—even to the point of death or "suicide," as we have seen—underwrites the indomitability of freedom.[38] In fact the possible destruction of the body by the will instantiates the "spiritual mediation" of actuality or immediacy.[39] Thus the will's right over its body, given the conceptual harmony of the individual and universal volition in spirit, cannot extend to an alien individual will.[40] "[Th]is is *my* will," Hegel adds: given my intrinsic freedom, no one else has the right to take possession of my natural immediacy. For this reason, as Hegel again insists here—making specific reference to New World slavery—"slaves have an absolute right to free themselves" or "break their chains [*Fesseln*] at any time."[41]

The slave remains central in the *Philosophy of Right*, underwriting the progression from the dialectic of person and property to the idea of the state. Indeed the relation of "master and slave," born of the "struggle for recognition," gives rise to the state as the "objective" articulation of recognitive self-consciousness[42]:

> Objective spirit—the content of right—should not again be apprehended in its subjective concept alone, and consequently human beings should not be determined as slaves; but for this [conceptual renunciation of slavery] to no longer be a mere *ought to be*, human beings must come to the realization that the idea of freedom is actual only as the state.[43]

The movement here from the "subjective concept" of spirit to its objectivity parallels the historical progression from the "idea" that human beings are free toward actualized

---

[35]Hegel, *Lectures on Natural Right and Political Science*, 77.

[36]Hegel, *Werke* 7: §54–6: 119–22.

[37]Hegel, *Werke* 7: §48: 111.

[38]Hegel, *Vorlesungen über Rechtsphilosophie 1818–1831*, 4: §42: 112; see also 4: §91: 272.

[39]Hegel, *Werke* 7: §43: 104.

[40]Hegel, *Werke* 7: §43–8: 104–11.

[41]Hegel, *Vorlesungen über Rechtsphilosophie 1818–1831*, 4: 239. This passage, too, has largely escaped scholarly attention.

[42]Hegel, *Werke* 7: §57: 124.

[43]Hegel, *Werke* 7: §57A: 126.

freedom from slavery in the state. Elsewhere, too, Hegel identifies the emerging self-consciousness of the slave as the "phenomenal and apparent beginning" of the state. Thus in *The Philosophy of Subjective Spirit*:

> It is through the *appearance* [*Erscheinung*] of this struggle for recognition and submission to a master that states [*Staaten*] in their incipient forms have emerged out of the social life of men. Consequently, the violence [*Gewalt*] that is the foundation [*Grund*] of this appearance [*Erscheinung*] is not the ground [*Grund*] of right, though it does constitute the necessary and justified moment by which self-consciousness makes the transition from the condition of being immersed in desire and singularity into that of its universality. This transitional self-consciousness is not the substantial principle, but the phenomenal or apparent beginning [*erscheinende Anfang*] of states.[44]

We will return to the nature of this "appearance" [*Erscheinung*] of the struggle for recognition and the "beginning" of states. For now it suffices that the *Knecht*, subjugated to a master, moves beyond this point of "beginning" through the process of "formation," or what Hegel repeatedly and interchangeably calls *Formieren* or *Bilden* and their cognates.[45] The slave's "formative activity" [*Formieren*] not only underwrites his self-knowing in the thing he produces,[46] but also gives rise to a community or system of need:

> Since the means of mastery, the *Knecht*, has also to be kept alive, one aspect of this relationship consists of the community of need [*Gemeinsamkeit*] and concern for its satisfaction. Crude destruction of the immediate object is therefore replaced by the acquisition, conservation, and formation [*Formieren*] of that object, and the latter is treated as the mediating factor within which the two extremes of independence and dependence unite themselves. The form of universality [*Die Form der Allgemeinheit*] in the satisfying of need is a perpetuating means, a provision that takes the future into account and secures it.[47]

The "formation" [*Formieren*] of an object isolates the pure "form of universality," the self-canceling architectonic delineation that moves between representation and thing, or language and matter. Through its endless formation and deformation, the object mediates between the "extremes" of self-consciousness—the slave's submission of its will to another's through the abjuration of the object ("dependence") and the master's

---

[44] Hegel, *The Philosophy of Subjective Spirit*, 3: §433, 63, translation modified.

[45] As Hegel makes clear, the formation of form [*Formierung*] relates to the education and formation of the self [*Bildung*]: "The formation of form includes also the human development of one's body and spirit," making one's potentialities and capacities "universal" through "education and formation [*Bildung*]" (Hegel, *Vorlesungen über Naturrecht Staatswissenschaft*, 26).

[46] Hegel *Werke* 3: 154.

[47] Hegel, *The Philosophy of Subjective Spirit*, 3: §434: 65.

apparent self-sufficiency through the willful consumption and destruction of the object ("independence"). These two modes, as inchoate forms of social and individual subjectivity, begin to reconcile in the social "community" founded on individual "need."

Hegel further specifies that this sociality serving "need" emerges upon the evolution of the *Knecht* from a slave to an "abstract self" that exercises its will, even in service to a master:

> In that there is now only one will, that of the master, it is at the same time independent, directed in accordance to its desires, and in this respect the slave [*Knecht*] is an instrument and not an end in itself; but this instrument is at the same time also consciousness, or at least possibly so, and thus inheres in the possibility of free will. He who has been subjugated [*Unterworfene*] can thus take back his own will, can revolt at any moment, the principle being the abstract self, which can say no to obligation that contravenes right: where he has no right, the slave [*Sklave*] has no duty. Thus the instrument serves the master willfully, remaining implicitly or in itself free self-consciousness, and this will of the servant [*dieser Wille des Knechts*] therefore has to be made to incline favorably to the master: the latter thus has to take care of him as a living being, take care of him as an implicitly free will. The servant [*Knecht*] is thus brought into a mutuality or community of provision [*die Gemeinsamkeit der Vorsorge*], so that he has purpose, validity, and honor—and is a member of the family. The slave [*Sklave*] can have no honor; the servant [*Knecht*] has his honor in fidelity. This gives rise to communal provision for the satisfaction of desire, which involves the forming of the object at hand [*Formirung des Objekts vorhanden*]. The object must be consciously assimilated, the future has to be provided for, constituting a universalization with respect to the satisfaction of needs.[48]

Here a number of Hegel's arguments respecting servitude converge. As in the *Philosophy of Right*, he suggests that the *Knecht* as "consciousness" takes a range of historical forms evolving from slavery.[49] Hegel reiterates that the slave, as an implicitly free will, has the innate right to "revolt"; indeed, the fear of defiance causes the master to "provide" enough to the slave to "incline him favorably" toward service. Accordingly the slave becomes a "willful" servant, a historical *Knecht*, whose "formation of the object at hand" gives rise to a system for the "satisfaction of needs" in which he voluntarily participates.[50]

The "community of need" corresponds to what Hegel in the *Philosophy of Right* will call "political economy" [*Staatsökonomie*], the first diremption of "civil society." The

---

[48]Hegel, *The Philosophy of Subjective Spirit*, 3: 342, translation modified.

[49]Here again the connection of the *Knecht* to slavery is far more complicated than has been recognized. In Hegel's usage here, the conceptual *Knecht*, first taking form as the slave, is not to be confused with the historical "servant" or *Knecht* who becomes a "member of the family."

[50]Hegel refers also to the "provision" "made for serfs [*Leibeigene*] and slaves [*Sklaven*]" in the 1817–1818 lectures in Heidelberg (Hegel, *Vorlesungen über Naturrecht Staatswissenschaft*, 165).

"formation of form" [*die Formierung*] indeed marks the basis for economic activity by translating property into an alienable object:

> When I engage in the formation of form [*Formierung*], the determination of a thing as mine acquires an externality subsisting in itself, thereby ceasing to be limited to my presence in *this* space and *this* time and to the presence of my knowledge and will. The imposition of form [*Formieren*] is the mode of taking possession most appropriate to the "idea," in that it unites within itself the subjective and the objective, even though it varies endlessly according to the qualitative character of the objects and the differences among subjective aims. Here, too, belongs the imposition of form [*Formieren*] on the organic, where what I do does not remain external to the form, but is assimilated by it: the tilling of the soil, the cultivation of plants, the taming, feeding, and keeping of animals; and also mediating processes for utilizing elemental materials or forces or making one material produce effects on another ... The human being, in his existence in himself, is natural, and thus external to his concept. Only through the development [*Ausbildung*] of his body and spirit, essentially, through self-consciousness's grasping itself as free, does he take possession of himself and become his own property and not anyone else's.[51]

In the opening of the *Phenomenology of Spirit*, the "thing" for consciousness evanesces before the discursive form articulated by the "this"; by contrast, in "Self-Consciousness" and in its corresponding moment here in the *Philosophy of Right*, the object, materializing the subjective will, acquires an apparently independent "externality [*Äußerlichkeit*]."[52] In the latter two texts, which express the dialectic of spirit from, respectively, its "subjective" and "objective" sides, the thing thus surfaces the individuated form of "being-for-self": in the shaped object, the subject attains to the form of an "existent being."[53]

On the one hand, as a body this self-consciousness "becomes capable of taking the form of a thing" and thus, Hegel continues, of enslavement.[54] On the other hand, the servile self-consciousness, by abjuring or alienating the object it forms—the disembodied, sensuous manifestation of its will—to the master, isolates the idea of the freedom of self-consciousness from objective particularity. Paralleling this movement, the imposition or formation of form [*Formieren*] in the later development of spirit in its "objective" mode articulates its innate freedom as a "person" capable of owning and thus ultimately of "alienating" (gifting, selling, and so on) a formed object as property. For this reason political economy, predicated on the formation and exchange of property and thus on the co-implication of objectivity and subjectivity, remains conceptually and materially entangled with the possibility of slavery.

---

[51] Hegel, *Werke* 7: §56: 121–2.
[52] Hegel, *Werke* 7: §56: 121.
[53] Hegel, *Werke* 3: 154.
[54] Hegel, *Werke* 7: §57: 124.

The "formation" or "imposition of form" [*Formierung*] underwrites the process of "formation" or "education" [*Bildung*] through which the human being "forms" his "body and spirit," acquiring "skills" and, in general, the capacity to "make the universal inside him" a "determinate and distinct" objective form through productive activity.[55] Self-consciousness in its universality must endlessly detach or "separate" itself even from this "activity of imposing form" [*die Tätigkeit der Formierung*][56]:

> The essence of spirit is not to *be*, but to posit itself by means of activity. It is only by forming or educating [*bilde*] myself that I become a *Meister* over my activities and can perform them in a manner appropriate to the object I want to work on. By imposing form [*Formierung*] I determine myself, I separate the determinate activities from me. These particularities, these skills belong to me, and they only occur because I have not remained in identity with myself.[57]

Through the fashioning of the object, the activity that isolates its "universal form," and the skill gained in doing so, the I "posit[s]" itself as a universal, an empty self to which no particularity can cling. In its universality, the "I" inheres neither in its objects nor skills (those that "belong to me"); these particularities accruing to the "I" must be externalized in order to prevent them from constituting and thus exercising "mastery" over the self.[58] Thus the "I," by virtue of formative activity, surfaces its universal, dynamic capacity to possess or accrue and then empty itself of particularity—in other words, to develop or change rather than merely cling to its "identity" with itself.

Crucially, since *Bildung* "concerns form" or, indeed, any aspect of the "I" in relation to its shaping of objectivity, the "formation" of the object [*Formierung*] constitutes the "formation" of the "I" [*Bildung*].[59] Thus Hegel makes the foundational and little noticed claim that "the formation of form *is* formation [of the self], or education as such" [*Diese Formierung ist die Bildung überhaupt*]; or, equally, "the form of universality imparted here to the particular *is* education" [*Diese Form der Allgemeinheit, die hier dem Besonderen gegeben ist, ist die Bildung*].[60]

The progression in the *Phenomenology of Spirit* from the slave's "formation of form" [*das Formieren*] to its discovery of its freedom in and from objectivity corresponds to this movement in the *Philosophy of Right* from aesthetic activity to *Bildung*.[61] Indeed the malleability of the developing self-consciousness characterizes all of its historical

---

[55]Hegel, *Vorlesungen über Naturrecht Staatswissenschaft*, 26.

[56]Ibid., 26.

[57]Ibid., 26. Note that the term *Meister* here again does not refer to the *Herr* that, driven by desire, owns and exploits the slave; rather *Meister* reflects the mastery over work in the attempted (and ultimately impossible) articulation of the "ideal" union of form and content, quintessentially in Greek art, economy, and political theory.

[58]Hegel, *Vorlesungen über Naturrecht Staatswissenschaft*, 26.

[59]Hegel, *Vorlesungen über Naturrecht Staatswissenschaft*, 116.

[60]Ibid., 116. Emphasis mine.

[61]Hegel, *Werke* 3: 154.

modes from slave, serf, and willful servant to member of civil society [*Bürger*] or "private person," whose "essential activity consists in imparting the form of universality to, and thereby conferring validity upon, arbitrary desires as well as needs and their satisfaction."[62] "Slaves" [*Sklaven*], "serfs" [*Leibeigen*], and "members of civil society" [*Bürger*] all "labor for their needs," even if only the latter work in "the feeling that their property is protected."[63] In the context of political economy, this "labor" constitutes an "abstract" "activity" that purges the self of "particular subjectivity": "one's own indeterminacy, imagination, and opinion must be given up, and one must direct one's work to a determinate end" for the sake of "the needs of others."[64] Accordingly this labor, the participation in the production of means, constitutes *Bildung überhaupt*, or the cultivation of "general" sensibility with respect to socially determined needs.

The intersubjectivity of self-consciousness, its relation to itself "through identity with another self-consciousness," mediates not only the production of "means," but also the development of those same socially inflected "needs":

> What we have to consider here are needs and the means of satisfying them. One human being's needs are mediated by others. The means of satisfying needs, i.e. work, is work for others in order to work for oneself; one procures one's needs through others. As universality, human beings should rise above their immediate single needs; this transcendence is initially only proliferation, or particularity … one concrete need is divided into many needs and these in turn into many others …. Division of need makes it more universal, more abstract … The quest to discover means of satisfying [needs] is stimulated anew by each new means. This proliferation of means is mediated, for the specific sphere of need is immediate need, the requirements of nature; what constitutes the mediation is that a self-consciousness relates to itself through identity with another self-consciousness … This mediation has its starting point as such in the contingency and inequality that are to be found among different individuals in regard to modifications and needs, in particular to the way they are satisfied or to kinds of enjoyment. This perception involves the contradiction implied by inequality with the other in the consciousness of equality, and justifies the drive to bring about and represent [*vorzustellen*] to oneself one's equality with others, the imitative drive, which affords the stimulus to obtain the same unknown enjoyment for oneself or in general to acquire what the other has. By dint of repetition the enjoyment becomes something subjectively universal, a habit [*Gewohnheit*] and need. It is then no less necessary to give this equality determinate existence for the other and to make oneself aware of being regarded and recognized [*anerkannt*] by the other as his equal.[65]

---

[62]Hegel, *Vorlesungen über Naturrecht Staatswissenschaft*, 116.

[63]Hegel, *Lectures on Natural Right and Political Science*, 214.

[64]Hegel, *Lectures on Natural Right and Political Science*, 174.

[65]Hegel, *Lectures on Natural Right and Political Science*, 167–9.

Following Adam Smith, Hegel argues that the market processes underpinning political economy increasingly meet human "needs" by optimizing the "means" of production, for instance through the division of labor.[66] Insightfully, he further frames these market processes as the attempt of a fragmented self-consciousness to achieve recognitive reconciliation with itself by harmonizing individual and collective activity. Through the endless attempt of irreducibly different subjects to gain "equality" with each other, political economy engenders ever-increasing needs, resulting in a proliferation of requirements and the means to satisfy them.

Hegel expounds on this process as follows: conscious of his fundamental identity with his other, the subject confronts the other's paradoxically dissimilar habits and satisfactions. To achieve equality, the subject then imitates the other, "confident that what [the latter] has must be pleasing," and aims for "recognition by the other as his equal."[67] This desire for recognition thus socializes humans to ever-increasing needs and means, the particularity of which entrenches inequality. As increasingly "abstract" "representations" of our recognizability to other self-consciousnesses, these dependencies have ever less to do with concrete "requirements of nature": addressing more than the need to keep warm, for instance, we wear "fashions" established by "others" in order to be recognized as identical.[68] Furthermore, through "repetition," enjoyments become "self-imposed needs," as in the case of psychologically or physiologically habit-forming or addictive products including, in Hegel's day as in ours, tobacco, alcohol, coffee, and sugar.[69]

Counter-intuitively, this apparent vortex of dependence underwrites the *Bildung* of self-consciousness by mediating its relation to objectivity through ever more "abstract" or "universal" modes of "representation" of needs and means. Already the "abstract person" imposes form on the object through its discursive "representation" [*Vorstellung*], the "marking of the thing with a sign [*Zeichen*] that is supposed to indicate that I have invested my will in it."[70] Translated into a sign with which it has no necessary relation, the object "does not count as a thing" but rather as "what it is supposed to signify."[71] In this respect "taking possession" through the "mark" of an arbitrary signifier reveals the "universality" of the object: translated into the universal currency of signs, it becomes, effectively, a commodity negated by use or consumption, "reduced" to a "means for the satisfaction of my need."[72] By imposing the discursive "form of universality" on both needs and means, self-consciousness underwrites their economic circulation as socially recognized values. Through this act of *Bilden*, self-consciousness experiences "means"

---

[66]Hegel, *Werke* 7: §198, 352. See also Herzog, *Inventing the Market*.

[67]Hegel, *Lectures on Natural Right and Political Science*,169.

[68]Hegel, *Lectures on Natural Right and Political Science*, 168.

[69]Hegel gives the examples of fashion and smoking (Hegel, *Lectures on Natural Right and Political Science*, 169). A significant part of our economy today depends on addiction and compulsion, from fatty and sugary food to television series and media accessed on portable devices.

[70]Hegel, *Werke* 7: §54: 119, 7: §58: 126.

[71]Hegel, *Werke* 7: §58: 126.

[72]Hegel, 7: §59: 128.

as discursively mediated "forms" through which it satisfies needs and "represents" its equality to others and to itself. This endless stream of means, produced and consumed, constitutes *Bildung* because no representation or form anchors self-consciousness to a particular object. Furthermore, the process cultivates a sensibility with respect to socially validated needs and thus, necessarily, enables self-consciousness to give "due scope" to the needs of others.[73]

While "*Bildung* relates to form," its "content," says Hegel, "can be of the most varied nature."[74] As we have seen, the inadequate affinity of form and content defines the "aesthetic"; and Hegel frames the latter as the dialectic of architecture and poetry, two aesthetic forms manifesting oppositional relations of form and content.[75] Architectural "form" emerges as demarcated sensuous matter gesturing endlessly at its discursive meaning or "content"; poetic "form," by contrast, translates "its sensuous element," the voice, into a "meaningless" discursive "sign," dissolving received objective content and articulating it anew.[76] Where built form, or apparently enduring demarcations of objectivity, gestures at potentially congruent but ultimately inadequate content, discursive or poetic form attempts endlessly to slough off or dissolve existing "sensuous" externality and so reduce possible objective content to a "pure letter," a hieroglyph with no material referent.[77]

In the dialectical circuit of the aesthetic, architecture relates material form to verbal content, while poetry relates verbal form to material content. The interpenetration of these oppositional modes constitutes the "architectonic" dimension of any attempt to relate form and content in the delineation of a meaningful world; accordingly form and content each traverse the bounds between concept and reality, or language and matter. This same entanglement of form and content will structure for Hegel the "architectonic" of the state's rationality. Thus in the preface of the *Philosophy of Right*:

> This, too, is what constitutes the more concrete meaning of what has been more abstractly referred to as *the unity of form and content*, for *form* in its most concrete sense is reason as cognition [*Erkennen*] that grasps conceptually [*begreifendes*], and *content* is reason as the substantial essence of ethical [*sittlichen*] as well as of natural reality; the conscious identity of the two is the philosophical idea.[78]

Here the movement between conceptual and "concrete" "form"—already evident in the paronomastic term *begreifen*, meaning both "to grasp" physically and "to comprehend"—parallels the translation of "content" from conceptual relationality

---

[73]Hegel, *Vorlesungen über Naturrecht Staatswissenschaft*, 115ff.

[74]"Die Bildung ist etwas Formelles und der Inhalt kann von der verschiedensten Natur sein" (Hegel, *Vorlesungen über Naturrecht Staatswissenschaft*, 116).

[75]Hegel, *Werke* 15: 235.

[76]Hegel, *Werke* 15: 235.

[77]Hegel, *Werke* 15: 235 and 13: 123.

[78]Hegel, *Werke* 7: 27.

("essence") to materiality ("substantial[ity]") and from notionally "ethical" to "natural reality." Referring to and converging imperfectly with each other, the interpenetration of these conceptual and material modes, prior to their "conscious identity" with each other, on Hegel's definition must be aesthetic.

In the *Philosophy of Right*, *Formieren* or *Bilden* therefore constitutes an aesthetic operation that propels the movement of political economy. The imposition of the "form of universality," the "pure form" moving between the discursive and material, delineates objective "content" in the world; the ensuing "concrete" "form" cannot be fully subsumed into or abstracted from its objective "content," resulting in their aesthetic coimbrication.[79] The term *Zeichen*, referring to a linguistic "sign" and a physical "mark," also moves between the linguistic and sensuous realms. The interpenetration of linguistic and physical form in the formation of abstract property—the circulating commodity of political economy—reflects the aesthetic entanglement of concept and matter in the "grasping" of a thing: "The taking possession through the discursive term or through marking [*Bezeichnung*] is the most perfect mode of doing so, for all others also have more or less the same effect of the sign or mark [*Zeichens*]. Whenever I grasp [*ergreife*] or form [*formiere*] a thing, the ultimate meaning is also a sign or mark to others for the purpose of excluding them and showing them that I have put my will into that thing."[80]

Just as the sign cannot achieve complete freedom from its referent, maintaining always a symbolic entanglement with materiality, so, too the object, through inventive "formation," holds the potential to express a new interpenetration of form and content, hence an aesthetic evolution of meaning for self-consciousness as producer and consumer. The resulting possibility of ever-new relations of form and content underwrites the aesthetic dimension of the "formation" or *Bildung* of self-consciousness, stimulating the "proliferation" of economic activity:

> At an immediate level, the proliferation of need leads to an equal proliferation or stimulation of infinitely varied and increasingly strenuous activity; at a theoretical level, this process involves a rapid movement through representations [*Vorstellungen*], the grasping of complex and universal relations, and the *Bildung* of the understanding [*Verstands*] and of language; but this process also engenders a need for occupation, in the shape of work, that must be measured to the needs of others and [thus] takes on a developed or refined [*gebildeten*], universal form.[81]

Here Hegel again relates *Bilden* as an aesthetic operation to the *Bildung* of consciousness as "understanding." The innovative conjunction of form and content creates an endless "proliferation" of new needs and new means; Hegel identifies *Bildung* as the virtue of this ever more "strenuous" economic activity. In the absence of the aesthetic dimension of

---

[79]Hegel, *Werke* 3: 154.

[80]Hegel, *Werke* 7: §58A: 127–8.

[81]Hegel, *Vorlesungen über Naturrecht Staatswissenschaft*, 124.

Bilden, political economy [*Staatsökonomie*] would consist in the "stimulation" of ever-increasing and pointless "activity."

How does the aesthetic intervention of an individual self-consciousness create a "universal form"? Already in his Jena lectures, Hegel describes the "cycle" through which the "inventions" of individual skill are codified, reproduced, and ultimately appropriated into a new "universal rule" [*allgemeine Regel*][82]:

> The recognition of labor and skill [*Das Anerkennen der Arbeit und Geschicklichkeit*] goes through the cycle in its universal dimension, [while consciousness goes through] the cycle's individual dimension through learning. Against the universal skill [*Geschicklichkeit*], the individual posits himself as a particular, he separates himself and makes himself more skillful than the others; he invents more useful tools; but what is truly universal in his particular skill is the invention [*Erfindung*] of a universal: others learn it, dialectically overcoming [the inventor's] particularity, and it immediately becomes a universal good.[83]

In the *Phenomenology*, the enslaved self-consciousness's "skill" [*Geschicklichkeit*], articulating the object's architectonic "form," discloses its fluidity and self-canceling impetus.[84] In this process the notional slave identifies not only his freedom from all apparently enduring form, but also the possibility of aesthetic production—harnessing, in the architectonic, both the externalizing force of architecture and the dissolving power of poetry. This same process obtains in the case of the historical "person" laboring in a modern economy: "he makes himself more skillful than the others; he invents more useful tools." The translation of means into a representational economy, driven by the intersubjective process of "recognition," underwrites the movement from "particular skill" to a "universal" "invention." The new tool "becomes the machine," ultimately freeing the human being from mechanical labor and its stultifying effects:[85]

> And so the work [of the factory laborer] becomes abstract, monotonous, and easier, in that there is only one operation, only one skill that the individual subject practices, and so he can acquire more facility in that single function. [By contrast], every craftsman [*Handwerker*] produces more concrete work; he often has to move between multiple tasks; [and] his knowledge must be manifold and extend over many objects. Accordingly, factory workers [*Fabrikarbeiter*] become dull and dependent on their factory, for nowhere else can they use this single skill. A factory presents a sorry picture of the dulling [*Abstumpfung*] of human beings … But when factory labor has reached a level of perfection and simplicity, then machines

[82]Hegel, *Jenaer Systementwürfe I: Das System der spekulativen Philosophie*, eds. K. Düsing and H. Kimmerle (Hamburg: Felix Meiner, 1986), 227.

[83]Ibid., 227–8.

[84]Hegel, *Werke* 3: 154.

[85]Hegel, *Vorlesungen über Naturrecht Staatswissenschaft*, 127.

can supplant the machine-like labor of human beings; this is the usual progression in factories. And [in this ceaseless cycle] through the end of this machine-like progression, human beings become free again.[86]

As a product of aesthetic "innovation," the "machine" promises to free the laboring self-consciousness from the "strenuous activity" to which it would otherwise be condemned by the proliferation of means. Mediated by representation, political economy indeed depends on the signifiable and thus tradeable "excess" or "superfluity [*Überfluß*] of means of enjoyment": "the contingent circumstance that one person has an excess of one means of satisfaction leads to the exchange against means that the other has in excess."[87] More generally, the aesthetic dimension of "formation" engenders "excess" as an element inherent to the representational function propelling the "system of need" in civil society.

Hegel's critique of political economy turns on the excess of these fundamentally representational or discursive operations, inflecting, as we will see, his theory of the state. This excess in the representational economy, driven by aesthetic "invention," knows no bounds: "This proliferation has no limit [*Grenze*], just as there is no limit between what is natural and what is based on representation [*Vorstellung*]—imaginary need [*eingebildetes Bedürfnis*]."[88] The subject, before she amasses enough capital to exert mastery over other laborers, remains a *Knecht*. At the same time, the desire for recognition drives her to imitate those who continue to accrue possessions: as her needs grow, she continues to labor, subjected to newer processes that require specialization and abstraction from the complete cycle of production.

The boundlessness of representational possibility, correlating to an "infinity" of perceived needs and means, causes humans to traverse spatial limits as well, covering "the whole earth to find the most suitable means for their needs, even for the most humble end ..."[89] While the earth, being spherical, presents no insurmountable limit or border [*Grenze*] for the geographical expansion of this representational economy, self-consciousness must confront the finitude of the earth's surface, the competition for land, and thus the need for "civil society," or the "reciprocal recognition of rights": "the whole earth is occupied, and [individuals] have in consequence to rely on civil society [*bürgerliche Gesellschaft*]."[90]

As a "communal" framework for reciprocal interdependence, "civil society" has as its basis "the task of securing the life and property of individuals."[91] For this reason civil society constitutes a "state" only "as understanding envisages it" [*Verstandesstaat*]—that is, a "state based on need" [*Notstaat*]. Here individuals as "independent agents," indulging their "particular subjectivity," "see" such "needs" as actual "necessities" instead

---

[86]Ibid.
[87]Ibid., 125.
[88]Ibid., 122.
[89]Ibid., 122.
[90]Ibid., 149, 160.
[91]Ibid., 112–3, 149; Hegel, *Werke* 7: §332: 499.

of as imaginary or contingent representations.[92] This "external" [*äußere*] state, rather than taking "the form of purpose in and for itself," centers on "property" as the foundation for meeting "needs"; but this "externality" translates merely into an "abstract universality, a universality that is only a means."[93]

Civil society "combs the earth" not only for new products and means to increase production, but also for new "consumers" to purchase "excess" goods.[94] Relating to "the needs of the entire world," civil society moreover spreads "artistic industriousness" [*Kunstfleiß*] from one corner of the globe to another.[95] The sector of "business" or "industry," occupied with "the imposition of form on the products of nature," constitutes "the chief sector in civil society."[96] Engaging in "trade," this sector becomes "cosmopolitan," transcending any particular "fatherland" or "state."[97]

Multiplying its representations, civil society also exposes its increasingly specialized pools of labor to stagnation or obsolescence due to innovation and mechanization.[98] Increasing concentrations of wealth and the ceaseless drive for monopolistic control over resources can make necessities too expensive for the poor.[99] Wealth can also spur population growth, which at times may outstrip the "availability of means."[100] These "excesses" of political economy, a function of its fundamentally representational or discursive mediation, can only be mitigated, never abolished; thus "civil society" leads inevitably to a certain degree of "poverty" and thus potentially a "rabble."[101] While a "rapid, clear system for the administration of justice and civil and political freedom in general" can increase the "prosperity" of civil business, the production of adequate means and the balancing of competing interests require a deliberate and collectively oriented "system of care and oversight."[102] Indicatively, provision must be made for "those whose livelihood has disappeared" due to mechanization.[103]

As part of its "system of care" for superfluous laborers, civil society is "driven" to develop a strategy of organized "colonization."[104] Likewise the poor can attempt to "migrate" to a "capital city" or "wealthy country" of their own accord.[105] Typically the

---

[92]"Civil society is in the first place the external state or the state as the understanding envisages it" (Hegel, *Vorlesungen über Naturrecht Staatswissenschaft*, 112).

[93]Hegel, *Vorlesungen über Naturrecht Staatswissenschaft*, 112–3; Hegel, *Werke* 7: 28.

[94]Hegel, *Vorlesungen über Naturrecht Staatswissenschaft*, 122; Hegel, Werke 7: §246: 391.

[95]Hegel, *Vorlesungen über Rechtsphilosophie 1818–1831*, 4: 520; Hegel, *Werke* 7: §246: 391

[96]Hegel, *Vorlesungen über Rechtsphilosophie 1818–1831,* 4: 519.

[97]Ibid., 4: 520.

[98]Hegel, *Vorlesungen über Naturrecht Staatswissenschaft*, 161, 166–7.

[99]Hegel gives the example of London: "As wealth increases, it concentrates" into fewer and fewer hands, and those who possess that "great capital" can buy assets more easily than can those without capital, "so the inequality between them increases" (Hegel, *Vorlesungen über Rechtsphilosophie 1818–1831*, ed. Karl-Heinz Ilting (Stuttgart: Frommann Verlag, 1974), 4: 494.

[100]Hegel, *Vorlesungen über Naturrecht Staatswissenschaft*, 164–5.

[101]Ibid., 160–2.

[102]Ibid.,164–5.

[103]Ibid., 166–7.

[104]Ibid., 164–5.

[105]Ibid., 161.

need for colonization or migration arises when a "mass of people" "cannot secure the satisfaction of their needs by their own labor once production surpasses the needs of consumption."[106] By implication, when that "mass of people" can neither satisfy its needs through work nor emigrate, they will wallow in poverty. Thus Hegel points to the "sickness" of the otherwise "booming" economy of England, whose "rabble" demonstrates "the depth of the abyss into which human nature can sink."[107]

Ultimately civil society attempts to end the infinite cycle of "imaginary need" and lessen poverty and inequality by developing "communal" [gemeinsame] associations or "corporations" [Korporationen], groups of people who share a similar vocation or "occupational sector."[108] Participation in such associations, which provide status, training, insurance, political advocacy and even possibly representation, militates against the "atomistic spirit" [Geist der Atomistik] of the market, according to which individuals pursue enjoyment only for themselves and seek recognition through the display of wealth rather than through social belonging.[109] But corporations disregard the interests of other corporations: organized labor associations privilege the interests of their own members over those of the collective. A similar conflict ensues between labor and capital: the latter, striving ceaselessly to monopolize markets and thus further concentrate itself, undermines or even seeks to abolish forms of organized labor through legislative influence in the Verstandesstaat.[110]

Family life and civil society, the two initial diremptions of ethical life [Sittlichkeit], both remain unstable in the absence of social norms harmonizing the individual and collective will in a governed polity. Hegel differentiates these two ethical forms with respect to their orientation toward "ground" or territoriality. The "family," the first diremption of "ethicality," literally seeks firm [festen] ground for the natural immediacy of its biological and physical bonds.[111] By contrast "civil society," as a merely "formulaic universality"

---

[106]Hegel, Werke 7: §248, 392.

[107]Hegel, Vorlesungen über Rechtsphilosophie 1818–1831, 3: 704.

[108]Hegel, Vorlesungen über Naturrecht Staatswissenschaft, 167–8, 122, 142.

[109]Hegel, Vorlesungen über Naturrecht Staatswissenschaft, 169; Hegel, Werke 7: §230ff, 382ff.

[110]Hegel, Vorlesungen über Naturrecht Staatswissenschaft, 169–70. Thus Hegel argues that with the "abolition of corporations" or vocational organizations in France and England, "the condition of the working class deteriorates, because it must then work for less, and the merchants can buy more cheaply." While this apparently serves the interests of "commerce," in fact "the work of business has gotten worse." In England, commerce has flourished, but only because of exclusive (and indeed imperial) access to a vast "world market"; otherwise the absence of labor cooperatives contributes to "the most horrendous poverty" and a "widespread rabble" (Hegel, Vorlesungen über Rechtsphilosophie 1818–1831, 3: 711–2, 4: 626).

[111]For Hegel the relation between "ethical life" and "ground" first emerges from the family's "external reality" in property. Indeed the family, as an "immediate" modality, "must" have property to live; but since the family is not an "abstract person," it rises above the latter's merely "abstract" need for property—a need emerging from "self-seeking" or "desire" (Hegel, Die Philosophie des Rechts: Die Mitschriften Wannenmann (Heidelberg 1817/18) und Homeyer (Berlin 1818/19), ed. Karl-Heinz Ilting [Stuttgart: Klett-Cotta Verlag, 1983], 142). In order for property to become "fixed" or "firm" [festen] rather than "abstract," ethical relationships must exist, for only ethicality, the relation of subject and object, can give concrete life to "immediate" needs and means. Ethicality first appears in the shared subjectivity of enduring love, where two people with no "natural" bond enter into marriage—a lifelong ethical relationship—of their own free will. The love commitment must be permanent in order to differentiate it from mere concubinage and create a shared sense of subjectivity in

based on the dogmas of the "understanding" and a boundless representational economy, takes to the sea[112]:

> The condition for the principle of family life is the earth, solid ground and soil [*Grund und Boden*]; likewise the natural element for industry, animating its outward impetus, is the sea ... [T]rade by sea, the greatest medium of communication, creates commercial links between distant countries, a relationship of right involving contracts. At the same time, trade [*Verkehr*] of this kind is the most potent means of *Bildung*; through it commerce acquires its world-historical significance.[113]

Spilling out "beyond itself," the "dialectic of civil society" pursues ever deeper "interconnection," including through "systematic" or "sporadic" "colonization" or the outmigration of its "excess" labor.[114] Where European states based on "need" and thus mere "understanding" emphasize this movement beyond territorial limits into the "boundless" sea, Asiatic states cling to their grounded boundaries:

> The sea gives us the picture-thought of the indeterminate, the unlimited, and infinite [*die Vorstellung des Unbestimmten, Unbeschränkten und Unendlichen*]; and as man feels *his own infinite* in that infinite, he is given the courage to venture beyond what is limited [*Beschränkte*]. The sea invites man to conquest and piratical looting [*Raub*], but also to profit and business. The land, the flat valley, binds him to the soil [*Boden*], involving him in an infinite number of dependencies, but the sea leads him out beyond these limited [*beschränkten*] circles. Those who take to the sea aim for profit and acquisition, but the means are inverted [*verkehrt*], for they risk losing both property and life ... This boundless [*unendliche*] surface [of the sea] is absolutely malleable—resisting no force [*Drucke*], not even a breath of wind. It appears boundlessly innocent, yielding, friendly, and affectionate; and it

---

the world; thus only marriage emerging out of a love bond can begin to unify the individual and collective will. The relation of this love bond as grounded ethicality to the development of states can be gleaned from their "founding myths," where "the institution of fixed [*festen*] property," attending the "advent of marriage," lays the foundations for "ethical social life" (Hegel, *Werke* 7; §170, 323–4). But the definition and circulation of family property, no matter how "firm," cannot be resolved except in "the sphere of civil society." And here the acquisition of property again centers on the activity of the "particular" "I," suspending the "ethical determination" of the family: "The right that accrues to the individual on the basis of the family unity ... emerges in the form of legal right" "only when the family begins to dissolve" (*Die Philosophie des Rechts: Die Mitschriften Wannenmann (Heidelberg 1817/18) und Homeyer (Berlin 1818/19)*, 250; Hegel, *Vorlesungen über Rechtsphilosophie 1818–1831*, 4: 395; Hegel, *Werke* 7: §159, 308). Here the lack of a "natural" bond between the parties to a marriage opens the institution, while keeping with Hegel's dialectic, to non-heteronormative possibilities, including gay marriage and adoption. The decoupling of marriage from sexual reproduction in the *Phenomenology of Spirit* (see Chapter 9) indeed adds foundational support for such a reading. A study of the relation between the "family," gender, and heteronormativity in Hegel lies beyond the scope of this book (on this topic, see *Hegel's Philosophy and Feminist Thought*).

[112]Hegel, *Werke* 7; §157, 306.

[113]Hegel, *Werke* 7; §247, 391.

[114]Hegel, *Werke* 7; §246, 391.

is exactly this pliability that turns [*verkehrt*] the sea into the most dangerous and violent element. To this deceitfulness and violence, man merely opposes a simple piece of wood; relies entirely on his courage and presence of mind; and thus passes from firm to unstable support, taking his artificial ground [*gemachten Boden*] with him. The ship, that swan of the sea, cutting the wave-plain in agile and round movements or inscribing circles upon it, is a tool whose invention [*Erfindung*] honors man's intrepidity as well as his understanding. This spilling out into the sea beyond the limitations [*Beschränktheit*] of land [*Erdbodens*] is lacking in the magnificent edifices [*Prachtgebäuden*] of Asiatic states, even as they themselves border [*angrenzen*] on the sea, like China. For them the sea is only the limit or ceasing [*Aufhören*] of the land …[115]

Where an attachment to the land creates bonds of "dependence," tying an individual to the obligations of family, the "infinite" sea offers "limitless" [*unendliche*] possibilities for material gain, not only through colonization and migration, but also through commerce and piracy. The ship, a "tool" or "invention" emerging out of the innovative and cosmopolitan forces of political economy, realizes as it honors only the "understanding." The movable and "artificial ground" [*gemachten Boden*] of this floating "tool" marks, accordingly, the deterritorialization of the *Verstandesstaat* and the global reach of its "system" of needs and means.[116] In this passage Hegel relates the state based on "needs and means," or the "external state," to the "perverse" logic of the "understanding," recalling the critique of the latter in the *Phenomenology of Spirit*: emerging from the necessities of political economy, the "external state" endlessly "inverts" means and ends in the infinite cycle of need and, by implication, the fluid sea into an "artificial ground" removed from any concrete community. Indeed the "pliability" of the sea leads to the deceitful "inversion" of placidity into tempestuous violence in a manner that threatens commerce (hence Hegel's play on *Verkehr*, meaning trade, and *Verkehrung*). In contrast, the Asiatic conception of the state relates to the fixity of its territorial limits: here Hegel evokes China's turn away from maritime exploration and international commerce during the Qing dynasty.[117] Even so, Asiatic states relate, as "magnificent edifices" [*Prachtgebäuden*],[118] to the quintessentially Oriental art of building; by implication, the

---

[115]Hegel, *Werke* 12: 118–9.

[116]Hegel, *Werke* §189, 346.

[117]Hegel was aware of the burgeoning trade on the Indian Ocean, the south China seas, and the Pacific rim prior to the arrival of Europeans. He may have learned of China's economic turmoil from Adam Smith. In the seventeenth century, the Qing dynasty further restricted trade, partly in response to European piracy and the violent trade practices that wrecked havoc on the Chinese economy (see Shi Zhihong, "China's Overseas Trade Policy," in *Inter-Asian Trade and the World Market*, ed. Latham and Kawakatsu [London: Routledge, 2006], 8–10). The effect of the European expropriation of silver from the colonies on the shift in global economic power from Asian to European economies after 1492 merits further investigation and treatment in narratives of colonial history. In the nineteenth century, Europeans—this time the British—forcefully penetrated China's borders to sell highly addictive opiates.

[118]Hegel uses the expression "den asiatischen Prachtgebäuden von Staaten" in Hegel, *Werke* 12: 119. See also the phrase "die Prachtgebäude der orientalischen Reiche" in ibid., 135.

borders [*Grenzen*, evoked by the verb *angrenzen*] of such states delineate an architectonic and thus ultimately fluid territorial "limit."

How does Hegel resolve the conflicting conceptions of the state in relation to the "ground" of the earth? Does the state require—and can it maintain—a "single political authority" [*einer Staatsgewalt*] over a territory?[119] If so, wouldn't such an exclusive ("single") power, anticipating Max Weber's well-known definition of the state, necessarily have to monopolize the authoritative use of force within a delimited territory?[120] On the other hand, how could such a state maintain its territorialized power in the face of the "spilling over" or incursions of a globalizing civil society, effecting the movement of peoples and goods across state borders? Given the dialectic of grounded and cosmopolitan *Sittlichkeit*, what constitutes for Hegel the "architectonic" state?

For Hegel the state as the "actuality of the ethical idea"—"ethical spirit as manifest, substantial will" in contrast to the merely "external state" "based on need"—emerges from the dialectical relation between the family tied to the soil and a deterritorialized civil society.[121] These modes of ethical life involve the violence of failed recognition between self-consciousnesses. As we have seen, the individual in the family begins, but ultimately fails to achieve mutual recognition through love: the family breaks down into abstract persons who possess property to the exclusion of others, such that all remain in a "state of nature." The attempt to satisfy necessities leads to political economy and consequently civil society: the system of needs and means, tending to concentrate capital in the hands of certain masters, cycles the laboring *Knecht* through various forms of servitude from slavery and serfdom to wage labor.[122]

This "appearance [*Erscheinung*] of the struggle for recognition" and then "submission to a master" mark the "apparent beginning" [*erscheinende Anfang*] of the state in its "incipient" form; accordingly the struggle for recognition and the ensuing dialectic of master and slave engenders the third moment of ethical life.[123] Hegel will repeatedly use the term *Erscheinung* to insist on the phenomenality or materiality of the state: but violent subjugation and the emergence of the "transitional self-consciousness" as it

---

[119]Hegel, *Werke* 1: 503. Hegel emphasizes "einer."

[120]Max Weber argues: "the state is that human community [*Gemeinschaft*] which (successfully) lays claim to the monopoly of legitimate physical violence within a certain territory, this 'territory' being another of the defining characteristics of the state. For the specific feature of the present is that the right to use physical violence is attributed to any and all other associations or individuals only to the extent that the state for its part permits this to happen. The state is held to be the source of the 'right' to use violence" (Max Weber, *Political Writings*, eds. Lassman and Speirs [Cambridge: Cambridge University Press, 1994] 310ff.).

[121]Hegel, *Vorlesungen über Rechtsphilosophie 1818–1831*, 4: 619–20.

[122]Civil society in the form of commerce and trade constitutes a "universal interaction and *Bildung* of humankind," resulting in "reciprocal recognition" (Hegel, *System der Sittlichkeit: Critik des Fichteschen Naturrechts*, ed. H. D. Brandt [Hamburg: Meiner Verlag, 2002], 13). But this universalism remains abstract, instructing the subject in the emptiness of form, but not in the realized vitality of the social or universal will in the "concrete freedom" of the state (Hegel, *Werke* §260, 406; see also *Werke* 10: §432, 219). In civil society, which emerges after the struggle to the death, the relation of mastery and slavery prevails in its objective counterpart, namely the relation of person and property.

[123]Hegel, *The Philosophy of Subjective Spirit*, 3: §433, 63. It is important to recall that these "moments" are not chronological: in fact civil society, says Hegel, requires a state, at least in its diremption as a *Verstandesstaat*.

labors to unify individuality and universality constitute only the concrete "beginning" and not the "substantial principle" of the state.[124] Hegel articulates the same point at greater length in the 1827–1828 lectures on *The Philosophy of Spirit*:

> Reason demands that reciprocal recognition be the result [of the struggle between self-consciousnesses]. But [violent struggle] constitutes only the phenomenal or external origin [*der erscheinende Anfang*] of the state, not its substantial principle. On the contrary, whatever drives the state to violence [*Gewalt*] and arbitrariness gradually makes itself superfluous through the development of reason. We must distinguish between the apparent beginning [of the state] [*die Erscheinung im Anfang*] and its genuine originating principle. We find the relation of mastery and slavery [*Herrschaft und Knechtschaft*] in the patriarchal condition. In earlier times the one who was subjugated became the slave [*Knecht*] of the other. There is a kind of mutuality or community [*Gemeinsamkeit*] posited here—the master only has property and the slave [*Sklave*] has none. The slave is not his own [*nicht sein eigen*], not free for himself [*für sich*]; he has sacrificed his freedom for his life. He has no will of his own. He has recognized the will of the other, and is a thing for the other, and so belongs to the other—this is a community [*Gemeinsamkeit*] based on needs and their satisfaction. This is not a universality that would be recognized in and for itself, [namely as a community based on] right or justice, but [merely] a

---

[124]On the relation of states and violence, see Hegel, *Die Vernunft in der Geschichte*, ed. J. Hoffmeister (Hamburg: Felix Meiner, 1955), 114. In this context, Hegel also discusses the use of the term *Erscheinung* with respect to the state: "The universal idea attains to phenomenal appearance [*Erscheinung*] in the state. In regards to the term *Erscheinung*, it should be noted that it does not have the meaning here that it has in its ordinary sense. [Ordinarily] we distinguish between force [*Kraft*] and appearance [*Erscheinung*], as if the former were essential and the latter inessential and external. But even in the category of force there is no concrete determination. On the other hand, where there is spirit—that is, the concrete concept—the *Erscheinung* itself is the essential ... The phenomenal aspect of the spirit is its self-determination, which is the element of its concrete nature: the spirit which does not determine itself is merely an abstraction of the understanding [*Abstraktum des Verstandes*] ... We therefore regard a *Volk* as a spiritual individual, and in this we do not emphasize here the external side, but rather what we have previously called the spirit of the people [*der Geist des Volkes*], i.e. its self-consciousness in relation to its own truth and being, and what it regards as truth in general, the spiritual powers that live and rule in a people. The universal which emerges and becomes conscious [*gewußt*] in the state, the form [*Form*] to which all assimilates, is that which constitutes the formation [*Bildung*] of a nation" (ibid., 114). Echoing his critique of the idea of "force" [*Kraft*] for the faculty of "understanding" in the *Phenomenology of Spirit*, Hegel argues that initially the state's *Erscheinung*, for all its violence, like the category of "force" [*Kraft*] remains a discursive ideality with "no concrete determination." Only when the state materializes as self-consciousness that knows itself as itself, and therefore does not require the coercion of other self-consciousnesses, could spirit "appear" as the phenomenal state in its more "essential," hence endlessly self-reflexive, sense. Here spirit realizes itself fully and concretely as "self-consciousness in relation to its own truth and being," or as the endlessly self-canceling form of spirit through *Bildung*. As we will see, H. B. Nisbet's translation of *Bildung* as "culture" here is deeply misleading, for it implies that "culture" is the static, phenomenal form of spirit, where in fact it is merely part of the self-negating and thus dynamic, ever-changing particularity that self-consciousness, in the *Bildung* of a "people" as a "nation" in history, endlessly sheds (Hegel, *Lectures on the Philosophy of World History: Introduction*, transl. H. B. Nisbet, 96). It is also important to note that Hegel describes the state here in its final determination as an "individual" that coheres with the "universal," hence as the "concrete" spirit of freedom in world-history. Elsewhere, as we will see, Hegel will frame the dialectic of the state in terms of "inner" and "outer" "right," an opposition resolved in world-history.

community [based on need]. The slave [*Sklave*] is a means [*Mittel*], and indirectly for the preservation of such means slaves [*Sklaven*] must be cared for; and thus the slave becomes a relative end. An interest to form [*formieren*] objects arises which provides the possibility of satisfying desire. Concern to preserve this activity is what holds master and servant [*Herr und Knecht*] together ...[125]

Though "states have originated in force"—through the "subjugation" and "domination" of slaves by masters—violence becomes increasingly "superfluous."[126] Emerging from the struggle to the death, slaves and masters bind themselves to each other through their interest in preserving the former's life as a "relative end." Here again Hegel gestures at the development of the *Knecht* from slave to laborer as the "community" evolves into the "system of need" and the contractual regimes of the *Verstandesstaat*. Ultimately the state, the mutual recognition of individuals, realizes itself as the free, rational, and universal will of each self-consciousness.[127] Thus "personal individualit[ies]" "know and will the universal ... recogniz[ing] it as their own substantial spirit."[128] For this reason the state becomes increasingly less reliant on coercion or force: "Often in its *representation* [*Vorstellung*], the state is held together by force, but what in fact holds it together is the fundamental feeling of order possessed by all; the state manifests the free will of all, rationality in its concreteness."[129] Thus, in the passage cited previously, "the violence [*Gewalt*] that is the ground [*Grund*] of this [initial] appearance [*Erscheinung*] [of the state] is not the ground [*Grund*] of right."[130]

This analysis countervails conceptions of the state as, for instance, a "community [*Gemeinschaft*]" that successfully monopolizes "legitimate physical violence within a certain territory."[131] In this latter conception, the state, as the author of "right" [*Recht*] and so the basis of its own legitimacy, merely asserts itself as the "source of the 'right' to use violence" and the sole power to make and coercively enforce the law within a demarcated territory. If recognitive self-consciousness, and not violence in the defense

---

[125]Hegel, *Lectures on the Philosophy of Spirit 1827–8*, transl. R. Williams (Oxford: Oxford University Press, 2011), 191, translation slightly modified.

[126]Hegel, *Lectures on the Philosophy of Spirit 1827–8*, 190. See also *Werke* 10: §432, 219: "although the state may arise by force, the state does not rest on force ... In the state what rules is the spirit of the people, custom [*Sitte*], and law [*Gesetz*]. There man is recognized and treated as a rational being, as free, as a person; and the individual, on his side, makes himself worthy of this recognition by overcoming the naturalness of his self-consciousness and obeying a *universal, the will that is in and for itself*, the law [*Gesetze*]; he thus behaves towards others in a manner that is universally valid, recognizing them—as he wishes others to regard him—as free, as persons."

[127]Hegel, Werke 7: §260: 406–7.

[128]Ibid.

[129]"Durch die Gewalt (ist die *Vorstellung* oft) (daß) (hänge) der Staat zustammen (hänge), doch das Haltende ist das Grundgefühl der Ordnung, das alle haben; der freie Wille Aller ist dabei, und sie wollen alle die Sache, das Vernünftige" (Hegel, *Vorlesungen über Rechtsphilosophie 1818–1831*, 3: 725). Emphasis mine. Hegel notably views South American states as weak because they are solely based on military force (Hegel, *Lectures on the Philosophy of World History: Introduction*, 166).

[130]Hegel, *The Philosophy of Subjective Spirit*, 3: §433, 63, translation modified.

[131]Weber, *Political Writings*, 310ff.

of bordered "ground,"[132] constitutes the "substantial principle" and phenomenality of the state beyond its mere "origin," what then marks the material "limit" of its law or "right" over against that of another state? Given the globalizing impetus of civil society, what then constitutes the "ground" of right?

The ground of right and the limits of cosmopolitanism

For Hegel the tension between grounded and cosmopolitan ethicality, or family and civil society, produces the state as the dialectic of "right" "inside the state" (or "internal state law" [*innere Staatsrecht*]) and "outside the state" (or "external state law," [*äußere Staatsrecht*]). Most commentators on Hegel have assumed that this dialectic of "inner" and "outer," rehearsing the "immediate" and so territorialized ethicality of the family, relates merely to the "ground" of the state: for them "internal state law" refers to the "right" obtaining in a demarcated territory, and "external state law" refers to the ultimate coherence of an "international" "human rights" regime agreed by cooperating militarized entities, each enforcing the law within geographically separated polities.[133]

Nowhere in his mature work, however, does Hegel argue that the state as an independent, ethical totality realizes itself through "single" authorities, each obtaining in a separate territory. In fact the notion of the state as violent power marks only the "representation" [*Vorstellung*] of the state, not its "actuality."[134] Grasping Hegel's conception of the "state" requires patiently studying the dialectic of the state as he presents it, with assiduous attention to his logical terms. Thus in the *Encyclopedia*:

> The state is (α) its internal organization as self-referential development—*right inside the state* [*innere Staatsrecht*] or the *constitution* [*Verfassung*]; (β) a *particular* individual [*besonderes Individuum*], and thus in relation to other particular individuals—*right outside the state* [*äußere Staatsrecht*]; (γ) but these particular spirits are only moments in the development of the universal idea of spirit in its actuality: *world-history* [*Weltgeschichte*].[135]

---

[132]Ibid.

[133]My reading of Hegel here owes a debt to the work of Andrew Buchwalter, Steven Hicks, and Robert Fines. See especially: Andrew Buchwalter, "Hegel's concept of an international 'We'"; Steven Hicks, "Hegel on Cosmopolitanism"; and Robert Fine, "Contra Leviathan: Hegel's Contribution to the Cosmopolitan Critique."

[134]Hegel, *Vorlesungen über Rechtsphilosophie 1818–1831*, 4: 725.

[135]Hegel, *Werke* 10: §536: 330. Compare Hegel's account of the dialectic of the state in the *Philosophy of Right*: "The idea of the state a) has immediate actuality and is the ethically individual state [*der individuelle Staat*] as a self-referential organism—the constitution [*Verfassung*], or right within the state; b) passes over into the *relationship* of separate states to other states—right outside the state [*äußere Staatsrecht*]; c) is the universal idea as genus and as absolute power in relation to individual states—spirit that gives itself its actuality in the process of world history" (Hegel, *Werke* 7: §259: 405–6). Here and elsewhere, I have borrowed Alan White's felicitous rendition of Hegel's state as an "ethical individual" (*Hegel's Philosophy of Right*, transl. Alan White [Newburyport: Focus, 2002], *passim*).

In a differently worded but substantively similar formulation in the *Philosophy of Right*, Hegel states that in its first diremption the state, as "internal right," only "has immediate actuality" [*unmittelbare Wirklichkeit*] "essentially" [*wesentlich*]:

> The state in its actuality is *essentially* [*wesentlich*] an ethically individual state, and beyond that a particular state. Ethical individuality should be distinguished from particularity; the former is a moment in the idea of the state, whereas the latter belongs to history.[136]

The state's "immediate" being reflects back into itself as essence. In this "ideality," it remains an ethical "individual" abstracted from history, an "inner constitution" merely "for itself" [*innere Verfassung für sich*] with no relation to an "other."[137] As the phantasm of the state in its self-sufficient actuality, "right inside the state" [*innere Staatsrecht*] marks only ideally the "real self-consciousness of all" or the "communal spirit."[138] Here this "right" manifests in "custom or ethical habit [*Sitte*] as it exists *immediately* in the individual self-consciousness": "it is in the knowledge and activity of the individual self-consciousness that the state has its mediate actuality."[139] This "ethical habit" contrasts with "positive law," which pertains to civil society or the *Verstandesstaat* based on need, since an abstract legal code only concerns persons and the legality of their property and private actions.[140] "Expressed and made known" in discursive form and backed by the threat of force, "positive law" succumbs to semantic inversion and perversion by the understanding.[141] Unlike a "contract" kept due to self-interest, coercion, or the fear of violence, "internal state law," as the "ideal" of living or organic "constitutional law," marks the convergence of "right" and perceived "duty."[142] Socialized to this constitutional law, self-consciousness effects the rational union of the individual and universal will: in their final dialectical articulation, "laws" mark "the substance of the individuals' *free*

---

[136]Hegel, *Werke* 7: §259A: 405. Emphasis mine. Note that "essence" is a logical term relating to "self-reflection." On the relation of the "idea" and particular history of the state, see also Hegel, *Werke* 7: §258: 400 and Hegel, *Lectures on the Philosophy of Spirit 1827–8*, 191.

[137]Hegel, *Werke* 7: §259: 404, §330: 497, §321: 490, §272: 432. Hegel's use of *für sich* evokes the fantasy of a self-referential and independent ideality; Hegel will differentiate between this disconnected "constitution" *für sich* and the state as *Für-sich-Sein*.

[138]Hegel, Werke 7: §260: 406–7.

[139]Hegel, *Lectures on Natural Right and Political Science*, 221. Emphasis mine.

[140]Hegel, *Werke* 10: §529–30, 324–6.

[141]Ibid.

[142]Hegel, *Lectures on Natural Right and Political Science*, 240; Hegel, *Werke* 7: §261: 408; "The contractual form of constitutional development is not in fact the rational, but merely a formal property" (Hegel, *Lectures on Natural Right and Political Science*, 242). For Hegel the constitution must be based on "freedom of the will"; the state must "cohere" on the basis of the latter. For this reason the constitution must be living—not an abstract code: "The state is an organism, i.e. the development of the idea into the articulation of its distinctions. Thus these distinct aspects of the state are its various powers with their functions and operations, through which the universal continuously produces itself in a necessary way, and maintains its identity because it is presupposed by its own production. This organism is the political constitution; it is produced perpetually by the state, while it is through [the constitution] that the state maintains itself" (Hegel, *Werke* 7: §269: 415).

willing within their bounds and of their disposition and so are displayed as prevailing custom."[143] The "content" posited by law as "right" [*Recht*], "impressed" [*eingebildet*] on the subjective will, thus becomes its "habit, disposition and character."[144]

As an ideality, however, the state in its determination as *innere Staatsrecht* cannot hold. On Hegel's analysis, the state "becomes exclusive," referring to itself in contradistinction to what lies outside it. It thus presents as a "sovereignty against others" [*Souveränität gegen außen*], a "being-for-self" [*Für-sich-Sein*] or individuality that knows itself in its distinction from "other states."[145] Thus in the dialectic of "right within the state," the fantasy of the state as the purportedly "immediate" articulation of "inner" freedom that is "for itself" yields the entity that knows itself as a relation mediated by otherness, a "Being-for-itself" (i.e., as an "in itself" and not "for another"). As an exclusivist sovereignty against otherness, the state posits itself as an enclosed "self-sufficient totality" [*selbständige Totalitäten*]. And yet a contradiction will emerge, since this "sovereignty," even as it posits itself as a totality or "in-itself," depends on the other for recognition; accordingly the *innere Staatsrecht*, as a false "ideality," does not materialize concrete freedom historically.[146]

Even so, the ideal state as an actual, exclusionary "individual," according to Hegel's remarkable critique, exercises force in time through the unstable, evanescent delimitation of otherness: "the force [*Gewalt*] through which any state manifests in its first entry into history *is* this self-sufficiency or independence [*Selbständigkeit*] in general, even if it is quite abstract and has no further inner development."[147] In other words, the ideality of the state as a demarcated and restricted "self-sufficiency" materializes the state as the "force" of exclusion, and not as the actuality of concrete freedom. This violent beginning accordingly does not belong to the history of freedom: "The origin of states [into history] is nothing historical: to history [*Geschichte*] belongs maturation [*Bildung*], which first falls to the progressive development of states."[148]

Thus the dialectic proceeds to *äußere Staatsrecht*, the view of the state as "right" explicitly mediated by the state's "outside." Here the state moves from ideality to

---

[143]Hegel, *Werke* 10: §538: 331.

[144]Hegel, *Werke* 10: §485: 303–4.

[145]Hegel, *Werke* 7: §321: 490. On the logical terms *für sich, Für-sich-Sein*, etc. see Inwood, *A Hegel Dictionary*, 133ff.

[146]Hegel, *Werke* 7: §330: 497. This itinerary toward "external right" of the state is already charted in the statement that the "objective will ... is rational only in that it is *in itself*, not only *for itself*" (Hegel, *Werke* 7: §258: 401); for this reason the rational (as opposed to exclusivist) state must realize right "in and for itself" (*Werke* 7: §258: 401–2; see also 7: §330: 497). Buchwalter astutely notices Hegel's use of the term "an sich" in his formulation of the state (in the diremption of "external right") as a self-sufficient totality "in itself" [*an sich*] (Buchwalter, "Hegel's concept of an international 'We,'" 160; see Hegel, *Werke* 7: §330: 497).

[147]"Die erste Gewalt, in welcher Staaten geschichtlich auftreten, ist daher diese Selbständigkeit überhaupt, wenn sie auch ganz abstrakt ist und keine weitere innere Entwicklung hat" (Hegel, *Werke* 7: §322: 491). Emphasis mine. On the *Erscheinung* of the state, see Hegel, *Die Vernunft in der Geschichte*, 114.

[148]"Der Ursprung der Staaten ist nichts Geschichtliches, zur Geschichte gehört Bildung, die erst in die Fortentwicklung der Staaten fällt aber so weit Ursprung der Staaten vorhanden ist, so findet es sich ..." (Hegel, *Vorlesungen über die Philosophie des Geistes: Berlin 1827/1828*, ed. F. Hespe and B. Tuschling [Hamburg: Felix Meiner, 1994], 170).

externality, and from self-referentiality to a recognitive relation with otherness. To effect the consonance of the individual and universal through the *Bildung* of "history," the state must materialize as a "particular state" in relation to other states: "without this relationship between it and its others," the state can never be an historical individual, just as a human being "who lacks contact with other persons" cannot be "an actual person."[149] Specifically, the state's "legitimacy" must be "completed" [*vervollständigt*] through "recognition by other states" in their particularity; mutuality or reciprocity appears to be a "guarantee" of each state's recognition as an "individual self-consciousness."[150] That recognition takes the form of "right outside the state."

What then resolves the opposition between "right inside the state" and "right outside the state"? What theory of the state emerges? The ideal "individual" state, the *innere Staatsrecht* referring only to itself, contrasts with the "particular" state, which refers to other states in order to produce itself as an independent or "self-sufficient" entity through external recognition. Only through the historical process of development and the mutuality attained through "right outside the state" can the "particular" state attempt to realize itself as a concretely free "individual."[151] Initially the "particular" state seeks "recognition" from other states as a merely "formal" or "abstract" "sovereign self-sufficiency" [*souveräner Selbständigkeit*], remaining therefore a self-consciousness merely "for another."[152] Excluding people who do not belong to its *Volk* or *Nation* or fall outside the protections of its "inner" constitution [*innere Verfassung*], the state is not yet spirit as self-consciousness that knows itself as itself, a "being in-and-for-itself" [*an und für sich Sein*] emerging from the mutual recognition of all self-consciousnesses.[153]

Moreover "right outside the state" remains contingent. There is no global or universal regime to "judge between states" or enforce conflicting, provisional articulations of "right"; at best states agree to "arbitrators or mediators," and even such multilateral or international actors "exercise their functions only contingently."[154] Treaties [*Traktate*] and other agreements between states are merely provisional "contracts": as "particular entities," states thus engage each other in a "state of nature," entering into or withdrawing

---

[149]Hegel, *Werke* 7: §331: 498.

[150]Hegel, *Werke* 7: §331: 498. Buchwalter flags the importance of the word "completed" here (Buchwalter, "Hegel's Concept of an International 'We,'" 160).

[151]See Hegel, *Werke* 7: §331: 498. Hegel explicitly relates the need for recognition by the particular state (in its orientation toward "right outside the state") here to §322, where the state from the standpoint of "inner right" articulates "sovereignty against others," except without seeking explicit mediation through other states.

[152]"The people as a state is spirit in its substantial rationality and immediate actuality, hence the absolute power on *earth*. Accordingly, one state is sovereign and self-sufficient against other states. Being as such *for the other* [*für den anderen*]—that is, to be *recognized* [*anerkannt*] by the other constitutes the state's first, absolute justification and legitimacy [*Berechtigung*]. But this justification is at the same time only formal, and the demand for this recognition of the state merely because it is a state, is abstract" (Hegel, *Werke* 7: §331: 498). Emphasis in original.

[153]"Whether the state is such a *being in and for itself* depends on its content, constitution, and state; and recognition [*Anerkennung*] [between two states], comprising an identity of both, also rests upon the view and the will of the other [state]" (Hegel, *Werke* 7: §331: 498). Hegel refers to ethicality "in and for itself" at the beginning of the chapter on ethicality.

[154]Hegel, *Werke* 7: §333: 500.

from agreements at will.[155] The rights of states manifest themselves "only in their particular wills and not in a universal will with constitutional powers over them. This universal determination thus does not go beyond an ought-to-be."[156] For this reason, Hegel rejects the possibility of a "perpetual peace" secured by a "league of nations" or world republic.[157] Just as any league of nations would necessarily "engender an opposite and create an enemy," so too any world republic would differentiate itself into parts seeking dialectical individuality or independence [*Selbständigkeit*] as a particular state.[158] In other words, a single global state as a purportedly single sociality would have to differentiate itself into multiple "individual" socialities seeking recognition from each other.

Though the non-dialectical condition of "perpetual peace" remains unobtainable, Hegel nonetheless acknowledges the rational necessity of multilateral efforts to institute "international law" or, more literally, the "peoples' rights" [*Völkerrecht*].[159] He indeed points to *Völkerrecht* as a second mode of "right beyond the state," beyond its initial diremption in contingent "treaties" or "conventions":[160]

> External state-rights rest partly on these positive treaties, but to that extent contain only rights falling short of true actuality (§545): and partly on so-called *international law* or peoples' rights [*Völkerrechte*], the universal principle of which is the presupposed recognition of states [*Anerkanntsein der Staaten*]. This recognition restricts their otherwise unconstrained action against one another in such a way that the possibility of peace remains [even in war]. It further distinguishes

---

[155]Hegel, *Werke* 7: §333: 499–500, §340: 503. See also Hegel's description of "nations" in a "state of nature" in the section on "Religion" in the *Phenomenology*. There nations identifying themselves with animal spirits manifest the spirit as "destructive being-for-self," divided into forms of existence that prey on the negativity of things as such and thus hate and fight each other to the death. Nations begin to emerge from that state of nature only through the advent of self-consciousness as the slave and its aesthetic activity as the *Werkmeister*. As it begins to produce objects, the self finds itself in the object: thus the production is also "the produced self, the self depleting its self in its productive activity, that is, the self become a thing," thus marking the birth of the spirit as *Werkmeister* (*Werke* 3: 508). In this diremption, spirit grasps itself as being that is *for itself*, and sees nature as material to be used, altered and fashioned into artificial productions. It then returns to the form of being-for-self, namely the animal, but this time constituting himself as the producer of the work incorporating the animal element (ibid., 3: 510–1).

[156]Hegel, *Werke* 7: §333: 499–500.

[157]Hegel, *Werke* 7: §333: 499–500. Here Hegel evokes Kant's well-known critique of "perpetual peace."

[158]Hegel, *Werke* 7: §324A: 493–4. As Avineri points out, Hegel criticizes "the theoretical premises of the Holy Alliance of post-1815 Restoration Europe" (Avineri, *Theory*, 201).

[159]I have chosen to translate *Völkerrecht* as both "international law," reflecting the standard German sense of the term, and the more literal "people's rights"—the latter to emphasize the socialization, in Hegel's view, that gives concrete life to international law. As we will see, the same process of social habituation underwrites the actuality of both constitutional and international law.

[160]In the 1822–1823 lectures, the section entitled "*Äußere Staatsrecht*" is divided into the following sections: "The Legal Status of International Law"; "The Questioning of International Law by Reason of State"; and "The Supranational Foundations of International Law" [*Der rechtliche Status des Völkerrechts; Die Infragestellung des Völkerrechts durch die Staatsräson; and Überstaatliche Grundlagen des Völkerrechts*] (Hegel, *Vorlesungen über Rechtsphilosophie 1818-1831*, 3: 832–6).

individuals as private persons from the state. *In general, [international law] rests on social habituation [Sitten].*[161]

Here *Völkerrecht* does not escape the contingency of any historical legal regime, subject as it is to violence and the merely arbitrary will. Crucially, however, the same contingency would "infect" "right inside the state" [*innere Staatsrecht*] or constitutional law: both internal and external state law remain subject to the mutual recognition of self-consciousnesses of each other's freedom, where each knows its own and the other's individual will as an expression of the universal will. Even in the fantasy of a self-sufficient state with no outside, a constitution may stipulate that an executive in a state must follow the ruling of an independent domestic court; but theoretically he may ignore it, just as he may disregard the ruling of an international court.[162] In both cases, the absence of "right" arises from a failure of recognitive self-consciousness. A written constitution is, in the first place, only a piece of paper; it obtains only to the extent it materializes as a living organism, the ethical substance of *Sitte*. For this reason all states, no matter how entrenched their constitutional ethos, remain subject to collapse: "The highest point a people can reach is to preserve their independence and sacrifice everything to it. But this independence is nothing absolute, and it can be destroyed. Something higher transcends it, world spirit, and where the latter emerges, the rights of the peoples [*die Rechte der Völker*] disappear."[163] Ultimately the *Rechte der Völker* to found independent states or achieve independence from an external power remains as contingent as *Völkerrecht*.

Notwithstanding the impossibility of any final, sustained realization of recognition, Hegel argues dialectically and speculatively that to find contingent, historical form, the "universal" will of the "ideal" *innere Staatsrecht* must converge with "universal right" [*allgemeinem Recht*] or *Völkerrecht*, the principle of which is the "recognition of states" [*Anerkanntsein der Staaten*].[164] The state's legitimacy, and thus its historical actuality as an ethical "individual," depends both on a "wholly internal relationship" of recognitive self-consciousness and on the "completion" of that legitimacy through its "recognition" by and of "other states."[165] This conflation of interiority and exteriority would result in the simultaneous "self-sufficiency" of states and their necessary implication in their respective interiors[166]:

But this recognition requires a guarantee that each state will also recognize the others who are to recognize it—that is, respect them in their independence, and thus no state can be indifferent to what is going on in the interior of the others.[167]

---

[161]Hegel, *Werke* 10: §547: 346, emphasis mine. See also Hegel, *Werke* 7: §333: 499–500. Compare Hegel's use of *völkerrechtliche* in §338: 502 and §339: 502.

[162]Andrew Jackson and Abraham Lincoln, for instance, both ignored the United States Supreme Court.

[163]Hegel, *Vorlesungen über Naturrecht Staatswissenschaft*, 255.

[164]Hegel, *Vorlesungen über Naturrecht Staatswissenschaft*, 247; Hegel, *Werke* 10: §547: 346.

[165]Hegel, *Werke* 7: §331: 498–9.

[166]Hegel, *Werke* 7: §331: 499.

[167]"Aber diese Anerkennung fordert eine Garantie, daß er die anderen, die ihn anerkennen sollen, gleichfalls anerkenne, d. i. sie in ihrer Selbständigkeit respektieren werde, und somit kann es ihnen nicht gleichgültig sein, was in seinem Innern vorgeht" (Hegel, *Werke* 7: §331: 498–9).

No state can "recognize" another state without knowing the extent to which its "individual" will coheres with the "universal will"; to be recognizably "universal," this "will" would have to be the same both "inside" and "outside" the state. In other words, the distinction between *innere* and *äußere Staatsrecht*, the latter as *Völkerrecht*, would have to collapse. In addition, both modes of "right" depend upon the *Bildung* of self-consciousness, hence its evolution toward socialized ethicality [*Sitte*]. Indeed the latter, taking root historically, articulates freedom from contingency and remains, therefore, more resilient than imposed constitutions, treaties, or contracts based solely on coercion or force.[168]

As "right" inside and outside the state converge, states tend toward increasing "uniformity":

> States in the modern world seek independence of one another ... This obstinate tendency toward an absolute position to autonomy they have in common with the Greek city-states ... But despite all the differences between the individual states ... there also obtains a unity among them, and therefore we should view *even political independence as a merely formal principle*. Today there is not the same absolute chasm between the states of Europe that prevailed between Greece and Persia. When one state is annexed to the territory of the other, it loses, to be sure, formal independence, but its religion, its laws, the concrete way of life remain intact. *The trend of states is, therefore, toward uniformity*. There prevails among them one aim, one tendency, which is the cause of wars, friendships, and the needs of dynasties. But there also prevails among them another uniformity, which parallels the idea of hegemony in Greece, except that now it is the hegemony of spirit.[169]

Hegel could easily be misread here as arguing that a certain view of freedom, and more particularly of right, belongs only to Europe (or by corollary the "West") as a racially or ethnically static polity. But he only refers to Europe as an example of what can obtain between modern states, over against the gulf between less evolved political entities like Greece and Persia in antiquity. That "Europe" exhibits a lack of an "absolute chasm" between states and thus merely a "trend" toward uniformity hardly qualifies the continent as the exclusive province of universal right and freedom, much less of their final realization in the state. More to the point, the unity of Europe over against

---

[168]Thus a constitution, a "labor of centuries" (Hegel, *Werke* 7: §274A: 440), cannot be "imposed." Furthermore, "the spiritual education of a people or nation, which has the utmost influence on the constitution (as it does on what is animated by it), renders a consitution that is suitable for some other people unworkable for this one. What is rational must be, but it has its existence only in the self-consciousness of a people" (Hegel, *Lectures on Natural Right and Political Science*, 247). See also: "There is nothing easier than to formulate the general principles of a constitution, for in our day these concepts have become conventional abstractions ... The constitution is the foundation, the basis on which everything transpires. All constitutions are also the inner developments of the national spirit, the foundation in which it expresses the stage of self-consciousness it has reached" (Hegel, *Lectures on Natural Right and Political Science*, 240).

[169]Hegel, *Vorlesungen über die Philosophie der Weltgeschichte*, ed. G. Lasson (Leipzig: Felix Meiner, 1920), 761, cited in Avineri, *Theory*, 207. Emphasis mine.

other peoples reflects the persistence of a global "state of nature," hence of a singular unfreedom. Finally, where Europe's idea of freedom emerges from a notion of abstract right based on property, its states remain mere *Verstandesstaaten* based on "need." In the march of spirit toward freedom, "political independence" remains, in general, a merely "formal" or "abstract" principle belonging to the "ideality" of a still immature *innere Staatsrecht*. Only "concrete life" marks true independence: and that ethicality, in the shared ethos of freedom, must extend to all of humanity: "Ethical life [*Sittlichkeit*] must be the ethical life of *everyone*; it exists in necessity as socialized ethos [*Sitte*]."[170]

The progression toward that freedom through *Bildung*, engendering this interpenetration of states, nonetheless depends on civil society as the mediating term of ethical life. Civil society apparently dissolves "immediate" relations of love, namely in the family, through its atomization of the individual. But this suspension of "ethical determination" is "simply an error, because—even though I believe I am adhering to the particular, in fact the universal and essential and the necessity of [social] connections remain primary" in civil society.[171] Through the "abstract" and "universalizing" process of the "formation" of object and subject in relation to each other, civil society teaches subjectivity to abandon its attachment to fixed determinations, including of the literal "ground." As we have seen, the "universal" form emerging from the labor of "formation" impels me to "abandon my particularity and place myself in the mode of agreement; I have therefore to give myself the *form of universality* … It is no longer the case [in civil society], as it was in the family, that what counts is what I *immediately* am."[172] Attempting to fulfill the family's need for "fixed" [*festen*] property, the individual enters the sphere of "abstract right," at which point the "family begins to dissolve."[173] Actualizing the "form of right" [*die Form Rechtens*], the individual attempts to grasp "an enclosed plot of ground," but cannot eschew its discursive mediation.[174] Thus Hegel in the Jena lectures glosses the movement past the recognition precariously achieved in the family as follows:

[A]n existent thing is shown to be my possession through a sign [*Zeichen*], for instance, my working [*Bearbeitung*] on it. What is designated as mine the other [*Andere*] must not damage. The designation [*Bezeichnung*], however, remains incidental: thus an enclosed plot of ground with no more than a furrow for a boundary [*Umschließung*] is designated as mine—and yet not, [for] the sign has an *unbounded* [*unbegrenzte*] range: putting up a post on an island signifies that I wish to take possession of it; likewise, in working on a metal mug I cannot separate the form [I have given the mug] from [the object itself]. Likewise in the case of a field I have worked on, [or a] tree, where does the imposed form begin and where does

---

[170]Hegel, *Vorlesungen über Natturecht Staatswissenschaft*, 280. Emphasis mine.

[171]Hegel, *Werke* 7: §181A: 339.

[172]Hegel, *Vorlesungen über Naturrecht Staatswissenschaft*, 147–8. Emphases mine.

[173]Hegel, *Werke* 7; §170: 323; 7: §159: 308. See also the family's need for "fixed ground" [*festen Boden*] in *Werke* 7: §253: 395.

[174]Hegel, *Werke* 7: §159: 308.

it end? The inner side of each clod is left untouched, or moved only a little—so too with the underside, it is not moved much, and so on ...[175]

Here the "limit" or "form" imposed on the "ground" through the "enclosure" or "furrow" reveals itself to be merely a "sign" with "unlimited" [*unbegrenzte*] semantic range and fluidity. To the extent that it differentiates "mine" and "yours," or "inner" and "outer," any "limit" [*Grenze*] or line, as an extension of a "point" in space and time, remains necessarily discursive and thus materially indeterminate: "where does the imposed form begin and where does it end?" For this reason, the act of taking "possession," akin to both the "taking-the-this" and the slave's *Formierung* in the *Phenomenology of Spirit* and the *Philosophy of Right*, discloses the universality of "form," hence its resistance to exclusive ownership. The laboring individual thus discovers, in the foundational moments of civil society, the impossibility of delineating the "ground" "immediately." Only upon the conscious unity of form and content in the fully realized state could any such demarcation articulate the freedom of self-consciousness.

Through its discursive economy, civil society thus endlessly deterritorializes the state—but not to the point the latter frees itself permanently from the "ideality" of its grounded determinacy. The dialectic of civil society and the state indeed reveals a contradiction internal to any "particular" polity in its historical development. On the one hand, the "ideal" of the state as the articulation of "inner right" develops from the "patriarchal" view of the polity as an extension of people linked by blood and shared soil; recuperating the dialectic of the family, this vision of the state underwrites its abstract conception as a demarcated territory.[176] As we have seen, a particular state seeking recognition but still clinging to this ideal self-sufficiency "in itself" exerts and remains vulnerable to force from within and without. Where it asserts the exclusivism of its *Volk*, the latter lives always under the sign of the state's violent purging of otherness. Moreover the staking out of ground occurs through violence: thus the state demarcates its borders, its "sovereignty against external otherness," through a militarized sector dedicated to the forceful "defense" of its territory.[177]

On the other hand, civil society's "system of needs" translates the state into a *Notstaat*, and thus an "external" as opposed to formally "independent" or "self-sufficient" state. Because of the increasing emptiness of its multiplying signifiers, civil society stimulates the "maturation" and mutual "recognition" of self-consciousness across the world: while "self-sufficient states" as idealities "are wholes whose needs are principally met" within their own borders, "civil society individuals are reciprocally interdependent" everywhere and "in the most varied respects."[178] As we have seen, civil society pursues the incursion

[175]Hegel, *Jenaer Systementwürfe III*, 199. Emphasis mine.
[176]The "patriarchal" state originates from families that reproduce and expand into multiple families and clans. A state based on the increasingly weak bond of kinship can only be held together by force and thus collapses. Ultimately the bond of kinship—or of common ancestry, as in certain racial theories—becomes a mere "representation." Cf. also the section entitled "The Law of Nations" in Immanuel Kant, *Metaphysical Elements of Justice* (Boston: Hackett, 1999), 151.
[177]Hegel, *Werke* 7: §320–2: 490, §326: 494–5. See also *Werke* 1: 472 and Hegel, *Lectures on Natural Right and Political Science,* 300 on the need for a "territorial militia."
[178]Hegel, *Werke* 7: §332: 499.

of "needs and means" across frontiers, thus spurring the spread of "external law." The "cosmopolitan" business element, whose branches often have conflicting interests, indeed seeks and requires an efficient system "for the administration of justice, and civil and political freedom in general"; thus business leads to a "system of supervision" for the movement of labor and capital, including goods, across the limits of the state.[179] Hegel refers specifically to the "dependence" of supply chains on competition, including from "foreign concerns," to ensure the efficient availability of goods at various stages of production; the regulation of imports and exports for the purpose of protecting industry or underwriting minimum standards of quality; and the establishment of treaties "to obtain benefits for its subjects by trade negotiations."[180] He also refers to the protection of intangible "intellectual property," the theft of which threatens the development of "science."[181] Acknowledging the presence of "merchants from abroad" at "annual fairs" and the power that a state has to "impel" "foreign manufacturers to enter [its territory] and use its nationals in their factories" through protectionism, Hegel gestures at the conditions for the transfer of intellectual property across borders, not least with respect to the "introduction of machines."[182] Thus the state attempts to balance competing economic interests—for instance between the agricultural and commercial class, importers and manufacturers—through a coherent regulatory regime necessarily connected to the international flow of labor and capital.[183]

The movement of peoples through "colonization," migration, and the coercion and transport of "bondsmen" and "slaves," all functions of civil society, further compromises the material "boundary" [*Grenze*] of the state.[184] As a merely "external state" based on "need," civil society, through the influence of certain business interests or corporations, can also drive the state to expand its borders or seize territory abroad for resources.[185]

---

[179]Hegel, *Lectures on Natural Right and Political Science*, 214.

[180]Hegel, *Vorlesungen über Naturrecht Staatswissenschaft*, 162–4.

[181]Ibid.

[182]Hegel, *Lectures on Natural Right and Political Science*, 216.

[183]International regimes, explicit or implicit, inflecting the movement of capital due to trade, taxation, and changes in monetary policy; the purchase or sale by other governments of each other's sovereign bonds and currencies; state purchases of non-governmental securities, including equities and derivatives of foreign corporations; and the ability of corporations to shift intellectual property or change domicile to exploit low tax jurisdictions all instantiate the interdependence of states on one another. Jürgen Habermas further points out that tax rates in one country inflect tax rates in another (see the very Hegelian line of argument in Habermas' "The Postnational Constellation and the Future of Democracy," in *The Postnational Constellation* [Cambridge: MIT Press, 2001], 58–112).

[184]See Hegel, *Lectures on Natural Right and Political Science*, 214, 216.

[185]Thus to protect its interests in Iran, in 1953 the British-owned Anglo-Iranian Oil company, today British Petroleum, leveraged its influence in the United Kingdom—and, through Winston Churchill, the United States—to topple Iran's democratically elected government and instate the Shah as absolute ruler of the country (see Stephen Kinzer, *All the Shah's Men: An American Coup and the Roots of Middle East Terror* [Hoboken: John Wiley & Sons, 2003]). Likewise the United Fruit Company, now Chiquita Brands International, spurred the Eisenhower administration to engineer a coup d'état in Guatemala in 1954 (Lars Schoultz, *Beneath the United States: A History of U.S. Policy toward Latin America* [Cambridge: Harvard University Press, 1998]). Hegel's point is that the impetus of imagined "need" in civil society will drive the state to the domination of other peoples.

Driven principally by "need," the state will even push its "border" into the sea, the medium of civil society: "All nations lay claim to right over the sea to the furthest limit to which their guns can protect them."[186] And the forced enslavement and expatriation of foreign populations, sponsored or not by the state, undermine any possibility that the latter could ever subsist historically as an "exclusive" and "self-sufficient totality," including of a pure *Volk* uncontaminated by otherness.

To grasp Hegel's argument here about the gulf between the "ideality" of the state as a "self-sufficient totality" and its actual materialization in the "particular" form of "right outside the state," consider the case of international tourism. The number of international border crossings will have grown from 25 million in 1950 to a projected 1.8 billion by 2030.[187] Visa-free travel has increased dramatically: out of the world's two hundred countries, citizens of approximately half—including South Africa, Mexico, Brazil, Turkey, Malaysia, and Russia—can now travel freely to more than a hundred countries.[188] In 2006 only forty countries could do so.[189] Citizens from Japan and Germany can travel almost everywhere on earth. Chinese tourists now embark on 150 million international excursions, spending far more abroad than Americans.[190] Currently 600,000 Chinese study abroad.[191] If China and India, together representing close to two-fifths of the world's population, continue to gain economic and geopolitical clout, they, too, are likely to secure visa-free travel for their citizens to an increasing number of countries. Indicative of the power of capital in the system of "needs and means," the wealthy from any country can obtain citizenship from some of the world's most industrialized countries for a payment or by making an investment. The European Union offers supranational citizenship to citizens of most of its countries. The global movement of peoples spurs, as a rational necessity, the increasing uniformity of legal regimes. There are sinister implications as well: as Hegel warns, the propensity in political economy toward the commodification of bodies for the fulfillment of masterly "desire" underwrites the persistence of slavery. Thus travel and electronic communication have also led to an explosion in sex tourism and trafficking across borders, giving impetus to an industry based on the enslavement and prostitution even of children.[192]

---

[186]Hegel, *Lectures on Natural Right and Political Science*, 69–70.

[187]Dirk Glaesser et al., "Global Travel Patterns: An Overview," in *Journal of Travel Medicine*, 2017, 1–5.

[188]See the Henley Passport Index, published annually by Henley Partners (www.henleypassportindex.com).

[189]Ibid.

[190]"China's high-spending tourists bring political clout," *The Economist*, February 23, 2019.

[191]"Surging numbers of Chinese abroad should be welcomed," *The Economist*, May 17, 2018.

[192]The spread of sexual tourism on a global scale—especially in relation to the prostitution of children—reflects exactly what Hegel means by the commodification of bodies resulting from civil society. The need to travel for sex with coerced minors points to the wide range of norms across the world relating to this perverse phenomenon. By the same token, Hegel's argument would suggest that, through the same globalizing process, norms around such practices could also converge. On sexual tourism, see Jacqueline Sanchez Taylor, "Tourism and 'Embodied' Commodities: Sex Tourism in the Caribbean," in *Tourism and Sex: Culture, Commerce and Coercion*, eds. S. Clift and S. Carter (London: Continuum, 2000), 41–53; and Angela Hawke and Alison Raphael, *Global Study on Sexual Exploitation of Children in Travel and Tourism* (Bangkok: ECPAT, 2016).

In response to the incursions of civil society, the state can attempt to regress toward the ideality of exclusivist self-sufficiency, violently expelling others and barring tourists, business travelers, and even diplomats and trade emissaries. Hegel characterizes this primitive state as a notionally impenetrable "building" [*Gebäude*], a walled territory closed off from penetration by ground or sea. Partially in reaction to a period of increasing international integration, marked especially by agreements for the freer movement of goods and people, the view of the state as such a bordered territory has gained increasing currency.[193]

The view of the state as a sealed "building" leads to the desire for external recognition of its polity's independence and self-sufficiency. Where the process fails, a violent "state of nature" ensues, leading possibly to the destruction of states. Where some mode of incomplete recognition obtains, some states dominate and others are dominated. Emerging from the relation between these "particular," apparently "independent" states, "right outside the state" [*äußere Staatsrecht*] negotiates the state's development precisely by undermining its boundaries, even in the case of the most powerful states. Thus "right outside the state" occurs as a dialectic of "positive right" [*positivem Recht*] and "universal right" [*allgemeinem Recht*].[194] Initially the state, attempting to secure recognition as both an abstract ideality and a "being-for-self" through treaties, remains subject to the vicissitudes of positive right, hence a "maelstrom" of "contingency" that in fact undermines the "self-sufficiency of the state."[195] Contributing to that "contingency," civil society develops "widespread connections and multifaceted interests" that "may be readily and considerably injured" as it spreads across the globe; since the line or limit between society and a particular state is "indeterminable," any such "injury" can be taken to impinge on the "recognition" of that state, again leading to war.[196] But war, for all of its horrors, can teach self-consciousness to conjoin its particular interests to those of the collective, thus contributing to the *Bildung* of self-consciousness.[197] Moreover the experience of war can impel the evolution of a more uniform ethos of *Völkerrecht*. Through rational development, particular states, concerned with each other's internal affairs in the quest for mutual recognition, socialize themselves increasingly to the agreed norms of war and peace.[198] The violence between states, as the logical outcome of their grounded articulation, thus evolves the state's "external right" toward "universal right."

At peace with its neighbors, the state still struggles against the incursions of a burgeoning civil society; the latter, in which "all pursue their own interests," remains "the locus of the conflict of the interests of particular spheres against one another and against the universal."[199] What then resolves the dialectic of civil society and the state?

---

[193]See the recent political discourse in the European Union and the United States.

[194]Hegel, *Vorlesungen über Naturrecht Staatswissenschaft*, 247.

[195]Ibid.; Hegel, *Werke* 7: §330: 497, §340: 503.

[196]Hegel, *Werke* 7: §334: 500.

[197]Hegel, *Werke* 7: §324: 491–4. Hegel adds that war dissolves international law, but not "ethical life" (Hegel, *Lectures on Natural Right and Political Science*, 305).

[198]Hegel, *Werke* 7: §338 and §338A: 502.

[199]Hegel, *Vorlesungen über Naturrecht Staatswissenschaft*, 255.

The two conceptions of the particular state—first, as a *Verstandesstaat* or *Notstaat* dedicated to the "cosmopolitan" interest of increasingly atomized "persons" and their property and, second, as an enclosed, violently defended territory—may comprise the fundamental political dialectic of our time. As we have seen, both views depend on a discursive economy: civil society engenders an infinite array of signifiers of "need" and the "means" to meet them; and the "representation" of the state [*Vorstellung*] as violently controlled territory depends upon a symbology of a monolithic authority and a distinct sociality or "people" within a fixed territory. Thus cartographic images of delineated ground, flags, anthems, statues, military emblems, founding myths, and even culinary and sartorial elements metaphorize the state, but only in terms of its "externalities" and not its "rational" "substance" or material.[200] For Hegel those who understand the state in terms of "the contingent appearances of need," such as the "need for protection," taking such elements "not as moments in the state's historical development, but as its substance," "overlook what makes the state infinite and rational in and for itself [*an und für sich*]."[201] The "essence" of the state remains self-consciousness: "empirical individuality" and its "contingent properties," such as "strength and weakness, wealth and poverty," or by implication racial, ethnic, or cultural attributes related to a people, must not, however, be confused with the "thought" of "individuality" in its universal and thus recognitive determination. Singling out von Haller's *Restoration of Political Science* [*Restauration der Staatswissenschaften*] (1816) for making precisely such errors, Hegel points out that any attempt to reduce the state to contingent appearances must fall into utter "inconsistency" and contradiction, where one is "at home now with the exact opposite of what" one approved "a moment ago."[202] Indeed, as we recall from his critique of the understanding, any attempt to describe an object of appearance as a set of non-dialectical properties must result in the inversion and perversion of the produced meaning, whether related to the "need" for the defense of territory or the unique particularities of a "people."

Hegel's conception of the state as an "architectonic structure or building [*architektonisches Gebäude*], a hieroglyph of reason," reflects precisely his grasp of the discursive mediation of the state's aesthetic "form." As an "architectonic structure," the state equates ultimately to a linguistic signifier, an endlessly self-emptying line or "limit." Any view of the state as a building or walled territory marks the understanding's reduction of the state to a reified "picture-thought" or "representation" [*Vorstellung*]. The "architectonic" in actuality articulates the freedom from the binary oppositions that yield the positivist delusions of the understanding. Attempts to reify the state's "architectonic structure" as a violently and immediately demarcated limit, whether of a territorial border or an autochthonous or culturally monolithic "people," thus countervail the unfolding of freedom in the state. For "right" cannot be realized on bordered land: "the sphere of right is not the soil [*Boden*] of nature, but the sphere of freedom."[203]

---

[200]Hegel, *Werke* 7: §258: 401–2.

[201]Ibid.

[202]Ibid.

[203]Hegel, *Lectures on Natural Right and Political Science*, 52.

The "architectonic" limit, isolated first in the pyramids of Egypt, gestures endlessly at its own self-cancellation. Disclosing the movability of the dialectical line between "inner" and "outer," hence what lies within and without the sign, the architectonic marks the freedom from static form and, accordingly, from any manifestation of particularity. Ultimately the state articulates the dialectical fluidity of its spatial determination: thus Hegel defines the state as a "hieroglyph of reason that presents [*darstellt*] itself in reality."[204]

The state moves from the "picture-thinking" [*Vorstellung*] of static limits or borders to precisely this architectonic "presentation" [*Darstellung*] of "reason"; the state thus "appears" [*erscheint*] as its constitutive dialectical delimitation. In its "incipient form," the state manifests as the opposition of inner and outer, or the violent enclosure of territory by a patriarchal master. Accruing particular determinations—including those related to national characteristics or culture—such a state becomes a "bad state" with "merely worldly being" but "no true reality," like an "amputated hand."[205] The "particular determinations" of these "incomplete states" have not yet attained "free self-sufficiency" by disclosing their contingency and thus inherence in universality: here the "idea of the state remains veiled."[206]

A more advanced state claiming "inner" self-sufficiency or independence and attaining to international recognition "appears" increasingly through the discursively articulated "limit" between civil society and the state. Through the *Bildung* of civil society, particular states begin to share conceptions of "right" grounded in the universal will; accordingly recognition becomes possible, as states identify their mutual freedom from particularity. As a result of their increasing "uniformity," states distinguish themselves through their dialectical opposition not to each other, but rather to an increasingly global civil society, the mediating term in the progression of ethicality.[207] This dialectical relation remains fluid: for this reason, states have even been born of corporations.[208] The endlessly reproduced, necessarily "indeterminate" line between civil society and the state must therefore mark the "form" in which the "historical" state endlessly reappears.[209] More generally, this discursive mode manifests as the narrative "history" and symbology of the state—a discourse that remains violent so long as the state clings to its particular

---

[204]Hegel, *Werke* 7: §279A, 449.

[205]Hegel, *Werke* 7: §270A: 428–9.

[206]Hegel, *Werke* 7: §260A: 407.

[207]See Hegel, *Werke* 7: §258: 399. The increasing "uniformity" of states that recognize each other underwrites the slow evanescence of the physical limits between them, giving rise to transnational federations and supranational states like the European Union.

[208]While "states have often emerged from corporations," the state is more than just a "multiplicity of externally connected corporations" (Hegel, *Vorlesungen über Naturrecht Staatswissenschaft*, 207–8); Hegel makes the same point implicitly in *Werke* 7: §258: 399–400.

[209]On the "indeterminability" of the line between civil society and the state, see Hegel, *Werke* 7: §334: 500. See also Timothy Mitchell, "The Limits of the State: Beyond Statist Approaches and Their Critics," *The American Political Science Review*, 1991, 85: 1: 77–96.

determinations over against the process of *Bildung* that propels civil society. Such states are insufficiently "developed [*ausgebildet*]" or "badly constructed [*konstruiert*]."[210]

For a "completed [*vervollständigt*] state," by contrast, "thought and consciousness belong essentially [*wesentlich*]," such that the "whole endlessly regenerates itself through its perpetual dissolution."[211] Here spirit as recognitive self-consciousness reaching for universality, endlessly sloughing off particular determinations, identifies the fluidity of any delimitation as the essential, shared principle of objectivity and subjectivity.[212] Where multiple self-consciousnesses attain to this wisdom through the *Bildung* of labor, they recognize themselves as inhering in this freedom from particularity, identifying in their universality the ground for their solidarity in the state. Here the *Bilden* of form and the *Bildung* of the subject as coincident aesthetic processes yield the "nation" as the pure form of universality:

> The universal which emerges and becomes known [*gewußt*] in the state, the form [*Form*] to which all assimilates, is that which constitutes the formation [*Bildung*] of a nation.[213]

For Hegel particular states that fail to unveil for themselves the fluidity of their "form" do not belie the "idea" of the architectonic state. For the latter in its historical appearance cannot realize the "idea" through any static union of form and content. Such a state, were it possible, would not be aesthetic, but a "pure" *Kunstwerk*, a term Hegel associates with the "ideal"[214] attempt, in Greek art and political theory, to banish the temporality of self-consciousness:

> The state in and for itself [*an und für sich*] is the ethical whole, the actualization of freedom; and it is the absolute aim or telos of reason that freedom should be actual. The state is spirit standing [*steht*] in the world and consciously realizing itself there … Only when spirit is present in consciousness, when it knows itself as an existent object, is it the state. Any consideration of freedom must begin not with individuality or the individual self-consciousness, but only the essence of self-consciousness; for whether humans know it or not, this essence is externally

---

[210] Hegel, *Werke* 7: §280: 451.

[211] Hegel, *Werke* 7: §270: 429.

[212] To recall, there are three moments of self-consciousness: the struggle to the death, recognitive self-consciousness, and universal self-consciousness (see *Werke* 10: 9–37).

[213] This comment concludes the long passage cited earlier on the state's *Erscheinung* (Hegel, *Die Vernunft in der Geschichte*, ed. J. Hoffmeister [Hamburg: Felix Meiner, 1955], 114).

[214] As we have seen, in the *Aesthetics* Hegel distinguishes the "aesthetic" from the "ideal," or "art in its highest determination," which reveals itself as the lifeless art of the past. In the *Phenomenology of Spirit*, "natural religion" marks the birth of the aesthetic through the non-representational art of architecture, or the architectonic "formation" of form by the *Werkmeister*; by contrast the "religion of art" expresses the ideal through mimesis, for instance in Greek sculptural representations of the divine. Hegel associates this "ideal" articulation of art [*Kunst*] with picture-thinking [*Vorstellung*], positivism, and the conflation of content and form, or person and property, that leads to slavery in Greek culture.

realized as a self-sufficient power in which single individuals are only moments. The stride [*Gang*] of God in the world—that is what the state is. The ground [*Grund*] of the state is the power of reason actualizing itself as will. In considering the idea of the state, we must not have our eyes on particular states or on particular institutions. Rather we must consider the "idea," this actual God, as itself. Any state may be declared bad depending on one's principles; one may find this or that insufficiency in it; and yet, with respect to one of the mature [*ausgebildeten*] states of our epoch, it has in it the moments essential to the existence of the state. But since it is easier to find deficiencies than to grasp the affirmative, we may easily fall into the error of looking at discrete aspects of the state abstracted from the inner organism of the state. *The state is no ideal or pure work of art [Der Staat ist kein reines Kunstwerk]*; it stands in the world and so in the sphere of willfullness, contingency, and error, and bad behavior may disfigure it in many respects. But the ugliest man, or the criminal, or an invalid, or a cripple, is still a living human being. The affirmative—life—subsists despite such defects, and it is this affirmative element that concerns us here.[215]

Alluding to the categories of the aesthetic, Hegel identifies "freedom" not in the "ideal" articulation of the "pure" *Kunstwerk*, but rather in the necessarily aesthetic attempt to materialize the "idea" through the imperfect convergence of form and content in history.[216] The mystified belief in the atemporal coherence of form and content through mimesis, shaping the corporeal form of self-consciousness out of the immediacy of nature, yields for the Greeks the artistic ideal of "individuality conditioned by beauty."[217] This principle governs their statues of God in human form as well their "beautiful democracy" [*schöne Demokratie*], in which "the individual will" is "unfettered" in "its particular idiosyncrasy" rather than harmonized in the state.[218] This "political *Kunstwerk*" necessarily attends the positivist conflation of object and subject that underwrites slavery: thus "slavery

---

[215]Hegel, *Werke* 7: §258A: 403–4. In emending the text to "Der Staat ist kein reines Kunstwerk," I have followed Ilting's edition of the manuscript (Hegel, *Vorlesungen über Rechtsphilosophie 1818-1831*, 4: 633). Emphasis mine.

[216]"It is *beautiful individuality [die schöne Individualität]* that constitutes the core of the Greek character ... [for them] all issues in works of art [*Kunstwerke*]; we can conceive it as a threefold entity: as the subjective work of art—that is, as the *Bildung* of man himself; as the objective work of art—that is, as the design of the world of the gods; finally, as the political work of art [*politische Kunstwerk*], the mode of the constitution and the individuals in it" (Hegel, *Werke* 12: 295). Elsewhere Hegel writes that in the Greek realm "the one substance" of spirit "has dispersed into many peoples, in whom the essential element is unrestricted, serene ethical life. The principle of personal right emerges, but still compounded with and subordinate to the substantial, *ideal* unity—a self-determination whose resolutions come from within itself, although not yet ascribed to self-consciousness but to an external, superior force. The constitution is on the one hand democratic, but on the other hand this democracy still contains slavery" (Hegel, *Lectures on Natural Right and Political Science*, 310). See also the characterization of Greek virtue as a *Kunstwerk* in Hegel, *Werke* 7: §150: 300.

[217]Hegel, *The Philosophy of History*, transl. J. Sibree (New York: Dover, 1956), 238.

[218]Hegel, *Werke* 12: 307ff., 311.

becomes a necessary condition" of "democracy" in its "ideal" articulation.[219] By contrast the "idea" of the state, notwithstanding its necessarily deficient "appearance," remains implicit in the architectonic rationality of modern states. Here the state concretizes the "essence of self-consciousness," or recognitive reconciliation, as the "ground" of freedom or right. Only the aesthetic, hence self-canceling articulation of reason through the state marks this true "ground"; thus Hegel equates the latter to the "power of reason."[220] Freedom emerges in the modern state's recuperation of the architectonic act of *Bilden*, evoked here in the notion of the "mature" [*ausgebildet*] state. For this reason, Hegel in the *Philosophy of Right* explicitly distinguishes the modern state as an "architectonic structure [*architektonisches Gebäude*], a hieroglyph of reason," from the "beautiful democracy" of Athens, which hypostatized the sensuous to such a point the Greeks "took their decisions from the observation of external phenomena such as oracles, the entrails of sacrificial animals, and the flight of birds."[221]

As the discursive materialization of the dialectic, the architectonic for Hegel performatively engenders history. Only freedom from static particularity, as the rational telos of self-consciousness, reflects the nature of and so organizes the movement of the dialectic, the instrument of thought. Accordingly the resolution of the dialectic of freedom as right in the state must occur through the narration of history, or *Geschichtserzählung*. The latter accounts for the *Bildung* of self-consciousness through exclusivist modes of right—distinctions between its "inside" and "outside"—toward its rational conclusion in freedom. Given this "aim," history must endlessly shed the primacy of any national, geographical, cultural, or racial determination as its organizing principle. In this sense, the architectonic state, as the concrete materialization of human solidarity, occurs as "universal" or "world-history" [*Weltgeschichte*].

Hegel's dense argument has led to much confusion, not least because of his apparent privileging of the "German realm" [*germanische Reich*] or "people" in the dialectic of world-history. Hegel's apparent hierarchy of peoples' spirits [*Volksgeister*]—beginning in the East and ending in the West—seems to echo the primacy of the necessarily "European" state. But Hegel could not be clearer about the "limitations" of any such "particular" determination:

The principles of the peoples' spirits [*Volksgeister*] are altogether limited [*überhaupt beschränkte*] because of the particularity in which they have their objective actuality and their self-consciousness as ethical individualities. Their deeds and destinies in their reciprocal relationships are the appearing [*erscheinende*] dialectic of finitude of these spirits. Out of this dialectic arises universal spirit, the spirit of the world … as free from limitation [*unbeschränkt*] …[222]

---

[219]Hegel, *Werke* 12: 311. The language of the text suggests that the "unfettered" will of the citizen participating in the democracy requires, dialectically, the "fettering" of the wills of others.

[220]*Grund* also means the foundation or basis of an argument, hence its "rationality"; see "Grund" in Hegel, *Science of Logic*, 444ff.

[221]Hegel, *Werke* 7: §279A: 449.

[222]Hegel, *Werke* 7: §340: 503.

The spirit of any people, including of the "German" people, remains an intrinsically "limited" particularity opposed to the "unlimited" principle of universality constituting the "idea" of the state. For any of his contemporary readers, Hegel's use of the phrase *germanische Reich* would have reflected explicitly this tension between the notion of a "particular" "people" and the idea of a single, territorialized "state." There was, of course, no such German state when Hegel published the *Philosophy of Right* in 1820 or lectured on history through the ensuing decade. From the late medieval period until 1806, most German-speaking peoples of Europe lived in the still multi-ethnic confederation of the "Holy Roman Empire," renamed the "Holy Roman Empire of the German Nation" [*Heiliges Römisches Reich Deutscher Nation*] in 1519. The victories of Napoleon, "the world-spirit" Hegel glimpsed on horseback after the battle of Jena in 1806, led to the dissolution of the empire in the same year. The Congress of Vienna marked the end of French hegemony and the inauguration of the *Deutsche Bund*, a loose confederation of thirty-nine German states with no central executive or judiciary, in 1815. The linguistic and cultural diversity known as the *deutscher Dualismus*, manifesting in the political and military rivalry between the Kingdom of Prussia and the Kingdom of Austria (known more particularly as the *preußisch-österreichischer Dualismus*), perpetuated the continuing cultural and political differentiation of the German "people."[223]

In 1830, Hegel nonetheless celebrates this contemporary "political condition in Germany" for the pluralism of its "sovereign states" and the universal "freedom of property and of person" that had replaced "feudal obligations."[224] He adds that in each of these states the prince, as the hypostatization of the universal will in an individual body, "matters little" given "firmly established laws," a "code of rights," increasing meritocracy, and "the settled organization of the state."[225] Hegel applauds the end of the Holy Roman Empire because it "embodied the spirit of subjective satisfaction," especially in "religion."[226] By implication, similar limitations would plague states grounded in the merely "subjective satisfaction" of national or racial identity as well. While "nationalism" has its uses—for instance, organizing a conquered people to throw off the yoke of French imperial oppression or domination—ultimately the "Germanic" principle eschews nationalism as the principle for a unitary state.[227] The "need to find identity [*Identität*]" in "spheres" like religion "has been found superfluous in modern states."[228]

---

[223]On the German Confederation, see, *inter alia*, Jürgen Angelow: *Der Deutsche Bund* (Darmstadt: Wissenschaftliche Buchgesellschaft, 2003) and Wolf D. Gruner: *Der Deutsche Bund: 1815–1866*. (Munich: C. H. Beck, 2010).

[224]Hegel, *The Philosophy of History*, 456.

[225]Ibid.

[226]Hegel, *Lectures on the Philosophy of World History: Introduction*, 203. The addition of *Deutscher Nation* to the "Holy Roman Empire" articulated the defense of territorialized Christendom as the unique mission of the German "people."

[227]Hegel, *The Philosophy of History*, transl. J. Sibree (New York: Dover, 1956), 455. Albert Memmi, echoing Hegel, considers nationalism a dangerous but necessary step in the overthrow of hegemony (see Memmi, *The Colonizer and the Colonized*, 152).

[228]Hegel, *Werke* 1: 478.

The "Germanic spirit" in fact consists in the "realization of absolute truth as the unlimited self-determination of freedom."[229] The "German peoples" are "the bearers of the Christian principle" because they understand the latter to be the "principle of spiritual freedom," the recognitive "reconciliation" [*Versöhnung*] of object and subject and thus between self-consciousnesses.[230] It is only that universal principle, not any shared cultural particularity, that underwrites the kinship of European states: "The European nations form a family *in accordance with the universal principle* underlying their legal codes, their ethicality [*Sitten*], and their development [*Bildung*]."[231] The territorial family, still an element of the state of nature, represents only the first step in the evolution of ethicality toward universal "right."

Translations of the term *Sitte* to mean "custom" and *Bildung* to mean "culture" or "civilization" in such passages have entrenched the confusion around Hegel's view of the relations between a "people" and the "state." Indeed such translations, implying a static set of characteristics particular to a people, register precisely the opposite of Hegel's intended meaning.[232] For Hegel stasis in cultural specificity can have nothing to do with the essence of self-consciousness or the mutual recognition that gives rise to a "people." Accordingly the state consistent with the Germanic spirit eschews cultural sameness. Indeed Hegel from his earliest political texts divorces the project of the state from the preservation or purification of a national "culture." Already in his "Critique of the Constitution of Germany" [*Kritik der Verfassung Deutschlands*] of 1799–1802, he uses the terms *Sitte* and *Bildung* in their respective sense of "custom" and "culture" to insist on the necessary heterogeneity of these elements in the modern state. Citing the admixture of customs, cultures, and languages already characteristic of the "large countries" of his day, he writes:

> In our times, the connection between members [of a state] may be equally loose, or even non-existent in regard to customs [*Sitten*], culture [*Bildung*], and language [*Sprache*]; and identity in these respects, which was once a pillar of a people's union [*Grundpfeiler der Verbindung eines Volks*], now counts as one of those fortuitous circumstances whose nature does not prevent a mass of people from constituting a state power [*Staatsgewalt*] ... Rome or Athens, and even any small modern state, could not have survived if the many languages in use in the

---

[229]Hegel, *Werke*, 12: 413.

[230]Hegel, *Werke*, 12: 413.

[231]Hegel, *Werke* 7: §339A: 502–3. Emphasis mine.

[232]H. B. Nisbet translates *Bildung* here as "culture" (Hegel, *Elements of the Philosophy of Right*, 371); in his translation of this passage, Alan White translates the term as "civilization" (*Hegel's The Philosophy of Right*, 257). As we have seen, H. B. Nisbet makes the same reductive gesture in his translation of *The Philosophy of History* (see, indicatively, Hegel, *Lectures on the Philosophy of World History: Introduction*, 96). For a sense of the idea of *Bildung* Hegel inherited, see, *inter alia*, Wilhelm von Humboldt, "Theory of Bildung," in *Teaching As A Reflective Practice: The German Didaktik Tradition*, ed. Ian Westbury, Stefan Hopmann, Kurt Riquarts (London: Routledge, 1999) and Raymond Geuss, "Kultur, Bildung, Geist," in *History and Theory*, 1996, 35: 2: 151–64.

Russian empire had been spoken within their frontiers, or if the customs of their citizens had been as heterogeneous as they are in Russia—or as customs [*Sitten*] and culture [*Bildung*] are even in any major city in a large country. Differences of language and dialect, the latter of which makes divisions more irritating than does total incomprehensibility, and diversity of customs [*Sitten*] and culture [*Bildung*] among the separate estates, which makes it almost impossible for humans to recognize one another except by their outward appearance—the most powerful of these heterogeneous elements could be overcome and held together in the enlarged Roman Empire only through overwhelming power, just as they are in modern states by the spirit and art of political organization. Accordingly, disparity of culture [*Bildung*] and customs [*Sitten*] has become a necessary product *and a necessary condition of* the existence of modern states.[233]

In this early text, which precedes the development of the theory of "recognition" and *Bildung* in the years leading up to the publication of the *Phenomenology, Sitte* indeed refers to "custom" and *Bildung* simply means "culture." But even in this early passage, Hegel insists that the modern state in fact requires freedom from any specificity of custom or culture. Within a few years *Sitte* for Hegel will come to mean "ethicality" rooted in universality; and *Bildung* will mean the "formation" of self-consciousness toward freedom from particularity. Accordingly cultural production, necessarily dynamic, will consist in the "forming" [*Bilden*] of form, hence the endless architectonic movement of the aesthetic. *Bildung* will thus emerge as the shared commitment to dynamism grounded in a "people" self-consciously embracing their necessary heterogeneity.

The conception of "culture" as "development" thus detaches particular elements of *Bildung* from any static relation to a "people." Cultural traditions held up as the quintessence of a people reflect only the mystified positivism of the Greeks, marking the inertia of innovation and the stifling of the aesthetic. Accordingly development— of a culture or people—requires contact with "foreignness." Indeed that principle of otherness quickened the Greek spirit, as Hegel argues in his lectures on history:

It is superficial and foolish to imagine that a beautiful and truly free life could result from a process as simple as the development of a pure race [*Geschlecht*] remaining within the limits of kinship and friendship ... Thus the Greeks, like the Romans, evolved from a *colluvius*—a confluence of the most diverse nations. Of the multitude of peoples which we encounter in Greece, [we cannot] specify which ones were originally Greek and which had immigrated from foreign countries and parts of the world, for the time we speak of belongs to the non-historical and obscure ... We have spoken of foreignness as an element of the Greek spirit, and it

---

[233]Hegel, *Werke* 1: 477–8. Emphasis mine. On the presence of African intellectuals in Europe, including in Germany in the eighteenth century, see Abbé Grégoire, *De la littérature des nègres* (Paris: Maradan, 1808). Tavares adduces evidence to suggest Hegel was familiar with this work (Tavares, "Hegel et l'abbé Gregoire," 491–509).

is well known that the beginnings of Greek *Bildung* are connected with the advent of foreigners ... tradition states that the various states were founded by such foreigners. Thus, Athens owes its origin to Cecrops, an Egyptian, whose history is shrouded in obscurity ... [Also mentioned is] Danaus, from Egypt; from him descend Akrisius, Danae, and Perseus. Pelops [from Phrygia] is said to have brought great wealth with him to the Peloponnesus, and to have acquired great respect and power there. Danaus settled in Argos. Especially important is the arrival of Cadmus, of Phoenician origin, with whom phonetic writing is said to have been introduced into Greece; Herodotus speaks of its Phoenician origin, and ancient inscriptions then extant are cited to support the assertion. Cadmus, according to the legend, founded Thebes. We thus observe a colonization by developed peoples [*gebildeten Völkern*], who were in advance of the Greeks in point of cultural maturation [*Bildung*]: though we cannot compare this colonization with that of the English in North America, for the latter have not been blended or interbred [*vermischt*] with the inhabitants, but have displaced and ousted [*verdrängt*] them; whereas the [African and Asian and other foreign] settlers in Greece mixed together with the autochthonous population ... These foreigners are reputed to have established fixed *centers* in Greece.[234]

Here the element of "foreignness," a constitutive element of the Greek spirit, marks the ground of its *Bildung* or development. *Bildung* does not provide positive content characterizing the Greek people; neither do the Greek "people" represent a pure "race" or community to whom any such culture would belong. Indeed their "miscegeny" [*Vermischung*] undermines narratives of a "Greek culture" grounded in "autochthony" and self-invention—and, by extension, its appropriation into accounts of a purely "Western civilization." Egypt emerges from its dialectical entanglement with Africa; so, too Greece, in Hegel's historical narrative, "has its basis in oriental substantiality."[235]

Thus in his mature work, he insists on a critical approach to the concept of "culture" underwriting its history. All concepts are discursive and thus semiotic: those of a particular "culture" or "people," as with all necessarily pyramidal signs, cannot banish their inherent "foreignness." People do construct and crystallize an "identity" by mystifying their origins, effacing their "foreignness," and defining themselves in terms of merely contingent elements like language, food, dress, and so on. But any such hypostatization of the sensuous without self-reflection—the idealizing impetus that defines the later Greek spirit and causes its downfall—suffers from the same irrationality as notions of "race" or "racial purity."

Furthermore, the "recognition" of self-consciousness that gives rise to any crystallized category of sociality, as we have seen, engenders and yields ultimately to its "inversion" and "perversion." In the case of a "people" understood as an exclusivist "race" [*Geschlecht*], recognition takes the form of sexual intercourse [*Geschlechtsverkehr*] that, given the

---

[234]Hegel, *Werke* 12: 278–81.
[235]Hegel, *Lectures on Natural Right and Political Science*, 310.

nature of desire, must necessarily traverse or "pervert" the norms attending any group's conceptual purity. Hegel's account of Greek history here follows closely the dialectic of civil society in the *Philosophy of Right*: recognition yields social organization, towns and cities develop, trade ensues, and the resulting "inequality" spurs "colonization." In the absence of the violent displacement [*Verdrängung*] of current inhabitants, sexual reproduction gives rise to "admixture" [*Vermischung*].[236] Greek "ethical life," tied to its geographical proximity to the sea and thus constituting a primitive version of modern civil society, in turn leads to further colonization and intermingling in Egypt, Asia, and the western Mediterranean.

Hegel differentiates here between two modes of colonization: one leading to intermixing and a new cycle of the *Bildung* of spirit, and another to the violent removal of the current inhabitants of a land. As a consequence of the excess of labor in the representational economy of the system of needs, colonization manifests the universalizing and hence globalizing impetus of civil society. But any such "cosmopolitan" drive must be grounded in the concrete life of the state:

> The relativity of the reciprocal relation between needs and the labor to satisfy them is first of all reflected into itself in infinite personhood, in abstract right. But it is this very sphere of relativity, as *Bildung*, that gives right its existence as something universally recognized, known, and willed …
>
> It is part of *Bildung*, of thinking [*Denken*] as the consciousness of the individual in the form of universality [*Form der Allgemeinheit*], that the I comes to be apprehended as a universal person, in which respect all are identical. Human beings count as human beings only because they are human beings, not because they are Jews, Catholics, Protestants, Germans, Italians, etc. This consciousness, for which thought [*Gedanke*] is what matters, is of infinite importance. It is defective only when it is crystallized or fixed [*fixiert*], for instance as a cosmopolitanism [*Kosmopolitismus*] in opposition to the concrete life of the state.[237]

Though it spurs the *Bildung* of the subject by facilitating the incursion of foreignness and thus the universality or emptiness of apparent materiality, cosmopolitan civil society—crystallized as a global system abstracted from all particularity—threatens to oppose the state's "concrete life." This explicit "cosmopolitanism" [*Kosmopolitismus*], beyond reducing the state to a mere vehicle for the proliferation of abstract needs and means, crystallizes certain commodified forms over against inherited and so treasured particularities. By contrast, the mature state, endlessly liberating itself from all fixed forms, unfolds through the dynamism of a concrete and thus lived heterogeneity.[238]

Hegel points here not to the abandonment of cultural continuities or traditions, but rather to the exploration of their inner dynamism: the recognition of the actual negativity of any

---

[236]Hegel, *The Philosophy of History*, 232–3.
[237]Hegel, *Werke* 7: §209: 360–1.
[238]Compare Kwame Anthony Appiah, "Cosmopolitan Patriots," in *Critical Inquiry*, 2007, 23: 3: 617–39.

"local" particularity or custom thus need not hinder free or spiritual enjoyment. Against the discursive economy of abstract *cosmopolitanism*, the self-conscious *cosmopolitan* impetus— fundamentally a mode of *Aufhebung*—seeks not to relinquish material particularity in itself, but dialectically to evolve its mediating categories, giving rise to new modes of particularity that disclose and articulate our freedom. As Hegel states in his 1817–1818 lectures on *Rechtsphilosophie*: "The universal element in the state does not allow the particular purposes to ossify as such, but ensures that they keep on dissolving in the universal."[239]

Likewise the dialectic of cosmopolitan civil society and the state resolves not through the impossible preservation of an "ideal" cultural particularity "in itself," but rather through this discursive and thus self-canceling materialization of "universality."[240] The endless articulation and negation of the "form of universality" mark the architectonic unfolding of spirit.[241] Through its endless *Aufhebung* of particularity, the movement of the architectonic propels the interpenetration of diverse traditions, genres, and languages through aesthetic inventions that permit further enjoyment and spiritual development. Far from rejecting difference in cultural expression as such, Hegel's theatrical universalism privileges precisely the innovations—in music, art, food, clothing, literature, and language—that a "people" come most to cherish. The "concrete life" of the state emerges only when its "people" do not then erroneously fossilize or possessively mark such inventions, mistaking them as constitutive of their "identity."

An emancipated "people" is thus bound only by its collective commitment to *Bildung* and solidarity in the freedom from dialectical stasis. Likewise the "people as a state" [*Volk als Staat*], or "spirit in its substantial rationality," does not differentiate itself through positive cultural differences from its neighbors, but seeks intercourse endlessly to slough off "fixity" or "ossification," hence the hypostatization of any cultural expression as a particular identity.[242] Accordingly *Bildung* as a process contrasts with the *Kultur* of "nomads" or exclusivist religious groups who attempt to define themselves as "one people" "in opposition to their neighbors"; these cannot be "recognized" as a "state" because their exclusivism precludes "the universal identity that is the prerequisite for recognition."[243]

---

[239] Hegel, *Lectures on Natural Right and Political Science*, 221.

[240] The conflict between cosmopolitanism and cultural particularity cannot be resolved through mere fiat. (Such a unifying gesture—an insistence on the merely abstract harmony of the particular and universal—would misunderstand the ironic dimension of what Hegel calls the "concept.") Rather the dialectic of cosmopolitanism and cultural particularity unfolds through an endless process of *Bildung* effected by certain performative modalities we have yet fully to articulate. Hegel's thought, I argue, provides a framework for the critique of such modes.

[241] On the "form of universality" [*Form der Allgemeinheit*], see Hegel, *Lectures on Natural Right and Political Science*, 165 and 221; *Werke* 7: §209: 360 and 10: §434: 224; and Hegel, *Jenaer Systementwürfe I*, 227.

[242] *Werke* 7: §331: 498.

[243] *Werke* 7: §331: 499. Hegel uses the term *Kultur* only twice in the *Philosophy of Right*: once to refer to the cultivation of plants; and here to refer to the superficial differences between groups. According to Raymond Geuss, the abandonment of the term *Kultur* in favor of *Bildung* in the period after Hegel owes much to his influence: "Hegelianism acknowledges the superficial plurality of historically specific folkways, forms of art, sociability, religion, and so on, but sees them all as having an underlying unity, as being mere forms of an historically developing structure, *Geist* … In such a scheme there is no place for a separate concept of *Kultur*" (Raymond Geuss, "Kultur, Bildung, Geist," 157).

For Hegel the first mode of colonization—the migration of people across the world—coheres with the "concrete life of the state," since the admixture of superficially different human beings fosters the *Bildung* and thus recognitive reconciliation of a people to its others. In this respect, *Bildung* requires miscegeny to propel the persistent "perversion" of any cultural, racialist, or other fixed dogma of particularity.[244] Colonization as the migration of peoples, fueled by the intrinsic limitations of political economy, helps to alleviate its excesses and thus constitutes an important element in the "system of care." The traversal of boundaries by peoples adapting to the universality of the mature state thus marks a laudable effect of cosmopolitan ethicality.

By contrast the second mode of colonization consists in the seizure of land, dispossession of other peoples, or imperial administration of other territories; this mode, which I will call "imperialism" or "colonialism," reflects the desire of "mastery" [*Herrschaft*] and thus the failure of recognitive self-consciousness to achieve universality. As we have seen, civil society, acting in its own interest, will leverage the *Verstandesstaat*'s military power beyond its borders. This form of "abstract" "cosmopolitanism" will exploit "particular" identities—even violently—to proliferate the system of needs and means. Through colonialism, elements of civil society will also develop and uncritically utilize a global cultural discourse—like the "civilizing mission" of the later nineteenth century or the alternately "liberalizing" and "democratizing" "mission" of our own day—to widen the "external state's" hegemony in the name of particular interests.[245]

Against the resulting desire for "world domination," the "German spirit" seeks the "hegemony" only "of self-conscious thought":

> The unity of the universal is also present in [this final stage of the German spirit], not as the unity of abstract world domination or mastery [*Weltherrschaft*], but as the hegemony of self-conscious thought. Rational purpose is now seen as valid, and privileges and particularities melt away before the universal goal of the state. *The people will "Right" in and for itself* [*Die Völker wollen das Recht an und für sich*]: particular treaties or conventions are valid, and principles constitute the content of diplomacy.[246]

Here the *germanische Reich* manifests the spirit of universality that seeks not dominion over others, but rather recognitive "reconciliation" [*Versöhnung*] between individual and collective self-consciousnesses.[247] As a public figure, Hegel casts his German audience as the *Volk* that do not define themselves "in opposition to other peoples"; thus he

---

[244]The "perversity" of miscegeny expresses itself in the persistence of "interracial" sex as a taboo still resistant to sublation.

[245]A theory of the relation between civil society and the state would also have to account for the state's appropriation of civil society as a means through which to demand recognition. I will propound such a theory below.

[246]Hegel, *Werke* 12: 418. Emphasis mine.

[247]Hegel, *Werke*, 12: 413.

privileges the "German spirit" only where it endlessly cancels its particularity. The narrative armature of his "world-history" must thus be read as a performative act that tasks his German students, fellow intellectuals, and public figures with the mission of critically dismantling constructs that impose rigid and superficial differences between "cultures" and "peoples," instead recognizing their "universal identity" in the endless *Bildung* of self-consciousness.

The advent of the "German Reich" in 1871 betrays Hegel's conception of the *germanische Reich* in every respect. Emerging out of the Franco-Prussian War, the *Deutsches Reich*, a state at least notionally based on the privileged relation of a unitary and autochthonous people to its "ground," already gestures at the genocidal horror of its "third" articulation under Adolph Hitler.[248] Hegel's still relevant but nonetheless unappreciated critique of the *innere Staatsrecht* sets forth the logic behind the increasing violence of this exclusivism.

In the same manner, later appropriations of Hegel to justify an exclusivist or pure "Western" or "European" "culture" betray his dismantling of precisely such categories through the universalizing spirit of world-history. "Western" continuity from "its" anachronistically appropriated Greek past strips the latter of its interpenetration with Africa and Asia over more than two millenia, from the adoption of the Phoenician alphabet to the implication of Greek thought in Arabic, Persian, Turkic, and other expressions from Spain and Mali to the upper Oxus.[249] And the deployment of "Western civilization" as a concept performatively constructs as it hardens opposition to "African," "Egyptian," "Islamic," "Chinese" or other "civilizations." The critique of such superficial and dialectically unstable categories has not impinged upon the continuing reification of "Western" culture. Not that we can dispense with racial, cultural, or civilizational categories; against the continuing reign of mere "understanding," Hegel's world-history teaches us to evoke precisely to erode such concepts, hindering their appropriation in the service of mastery.

Texts from Hegel's corpus that apparently privilege "German," "European," or "Western" people may well have contributed to the crystallization of racial categories and the ensuing imperialism and genocides of the nineteenth and twentieth centuries.[250] Assertions to

---

[248]On autochthony see Peter Geschiere, *The Perils of Belonging: Autochthony, Citizenship, and Exclusion in Africa and Europe* (Chicago: University of Chicago Press, 2009).

[249]See Martin Bernal's *Black Athena: The Afroasiatic Roots of Classical Civilization*, Vol. 1: *The Fabrication of Ancient Greece 1785–1985* (Brunswick: Rutgers University Press, 1987). This first installment of *Black Athena* has remained largely free from the controversy of the later volumes. On the debates around Martin Bernal, see *Black Athena Comes of Age: Towards a Constructive Re-assessment*, ed. Wim M. J. van Binsbergen (New York: LIT Verlag, 2011). On the artificial stripping out of the Islamic world from European history, see Marshall Hodgson's classic *Rethinking World History: Essays on Europe, Islam and World History* (Cambridge: Cambridge University Press, 1993).

[250]The views attributed to Hegel about the sub-human nature of the African are akin to those repeated by Germans during the genocide of the Herero people (see Horst Drechsler, *Let Us Die Fighting: The Struggle of the Herero and Nama against German Imperialism, 1884–1915* [Berlin: Akademie-Verlag, 1980]; Jürgen Zimmerer, "Annihilation in Africa: The 'Race War' in German Southwest Africa (1904–1908) and Its Significance for a Global History of Genocide," in *Bulletin of the German Historical Institute*, 2005, 37: 51–7).

the contrary ignore the performative power of Hegel's statements, especially when read in isolation, on the "barbaric" nature of the African. Indicatively, L. Q. C. Lamar from Mississippi reads selections from Hegel's *Lectures on the Philosophy of History* in the United States Congress in 1860 to justify the bondage of Africans as necessary for the "development" of "negroes."[251] But Lamar, ignoring the terms even of the cherry-picked passages he reads, fails to grasp that Hegel's conception of "*Bildung*," his "idea" of freedom, and its telos in the "rational state" identify "right" not in slavery, but rather in the mutual recognition by human beings of their intrinsic freedom. Lamar evokes only the philosopher's statements on the "barbarism" of Africans, eliding his condemnation of the "savagery" of slavers and of Christian practices throughout history and up to the burning of witches in the late eighteenth century.[252] Nor does Lamar register Hegel's insistence on the innate freedom of all human beings, the fluidity of the "so-called races," the virtue of miscegeny, and the right of slaves to revolt in the struggle for recognitive reconciliation.[253]

This evident ignorance of Hegel's philosophy does not stop Lamar, a future Senator and Supreme Court Justice, from asserting that Hegel's lectures constitute "an imperishable monument of human genius."[254] Lamar may seem like too easy a target; but like this noted slaver, many of today's popular defenders of "Western" philosophy as a self-invented, hermetically sealed totality have not read or do not understand the texts they celebrate, even or especially where instruction is provided on the dialectical nature of the concept.[255] The failure to internalize even this lesson in critical thinking, elementary since at least Hegel, has led to interminable discussions about the "influence" of one intellectual canon, culture, or civilization on another, even as partisans fail to grasp that each such category, by virtue of definitional fiat, can always be made to appear impervious to extrinsic penetration. In the case of the components of "Western civilization," today's parlous state of affairs protects not only the corpus, but also the existing disciplines of Greek, Latin, and medieval and Enlightenment philosophy, literature, art, and history from "foreign" elements.[256] Considered critically, however, all such categories lack a fixed referential anchor and remain dialectically porous, hence subject to canonical reorganization on lines other than the positive, verified "transmission" of knowledge from one purportedly autonomous subject to another.

---

[251]Michael Hoffheimer, "Martin Luther King Jr.'s Favorite Philosopher," *The Owl of Minerva*, 1993, 25: 1: 118–9.

[252]On Hegel's use of the same vocabulary for Christian practices and European slavers, see Chapter 9.

[253]Hegel, *Berliner Schriften 1818–1831* (Hamburg: Felix Meiner, 1997), XI: 531.

[254]Hoffheimer, "Martin Luther King Jr.'s Favorite Philosopher," 118.

[255]The academic use of the category "Western" echoes, performatively underwrites, and entrenches the brand of exclusivism now articulated by the current political leader of the United States, e.g., "THE WEST WILL NEVER BE BROKEN. Our values will PREVAIL. Our people will THRIVE and our civilization will TRIUMPH!" (https://twitter.com/realDonaldTrump/status/883012994145280000/video/1, July 6, 2017; emphasis in original).

[256]On the tautology relating "Western" myths of self-invention and autonomous subjectivity, see my "From Bayt to Stanza: Arabic Khayāl and the Advent of Italian Vernacular Poetry," forthcoming in *Exemplaria*. Establishing a framework for the critique of the genealogies of "Western" culture, the essay identifies epistemological continuities between Arabic literature and early Italian vernacular poetry, including the sonnet—perhaps the "Western" literary form par excellence.

The abstract cosmopolitanism of "world" philosophy, literature, religion, or history—understood as an amalgam of still distinct, monolithic traditions—does not countervail this problematic approach to the *Bildung* of the citizen. The latter must be schooled in the dialectic and its implication in the concepts and fluidities of representation, subjectivity, history, and culture; thus can the citizen learn how such notions in their positivist modes artificially, rigidly, and dangerously separate one people from another. Only the critically self-conscious narratives that penetrate such ossified categories can advance the cause of freedom in the developing state.

Hegel, Haiti, and the narrative of reconciliation

To break the fetters of inherited divisions, our task, following Hegel, must be to engender the recognitive reconciliation of *Herr* and *Knecht* through the discursive critique of the narratives of mastery. Here Hegel's work is exemplary. The dialectic of slavery and freedom—central to his work—must, by virtue of his own system, take concrete, historical form. What form would this dialectic take in the age of the modern state? Several scholars have insisted on Hegel's awareness of the Haitian revolution at the time he wrote the dialectic of master and slave in the *Phenomenology*. We have yet to identify adequately, however, how that material corollary inflects our reading of the theory of recognition and its place in Hegel's system.[257] What, then, would it mean to read Hegel's dialectical progression of freedom in terms of its Haitian referent?

We begin with two hypotheses. First, the Haitian slave indeed does represent a historical form of Hegel's *Knecht*, as some have suggested, but only by virtue of the slaves' collective effort at self-emancipation; by corollary, the Haitian slave marks the socialized self-consciousness of the liberated *Knecht* only to the extent that the independent Haitian polity, attempting to gain "recognition," marks a historical form of Hegel's recognitive "state."[258] Second, the relation of Hegel's writings to contemporary slavery is not merely referential; as retrospective and thus prototypical narratives of the slave's progression toward the state, his texts performatively enact the movement toward recognitive reconciliation.

At stake here is not only the interpretation of Hegel's work, but also the relation of subjectivity and political theory in his wake, especially in postcolonial and specifically African studies. To begin with, Hegel assigns the task of discovering freedom—as the aesthetic act of *Bilden,* over against the flawed diremptions of the Enlightenment or of the Terror in France—to the modern slave, a figure he connects essentially with the African. Thus in the previously cited passage from the lectures of 1827, Hegel identifies the roots of "reciprocal recognition," the "substantial principle" of the "state," in the dialectic of mastery and slavery [*Herrschaft und Knechtschaft*].[259] To recall: the *Knecht*, in its quintessential form as a "slave" [*Sklave*], does not own himself; he subordinates his

---

[257] My purpose here is to substantiate and build on the claims of Tavares, Buck-Morss, Nesbitt , and Jenson.

[258] It bears remembering that for Hegel only "ethical existence [constitutes] the state as such" [*Das sittliche Dasein ist der Staat überhaupt*] (Hegel, *Vorlesungen über Naturrecht Staatswissenschaft*, 280).

[259] Hegel, *Vorlesungen über die Philosophie des Geistes: Berlin 1827/1828*, 171–2.

"freedom" to his "life" and "has no will of his own." He recognizes the other and "is a thing for the other"; he "belongs to the other." Master and slave collude to keep the latter alive; in this "community of need," the "slave [*Sklave*]" develops "an interest to form [*formieren*] objects … which provides for the possibility of satisfying desire," until:

> The slave [*Knecht*] suspends his inner immediacy, which consists of desire and self-seeking; these relate only to his immediate particularity. With this suspension, the slave makes the transition to universal self-consciousness. The essential element of this transition falls on the side of the slave … the master does not negate desire in its inner dimension, nor does he negate self-seeking or the particularity of the will. The dialectical overcoming [*Aufheben*] of the self-seeking particularity of the will occurs in the slave [*Knecht*] …[260]

And in the section on "Self-Consciousness" in the 1830 version of the *Encyclopedia*:

> The master [*Herr*] confronting the slave [*Knecht*] was not yet genuinely free, for he was still far from seeing his own self in the other. Only through the slave's achievement of freedom does the master, too, become completely free.[261]

While the master progresses toward freedom through the "community of need" that drives the *Bildung* of self-consciousness, he only achieves emancipation through "the dialectical overcoming [*Aufhebung*] of the immediate will objectified for him in the slave."[262] The latter's liberation—his detachment from his corporeal immediacy and thus willingness to die for his own freedom—enables the master to "recognize" the slave's "*Aufhebung* as the truth in regard to [the master], too": thus the master also "submits his own selfish will to the law of the will that is in and for itself."[263] Only at that moment—in which individual and collective wills cohere—can the truly rational "state" appear.

Notwithstanding such passages, many readers of Hegel do not connect the dialectic of *Herr* and *Knecht* with actual slavery, much less to the concrete materialization of the state. But the central, organizing idea in Hegel is that spirit, in all of its diremptions, must take material form in time. Indeed philosophy must "find itself" in the "present," abstracting an "ideality" over against the "real"; that ideality in turn "builds [*erbaut*] the same world, grasped in its essence, in the shape of an intellectual realm."[264] If we are to take Hegel at his word, the relation in the *Encyclopedia* between the collective will on the part of slaves to die for their freedom and the birth of the rational state cannot but evoke Haiti's demand for the recognition of its freedom and independence during the first quarter of the nineteenth century.

---

[260] Ibid., 172.

[261] Hegel, *Werke* 10: §436R: 226–7.

[262] Hegel, *Werke* 10: §435R: 225–6.

[263] Hegel, *Werke* 10: §435R: 225–6.

[264] Hegel, *Werke* 7: 28. Hegel's point here is crucial: the philosophical ideal submits to the idea and vice versa. The program for the unfolding of freedom requires nothing more than what is already immanent in the dialectic. What is rational, in other words, exists as possibility.

The Haitian revolution and the question of slavery loomed far larger in scholarly German consciousness than it does today. Scholars have pointed to numerous sources for Hegel's information on the horrors of American and Caribbean slavery and on the Haitian revolution in particular, including *Minerva*, "the most important political journal at the turn of the century."[265] Haiti features prominently in *Minerva* from its inception in 1792 and through Hegel's entire career. The first article on the Haitian slave revolt, published in the journal's inaugural issue, expresses support for the rights of "people of color" and the agitations of *Les Amis des Noirs*, including the Abbé Grégoire.[266]

In an addition to the 1830 *Encyclopedia*, Hegel lauds the Haitian state in the following terms:

[Africans] cannot be denied a capacity [*Fähigkeit*] for *Bildung*; not only have they, here and there, adopted Christianity with the greatest gratitude, speaking movingly of the freedom [*Freiheit*] they have thus acquired after a long spiritual servitude [*Geistesknechtschaft*], but in Haiti they have even formed a state on Christian principles ...[267]

Here Hegel views the Haitian state "based on Christian principles" as an African emergence from "spiritual *Knechtschaft*": the African *Knecht*, unconscious of his freedom in "Africa proper," only attains to "freedom" in the "state" through a crossing over the seas and subjection to modern slavery, a particularly cruel mode of cosmopolitan *Bildung*.[268]

---

[265] Buck-Morss points out that the journal's readers and contributors included the German political and intellectual elite: amongst *Minerva*'s regular readers were King Wilhelm III, Goethe, Schiller, Klopstock, Schelling, and Hegel (*Hegel, Haiti, and Universal History*, 45). Other sources include Marcus Rainsford, *An Historical Account of the Black Empire of Hayti*: (1805), now available in a new edition by P. Youngquist and G. Pierrot (Durham: Duke University Press, 2013). See also d'Hondt, *Hegel secret*, 9ff.

[266] "Historische Nachrichten von den letzten Unruhen in Saint Domingo. Aus verschiedenen Quellen gezogen," in *Minerva*, 1792, 1: 296–319, an issue Hegel read (d'Hondt, *Hegel Secret*, 9–12); see Buck-Morss, *Hegel, Haiti, and Universal History*, 42. For Hegel's interest in the French abolitionists, see Tavares, *Hegel, critique de l'Afrique* and his "Hegel et l'abbé Grégoire."

[267] Hegel, *Werke* 10: 60. Crucially, Hegel here connects Haiti explicitly with the African spirit.

[268] Hegel adds here that Africans in the state of nature cannot have an "inner" drive for *Kultur*. Herbert Uerlings adduces this text as evidence of Hegel's tendency to self-contradiction due to Eurocentricity and then concludes—in an astonishing leap—that this phrase articulates Hegel's "delegitimiz[ation]" of the Haitian Revolution" (Uerlings, "Anerkennung und Interkulturalität," 95). Rather than being inexplicably inconsistent in the same breath here, Hegel argues that Africans, given their origin in the non-dialectical and non-historical state of nature he calls "Africa proper," by definition do not author and fix their own dialectical differentiation or *Kultur* as a people: *Kultur* is for Africans a matter of entirely external interpellation. Hegel thus implies that any cultural attributes of Africans remain contingent (see my earlier discussion of the difference between *Kultur* and *Bildung*). By contrast, the defining human capacity for *Bildung* or spiritual maturation through the experience of the dialectic "cannot be denied" to Africans: the process of *Bildung* begins when Africans step into history as slaves and as they attain, through *Bilden*, a collective consciousness of their own actual independence—a freedom they are tasked historically to awaken in their benighted masters. Uerlings, in many cases following Tibebu, makes other arguments rejecting the positive place of the Haitian state in Hegel's thought, of which I will here engage three: 1) For Uerlings, Hegel's exuberance on seeing Napoleon, the "world soul" on "horseback," in 1806 suggests that the German philosopher supported the French emperor's desire to reconquer Haiti and re-enslave its population (Hegel, *Briefe von und an Hegel*, ed. J. Hoffmeister. Hamburg: Meiner, 1969–71, 120). But Hegel's thrill upon seeing Napoleon does not necessarily translate into support for all of Napoleon's policies. (I would have been thrilled to see Barack Obama in person during his Presidency; that does not mean I supported his use of drones abroad.) Moreover Hegel explicitly views the emperor's forced

Two articles in *Minerva* from the 1820s that have escaped scholarly attention shed light on Hegel's formulation here.[269] A sixty-page 1825 article in *Minerva* entitled "Account of the Negotiations between France and the Haitian State" opens by calling out the historical importance of "the negro and mulatto republic's" disruption of the "antiquated political system of states" [*alte politische Staatensystem*].[270] In the journal's view, the shock to the "system" of nation-states stemmed from the demand, on the part of transplanted Africans, for "recognition" of Haiti as an equal, "independent state."[271]

---

diffusion of "liberal institutions" as the emanation of an "abstraction" that cannot fundamentally impose onto self-consciousness either freedom or slavery (Hegel, *Werke* 12: 533–5). For Hegel, Napoleon could no more force freedom upon a people unsocialized to their independence than he could impose bondage on a people certain of their freedom (ibid.). The fact that Napoleon had failed to impose a constitution in Spain or Italy or slavery in Haiti does not change his importance as the apotheosis of a world-historical force that, in its failure, nonetheless prompts the movement of history. 2) Uerlings further argues that Hegel's failure to mention the Haitian revolution prior to 1830 proves that he viewed it negatively; at a minimum, since Hegel mentions the French Revolution and not Haiti in his discussion of world-history, "Saint-Domingue [cannot be] the site of God's theodicy" (Uerlings, "Anerkennung und Interkulturalität," 93). There are several problems with this argument: (a) In the *Phenomenology*, Hegel does not mention any historical events by their proper name; (b) as we have seen, Hegel explicitly connects the *Knecht* in the *Phenomenology* to New World slavery in the *Philosophy of Right* and implicitly in numerous lectures on the *Encyclopedia*; (c) it is Uerlings, not Hegel, that restricts what the latter calls the "French revolution" to Europe—a move that, excluding Saint-Domingue and its inhabitants, requires at least some measure of historical justification (see my discussion below); and (d) Hegel's failure to allude less cryptically to Haiti in the *Phenomenology* (for instance, by use of the word *Sklave*) may have been for fear of Napoleon's army, just as his circumspection with respect to explicitly lauding a violent slave revolution in the published *Philosophy of Right* may have been for fear of the censors. Uerlings dismisses this last point, made by Tavares and Buck-Morss, without argumentation. In the same letter to Niethammer, Hegel in fact refers explicitly to the "fear" with which he mailed the manuscript of the *Phenomenology* as Napoleon was scaling the walls of Jena (Hegel, *Briefe*, 120). And the Carlsbad Decrees of 1819, which led to the arrest of a number of Hegel's friends and students, could not but have inflected Hegel's formulations in the *Philosophy of Right*, published the next year. 3) For Uerlings, Hegel's preference for the gradual to the sudden abolition of slavery reflects his discomfort with or even hostility to slave revolt. Now, in the cited passage on "abolition" Hegel actually writes, "Since the essence of man is freedom, slavery is in and of itself wrong; but man must first become ripe for it. So the gradual abolition [*Abschaffung*] of slavery is more appropriate and correct than its sublation through immediate abolition [*Aufhebung*]" (Hegel, Werke 12: 129). Using the crucial term *Aufhebung* here, Hegel critiques the notion that instant legislative manumission, eschewing what he elsewhere identifies as the recuperative perversions of the dialectic, will effect instant emancipation: indeed he insists that the "annulment" or *Aufhebung* of a law amounts also to its preservation, as the double meaning of *Aufhebung* suggests (Hegel, *Werke* 8: §96: 204–5). The legal abolition of slavery thus does not amount to its dialectical overcoming [*Aufhebung*], yielding rather to new discursive and material regimes of implicitly or explicitly forced labor. In the absence of an increasingly collective self-consciousness of freedom on the part of an interpellated group (without which actual emancipation cannot happen), legislated freedom will not advance the cause of freedom; accordingly a "gradual" process of abolition and emancipation—geared genuinely toward the care and *Bildung* of the slave—is preferable to sudden manumission. Whether one agrees with Hegel or not, it should be clear that this statement is entirely consistent with his views that a collective self-consciousness that prefers death to bondage—resisting violently if necessary—is less likely to remain enslaved; and that this action on the part of the enslaved remains a much surer—albeit still long and arduous—route to freedom than abolition. I will address the persistence of forced labor after the abolition of slavery (or in the absence of its legality) below.

[269]See "Skizze von Hayti in Beziehung des moralischen und politischen Characters seiner Bewohner," in *Minerva*, 1822, 123: 454–85; and "Darstellung der zwischen Frankreich und Hayti Statt gefundenen Unterhandlungen," in *Minerva*, 1825, 135: 329–91.

[270]"Darstellung," in *Minerva*, 1825, 135: 329. All translations from *Minerva* mine, unless otherwise indicated.

[271]Ibid., 135: 330.

The article points to the Haitians' race and former enslavement as the contradiction underwriting that "system." On the one hand, the European powers and the United States, given their significant interests in slavery in the Caribbean or on the American mainland, dared not recognize the independence of the slaves or their republic, wishing rather to subjugate them anew; on the other hand, none of the imperial powers could ignore Haiti's economic importance.[272] According to the piece:

> Haiti had made immeasurable progress [by 1816]. Order showed itself in all parts of the administration, population and civilization grew rapidly, and commerce flourished. American, English, Dutch and French people visited the island at that time, and especially the English and French vied for primacy ...[273]

Hegel's brief but nonetheless laudatory reflection on the Haitian "state" in 1830 aligns with such unstintingly sympathetic views expressed in *Minerva* in the 1820s. To take various instances from the articles on Haiti published in 1822 and 1825:

> Haiti has begun to shake free from those wretched prejudices against the equality of human rights which obtain no matter the color of the skin—prejudices that have survived only through sophistical artifices and blind superstition—and to satisfy the demands of universal, rational human rights.[274]

> Twenty-five years ago, the Haitians were still immersed in the deepest ignorance and they had no concept of human society, their physical and moral abilities having been dulled through oppressive slavery [*Knechtschaft*]. Now they have learned to read and write over a period of a few years; they have become notaries, judges, civil servants, some practicing painting and sculpture; others are builders, mechanics, and linen weavers; others work on sulfur mines, and make saltpeter and gunpowder, as in Europe, without any other help than chemical and mineralogical books. In the art of war their progress is no less great.[275]

> [T]he deepest peace prevailed throughout the island. From the year 1811 onward, civilization made rapid progress in St. Domingo. Both Christophe and Pétion seemed anxious to support industry, morality, and science in their field ...[276]

---

[272] At the outset of the slave revolution, Saint-Domingue produced between 40 and 50 percent of the world's sugar and between 50 and 60 percent of the world's coffee (David Geggus, "The British Government and the Saint Domingue Slave Revolt, 1791–1793," in *The English Historical Review*, 1981, 96: 379: 285; Trouillot Michel-Rolph, "Motion in the System: Coffee, Color, and Slavery in Eighteenth-Century Saint-Domingue," in *Review: A Journal of the Fernand Braudel Center* [Binghamton: Fernand Braudel Center, 1982], 5: 3: 337).

[273] "Darstellung," in *Minerva*, 1825, 135: 350–1.

[274] "Skizze von Hayti," in *Minerva*, 1822, 123: 484.

[275] "Darstellung," in *Minerva*, 1825, 135: 351–2.

[276] Ibid., 135: 332.

Any impartial observer will necessarily have to admire the civilization in Christophe's states.[277]

The code consists of simple, clear laws appropriate to the customs and character of the people … all are founded on justice and humanity …. several manufactures have been erected, which give rise to the most beautiful hopes.[278]

In the southern part the government was mild; the reasonable laws which the people gave themselves were punctually obeyed; there was true freedom everywhere; the people were benevolent, the administration paternal, the president popular, and in every sense a leader, who appeared to be created to rule free men …[279]

[with respect to] public education … in both parts of the island, seven Lancaster schools were created, and around Cap Henri a Collegium has been established, where ancient languages, medicine, surgery, the pharmaceutical sciences, and mathematics are taught.[280]

The articles on Haiti in *Minerva* published after 1804 detail the persistence of European threats to reconquer the island, as well as the determination of the new Republic not only to protect itself through military preparation, but also to convey discursively to any threatening power the Haitian people's willingness to die in the defense of its freedom. The 1825 article cites, for instance, a diplomatic letter from the Haitian Secretary of Foreign Affairs to the French King after the fall of Napoleon in 1814. The missive relates, first, the Haitians' ceaseless preparations "for war," so as "to offer the strongest resistance in the event of an attack"; and, second, an openness to a new relation based on equality: "France has taken another form; his Majesty [of Haiti] hopes to find in [the new French regime] a just and philanthropic government that will fully convince itself that no violence can compel us again to submission."[281] The article in *Minerva* continues:

Similar sentiments animated the southern provinces. The government formally declared that at the first appearance of a hostile army, they would burn down the houses and destroy anything that could not be brought into the mountains … An English merchant who related these measures in a letter said at the same time about President Pétion: "I have never seen a more virtuous or more amiable man; he is the idol of the people, but would certainly be deposed on the spot, if he were

---

[277]Ibid., 135: 333–4.
[278]Ibid., 135: 335.
[279]Ibid., 135: 355.
[280]Ibid., 135: 352.
[281]Ibid., 135: 339.

considered capable of returning the colony to France. If anyone doubts that the measure of destruction is beneficial, he answers: 'Look at Moscow, if that had not been destroyed, Napoleon would still be the tyrant of Europe.'"[282]

The article also describes a "Proclamation" published in the *Royal Gazette* in Haiti in the same year. As cited, this text characterizes the people's response to "our irreconcilable enemies, the planters, who for twenty five years have not yet given up the idea of re-establishing slavery," as follows: "we will all perish or remain independent and sovereign [*unabhängig*]."[283]

The link in such expressions between the independence of the slave and the sovereignty of the state, reflecting a collective agency Hegel identifies as the essence of freedom in ethical life, could not have been lost on him. Repeatedly the article in *Minerva* cites Haitian texts connecting the impossibility of re-enslavement to the demand for recognition of the new state. The Haitian experience from 1789 to 1825 indeed instantiates, as no other example historically to that point, the entire cycle in Hegel's philosophy between *Knechtschaft*—a name in *Minerva*, too, for the slavery of Africans—and the attainment of recognitive reconciliation between states as collective modalities of self-consciousness.[284]

The centrality of this cycle from *Knechtschaft* or *Sklaverei* to the realization of the state in Hegel's thought marks a narrative reflection of Haiti's discursive attempts at reconciliation. One scholar has brilliantly connected Jean-Jacques Dessalines' conception of freedom—in an 1804 text published in German translation in the February 1805 edition of *Minerva*—to Hegel's dialectic of master and slave in the *Phenomenology*.[285] Dessalines' voice rings out through the layers of mediation: the Haitians, he declaims, "had resuscitated freedom by infusing their own blood in it"; they were "proud to recover their freedom, jealous to maintain it, and determined to overcome anyone who would try to ravish it from them

---

[282]Ibid., 135: 339–40.

[283]Ibid., 135: 341.

[284]In a passage that has been subject to misreading, Hegel indicates that the philosophical view of history cannot consider the "New World," the "land of the future," any more than it can engage the "past," taken merely as "what has happened" [*Geschehene*]; rather philosophy must center on "what is"—that is, what presents itself to "reason." But in fact philosophy, engaging the received archive, aims at the "present" appropriation of what has happened or could happen; in this manner it draws the possibility immanent in the dialectic into a speculative narrative of "reason" (Hegel, *Werke* 12: 114). Any such speculation proleptically gestures at the possibility and thus futurity immanent in present articulation; that "present," as an expression of latent sociality or community, "raises itself" up and "is essentially reconciled, brought to consummation through the negation of its immediacy, consummated in universality, but in a consummation that is not yet achieved, and which must therefore be grasped as *future*—a now of the present that has consummation before its eyes; but because the community is posited now in the order of time, the consummation is distinguished from this 'now' and is posited as future" (Hegel, *Lectures on the Philosophy of Religion* [Los Angeles: University of California Press, 1987] 3: 188). For this reason Hegel can speak of merely posited political institutions as actualities in the *Philosophy of Right*. (On the idea of the immanent futurity of philosophical speculation, see Malabou, *The Future of Hegel*, 6ff.) As I have shown, the idea of the "state" in the *Philosophy of Right* cannot be reduced only to Haiti or any other particular state; rather the "state," as a dialectic of "internal" and "external" "right" for any possible polity, must be read as a speculative principle gesturing proleptically at all immanently "postcolonial" or "free" states.

[285]Deborah Jenson, "Hegel and Dessalines," 269–75.

again." Thus had they revealed their French masters as the true slaves: "Slaves! ... let us leave that qualifying epithet to the French themselves: they had conquered to the point of ceasing to be free."[286] Dessalines' complex formulation, written before Hegel recasts the dialectic of recognition in terms of master and slave, presents "freedom" as an idea concretized and made substantial by the blood of slaves. The convergence of concept and materiality here reveals mastery as the experience of an ultimately spiritual servitude. But the Haitians, insists Dessalines, had saved freedom as such for everyone. The French needed only to reconcile themselves to freedom from mastery and recognize the Haitian state. Hegel's entire career—from the publication of the *Phenomenology of Spirit* in 1807 and the *Philosophy of Right* in 1820 to the last version of the *Encyclopedia* in 1830—can be read as an echo and elaboration of this idea of freedom.

Haiti's example—along with the black republic's material support for liberation movements in the Americas—hastened the independence of numerous states in the years preceding the publication of the *Philosophy of Right*.[287] By 1815, most of the colonies from Mexico to Brazil and Chile had emancipated themselves from their European masters. Accordingly Hegel, who lauds the independence of the American colonies, views future colonization and decolonization as the predictably dialectical movement from cosmopolitan civil society to the "state." In the *Philosophy of Right*, he further links the asymmetrical relation of the mother country and its colony to the dialectic of master and slave: "the inequality of right ... has resulted in war and eventual independence, as the example of the English and Spanish colonies shows. The liberation [*Befreiung*] of the colonies proves to be the greatest advantage for the mother state, just as the emancipation of the slaves [*Freilassung der Sklaven*] proves to be of greatest advantage for the master [*Herr*]."[288] The process of independence and recognition, in other words, reiterates the dialectic of *Herr* and *Knecht* at the level of ethical sociality: "liberation" [*Befreiung*] and "emancipation" [*Freilassung*], as the German cognates suggest, bespeak each other.[289] Hegel's remark, made in 1824–1825 during the well-publicized negotiations for the recognition of Haiti, is notable for its elision of any reference to France or its former colony on Saint-Domingue. Hegel implicitly demarcates the experience of the English and Spanish colonies—by then mostly independent and widely recognized states—from the example of Haiti, where a group of African slaves had, as of the time of the remark, emancipated themselves but still failed to achieve recognition as a state from any major power. Hegel will only refer to Haiti as the realization of the postcolonial "state" on the Christian principles of innate freedom and universal right after its official recognition by

---

[286]Ibid., 273.

[287]Eleazar Córdova Bellow, *La Independencia de Haití y su influencia en Hispanoamérica* (Caracas: Venezeula, 1967). Reflecting Haiti's continuing world-historical importance, Greek revolutionaries reached out to President Boyer in the 1820s for assistance in the struggle against the Ottomans. For Boyer's response, see E. G. Sideris and A. A. Konsta, "A Letter from Jean-Pierre Boyer to Greek Revolutionaries," in *Journal of Haitian Studies*, 2005, 11:1: 167-71. I am obliged to Roger Célestin for this reference.

[288]Hegel, *Werke* 7: §248A: 393.

[289]Hegel defines "ethical life," after all, as "the idea of freedom": "Die Sittlichkeit ist die *Idee der Freiheit*" (Hegel, *Werke* 7: §142, 292).

France.[290] Taken together, Hegel's remarks from before and after he would have learned of Charles X's decree distinguish the postcolonial state as an exemplary culmination of the *Bildung* through which the "African" *Sklave* attains to a more self-conscious and mutually recognitive "emancipation" [*Freilassung*].[291]

Readers of the 1825 article on Haiti in *Minerva*, including Hegel, would indeed have noted its emphasis on the spirit of reconciliation in Haitian communications with France from 1814 to 1825. One letter insists that "the Government of the Republic" expressed "only the unwavering will of the people" for "clear and unconditional" recognition of Haiti's independence.[292] Rather than ally itself with another European power in the face of French intransigence, Haiti nonetheless desired "sincere reconciliation" with its former colonialist master.[293] Haiti's President—in a gesture many of his countrymen protested—offered monies and advantages in trade to incentivize France and effect this reconciliation. Even so, Haiti did not waver on the content of the public recognition demanded by its people of the French King: according to *Minerva*, Haitian diplomats insisted on "a royal ordinance, whereby His Majesty the King of France recognizes the people of Haiti as free and independent, and renounces from this moment and forever both for himself and for his descendants all claims of France on the island of Haiti."[294] The article concludes with an editorial note acknowledging, as Hegel would have, the contingency of any such recognition of independence. The editor, apparently unaware of the amount of the "indemnity" to be paid by Haiti, warns that only future "treaties" and "diplomatic acts" would bear out the sincerity of the King's Ordinance. But if the recognition were to succeed for both parties, it would "set up a model for other governments' abjuration of colonies declaring their own emancipation."[295]

Hegel's work, effecting a similar reconciliation of "African" and "European" voices in the history of emancipation, denudes freedom of any historical specificity or fixity. Already his vision of Haiti as an "African" state built on "Christian" principles brings together the incipit and telos of religious history, from the unconsciousness of "fetishism" to the self-consciousness of the "revealed religion."[296] Any self-conscious

---

[290]As is evident in the communications between them—published, as we have seen in *Minerva*—France's recognition of Haiti marks an acknowledgment of a certain shared ethos—from political economy to ideas of "right" grounded in the trans-Atlantic revolutions of the late eighteenth century. Not that Charles X's decree marked any certain guarantee of Haiti's independence; but then no state enjoys any such guarantee.

[291]The "African," of course, remains free of any cultural or historical content beyond that of self-consciousness engaged in the *Bilden* of freedom.

[292]"Darstellung," in *Minerva*, 1825, 135: 364.

[293]Ibid., 135: 364.

[294]Ibid., 135: 381.

[295]Ibid., 135: 391.

[296]In his remarks, Hegel explicitly contrasts the Christianity of self-emancipated Africans in Haiti to the fetishism of those in the state of nature of Africa proper (Hegel, *Werke* 10: 60). Here again the philosophy of history circles back to its beginning, as both Christianity and African religion effect a convergence in time of subject and object: Christianity self-consciously through the reconciliation of spirit and the body of man; and African religion unconsciously through the investment of "supernatural power" in the fetish (Hegel, *Werke* 12: 123).

history of freedom must likewise assess critically the reconciliation of inner and outer *Staatsrecht*, however contingent, modeled by the Haitian state: the latter, admitting of "no predominant religion" and first allowing "freedom of worship" in the 1805 Constitution, realizes the "Christian principle" that centers on the individual as an infinite end, rather than a racialized particularity.[297] Haiti's recognitive resolution with France, however contingent and problematic, achieves that universality *in potentia* in the narration of world-history. For Hegel less mature conceptions of freedom—grounded in abstract right, formulaic morality, or absolute freedom in subjectivity—lead, in the case of the Enlightenment, to merely empty formalism; in the case of the American Revolution, to the "atomized" subjects of the *Verstandestaat*; and in the case of the revolution in France, to the Reign of Terror.[298] The Haitian revolution cannot be fully demarcated from these other revolutions; rather Haiti—born of slavery and emancipation—marks their incipit and culmination. Here it bears noting, in light of Hegel's notion of world-history, that the complete uncoupling of the French and Haitian Revolutions only entrenches the hierarchies that give rise to race-based slavery and colonialism in the first place. Mulattoes and free blacks in Paris—including figures like Julien Raimond and Vincent Ogé—inflected debates on the nature of freedom through their activism in the *Société des Colons Américains* and influence on *Les Amis des Noirs*; to strip these debates and figures out of the history of the French Revolution misrepresents its central problematic and, worse, rehearses the very gesture of non-recognition thwarting the cause of freedom today.[299]

In contrast to the prevailing history of freedom in Hegel's wake, his works, as narratives of recognitive "reconciliation," attempt performatively to advance the progression of

---

[297]See Bob Corbett, "The 1805 Constitution of Haiti," http://faculty.webster.edu/corbetre/haiti/history/earlyhaiti/1805-const.htm. The right to "freedom of worship" also appears in the 1816 Constitution of Haiti: see "Révision de la Constitution Haïtienne de 1806 (1816)," https://haitidoi.com/constitutions/1816-2/.

[298]Thus with respect to the Americans after their Revolutionary War, "the basis of their existence as a united body lay in the necessities that bind man to man, the desire of repose, the establishment of civil rights, security and freedom, and a community arising from the aggregation of individuals *as atomic constituents*; so that the state was merely something external for the protection of property ... [T]he fundamental character of the community [consists in] the endeavor of the individual after acquisition, commercial profit, and gain; the preponderance of private interest [devotes] itself to that of the community only for its own advantage. We find, certainly, legal relations—a formal code of laws; but respect for law exists apart from genuine probity, and the American merchants commonly lie under the imputation of dishonest dealings under legal protection" (Hegel, *The Philosophy of History*, 84, emphasis mine).

[299]Readers of the *Phenomenology*, viewing the referent of "Absolute Freedom and Terror" as the French Revolution, demarcate it as a purely European phenomenon divorced from the travails of the (for them historically unspecified) *Knecht* in the section on "Self-Consciousness." Such readers do not register the paradigmatic nature of both "Self-Consciousness" and "Absolute Freedom and Terror." Adopting precisely the Eurocentricity attributed to Hegel, they neglect the universal and thus potentially global inflections of the revolution for "absolute freedom" in Hegel's text, evident in his reference to spirit's renewed experience of the slavish "fear of the master" [*die Furcht des Herrn*] (Hegel 3: 438) (see my "The Franco-Haitian Revolution: Hegel, Fanon, and the Problem of Recognition," forthcoming). On the activity of figures like Raimond and Ogé in the early days of the revolution in France, see David Geggus, "Racial Equality, Slavery, and Colonial Secession during the Constituent Assembly," *The American Historical Review*, 1989, 94: 5: 1290–308, especially 1299ff.

self-consciousness from mere "desire" and toward "universal self-consciousness." In his philosophy of freedom, the German philosopher echoes the voices of transplanted Africans dialectically overcoming their interpellated otherness. Through this narrative gesture, he articulates the "German" spirit's negation of its historical particularity. Thus the "African spirit"—the non-dialectical, non-historical principle that first gives rise to the idea of freedom in Egypt and then further traverses the limits of East and West— reconciles with the "German spirit" in the *Weltgeist* of "world history."[300]

This perspective illuminates the relation of *Weltgeschichte* to the dialectic of the state in the conclusion of the *Philosophy of Right*. Given the endless self-negation of their historical "forms," the "spirits of peoples in their variegated actuality" are "present" in "world-history" "as only ideal; and the movement of spirit within this element is to show this ideality."[301] Through history, "peoples" and their "geographical and anthropological worldly being" appear as "immediate, natural actuality," but all immediacy and "being" succumb to the negativity of the "this" and hence the *Aufhebung* of spirit.[302] World-history as spirit "is nothing but its activity of knowing itself absolutely, and thus of freeing its consciousness from the form of natural immediacy as it returns to itself."[303] Thus the most apparently reified categories of history become hypostatized "ideals" dissipating before the rationality of "universal spirit."[304] Like Greek "ideal" sculpture or the Roman "penates," the "spirits of peoples" are shown to be false or contingent gods, merely "particular" moments in the dialectical unfolding of reason.[305] Accordingly, world-history unveils the freedom of self-consciousness from any fixed geographical or anthropological determinations.

Why then must world-history in its final diremption articulate "concrete spirit" in the form of the "architectonic" state?[306] As the "development" of "freedom," *Weltgeschichte* takes place through "moments of reason and so of spirit's self-consciousness"; "this development," Hegel adds, "is the interpretation [*Auslegung*] and actualization of universal spirit."[307] The spirit of world-history co-implicates discursive "interpretation" and actuality, historical discourse and event, or sign and referent through the "form of occurrence"—what Hegel elsewhere calls its aesthetic and thus performative "narration" [*Geschichtserzählung*].[308] This form of history, as we have seen, must be architectonic, underwriting the fluidity of the categories of world-history.[309] As a "hieroglyph of reason," the state emerges as a

---

[300]"World-history," as the "history of spirit," "is its own act. Mind as spirit, spirit as mind [*Geist*] is only what it does …" Thus Hegel imagines history as a performative act, a self-conscious "interpretation of itself to itself" (Hegel, *Werke* 7: §343, 504).

[301]Hegel, *Werke* 7: §341: 503.

[302]Hegel, *Werke* 7: §346: 505.

[303]Hegel, *Werke* 7: §352: 508.

[304]Hegel, *Werke* 7: §342: 504.

[305]Hegel, *Werke* 7: §341: 503.

[306]Hegel, *Werke* 7: §360: 512.

[307]Hegel, *Werke* 7: §342: 504.

[308]Hegel, *Werke* 7: §346: 505.

[309]My reading takes seriously Hegel's view of "world-history" as the resolution of the dialectic of inner and outer *Staatsrecht*.

discursively mediated union of the individual and universal self-consciousness. Here the principle of architectonic fluidity associated with the African Memnon and slave—the *Werkmeister* of history—underwrites the Germanic principle of the state as the "image [*Bild*] and actuality of reason."[310] The emancipated slave, it will be recalled, identifies the aesthetic dimension of recognitive agency. Already through self-liberation, the slave frees the master from his dependence; but slave and master can only attain to self-consciousness of their own freedom through the recognitive and retrospective narrative or history that effects their reconciliation.[311] Hegel's narrative—modeling retrospectively the African's movement from slavery to freedom in the recognitive and thus universal state—instantiates precisely how such liberations slough off their particularity with respect to "peoples," freeing humanity from the categories and thus shackles of history.

Postcoloniality, architectonics, and the open border

Having safeguarded its independence in the early nineteenth century, Haiti nonetheless could not thrive. The terms of France's recognition in 1825 saddled the new republic with debt. Moreover Haiti could not compete with an increasingly global supply of cheap labor exploited by imperial powers. The United Kingdom and the United States abolished the slave trade, as both powers feared the ardent independence, manifest in Haiti, of Africans not born to race-based plantation slavery.[312] The collapse in the economies of India in the late eighteenth century and of China in the nineteenth century unleashed a flood of cheap labor on the world market. The increasingly global British *Verstandesstaat* extended the slave trade in all but name, importing effectively permanent indentured servants known pejoratively as "coolies" from Asia to the Caribbean as early as 1807. This system of de facto forced labor spread globally, from South America and the Caribbean to Africa.[313]

---

[310]Hegel, *Werke* 7: §360: 512.

[311]See Chapters 8 and 9.

[312]See Edgar Erickson, "The Introduction of East Indian Coolies into the British West Indies," *The Journal of Modern History*, 1934, 6: 128; Robin Blackburn, "The Force of Example," in *The Impact of the Haitian Revolution*, 18; and David Brion Davis, "Impact of the French and Haitian Revolutions," in *The Impact of the Haitian Revolution*, 5–6.

[313]On the development of discursive and material regimes of forced labor after the various acts of emancipation in the nineteenth and twentieth centuries, see, *inter alia*, Douglas Blackmon, *Slavery by Another Name: The Re-Enslavement of Black Americans from the Civil War to World War II* (New York: Doubleday, 2008); David Oshinsky, *Parchman Farm and the Ordeal of Jim Crow Justice* (New York: Free Press, 1996); Nitin Varma, *Coolies of Capitalism: Assam Tea and the Making of Coolie Labor* (Berlin: De Gruyter, 2017); and *Coolies: How Britain Reinvented Slavery* [documentary] (London: BBC, 2002). On the policy of holding women and children hostage and forcing men to collect rubber—a policy that contributed to halving the population of the Congo—see Adam Hochschild, *King Leopold's Ghost: A Story of Greed, Terror, and Heroism in Colonial Africa* (Boston: Houghton Mifflin, 1999). Methods used in the Congo were copied in French Equatorial Africa. René Vautier's 1950 documentary entitled *Afrique 50* exposed forced labor practices—imposed through brutal and random violence—in the French colonies, his voice recounting untold horrors he witnessed: "Ici, le chef de village, Sikali Wattara, a été enfumé et abattu d'une balle dans la nuque, une balle française ... Ici, une enfant

In the United States, the restriction of the importation of new slaves and need to extend the life of those born into bondage may have necessitated an increase in paternalism, perhaps reducing the incidence of life-threatening brutality.[314] By the same token, slave breeding and rape, including of girls as they reached puberty, become all the more necessary to ensure reproduction.[315] Slaves were increasingly valuable commodities to be propagated, but as productive beasts—not human beings. The slave population in the United States quadrupled from the end of the slave trade to the eve of the Civil War; their ranks by 1860 included 400,000 acknowledged "mulattoes."[316]

As sugar production by slaves and coolies increased elsewhere in the Caribbean, Haiti's domestic industry, a principal source of export earnings, collapsed.[317] Haitian coffee, requiring less labor, continued to be competitive on the world market, but generated too little to service the state's overwhelming debt to France.[318]

Moreover Haiti, notwithstanding its efforts, could not ultimately participate as an equal in a world political system dominated by the racially interpellated and increasingly colonialist order of European states based on need. The United States, which refused to recognize Haiti until 1862, became by the end of the nineteenth century the dominant force in the Americas. In 1915 this emergent power secretly funded the purchase of Haiti's principal bank as a cover to invade and occupy the island for twenty years. Today Haiti remains one of the poorest countries on earth. In the end, the "postcolonial" state founded by slaves did not escape the effects of colonialist hegemony.[319]

The failure of the Haitian state reflects the persistence of the *Verstandesstaat* and its global proliferation of needs and means. Haiti's fate thus prompts questions about the possibility of a "postcolonial" global order in the wake of the apparent decolonization of states during the second half of the twentieth century. On the one hand, the colonialism of Hegel's day—the seizure and administration of the land of other peoples by the state

---

de sept mois a été tuée, une balle française lui a fait sauter le crâne … Ici, du sang sur le mur, une femme enceinte est venue mourir, deux balles françaises dans le ventre … Sur cette terre d'Afrique, quatre cadavres, trois hommes et une femme assassinés en notre nom à nous, gens de France!" (*Afrique 50* [documentary], dir. René Vautier [France: Ligue française de l'Enseignement, 1950]). The film was banned in France until the end of the twentieth century. On the use of forced labor practices on poor "white" Europeans despite the illegality of slavery prior to the nineteenth century, see Don Jordan and Michael Walsh, *White Cargo: The Forgotten History of Britain's White Slaves in America* (New York: New York University Press, 2008).

[314]Or so Hegel would have surmised, since he links a concern for the slave's life with the development of a "community of need." In the absence of hard evidence, any specific claims along these lines must remain hypothetical.

[315]On "slave breeding," see Manning Marable, *How Capitalism Underdeveloped Black America: Problems in Race, Political Economy, and Society* (Boston: South End Press, 2000), 72ff.; Dannell Moon, "Slavery," in *Encyclopedia of Rape*, ed. Merril Smith (Westport: Greenwood Publishing Group, 2004), 234; and Sharon Block, *Rape and Sexual Power in Early America* (Chapel Hill: University of North Carolina Press, 2006).

[316]According to the 1860 census, 411,000 slaves were classified as mulatto, out of a total slave population of 3,900,000 (Marable, *How Capitalism Underdeveloped Black America*, 74).

[317]Alex Dupuy, *Haiti in the World Economy: Class, Race, and Underdevelopment since 1700* (Boulder: Westview, 1989), 92.

[318]James Graham Leyburn, *The Haitian People* (New Haven: Yale University Press), 1945, 114.

[319]For a general history of Haiti, see Phillippe Girard, *Haiti: The Tumultuous History* (New York: Palgrave, 2010).

or its proxies for the purpose of settlement or profit—appears now to be a diminishing (though far from extinguished) global phenomenon. On the other hand, powerful states continue to dominate weak ones: the United States projects geopolitical power through hundreds of military installations around the world; France does the same in its former territories in Africa.[320] Colonialism emerges, now as ever, from a cycle in which economic leverage and military strength reinforce each other, a process we can still frame, following Hegel, in terms of the dialectic of civil society and the state: thus civil society, concentrated in strong states "based on need," reinforces the global military reach of the state and its allies; and the state, separately or through alliances and trade blocs, exerts economic and military leverage to secure advantages for elements of civil society holding sway in the state.[321] For Hegel this process leads to a "state of nature" and, by implication, the *Herrschaft* of some nations as "ethical individuals" over others.[322]

With the end, often violent, of European countries' direct administration of states in Africa, Asia, and the Americas, norms have shifted away from the racial supremacism of colonial discourse. Concurrently, titular "decolonization" has spurred the migration of millions of people from dominated countries to Europe and the United States. The resulting admixture of what Hegel would consider superficially different "peoples" has prompted a crisis in the conception of the state as either an "ideality" of internal right and thus exclusionary self-sufficiency or a cosmopolitan *Verstandestaat* based on need. Proponents of the former, "internal" mode want the state to exercise control over the flow of immigration through a "secure border," ensuring that immigration does not threaten the dominance, for instance, of "whites" or Christians in the host country or its prevalent national "culture." Proponents of the latter, "external" mode insist on a reasonable flow of immigration, legal or even otherwise, to optimize access to youthful or skilled labor in the service of a globally expanding civil society.

Each of these views of the state depends on a discursive economy of mediated properties, whether of an "ideal" individual state purportedly belonging to a people or of a system of abstract needs and means. As we have seen, the corresponding internal and external modes of the state thus remain dialectically entangled, together producing the violent and unstable "particular state" through aesthetic symbology. All such symbols, however, gesture endlessly at content and thus cannot underwrite the identity of a people; even a written constitution, abstracted from lived ethicality in a free state, lends itself to "perversion" or *Verkehrung*. A "people" defining its "identity" in terms of symbology does so at the expense of the "universal identity" that, grounded in the self-consciousness of freedom, defines the human. Insisting on their internal sameness in differentiation from otherness, the constituents of a "people," as they turn to recognize

---

[320]The United States also has a long history of imperial conquest and continues to administer territories in the Pacific and Caribbean: see Daniel Immerwahr, *How to Hide an Empire* (New York: Farrar, Straus, and Giroux, 2019); and *U.S. Department of Defense Base Structure Report*, "A Summary of the Real Property Inventory," 2015. On the persistence of French power in its former colonies in Africa, see François-Xavier Verschave, *La Françafrique: Le plus long scandale de la République* (Paris: Stock, 2003).

[321]See Mitchell, "The Limits of the State"; Verschave, *La Françafrique*.

[322]Hegel, *Die Philosophie des Rechts: Die Mitschriften Wannenmann (Heidelberg 1817/18) und Homeyer (Berlin 1818/19)*, 247.

each other, confront further layers of irreducible difference. There is, in the end, no difference between identity and difference, as Hegel teaches us in the *Science of Logic*.

In addition, neither vision of the state centers on the idea of "right" grounded in the freedom of self-consciousness and the universality of the human being. Here even the discourse of "human rights" betrays its limitations and susceptibility to perversion. The 1951 Convention Relating to the Status of Refugees and the 1966 International Covenant on Civil and Political Rights enact, respectively, the entitlement to asylum and the freedom of movement as universal human rights; exploiting the elasticity of definition to limit these "rights," however, essentially no wealthy country allows refuge or freedom of movement to citizens of poor countries on the basis of hunger, disease, unemployment, natural disaster, or environmental degradation, even where the prospective host nation bears some share of responsibility for such conditions.[323] More generally, the contribution of a global civil society to the misery of human beings—often leveraging a colonialist platform—has not translated into a global right to escape such privation in fact. Thus demand in rich countries for illegal narcotics bolsters international networks of organized criminality that weaken neighboring states used for supply or logistics; but the behavior of citizens in rich countries has not led to the recognition of any concrete rights for affected citizens in poor ones. Subsidies and protections for internal agriculture within rich countries and the dumping of excess supply onto world markets negates what is frequently a competitive advantage of poor countries; the resulting hindrance to economic development, leading to malnutrition and stunted brain development, still does not—according to actual conceptions of "right" in the rich world—violate the tangible rights of children in poor states. A "particular state," so long as it clings to the "ideality" of its "internal right" and "sovereignty over others," will leverage the discourse of "universal" human rights for mercenary purposes, signaling, too, moral superiority with respect to dominated countries. If "external right," including international law based on what Hegel calls "peoples' rights," remains contingent on the arbitrary will and does not concretize globally and universally, the "particular state" will only attempt to articulate "internal right"—that is, rights pertaining merely to a singly polity.

Current developments of supranational states, too, remain vulnerable to Hegel's critique of *Staatsrecht*. As we have seen, any "federation" of states or "league" must posit an enemy, an externality or otherness to be dominated.[324] For instance, the European Union has dedicated resources toward developing a "European" identity, including through student exchanges within the continent; but any such discourse performatively differentiates its polity from African, Asian, Latin American, and other populations and states.[325] The supranational body and its member states thus struggle to emerge from the

---

[323]On the unreliability of definitions, legal or otherwise, to guarantee "right," see Hegel, *Werke* 7: §2A: 30–1.

[324]Hegel, *Werke* 7: §333: 499–500.

[325]The very title of Jürgen Habermas' *The Divided West* interpellates an Asian, African, and Latin American "other" against which the "West" must unify. On the other hand, Habermas remains a point of reference for current debates around international political organization. On "recognition" (with all of its Hegelian overtones of domination) and the modern state, cf., *inter alia*, Jürgen Habermas, "Struggles for Recognition in the Democratic Constitutional State," in *Multiculturalism*, ed. Charles Taylor (Princeton: Princeton University Press, 1994), 107–48; Jürgen Habermas, *The Inclusion of the Other* (Cambridge: MIT Press, 2000); and Axel Honneth, *The Struggle for*

dialectic between, on the one hand, the ideality of self-sufficient, internal right predicated on exclusivist identity and , on the other, the cosmopolitan *Verstandesstaat*—an apparent opposition accentuated by insistent national identities. In the absence of a resolution to this conflict between the "internal" and "external" modes of *Staatsrecht*, the European Union will either realize a politically integrated, exclusivist state with an increasingly powerful central executive, judiciary, and legislature or remain a weak federation.[326] In the former case, the European Union would largely follow the example of the United States, a *Verstandesstaat* with global military and economic reach; in the latter case, the federation would remain more likely to suffer the withdrawal of its members.[327]

Until and unless the modern state resolves the dialectic of right through self-conscious ethicality, the "postcolonial state"—understood as the recognitive harmony of states free from colonialism—cannot materialize. The United States, the European Union, and possibly a newly emergent China as extensions of a fractured civil society will continue to undermine freedom in weaker states through predatory trade practices and agreements, resource appropriation, foreign corrupt practices, and environmental degradation.

For Hegel the dialectic of "internal" and "external" *Staatsrecht* resolves only through the architectonic movement of the rational state. Here self-consciousness produces recognitive narratives of world-history as the aesthetic realization of the state. These recognitive regimes, exposing the "ideality" and thus phantasmatic dimension of the particular, underwrite the solidarity of a people in their common humanity. In an initial phase, the experience of civil society forms the subject as an abstract "person," to the point she matures beyond the mere "understanding" of "right" as an extension of the system

---

Recognition: The Moral Grammar of Social Conflicts (Cambridge: Polity Press, 2005). The theory of recognition has been extended to the analysis of religious minorities: in a nuanced article on the "non-recognition" of Muslims in Denmark, Heiko Henkel—engaging Honneth, Habermas, and other contemporary thinkers on recognition and the European project—argues that Danish Muslims have experienced marginalization from the "ethnically" Danish majority or, worse, a "non-recognition" felt in the widespread and often harsh critique of religious Muslim practices, ranging from public condemnations of the Muslim headscarf as unsuitable for Danish society to the bureaucratic regulations that require Muslims to arrange burials through a pastor of the Danish *Folkekirke*, the Lutheran state church (Heiko Henkel, "Fundamentally Danish? The Muhammad Cartoon Crisis as Transitional Drama," *Human Architecture: Journal of the Sociology of Self-Knowledge*, 2010: 8: 2: 67–82). This non-recognition "is most visible in the intensely negative representation of Muslims in the Danish media ... and the almost ubiquitous display of suspicion towards practicing Muslims since the September 11th attacks. The publication of the Muhammad cartoons, and the subsequent official and public support for Jyllands-Posten, were broadly perceived by Danish Muslims as a dramatically staged escalation of this non-recognition of Muslim residents of Denmark as Muslims" (ibid. 69).

[326]Thus Dani Rodrik argues that a country can have economic integration, democracy, or a nation-state, but not at all three: a country can choose (1) integration and democracy through elected representatives to supranational institutions, but give up on the nation-state; (2) a nation-state and democracy, but give up on the benefits of broader economic integration; or (3) integration and a nation-state, but relinquish democratic control to bureaucrats in supranational institutions (Dani Rodrik, *The Globalization Paradox: Democracy and the Future of the World Economy* [New York: Norton & Co, 2012]). If Europe goes the way of the first option, the European Union emerges as a powerful "particular state" exerting increased economic and military force worldwide. A number of nationalists, notably in Britain, France, and Italy, support the second option—which amounts to leaving the European Union—even where they acknowledge the economic costs. There are, at least now, few partisans in Europe favoring the third option.

[327]Particularly during times of economic crisis or social upheaval, as with so-called "Grexit," "Brexit," and so on.

of needs and means. In the more advanced dialectic of world-history, by contrast, self-consciousness in its maturity seeks recognitive reconciliation and "universal identity."

What modalities of *Bildung* toward the realization of the postcolonial state emerge from Hegel's work? On Hegel's example, the humanities must engage critically the dialectical differentiation of philosophy, literature, art, science, and history into "Western," "Eastern," "European," "African," or other particular categories. So, too, the canons of "world" literature, philosophy, or art, in order to avoid serving a merely abstract cosmopolitanism, require ceaseless scholarly subversion of the limits between their subsidiary categories. The humanities must perform such deconstructions for students and the citizenry as part of the *Bildung* of self-consciousness. For his part Hegel, as we have seen, cites the coimbrication of Greek and Afro-Asiatic cultural production; of the Arabic and Latin intellectual tradition, including in "philosophy" and "science"; and of Persian poetry and contemporary German literature to erode purportedly endogenous canons of philosophy or literature and instantiate "freedom" from dialectical stasis as the emancipatory "essence" of world-history. Beyond the fairly elementary capacity to critique general categories like race or culture through textual analysis, such approaches in the construction and deconstruction of knowledge require rigorous training in multiple languages, critical theory, and the methods of dialectical argumentation.[328]

In this vein, the progression toward "recognitive reconciliation" requires decoupling the idea of freedom in academic and popular discourse from its purported and exclusivist "Western" origin and specificity. Such "immature" conceptions of freedom become the property of one particular culture, people, or race to then bestow magnanimously—or not—on another. Hegel's narratives of reconciliation model the movement from colonialism as a mode of abstract cosmopolitanism toward concrete freedom in recognition: both the *Phenomenology of Spirit*, largely free from particular references, and the *Philosophy of Right* offer retrospective narratives of freedom as performative archetypes of its historical realization.

The increasing demand by aggrieved populations and formerly colonized countries for new histories, apologies, reparations, the return of stolen artifacts, or the removal of monuments and symbols points to a crisis centered on the problem of recognitive reconciliation. Moreover the rapid proliferation of agents—individual, institutional, and governmental—and transnational channels for the production and distribution

---

[328]Too few doctoral students in the United States and Europe, even as they compete for an increasingly limited number of academic positions, obtain the linguistic mastery and philosophical preparation that might lead precisely to such interventions in world-history. Students of the ancient world would do well to heed the cautionary remarks of the American linguist Edward Sapir: "When we realize that an educated Japanese can hardly frame a single literary sentence without the use of Chinese resources, that to this day Siamese and Burmese and Cambodian bear the unmistakable imprint of the Sanskrit and Pali that came in with Hindu Buddhism centuries ago, or that whether we argue for or against the teaching of Latin and Greek, our argument is sure to be studded with words that have come to us from Rome and Athens, we get some indication of what early Chinese culture and Buddhism and classical Mediterranean civilization have meant in the world's history. There are just five languages that have had an overwhelming significance as carriers of culture. They are classical Chinese, Sanskrit, Arabic, Greek, and Latin" (Edward Sapir, *Language: An Introduction to the Study of Speech* [New York: Harcourt, Brace and Company, 1921], 207). In this vein, students of medieval Europe would do well to study Arabic.

of historiographical materials signals a seismic shift in the relation of subjectivity and history. In particular, the de-centering of historiographical production threatens long-standing narratives grounding the twin notions of individual and national sovereignty in subjective classifications of desire, gender, race, religion, and culture—markers of identity tied, in turn, to fixed objective determinations of corporeality and territory. For the colonizers of the earth and their heirs, this encounter with the disembodied and ungrounded agency of the subject and state marks a revolution.

Given the aporia of reconciliation and the ungovernable socialization of agency, how to articulate any program of *Bildung* for the realization of freedom? Hegel's infamous insistence on the belatedness of philosophy expresses an apparent impotence before the task. Derrida, too, likens the project of reconciliation, framed as "forgiveness," to an impossible dream:

> Ce dont je rêve, ce que j'essaie de penser comme la "pureté" d'un pardon digne de ce nom, ce serait un pardon sans pouvoir: *inconditionnel mais sans souveraineté*. La tâche la plus difficile, à la fois nécessaire et apparemment impossible, ce serait donc de dissocier *inconditionnalité* et *souveraineté*. Le fera-t-on un jour? C'est pas demain la veille, comme on dit. Mais puisque l'hypothèse de cette tâche imprésentable s'annonce, fût-ce comme un songe pour la pensée, cette folie n'est peut-être pas si folle.[329]

> What I dream of, what I try to think of as the "purity" of a forgiveness worthy of its name, would be a forgiveness without power: *unconditional but without sovereignty*. The most difficult task, at once necessary and apparently impossible, would be to dissociate *unconditionality* and *sovereignty*. Could we accomplish such a thing one day? Not tomorrow, as they say. But since the hypothesis of this unpresentable task announces itself, if only as a dream for thought, this madness is perhaps not so mad.

Here the "hypothesis" of impossibility already points to a horizon of possibility: the "unpresentable task" presents itself. Hegel goes much further, positing this endlessly deferred limit as the internal end of the enterprise of thought. The "result" of history, as we have seen, must also mark its beginning: philosophical truth "has its end for its beginning … the result is the same as the beginning, because the beginning is an end."[330] This non-chronological "end"—what I have called the "telos" of history and philosophy—consists in the freedom of the historical event from any received form, including of given time. Like the translator attempting faithfully to translate an original text, the philosopher's equally possible–impossible task is to find in the event, belatedly and after the "fact," the elements of its undoing.[331] Freeing any configuration from its own necessity, the philosopher

---

[329]Jacques Derrida, *Foi et Savoir, suivi de Le Siècle et le Pardon* (Paris: Seuil, 2000), 133. Translation mine.

[330]Hegel, *Werke* 3: 23, 26.

[331]Thus the title of Walter Benjamin's widely read essay on translation refers to the *Aufgabe das Übersetzers*—both the task and renunciation of translation (see Paul de Man, *The Resistance to Theory*, 80).

identifies agency as an irrepressible possibility of history, emergent where it seems most hidden from view. Resignation before contingency, as an articulation of freedom in history, thus belies the power in *potentia* of any quiescence before the real. All actions, moreover, require resignation with respect to the future; so, too, resignation—the willful limitation of the will—constitutes an action: even the slave's labor, giving rise to the aesthetic, marks an impetus toward freedom from mastery. For this reason, Hegel insists on the necessity of contingency:[332] hence the dialectic of freedom urging, equally, the slave laboring over the object and the philosopher writing in the shadow of the world-soul on horseback.

Any telling of the past, whether through anthropology, sociology, political science, or other discipline, performatively resignifies given narratives of history in a manner that not only disrupts, but also consolidates inherited structures. However diffuse and multi-centered, any social program or orientation for reconciliation—a natural propensity, Hegel would say, of an increasingly cosmopolitan civil society—likewise remains subject to ironic perversion, reappropriation, and crystallization in the service of power. But every action or inaction expresses power through a contingent historical narrative suffused, accordingly, with the dream of reconciliation: "I that is We and We that is I."[333]

As an endless process, reconciliation requires recognition. What then would be the rational requirements internal to the production of world-history? In the context of colonial experience, the task must be to uncover, classify, translate, and disseminate archival materials[334] for historiography toward the development of shared narratives of history.[335] No efforts could or should be limited to institutional or state control: scholars, intellectuals, and activists can do much to realize such efforts through international collaboration. The process of reconciliation cannot yet be uncoupled, however, from the sovereign state: on Hegel's critique, reconciliation, as the materialization of "external right" between states, would require the joint sponsorship of imperial and colonized states and their institutions. "Recognition" at the level of "right" articulates precisely in order to dissolve what Derrida frames as "sovereign" "power."

The dialectic of "right" in world-history thus gestures at certain possibilities. Transnational commissions for truth and reconciliation, adding transparently to the archive and subject to the critique of other forces in civil society, can expose violations of right by colonial powers, resistance movements, and postcolonial regimes in the context

---

[332]Thus Hegel refers to the "unity of necessity and contingency" (Hegel, *Werke* 6: 213; see also 214–6). See Quentin Meillassoux, *After Finitude: An Essay on the Necessity of Contingency* (London: Bloomsbury, 2010).

[333]It bears mentioning that Hegel in the *Philosophy of Right* does not describe, much less defend, the actual institutions of the contemporary Prussian monarchy; rather his "outline" of the institutions of the rational state—whose accomplishment is left to the "German spirit"—performatively articulates a programmatic proposal for reform. Hegel's typical discursive strategy is to set forth specific "requirements" for the reformed state as a matter of rational necessity (see, indicatively, the use of the verb *erforden* in Hegel, *Werke* 7: §289: 458).

[334]Many such archives remain inaccessible to researchers, including in the UK and Belgium: see, indicatively, Ian Cobain and Richard Norton-Taylor, "Files that may shed light on colonial crimes still kept secret by UK," in *The Guardian*, April 25, 2013.

[335]All such narratives would collapse ultimately into that of the *Bildung* of self-consciousness toward freedom in recognitive reconciliation.

of collective experience. Discursive interventions can incorporate and develop methods in restorative justice and post-conflict recovery toward the goal of mutual recognition between imperial and colonized states, as well as the reconciliation of the citizens of weaker states to a joint purpose. The global dissemination of aesthetic expressions, popular or otherwise, can help habituate societies across the world to increasingly international norms and thus laws. The failure of any such positive program only reveals spiritual maturation as the immanently shared cause of all: *Bildung* takes place, Hegel demonstrates, through the imperfect advances of recognitive self-consciousness. The aim of world-history remains to teach citizens across states to uncouple self-consciousness from the merely "subjective," exclusivist satisfactions of national pride, racial identity, and territorial belonging.

The transnational production of world-history and international "right"—through the institutions of civil society and the state—contributes performatively to the concretization of the "rational" state through open borders. Beginning as violently demarcated ground, the state posits the self-canceling frontier as its rational telos, the paradoxical manifestation of right through world-history.[336] Only through the endless articulation and cancellation of its material limits can the "architectonic" state realize freedom on earth. In the absence of the free movement across frontiers, the state cannot resolve the dialectic between an exclusivist program of "inner right" [*innere Staatsrecht*] and the "external" demand for recognition of its legitimacy or "right" [*äußere Staatsrecht*]. On the one hand, "inner" right translates to the conception of the state as an ultimately "ideal" territoriality, a reification of the "ground of right" as a border between a "people" and its others. As a matter of definition, the exercise of privileged right within any appropriated and delimited part of the earth betrays the principle of universal right. Moreover the exclusivist conception of the state as defended ground, safeguarding the integrity of a people, leads only to the purging of its internal and inexhaustible otherness and ultimately the self-immolation of the state.[337] On the other hand, the "external" demand for recognition can only ground the state's legitimacy in its articulation of necessarily universal "right": states will collectively and mutually recognize their legitimacy if their system of right reflects a shared ethos, hence a coherence of individual and universal will. Any other mode of recognition remains partial or contingent, resulting in violent domination on the international stage. States can only be free if all states are free; a people can be free only if all people are free; and a human being can be free only if all human

---

[336]Hegel summarizes the paradoxical logic of the self-canceling limit as follows: "[The limit] is the mediation through which a something and its other both *are* and *are not*" [*Sie ist die Vermittlung, wodurch Etwas und Anderes sowohl ist als nicht ist*] (Hegel, *Werke* 5: 136; see also *Werke* 5: 142ff. and *Werke* 3: 75).

[337]For Hegel the critique of *bürgerliche Gesellschaft* must be approached from the perspective of ethical sociality in the state, or the cohesion of the individual and universal will in a social polity. For Marx the politicization of civil society through universal suffrage renders "inessential" its distinction from the state, leading to the dialectical overcoming or dissolution of both (Karl Marx, *Critique of Hegel's "Philosophy of Right,"* ed. J. O'Malley [Cambridge: Alden & Mowbray, 1967], 121). Marx's critique of Hegel lies beyond the scope of the present study.

beings are free.[338] "External" right only achieves the uniformity and thus universality of right through the *Bildung* of self-consciousness toward the realization of freedom.

An open border, as an endlessly self-canceling limit, demarcates spatially and thus symbolically the solidarity and shared sociality of a people, both internally and externally. The more a "people" begins to realize freedom, sloughing off the attachment to particularity, the less its members require spatial contiguity. Accordingly states may enter into overlapping territorial legal regimes. If a "people" is bound by its collective commitment to the *Bildung* of self-consciousness, then its members may belong to multiple legal socialities exercising "right." Thus Tunisia, in its radical 2014 Constitution, imagines belonging to a Maghrebi and larger Arab union as a "step" toward achieving "complementarity" between the "African" and "Muslim" "peoples."[339]

In contrast to the image of the state as a "magnificent" or monumental "building" [*Prachtgebäuden*] sealed off against foreignness, the "architectonic" state endlessly delimits its territory only to transcend the worldly being of its ground. As necessarily inadequate affinities of form and content, those aesthetic delimitations of space must endlessly and objectively appear—even if only on a map—in order repeatedly to evanesce as human subjects traverse them. Only through that self-canceling separation can states rehearse their mutual recognition. Accordingly an "open border," as the manifestation of the architectonic state, realizes the paradoxical "concept" in world-history.

The program emerging here requires, first, scholarly investigation of the philosophical, social, legal, economic, cultural, and political consequences of open borders leading to, second, commitments on the part of states to achieve a global regime of open borders within a specified period of time.[340] Far from being utopic, "open border" policies have already been promulgated in certain concrete, if limited forms—from the Convention on the Status of Refugees to the Schengen Agreement suppressing internal borders in Europe. Tellingly, fears of an exodus from poor countries in Eastern to Western Europe on the advent of the Schengen area have proven ill-founded, and yet the benefits to Central and Eastern European civil society have been immense.[341] Countries already participate in overlapping trade regimes that involve the increasing movement of people across borders. Notwithstanding current fears, annual crossings of the US–Mexico border, for

---

[338]"I am only truly free when the other is also free, and is recognized as such by me" (Hegel, *The Philosophy of Subjective Spirit*, 3: 57).

[339]"La République Tunisienne fait partie du Maghreb Arabe, elle œuvre à la réalisation de son union et prend toutes les mesures pour la concrétiser … En vue de soutenir l'Union maghrébine, qui constitue une étape vers l'union arabe et vers la complémentarité entre les peuples musulmans et les peuples africains … Au nom du Peuple, nous édictons, par la grâce de Dieu, la présente Constitution" (https://www.constituteproject.org/constitution/Tunisia_2014.pdf, PDF generated: 27 Jul 2018).

[340]For a review of the available studies on the economic impact of increased global labor mobility, see Michael Clemens, "Economics and Emigration: Trillion Dollar Bills on the Sidewalk?" *Journal of Economic Perspectives*, 2011, 25: 3: 83–106.

[341]Newer entrants to the European Union have experienced substantial development of their economies and civil societies generally. Indicatively, see M. Kahanec and M. Pytliková, "The economic impact of east–west migration on the European Union," *Empirica*, 2017, 44: 407.

instance, number in the hundreds of millions.[342] Plural legal regimes already co-exist in federalist systems like the United States and for signatories to international legal regimes.[343] The burgeoning institution of visa-free travel with identifying documents and biometric registration at borders provides a model for allowing the free movement of peoples while maintaining the state's security and surveillance apparatus—a problematic, but nonetheless significant step toward the realization of open borders. Internationally chartered academies and universities enabling or requiring study in multiple countries negotiate visa-free travel for their students from otherwise confined populations.[344]

The positing of an open border, surfacing the paradoxical logic of the limit, radically concretizes the idea of "right" in the state; it thus militates against the perverse appropriation of an otherwise abstract code of human rights by hegemonic powers. Enabling the migration of peoples will help to relieve poverty created by the global system of needs and means and, to balance labor flows, spur the development of more favorable trade regimes for poor countries and more sophisticated international systems of supervision and "care." Expanding regimes of open borders, as the architectonic realization of freedom, would moreover subordinate civil society to the goals of the rational state, focusing efforts worldwide on the economic, cultural, and social preparation of humanity for the free movement of peoples. Was it not the prospect of open borders that spurred rich countries in the European Union to invest in the poorer states in the south and east of the continent? The development of civil society in poor countries with the aim of an international regime of open borders would occur with the aim of universal right free of geographical or anthropological fixity.

The abstract cosmopolitanism of the current global order allows citizens of rich states almost unfettered access to any country on earth; millions travel abroad for leisure, education, research, or business annually. At the same time, hundreds of thousands of human beings escaping privation and violence risk their lives annually to enter the world's rich states. Tens of thousands have perished in the waters of the Mediterranean and Pacific and the deserts of North America. Rich states incarcerate thousands of migrants, sometimes in facilities resembling concentration camps. Tens of millions of undocumented and even documented migrants living on the soil of the world's most free states frequently do not have the same rights as citizens.

This political regime depends on a conception of citizenship based not in concrete right or universal freedom, but rather in the mystifications of identity and property. Driven by fear and desire and blind to the discursive mediation of their objects, the contemporary

---

[342]On US–Mexico border crossings, see Alfredo Corchado, *Homelands: Four Friends, Two Countries and the Fate of the Great Mexican-American Migration* (London: Bloomsbury, 2018) and Andrew Selee, *Vanishing Frontiers: The Forces Driving Mexico and the United States Together* (New York: Public Affairs, 2018).

[343]This phenomenon, known as legal pluralism, has a long history. See, *inter alia*, Sally E. Merry, "Legal Pluralism," *Law & Society Review*, 1988, 22: 869–96; Gad Barzilai, *Communities and Law: Politics and Cultures of Legal Identities* (Ann Arbor: University of Michigan Press, 2003); and Jessica Marglin, *Across Legal Lines: Jews and Muslims in Modern Morocco* (New Haven: Yale University Press, 2016).

[344]The University of Central Asia, for instance, was recently formed as a partnership between Kazakhstan, the Kyrgyz Republic, and Tajikistan.

citizen demands a state expelling otherness and yet safeguarding the abstract right to property through a cosmopolitan civil society. This contradiction articulates violence through multiple layers of delegated power. The reduction of the idea of freedom to the interests of property depends, as Hegel warns, upon the commodification of the human body; thus forced laborers, including child slaves, still toil worldwide to produce goods for or give sexual satisfaction to the citizens of rich countries. We cannot lay claim to freedom when it depends on binding suffering human beings to weak and still dominated states. Freedom must be universal and concrete or still elude our grasp.

CONCLUSION: AESTHETICS AND SOVEREIGNTY

The conception of the state as an aesthetic and recognitive phenomenon has profound implications for political projects centered on freedom from domination. On Hegel's analysis, sovereignty emerges not against otherness, but through a legibly universal commitment of states to the *Bildung* of their citizens. The dialectic of inner and outer "right" through the state in the *Philosophy of Right* resolves only where the world's most powerful nations attain to mutual recognition with their weaker counterparts. For Hegel universal right materializes through the liberation of self-consciousness from crystallized categories of world-history, narrations of recognitive reconciliation as realizations of freedom, and the endless dialectical overcoming of the state's delimitation from its outside. Ultimately the logic of Hegel's critique of the state underwrites the movement toward open borders.

Hegel's retrospective history of freedom, beginning with slavery as its dialectical contrary, centers on the form of the African *Knecht* reduced to thinghood and property. The narrative arc or circle ends with the slave's establishment of a state and world-historical attempt at recognitive reconciliation. Hegel conceives of "Africa proper"—its then still unpenetrated interior—as the non-historical, negative principle that, joined with "Oriental solidity" in Egypt, first animates the *Werkmeister*. Enabling the fissuring of spirit and matter in the Egytian pyramid, the surviving "African element" there gives rise to the dialectic as the "architectonic" delimitation of space and time, hence the aesthetic articulation of history. Where Egypt becomes the "land of dialectic," "Africa proper," lacking an archive and thus eschewing representation, remains a utopia or non-place beyond the reach of the dialectic of history.[1] Here form and content, subject and object, and the individual and universal unconsciously fuse. In the absence of narratable history and thus discursive mediation, spirit here remains closed to self-consciousness.

And yet Africa, inhering in the universal spirit, initiates the dialectic of freedom and its first awakening in the slave. As the non-dialectical principle internal to the concept, Africa prompts the movement of the dialectic through its entire history, endlessly evolving the limits between opposed terms. Thus the African Memnon, as the figure of the architectonic, migrates to Egypt and Greece, traversing the line between East and West. Likewise the African slave, stepping into history as the spirit yearning for freedom,

---

[1] Hegel, *Werke* 12: 309.

progresses through various modes of emancipation, beginning with the attempt to detach consciousness from corporeality and ending with the recognitive reconciliation with otherness through concrete sociality. Ultimately the African finds freedom from particularity in the postcolonial state founded on the universality of all human beings. Here the non-dialectical and historical spirits of *Weltgeschichte* reconcile in universal self-consciousness.

Why would Hegel figure the movement of history in geographic and anthropological terms? And why choose Africa? He could have chosen any utopic topos centered on peoples then lacking an accessible archive. To begin with, for Hegel the idea of "Africa" remains vulnerable to two converging perversions of the understanding. First, the positivism of mere understanding reduces spirit to skulls, bones, and skin color, resulting in implicit or explicit racialism; and second, the dialectic of abstract right in the state "based on understanding" [the *Verstandesstaat*], as a cosmopolitan and ultimately colonizing extension of political economy, cannot rigidly separate its categories of person and property and so produces the modern slave. More than the indigenous peoples of the Americas, Africans survive the brutality of the colonial onslaught and the regime of forced labor; thus the understanding historicizes the African as racially inferior and even sub-human—a beast made for commodification through chattel slavery. Hegel critiques both racialism and the dialectic of person and property in, respectively, the *Phenomenology of Spirit* and the *Philosophy of Right*; more explicitly, in the *Encyclopedia* he sets forth the contingency and inconsequence of dark skin and the equal rights of Africans to freedom. Flouting positivism, the establishment of Haiti as an independent state by African slaves and their demand for recognitive reconciliation typify the dialectical overcoming of the perversions of the understanding and thus the possibility of concrete, universal freedom on earth.

Furthermore Africa as a topos marks the freedom from history and its crystallized particularities. For Hegel as he writes, Africa "proper" posits an unrecoverable past, traversing the limits of history even as it produces none. His account of Africans in the resulting "state of nature" reflects his critique of this condition as the struggle to the death between self-consciousnesses prior to their reconciliation in ethical sociality. Crucially, he attributes this absence of *Sittlichkeit* in Africa to slavery; and it is "Europeans," he reminds us, that "lead" Africans into what he calls the "savagery" of historical bondage.[2] Hegel's frequently baseless account of the conditions of Africans may also reflect cultural or racial animus; but any such stubborn particularity on his part does not contravene the critique of static, hierarchical differentiation his project frames as the enemy of freedom. More to the point, the reproduction of the view of Africa as the non-historical "state of nature"—the ideological assumption of the race-based slave regime—enables Hegel to mount a withering critique of the relation of slavery, political economy, and the international order and justify the radical right of enslaved peoples to revolt, found independent states, and seek recognition from European powers. As the "understanding" of Africa represented in Hegel's work finds its inverted corollary in the Haitian state,

---

[2]Hegel, *Werke* 12: 125 and 487, where Hegel uses the term *Roheit* as a predicate for *Knechtschaft*.

so, too, geographical and anthropological determinations, revealed as mere "idealities," unravel before the movement of universal spirit in "world-history."

How does this recognitive translation of mere understanding—responsible for all manner of wrong in the name of right—illuminate approaches to the problem of freedom in the contemporary geopolitical context? More precisely, how might Hegel's narrative of Africa inflect its current conception and prospects for sovereignty?

The discursive realization of "Africa" today exhibits numerous similarities with its figural valences in Hegel's system. Cameroonian artist Barthélémy Toguo's organic installation entitled "The Last Supper" [*La Cène*], shown in Figure 10, instantiates the critical rigor of many such articulations of "Africa." Toguo conceived the piece for "Dak'art Green: Art and Vegetable Matter" [*Dak'Art Vert: Art et Matière Végétal*], an exhibit at the 2014 Biennale of Contemporary African Art in Dakar, Senegal. "Dak'Art Green" took place in the gardens of experimental botany near the medical school at the campus of Cheikh Anta Diop University. According to Daouda Ndiaye, the "scénographe" for *Dak'Art Vert*, artists displaying their works in the gardens were asked to create an "ephemeral," "biodegradable art installation" with "materials found on site."[3] The showcased works exist now only through their photographic representation.

"Installed" under a centuries-old baobab tree, Toguo's "The Last Supper" consists of a number of red bean plants sprouting from the ground in the form of the African continent. The latter appears as a detached island-like totality except for a second bed figuring the large easterly island of Madagascar. Fifty-four chairs, one for each of Africa's sovereign states, surround the two islands.

The piece posits Africa as an organic evanescence, a shaped garden that will disappear before our eyes. Indeed the title of the piece suggests that Africa will be a meal, literally to be eaten and digested. The red beans or *haricots rouges* refer to an African staple, recalling, too, the seeds fed to enslaved human beings trafficked across the ocean. Toguo proposed to harvest the beans for a "Last Supper" at the end of the Biennale. As an aesthetic production, Africa thus subsists as a negativity *in potentia*.

Alternating between high and low, the chairs undulate around the continent like the waves of its surrounding waters. The fifty-four chairs recall the colonial origin of the territorialized states, marking their historical continuity with the slave ships of the same story of conquest and subjugation. The empty national seats evoke as they mark the absence of the African subject, the latter like fettered captives once lost at sea: no longer on stable ground, they disappear into the unstable watery surface. Slave and subject, ghosts of this ironic Last Supper, haunt the circle of floating chairs.

As a biodegradable garden sprouting and then dissipating before our eyes, Africa offers no stable ground for its subjects. The vegetal matter constituting that ground,

---

[3]Daouda Ndiaye explains: "Le principe était simple: nous avons demandé aux artistes de travailler dans le jardin des plantes utiles de la faculté de médecine et de pharmacie de Dakar, avec des matériaux trouvés sur place et biodégradables" (cited in Nicholas Michel, "Arts Plastiques: Dak'Art Prend le Vert," *Jeune Afrique*, May 15, 2014: http://www.jeuneafrique.com/163765/culture/arts-plastiques-dak-art-prend-le-vert/, accessed October 10, 2018; translation mine).

like the bread and wine of the Christ, vanishes when eaten. The place can be grasped only upon the annulment of its appearance or representation. Through this endless resurrection in death, Africa emerges as the idea of no-place that nonetheless takes place—as ground exceeding its immediate articulation.

The piece thus interrogates the place and temporality of the African subject. Never autochthonous, she suffers the displacements of exile and return. And her subjectivity unfolds through an extrinsic, endlessly negated interpellation. She neither grasps nor yields to history.

Taking place at a Biennale of "African" art, the most prominent of its kind, and at the university named after the great Afrocentric thinker Cheick Anta Diop, Toguo's Africa realizes itself through an ultimately communal self-reflection. Ambiguously inviting students and foreign observers to sit and so take the place of the citizens of Africa's fifty-four states, the chairs prompt questions as to what constitutes an African subject in the first place. Is it autochthony? Race? Nationality? Or the dialectic of the subject on African ground?

Another question confronts the observer: Do the chairs form part of the work of art? Where does the ground of the work of art begin and end? The rectilinear lines of the chairs and the circle they draw around the continent point to the artificial form of the garden, the line that demarcates the shape of Africa. By throwing into crisis the lines between "art" and "vegetable matter" in the title of the exhibit, the chairs question the conceptual and material boundaries of the installation: they displace the line of the Africa-shaped garden as a work of art to the equally fluid line of the circle of chairs. Engaging the dialectic of art and nature evoked by Dak'Art Vert, Toguo further insists on the aesthetic dimension of what is only apparently natural form. The art of the shaped garden reveals the artificial mediation of all immediacy, beginning with its very ground. The visitor—local and foreigner alike—thus finds himself doubly removed: first, from the continent on which he purportedly stands, and second, from the seat he must again empty, if he is to observe the work from all of its outsides.

Gesturing at the fluidity of all geographical demarcations, the work ironizes the frontiers and thus territoriality of the nations constituting Africa. Indeed the fifty-four chairs parody its unity and totality: as of the date of the exhibition, there were indeed fifty-four African states in the United Nations and fifty-four in the African Union; they were just not the same states.

The African, Toguo suggests, neither dwells in a single body nor possesses her ground. Rather she materializes dynamically, through an endless process of evanescence and renewal that traverses the bounds of any individual body or people; a social phantasm, she elevates "I" to "We" and "We" to "I."

Africa concretizes the dynamism of the subject and state as they endlessly articulate and cancel their corporeal or territorial limits. As the concrete idea of no-place, Toguo's Africa marks the possible freedom from the arbitrary and particular, overcoming what Hegel would call subjective demarcations of culture and objective delimitations of territory.

Pointing to the universal negativity of the human subject, Toguo's empty chairs, inviting the foreign, articulate Africa's relative freedom from narratives of self-invention and of racial and cultural autochthony. As an aesthetic interpenetration of ideal and empirical ground, Africa signifies resistance to the false gods of static, immediate form.

Thus sovereignty emerges—from reciprocity.

Dispersing and returning, the African subject refuses mimicry. Reaching for more spiritual modes of recognition, she may yet reconcile humanity to its actual freedom.

Figure 10 *The Last Supper.* Barthélémy Toguo, *Dak'Art Vert*, 2014. Rendering by Boaz Balachsan.

SELECT BIBLIOGRAPHY

Afrique 50 [Film] Dir. René Vautier. France: Ligue française de l'enseignment, 1956.

Adorno, Theodor. *Hegel: Three Studies*. Translated by S. W. Nicholsen. Cambridge: MIT Press, 1993.

Adorno, Theodor. *Einführung in die Dialektik*. Berlin: Suhrkamp, 2015.

Adorno, Theodor. *Negative Dialectics*. Translated by E. B. Ashton. London: Routledge, 1974.

Agamben, Giorgio. *Language and Death: The Place of Negativity*. Translated by Karen E. Pinkus. Minneapolis: University of Minnesota Press, 1991.

Allen, Richard. "Slaves, Convicts, Abolitionism, and the Global Origins of the Post-Emancipation Indentured Labor System." *Slavery and Abolition* 35, no. 2 (2014): 328–48.

Almond, Ian. *The History of Islam in German Thought: From Leibniz to Nietzsche*. London: Routledge, 2010.

Anfänge bei Hegel. Edited by Wolfdietrich Schmied-Kowarzik and Heinz Eidam. Kassel: Kassel University Press, 2009.

Apollodorus. *The Library of Greek Mythology*. Translated by Robin Hard. Oxford: Oxford University Press, 1997.

Appiah, Kwame Anthony. "Cosmopolitan Patriots." *Critical Inquiry* 23, no. 3 (2007): 617–39.

Aravamudan, Srinivas. *Tropicopolitans: Colonialism and Agency, 1688–1804*. Durham: Duke University Press, 1999.

Art and Logic in Hegel's Philosophy. Edited by Warren E. Steinkraus and Kenneth I. Schmitz. Atlantic Highlands, NJ: Humanities Press, 1980.

Auerbach, Eric. "Figura." In *Scenes from the Drama of European Literature*, 11–76. Minneapolis: University of Minnesota Press, 1984.

Austin, J. L. *How to Do Things with Words*. Edited by J. O. Urmson and M. Sbisà. Cambridge: Harvard University Press, 1975.

Avineri, Shlomo. *Hegel's Theory of the Modern State*. Cambridge: Cambridge University Press, 1972.

Bakhtin, Mikhail. *The Dialogic Imagination: Four Essays by M. M. Bakhtin*. Translated by Michael Holquist and Caryl Emerson. Austin: University of Texas Press, 1983.

Beekes, Robert S. P. *Comparative Indo-European Linguistics*. Philadelphia: John Benjamins Publishing, 1995.

Benjamin, Walter. *The Arcades Project*. Translated by Howard Eiland and Kevin McLaughlin, 2 vols. Cambridge: Harvard University Press, 2000.

Bénot, Yves. *La Révolution Française et la Fin des Colonies*. Paris: Editions La Découverte, 1988.

Benveniste, Émile. *Problèmes de linguistique générale*, 2 vols. Paris: Gallimard, 1974.

Bernal, Martin. *Black Athena: The Afroasiatic Roots of Classical Civilization*, vol. 1: *The Fabrication of Ancient Greece 1785–1985*. Brunswick: Rutgers University Press, 1987.

Bernasconi, Robert. "Hegel at the Court of the Ashanti." In *Hegel After Derrida*. Edited by S. Barnett, 41–63. London: Routledge, 1998.

Bernasconi, Robert. "The Return of Africa: Hegel and the Question of the Racial Identity of the Egyptians." In *Identity and Difference*. Edited by P. T. Grier, 201–16. Albany: SUNY Press, 2007.

Black Athena Comes of Age: Towards a Constructive Re-assessment. Edited by Wim M. J. van Binsbergen. New York: LIT Verlag, 2011.

Blackburn, Robin. *The Overthrow of Colonial Slavery: 1776–1848*. London: Verso, 1988.

Blanchard, Pascal et al. *Sexe Race et Colonies: La domination des corps du XVe siècle à nos jours*. Paris: La Découverte, 2018.

Bloch, Ernst. *Subjekt-Objekt: Erläuterungen zu Hegel*. Berlin: Aufbau-Verlag, 1951.

Block, Sharon. *Rape and Sexual Power in Early America*. Chapel Hill: Omohundro Institute and University of North Carolina Press, 2006.

Bodammer, Theodor. *Hegels Deutung der Sprache: Interpretationen zu Hegels Äusserungen über die Sprache*. Hamburg: F. Meiner, 1969.

Brandom, Robert. *Articulating Reasons: An Introduction to Inferentialism*. Cambridge: Harvard University Press, 2000.

Brodsky, Claudia. "Architecture and Architectonics: 'The Art of Reason' in Kant's *Critique*." In *Canon*, vol. 3 of *The Princeton Journal: Thematic Studies in Architecture*. Edited by Taisto Mäkelä, 103–17. New York: Princeton Architectural Press, 1988.

Brodsky Lacour, Claudia. *Lines of Thought: Discourse, Architectonics, and the Origin of Modern Philosophy*. Durham: Duke University Press, 1996.

Brodsky Lacour, Claudia. "Architecture in the Discourse of Modern Philosophy: Descartes to Nietzsche." In *Nietzsche and "An Architecture of Our Minds*. Edited by Alexandre Kostka and Irving Wohlfarth, 19–34. Los Angeles: Getty Research Institute, 1999.

Brodsky Lacour, Claudia. "From the Pyramids to Romantic Poetry: Housing the Spirit in Hegel." In *Rereading Romanticism*. Edited by Martha B. Helfer, 327–66. Amsterdam: Rodolpi, 2000.

Brodsky Lacour, Claudia. *In the Place of Language: Literature and the Architecture of the Referent*. New York: Fordham University Press, 2009.

Bruns, Gerald. *Heidegger's Estrangements: Language, Truth, and Poetry in the Later Writings*. New Haven: Yale University Press, 1989.

Buchwalter, Andrew. "Hegel's Concept of an International 'We.'" In *Identity and Difference: Studies in Hegel's Logic, Philosophy of Spirit, and Politics*. Edited by P. T. Grier, 155–76. Albany: SUNY Press, 2007.

Buchwalter, Andrew. *Dialectics, Politics, and the Contemporary Value of Hegel's Practical Philosophy*. London: Routledge, 2012.

Buck-Morss, Susan. "Hegel and Haiti." *Critical Inquiry* 26, no. 4 (2000): 821–65.

Buck-Morss, Susan. *Hegel, Haiti, and Universal History*. Pittsburgh: University of Pittsburgh Press, 2009.

Burke, Kenneth. *The Philosophy of Literary Form: Studies in Symbolic Action*. Berkeley: University of California Press, 1941.

Burke, Kenneth. *Language and Symbolic Action: Essays on Life, Literature and Method*. Berkeley: University of California Press, 1966.

Butler, Judith. *Subjects of Desire: Hegelian Reflections in Twentieth-Century France*. New York: Columbia University Press, 1987.

Butler, Judith. "Gender Is Burning: Questions of Appropriation and Subversion." In *Bodies That Matter: On the Discursive Limits of Sex*, 121–40. New York: Routledge, 1993.

Butler, Judith. *Excitable Speech: A Politics of the Performative*. New York: Routledge, 1997.

Butler, Judith. *Antigone's Claim*. New York: Columbia University Press, 2000.

Cavell, Stanley. "What Did Derrida Want of Austin?" In *Philosophical Passages: The Bucknell Lectures in Literary Theory*, 42–65. Cambridge: Basil Blackwell, 1995.

Clemens, Michael. "Economics and Emigration: Trillion Dollar Bills on the Sidewalk?" *Journal of Economic Perspectives* 25, no. 3 (2011): 83–106.

Comay, Rebecca. *Mourning Sickness: Hegel and the French Revolution*. Stanford: Stanford University Press, 2011.

Comay, Rebecca and Frank Ruda. *The Dash—The Other Side of Absolute Knowing*. Cambridge: MIT Press, 2018.

Cook, D. J. *Language in the Philosophy of Hegel*. The Hague: Mouton, 1973.

Select Bibliography

"Darstellung der zwischen Frankreich und Hayti Statt gefundenen Unterhandlungen." *Minerva: Ein Journal historischen und politischen Inhalts* 135 (1825): 329–91. Edited by Johann Wilhelm von Archenholz.

d'Hondt, Jacques. *Hegel secret: Recherches sur les sources cachés de la pensée de Hegel.* Paris: Presses universitaires de France, 1986.

de Man, Paul. *Aesthetic Ideology.* Edited by Andrzej Warminski. Minneapolis: University of Minnesota Press, 1966.

de Man, Paul. *Allegories of Reading: Figural Language in Roussea, Nietzche, Rilke and Proust.* New Haven: Yale University Press, 1979.

de Man, Paul. *Blindness and Insight: Essays in the Rhetoric of Contemporary Criticism.* Minneapolis: University of Minnesota Press, 1983.

de Man, Paul. *The Resistance to Theory.* Minneapolis: University of Minnesota Press, 1986.

de Man, Paul. *Critical Writings: 1953–1978.* Edited by Lindsay Waters. Minneapolis: University of Minnesota Press, 1989.

de Nys, M. J. "Force and Understanding: The Unity of the Object of Consciousness." In *Method and Speculation in Hegel's Phenomenology.* Edited by Merold Westphal, 57–70. Atlantic Highlands: Humanities Press, 1982.

Deleuze, Gilles. *Le pli: Leibniz et le baroque.* Paris: Minuit, 1988.

Deleuze, Gilles and Félix Guattari. *A Thousand Plateaus.* Translated by Brian Massumi. Minneapolis: University of Minnesota Press, 1980.

Derrida, Jacques. *Speech and Phenomena and Other Essays on Husserl's Theory of Signs.* Translated by David Allison. Evanston: Northwestern University Press, 1973.

Derrida, Jacques. *Writing and Difference.* Translated by Alan Bass. Chicago: University of Chicago Press, 1978.

Derrida, Jacques. *Disseminations.* Translated by Barbara Johnson. Chicago: University of Chicago Press, 1981.

Derrida, Jacques. *Positions.* Translated by Alan Bass. Chicago: University of Chicago Press, 1981.

Derrida, Jacques. *Margins of Philosophy.* Translated by Alan Bass. Chicago: University of Chicago Press, 1982.

Derrida, Jacques. *Limited Inc.* Evanston: Northwestern University Press, 1984.

Derrida, Jacques. "Des Tours de Babel." In *Difference in Translation.* Translated and edited by Joseph F. Graham, 165–248. Ithaca: Cornell University Press, 1985.

Derrida, Jacques. "Architecture Where the Desire May Live." *Domus* 671 (1986): 17–25.

Derrida, Jacques. *Glas.* Translated by John Leavey, Jr. Lincoln: University of Nebraska Press, 1986.

Derrida, Jacques. "Cinquante-deux aphorisms pour un avant-propos." In *Psyché,* 509–18. Paris: Galilée, 1987.

Derrida, Jacques. "Point de folie – maintenant l'architecture." In *Psyché,* 477–93. Paris: Galilée, 1987.

Derrida, Jacques. *The Truth in Painting.* Translated by Geoff Bennington and Ian McLeod. Chicago: University of Chicago Press, 1987.

Derrida, Jacques. "Signature Event Context." In *Limited Inc.* Edited by Gerald Graff, 1–23. Translated by Samuel Weber and Jeffrey Mehlman. Evanston: Northwestern University Press, 1988.

Derrida, Jacques. *Memoirs of the Blind: The Self-Portrait and Other Ruins.* Translated by Pascale-Anne Brault and Michael Naas. Chicago: University of Chicago Press, 1993.

Derrida, Jacques. *Of Grammatology.* Translated by Gayatri C. Spivak. Baltimore: Johns Hopkins University Press, 1998.

Derrida, Jacques. *Foi et Savoir, suivi de Le Siècle et le Pardon.* Paris: Seuil, 2000.

Derrida, Jacques. *The Politics of Friendship.* London: Verso, 2006.

Desmond, William. *Art and the Absolute: A Study of Hegel's Aesthetics.* Albany: State University of New York Press, 1986.

Diodorus Siculus. *The Library of History*. Translated by C. L. Sherman. Cambridge: Harvard University Press, 1985.

Diouf, Sylviane. *Servants of Allah: African Muslims Enslaved in the Americas*. New York: New York University Press, 1998.

Dorigny, Marcel. *Révoltes et révolutions en Europe et aux Amériques (1773–1802)*. Paris: Belin, 2004.

Dorigny, Marcel and Bernard Gainot. *La Société des Amis des Noirs: 1788–1799*. Paris: UNESCO, 1998.

Drechsler, Horst. *Let Us Die Fighting: The Struggle of the Herero and Nama against German Imperialism, 1884–1915*. Berlin: Akademie-Verlag, 1980.

Drescher, Seymour. *Econocide: British Slavery in the Era of Abolition*. Pittsburgh: University of Pittsburgh Press, 1977.

Dubois, Laurent. *A Colony of Citizens: Revolution and Slave Emancipation in the French Caribbean*: 1787–1804. Chapel Hill: University of North Carolina Press, 2004.

Dubois, Laurent. *Avengers of the New World: The Story of the Haitian Revolution*. Cambridge: Belknap Press. 2004.

Endings: Questions of Memory in Hegel and Heidegger. Edited by Rebecca Comay and John McCumber. Evanston: Northwestern University Press, 1999.

Erickson, Edgar. "The Introduction of East Indian Coolies into the British West Indies." *The Journal of Modern History* 6 (1934): 127–46.

Fanon, Frantz. *Black Skin, White Masks*. Translated by R. Philcox. New York: Grove Press, 2008.

Farneth, Molly. *Hegel's Social Theory: Religion, Conflict, and Rituals of Reconciliation*. Princeton: Princeton University Press, 2017.

Felman, Shoshana. *The Literary Speech Act: Don Juan with J.L Austin, or Seduction in Two Languages*. Translated by Catherine Porter. Ithaca: Cornell University Press, 1983.

Feuerbach, Ludwig. "Towards a Critique of Hegel's Philosophy." In *The Fiery Book: Selected Writings of Ludwig Feuerbach*, 53–94. London: Verso, 2013.

Fichte, Johann Gottlieb. *Sämtliche Werke*, 8 vols. Berlin: De Gruyter, 1965.

Fine, Robert. "Contra Leviathan: Hegel's Contribution to the Cosmopolitan Critique." In *Hegel and Global Justice*. Edited by Andrew Buchwalter, 49–64. New York: Springer, 2012.

Fischer, Sibylle. *Modernity Disavowed: Haiti and the Cultures of Slavery in the Age of Revolution*. Durham: Duke University Press, 2004.

Flay, Joseph C. "Hegel's Inverted World." *Review of Metaphysics* 23 (1970): 662–78.

Freud, Sigmund. "Fetishism." In *The Standard Edition of the Complete Pscyhological Works of Sigmund Freud*, vol. 21. Edited by James Strachey, 147–58. London: Hogarth Press, 1975.

Gadamer, Hans-Georg. *Hegel's Dialectic: Five Hermeneutical Studies*. Translated by P. Chrisopher Smith. New Haven: Yale University Press, 1976.

Gadamer, Hans-Georg. *Truth and Method*. Translated by Joel Weinsheimer and Donald G. Marshall. New York: Continuum, 1976.

Gaffield, Julia. *Haitian Connections in the Atlantic World*: *Recognition after Revolution*. Chapel Hill: University of North Carolina Press, 2015.

Gainot, Bernard. *La Révolution des Esclaves: Haïti, 1763–1803*. Paris: Vendémaire, 2017.

Gasché, Rodolphe. "Setzung and Übersetzung: Notes on Paul de Man." *Diacritics* 11, no. 4 (1981): 36–57.

Gasché, Rodolphe. "Hegel's Orient or the End of Romanticism." In *History and Mimesis*. Edited by Irving J. Massey and Sung Wong Lee, 17–29. Buffalo: State University of New York, 1983.

Gasché, Rodolphe. "In-Difference to Philosophy: de Man on Kant, Hegel, and Nietzsche." In *Reading de Man Reading*. Edited by Lindsay Waters and Wlad Godzich, 259–94. Minneapolis: University of Minnesota Press, 1989.

Gasché, Rodolphe. "On Mere Sight: A Response to Paul de Man." In *The Textual Sublime: Deconstruction and Its Differences*. Edited by Hugh J. Silverman and Gary E. Aylesworth, 109–15. Albany: State University of New York Press, 1990.

Gasché, Rodolphe. "Some Reflections on the Notion of Hypotyposis in Kant." *Argumentation* 4 (1990): 85–100.

Gasché, Rodolphe. *The Idea of Form: Rethinking Kant's Aesthetics*. Palo Alto: Stanford University Press, 2003.

Geschiere, Peter. *The Perils of Belonging: Autochthony, Citizenship, and Exclusion in Africa and Europe*. Chicago: University of Chicago Press, 2009.

Geggus, David. "Racial Equality, Slavery, and Colonial Secession during the Constituent Assembly." *The American Historical Review* 94, no. 5 (1989): 1290–308.

Geuss, Raymond. "Kultur, Bildung, Geist." *History and Theory* 35, no. 2 (1996): 151–64.

Ghachem, Malick W. *The Old Regime and the Haitian Revolution*. Cambridge: Cambridge University Press, 2012.

Gillespie, Michael Allen. *Hegel, Heidegger, and the Ground of History*. Chicago: University of Chicago Press, 1984.

Gilroy, Paul. *The Black Atlantic: Modernity and Double Consciousness*. Cambridge: Harvard University Press, 1995.

Girard, Philippe. *Haiti: The Tumultuous History*. New York: Palgrave, 2010.

Glockner, Hermann. *Beiträge zum Verständnis und zur Kritik Hegels sowie zur Umgestaltung seiner Geisteswelt*. Bonn: Bouvier, 1965.

Golias, Theophilus. *Onomasticon latino-germanicum*. 1585.

Gordon, Cyrus. *The Common Background of Greek and Hebrew Civilization*. New York: W. W. Norton, 1962.

A Greek-English Lexicon with a Revised Supplement. Edited by Henry G. Liddell and Robert Scott, rev. by Henry S. Jones. Oxford: Clarendon Press, 1996.

Grégoire, Henri. *De la littérature des nègres*, Paris: Maradan, 1808.

Griffith, R. D. "The Origin of Memnon." *Classical Antiquity* 17, no. 2 (1998): 212–34.

Grosz, Elisabeth. *Architecture from the Outside: Essays on Virtual and Real Space*. Cambridge: MIT Press, 2001.

Guédé, Alan. *Monsieur de Saint-George, le Négre des lumières*. Paris: Acte Sud, 1999.

Gusti-Klara, Gaillard. *L'Expérience Haïtienne de la dette extérieure*. Port-au-Prince: Impremirie Henri Deschamps, 1988.

Habermas, Jürgen. "Struggles for Recognition in the Democratic Constitutional State." In *Multiculturalism*. Edited by Charles Taylor, 107–48. Princeton: Princeton University Press, 1994.

Habermas, Jürgen. *The Inclusion of the Other*. Cambridge: MIT Press, 2000.

Habermas, Jürgen. *The Postnational Constellation*. Cambridge: MIT Press, 2001.

Habermas, Jürgen. *The Divided West*. Malden: Polity, 2006.

Haitian History: New Perspectives. Edited by Alyssa G. Sepinwall. London: Routledge, 2013.

Hannig, Rainer. *Grosses Handwörterbuch Ägyptisch-Deutsch: die Sprache der Pharaonen*. Mainz: P. von Zabern, 1995.

Harris, H.S. *Hegel's Ladder*, 2 vols. Cambridge: Hackett, 1997.

Hegel after Derrida. Edited by Stuart Barnett. London: Routledge, 1998.

Hegel and Aesthetics. Edited by William Maker. Albany: State University of New York Press, 2000.

Hegel's Philosophy and Feminist Thought. Edited by K. Hutchings and T. Pulkkinen. London: Palgrave Macmillan, 2010.

Hegel, G. W. F. *Werke: Vollständige Ausgabe*, 18 vols. Berlin: Verlag von Duncker und Humblot, 1832–1845.

Hegel, G. W. F. *Vorlesungen über die Philosophie der Weltgeschichte*. Edited by G. Lasson. Leipzig: Felix Meiner Verlag, 1920.

Hegel, G. W. F. *Jenenser Realphilosophie II, Die Vorlesungen von 1805–1806*. Edited by J. Hoffmeister. Leipzig: Felix Meiner Verlag, 1931.

Hegel, G. W. F. *Jenenser Realphilosophie I, Die Vorlesungen von 1803–1804*. Edited by J. Hoffmeister. Leipzig: Felix Meiner Verlag, 1932.

Hegel, G. W. F. *Philosophy of Right*. Translated by T.M. Knox. Oxford: Clarendon Press, 1942.

Hegel, G. W. F. *Die Vernunft in der Geschichte*. Edited by J. Hoffmeister. Hamburg: Felix Meiner, 1955.

Hegel, G. W. F. *Lectures on the History of Philosophy*. Translated by E. S. Haldane and F. H. Simpson. London: Routledge, 1955.

Hegel, G. W. F. *The Philosophy of History*. Translated by J. Sibree. New York: Dover, 1956.

Hegel, G. W. F. *Sämtliche Werke*. Stuttgart: Frommans Verlag, 1957.

Hegel, G. W. F. *Hegel's Science of Logic*. Translated by A. V. Miller. Atlantic Highlands, NJ: Humanities Press International, 1969.

Hegel, G. W. F. *Werke in zwanzig Bändig*, 20 vols. Edited by E. Moldenhauer and K. M. Michel. Frankfurt am Main: Suhrkamp, 1969–71.

Hegel, G. W. F. *Vorlesungen über Rechtsphilosophie 1818–1831*. Edited by Karl-Heinz Ilting. Stuttgart: Frommann Verlag, 1974.

Hegel, G. W. F. *Lectures on the Philosophy of World History: Introduction*. Translated by H. B. Nisbet. Cambridge: Cambridge University Press, 1975.

Hegel, G. W. F. *Aesthetics: Lectures on Fine Art*. Translated by T.M. Knox. Oxford: Clarendon Press, 1975.

Hegel, G. W. F. *The Philosophy of Subjective Spirit*. Edited and translated by M. J. Petry. Boston: D. Reidel, 1978.

Hegel, G. W. F. *Vorlesungen über Naturrecht Staatswissenschaft: Heidelberg 1817/1818 mit Nachträgen aus der Vorlesung 1818/1819*. Edited by Becker et al. Hamburg: Felix Meiner Verlag, 1983.

Hegel, G. W. F. *Die Philosophie des Rechts: Die Mitschriften Wannenmann (Heidelberg 1817/18) und Homeyer (Berlin 1818/19)*. Edited by Karl-Heinz Ilting. Stuttgart: Klett-Cotta Verlag, 1983.

Hegel, G. W. F. *Jenaer Systementwürfe I: Das System der spekulativen Philosophie*. Edited by K. Düsing and H. Kimmerle. Hamburg: Felix Meiner Verlag, 1986.

Hegel, G. W. F. *Jenaer Systementwürfe III: Naturphilosophie und Philosophie des Geistes*. Edited by Rolf-Peter Horstmann. Hamburg: Felix Meiner Verlag, 1987.

Hegel, G. W. F. *Vorlesungen über die Philosophie des Geistes: Berlin 1827/1828*. Edited by F. Hespe and B. Tuschling. Hamburg: Felix Meiner Verlag, 1994.

Hegel, G. W. F. *Lectures on Natural Right and Political Science: Heidelberg 1817–1818 with Additions from the Lectures of 1818–1819*. Translated by J. Stewart and P. Hodgson. Berkeley: University of California Press, 1995.

Hegel, G. W. F. *Berliner Schriften 1818–1831*. Hamburg: Felix Meiner Verlag, 1997.

Hegel, G. W. F. *System der Sittlichkeit: Critik des Fichteschen Naturrechts*. Edited by H. D. Brandt. Hamburg: Felix Meiner Verlag, 2002.

Hegel and Capitalism. Edited by Andrew Buchwalter. Albany: State University of New York Press, 2015.

Hegel and Global Justice. Edited by Andrew Buchwalter. New York: Springer, 2012.

Hegel and the Infinite: Religion, Politics, and Dialectic. Edited by Slavoj Žižek et al. New York: Columbia University Press, 2011.

Hegel and Resistance. Edited by Bart Zantvoort and Rebecca Comay. London: Bloomsbury Academic, 2018.

Hegel's Philosophy and Feminist Thought. Edited by K. Hutchings and T. Pulkkinen. London: Palgrave Macmillan, 2010.

Hegel's Philosophy of Spirit. Edited by Peter G. Stillman. Albany: State University of New York Press, 1987.

Select Bibliography

Hegel: The Letters. Translated by C. Butler and C. Seiler. Bloomington: Indiana University Press, 1984.

Heidegger, Martin. *Identity and Difference*. Translated by Joan Stambaugh. New York: Harper and Row, 1969.

Heidegger, Martin. *On the Way to Language*. Translated by Peter D. Hertz. New York: Harper & Row, 1971.

Heidegger, Martin. *Poetry, Language, Thought*. Translated by A. Hofstadter. New York: Harper & Row, 1971.

Heidegger, Martin. *Hegel's Phenomenology of Spirit*. Translated by Parvis Emad and Kenneth Maly. Bloomington: Indiana University Press, 1988.

Heidegger, Martin. *The Concept of Time*. Translated by William McNeill. Oxford: Blackwell, 1992.

Heidegger, Martin. *Gesamtausgabe*. Frankfurt: Vittorio Klostermann GmbH, 2009.

Heinrich, Dieter. *Hegel im Kontext*. Frankfurt: Suhrkamp, 1971.

Helfer, Martha. *The Retreat of Representation: The Concept of* Darstellung *in German Critical Discourse*. Albany: State University of New York Press, 1996.

Henkel, Heiko. "Fundamentally Danish? The Muhammad Carton Crisis as Transitional Drama." *Human Architecture: Journal of the Sociology of Self-Knowledge* 8, no. 2 (2010): 67–82.

Herzog, Liza. *Inventing the Market: Smith, Hegel, and Political Theory*. Oxford: Oxford University Press, 2016.

Hicks, Steven. "Hegel on Cosmopolitanism." In *Hegel and Global Justice*. Edited by Andrew Buchwalter, 21–47. New York: Springer, 2012.

Hirt, Aloys. *Geschichte der Baukunst bei den Alten*, 3 vols. Berlin: G. Reimer, 1821–27.

"Historische Nachrichten von den letzten Unruhen in Saint Domingo. Aus verschiedenen Quellen gezogen," *Minerva: Ein Journal historischen und politischen Inhalts*, 1, 1792: 296–319. Edited by Johann Wilhelm von Archenholz.

History and System: Hegel's Philosophy of History. Edited by Robert Perkins. Albany: State University of New York Press, 1984.

Hochschild, Adam. *King Leopold's Ghost: A Story of Greed, Terror, and Heroism in Colonial Africa*. Boston: Houghton Mifflin, 1999.

Hodgson, Marshall. *Rethinking World History: Essays on Europe, Islam and World History*. Cambridge: Cambridge University Press, 1993.

Hoffheimer, Michael. "Martin Luther King Jr.'s Favorite Philosopher." *The Owl of Minerva* 25, no. 1 (1993): 118–19.

Hollier, Denis. *Against Architecture: The Writings of George Bataille*. Translated by Betsy Wing. Cambridge: MIT Press, 1989.

Honneth, Axel. *The Struggle for Recognition: The Moral Grammar of Social Conflicts*. Cambridge: Polity Press, 2005.

Hulin, Michel. *Hegel el l'Orient*. Paris: J. Vrin, 1979.

Hyppolite, Jean. *Logique et existence*. Paris: Presses Universitaires de France, 1961.

Hyppolite, Jean. *Genesis and Structure of Hegel's Phenomenology of Spirit*. Evanston: Northwestern University Press. 1974.

Hyppolite, Jean. *Introduction to Hegel's Philosophy of History*. Translated by Bond Hariss and J. B. Spurlock. Gainesville: University Press of Florida, 1996.

Identity and Difference: Studies in Hegel's Logic, Philosophy of Spirit, and Politics. Edited by P. T. Grier. Albany: State University of New York Press, 2007.

The Impact of the Haitian Revolution in the Atlantic World. Edited by David Geggus. Columbia: University of South Carolina Press, 2001.

Jakobson, Roman. *Selected Writings*, 8 vols. Berlin: Mouton de Gruyter, 1962–1988.

James, C. L. R. *Black Jacobins*. New York: Vintage, 1989.

Jameson, Frederic. *Valences of the Dialectic*. London: Verso, 2009.

Jameson, Frederic. *The Hegel Variations*. London: Verso, 2010.

Jenson, Deborah. "Hegel and Dessalines: Philosophy and the African Diaspora." *New West Indian Guide* 84, no. 3/4 (2010): 269–75.

Jenson, Deborah. *Beyond the Slave Narrative*. Liverpool: Liverpool University Press, 2011.

Johann Gottlob Schneiders Handwörterbuch der griechischen Sprache: nach der dritten Ausgabe des größeren Griechischdeutschen Wörterbuchs mit besonderer Berücksichtigung des Homerischen und Hesiodischen Sprachgebrauchs und mit genauer Angabe der Sylbenlängen, revised and expanded by Franz Passow. Leipzig: Friedrich Christian Wilhelm Vogel, 1819.

Johnson, Barbara. *The Critical Difference: Essays in the Contemporary Rhetoric of Reading.* Baltimore: Johns Hopkins University Press, 1980.

Johnson, Walter. *Soul by Soul: Life inside the Antebellum Slave Market.* Cambridge: Harvard University Press, 1999.

Johnson, Walter. "On Agency." *Journal of Social History* 37, no. 1 (2003): 113–24.

Johnson, Walter. *River of Dark Dreams: Slavery and Empire in the Cotton Kingdom.* Cambridge: Harvard University Press, 2017.

Kant, Immanuel. *The Critique of Pure Reason.* Translated by Norman Kemp Smith. New York: St. Martin's Press, 1965.

Kant, Immanuel. *Werkausgabe in zwölf Bänden.* Edited by Wilhelm Weischedel. Frankfurt: Suhrkamp Taschenbuch, 1974.

Kant, Immanuel. *The Critique of Judgement.* Translated by Werner S. Pluhar. Indianapolis: Hackett Publishing, 1987.

Kant, Immanuel. *Lectures on Logic.* Translated by J. M. Young. Cambridge: Cambridge University Press, 1992.

Kant, Immanuel. *Metaphysical Elements of Justice.* Boston: Hackett, 1999.

Kinzer, Stephen. *All the Shah's Men: An American Coup and the Roots of Middle East Terror.* Hoboken: John Wiley & Sons, 2003.

Kleist, Heinrich von. *Die Verlobung in St. Domingo.* Stuttgart: Reclaim, 2012.

Kojève, Alexandre. *Introduction à la Lecture de Hegel.* Edited by R. Queneau. Paris: Gallimard, 1947.

Kristeva, Julia. *La Révolution du Langage Poétique.* Paris: Seuil, 1974.

Lacan, Jacques. *Écrits: A Selection.* Translated by Alan Sheridan. New York: W. W. Norton, 1977.

Ladha, Hassanaly. "Hegel's *Werkmeister*: Architecture, Architectonics, and the Theory of History." *October* 139 (2012): 15–38.

Ladha, Hassanaly. "Allegories of Ruin: Architecture and Knowledge in Early Arabic Poetry." *Journal of Arabic Literature* 50, no. 2 (2019): 89–122.

Ladha, Hassanaly. "From Bayt to Stanza: Arabic Khayāl and the Advent of Italian Vernacular Poetry," forthcoming in *Exemplaria*.

Lambert, Johann Heinrich. *Anlage zur Architektonic.* Riga: Johann Friedrich Hartknoch, 1771.

Lefebvre, Henri. *The Production of Space.* Translated by Donald Nicholson-Smith. Oxford: Basil Blackwell, 1991.

Luckácz, Georg. *The Young Hegel: Studies in the Relation between Dialectics and Economics.* London: Merlin Press, 1975.

Lyotard, Jean-François. *Economie libidinale.* Paris: Minuit, 1974.

Lyotard, Jean-François. *Leçons sur l'Analytique du Sublime.* Paris: Galilée, 1991.

Madiou, Thomas. *Histoire d'Haiti.* Pétion-Ville: Editions Henri Deschamps, 1988.

Malabou, Catherine. *The Future of Hegel: Plasticity, Temporality, and Dialectic.* London: Routledge, 2005.

Manchester P. "Kant's Conception of Architectonic in its Historical Context." *In Journal of the History of Philosophy* 41 (2003), 187–207.

Marglin, Jessica. *Across Legal Lines: Jews and Muslims in Modern Morocco.* New Haven: Yale University Press, 2016.

Marx, Karl. *Critique of Hegel's Philosophy of Right.* Edited by Joseph O' Malley. Cambridge: Cambridge University Press, 1970.

Select Bibliography

Marx, Karl. *Capital: A Critique of Political Economy*, vol. 1: *The Process of Capitalist Production*. Translated by Samuel Moore and Edward Aveling. New York: International Publishers, 1984.

McCarney, Joseph. *Hegel on History*. London: Routledge, 2000.

Meillassoux, Quentin. *After Finitude: An Essay on the Necessity of Contingency*. London: Bloomsbury, 2010.

Memmi, Albert. *The Colonizer and the Colonized*. Boston: Beacon Press, 1991.

Merry, Sally E. "Legal Pluralism." *Law & Society Review* 22 (1988): 869–96.

Michel, Nicholas. "Arts Plastiques: Dak'Art Prend le Vert." *Jeune Afrique*, May 15, 2014: Available online: http://www.jeuneafrique.com/163765/culture/arts-plastiques-dak-art-prend-le-vert/ (accessed October 10, 2018).

Mitchell, Timothy. "The Limits of the State: Beyond Statist Approaches and Their Critics." *The American Political Science Review* 85, no. 1 (1991): 77–96.

Murray, David. "Hegel: Force and the Understanding." In *Reason and Reality*. Edited by G. N. A. Vesey, 163–73. London: Macmillan, 1972.

Nancy, Jean-Luc. *Hegel: L'inquiétude du négatif*. Paris: Hachette, 1997.

Neuhouser, Frederick. *Foundations of Hegel's Social Theory: Actualizing Freedom*. Cambridge: Harvard University Press, 2000.

Nesbitt, Nick. *Voicing Memory: History and Subjectivity in French Caribbean Literature*. Charlottesville: University of Virginia Press, 2003.

Nesbitt, Nick. "Troping Toussaint, Reading Revolution." *Research in African Literatures* 35, no. 2 (2004): 18–33.

Nesbitt, Nick. *Universal Emancipation: The Haitian Revolution and the Radical Enlightenment*. Charlottesville: University of Virginia Press, 2008.

Newmark, Kevin. *Irony on Occasion*. New York: Fordham University Press, 2012.

Nietzche, Friedrich. *Thus Spoke Zarathustra: A Book for All and None*. Translated by Walter Kaufmann. New York: Modern Library, 1995.

Nietzche, Friedrich. *Basic Writings of Nietzche*. Translated by Walter Kaufmann. New York: Modern Library, 2000.

O' Brien, George D. *Hegel on Reason and History*. Chicago: University of Chicago Press, 1975.

Obikili, Nonso. "The Impact of the Slave Trade on Literacy in West Africa: Evidence from the Colonial Era." *Journal of African Economies* 25, no. 1 (2016): 1–27.

Oxford Dictionary of English Etymology. Edited by C. T. Onions. New York: Oxford University Press, 1966.

Phillips, Anthony. "Haiti, France and the Independence Debt of 1825." 2018 Available online: https://canada-haiti.ca/sites/default/files/Haiti, Franceand the Independence Deb to f1825_0.pdf (accessed July 17, 2018).

Pinkard, Terry. *Hegel's Phenomenology: The Sociality of Reason*. Cambridge: Cambridge University Press, 1996.

Pippin, Robert. *Hegel's Idealism: The Satisfactions of Self-Consciousness*. Cambridge: Cambridge University Press, 1989.

Pippin, Robert. "Recognition and Reconciliation: Actualized Agency in Hegel's Jena Phenomenology." In *Recognition and Power: Axel Honneth and the Tradition of Critical Social Theory*. Edited by B. Brink and D. Owen, 57–68. Cambridge: Cambridge University Press, 2007.

Pippin, Robert. *Hegel's Practical Philosophy: Rational Agency as Ethical Life*. Cambridge: Cambridge University Press, 2008.

Pippin, Robert. *Hegel on Self-Consciousness: Desire and Death in the Phenomenology of Spirit*. Princeton: Princeton University Press, 2011.

Piquet, Jean-Daniel. *L'Émancipation des noirs dans la révolution française*. Paris: Éditions Karthala, 2002.

The Political Archive of Paul de Man: Property, Sovereignty, and the Theotropic. Edited by Martin McQuillan. Edinburgh: Edinburgh University Press, 2012.

Pope, Jeremy. "Ägypten and Aufhebung: G. F. W. Hegel, W. E. Du Bois, and the African Orient." *The New Centennial Review* 6: 3 (2006): 149–92.

Rainsford, Marcus. *An Historical Account of the Black Empire of Hayti.* Edited by P. Youngquist and G. Pierrot. Durham: Duke University Press, 2013.

Rathore, Aakash and Rimina Mohapatra. *Hegel's India: A Reinterpretation, with Texts.* Oxford: Oxford University Press, 2017.

Reading de Man Reading. Edited by Wlad Godzich. Minneapolis: University of Minnesota Press, 1989.

Reid, Jeremy. *The Anti-Romantic: Hegel against Ironic Romanticism.* London: Bloomsbury Academic, 2014.

Rhys, Jean. *Wide Sargasso Sea.* Edited by Judith Raiskin. New York: W. W. Norton, 1999.

Ribbe, Claude. *Le Chevalier de Saint-George.* Paris: Perrin, 2004.

Robinson, Cedric. *Black Marxism: The Making of the Black Radical Tradition.* Chapel Hill: University of North Carolina Press, 1983.

Rosenmeyer, Patricia. *The Language of Ruins: Greek and Latin Inscriptions on the Memnon Colossus.* Oxford: Oxford University Press, 2018.

Rozenzweig, Franz. *Hegel und der Staat.* Berlin: Suhrkamp, 2010.

Ruda, Frank. *Abolishing Freedom: A Plea for a Contemporary Use of Fatalism.* Lincoln: University of Nebraska Press, 2015.

Sala-Molins, Louis. *The Dark Side of the Light: Slavery and the French Enlightenment.* Translated by John Conteh-Morgan. Minneapolis: University of Minnesota Press, 2006.

Saussure, Ferdinand. *Cours de linguistique générale.* Edited by Tullio de Mauro. Paris: Payot, 1985.

Schlegel, Friedrich. *Kritische Ausgabe.* Edited by E. Behler et al. Paderborn: F. Schöningh, 1958.

Selee, Andrew. *Vanishing Frontiers: The Forces Driving Mexico and the United States Together.* New York: Public Affairs, 2018.

Sideris, E. G. and A. A. Konsta. "A Letter from Jean-Pierre Boyer to Greek Revolutionaries." *Journal of Haitian Studies* 11, no. 1 (2005), 167-71.

"Skizze von Hayti in Beziehung des moralischen und politischen Characters seiner Bewohner." *Minerva: Ein Journal historischen und politischen Inhalts* 123 (1822): 454–85. Edited by Johann Wilhelm von Archenholz.

Slave Revolution in the Caribbean 1789–1804: A Brief History with Documents. Edited by Laurent Dubois and John Garrigus. New York: Bedford/St. Martin's, 2006.

Snowden, Frank. *Blacks in Antiquity: The Ethiopians in Greco-Roman Experience.* Cambridge: Harvard University Press, 1970.

Speight, C. Allen. *Hegel, Literature, and the Problem of Agency.* Cambridge: Cambridge University Press, 2001.

Speight, C. Allen. "Artists, Artisans, and Hegel's History of Art." *Hegel Bulletin* 34, no. 2 (2013), 203–22.

Stern, Robert. *Hegel and the Phenomenology of Spirit.* London: Routledge, 2002.

Stone, Allison. "Hegel and Colonialism." *Hegel Bulletin,* June 2017. Available online: doi:10.1017/hgl.2017.17 (accessed October 10, 2018).

Strabo. *The Geography of Strabo,* 8 vols. Translated by Horace L. Jones. Cambridge: Harvard University Press, 2001.

Tavares, Pierre-Franklin. *Hegel, critique de l'Afrique: Introduction aux études critiques de Hegel sur l'Afrique.* Unpublished dissertation. Sorbonne, Paris, 1989.

Tavares, Pierre-Franklin. "Hegel et Haïti ou le silence de Hegel sur Saint-Domingue." *Chemins Critiques* 2 (1992): 113–31.

Tavares, Pierre-Franklin. "Hegel et l'abbé Grégoire: question noire et révolution française." *Annales historiques de la Révolution française* 293/294 (1993): 491–509.

Tavares, Pierre-Franklin. "À propos de Hegel et Haïti: Lettre de Pierre Franklin Tavares à Jean Ristat." *L'Humanité*, December 2, 2006.

Tibebu, Teshale. *Hegel and the Third World: The Making of Eurocentrism in World History*. Syracuse: Syracuse University Press, 2011.

Tieck, Ludwig. *Die verkehrte Welt*. Berlin: De Gruyter, 1964.

Tonelli, G. Kant's Critique of Pure Reason *within the Tradition of Modern Logic*. Edited by D. Chandler. New York: G. Olms, 1994.

Uerlings, Herbert. "Anerkennung und Interkulturalität: Überlegungen mit Blick auf 'Haiti' bei Hegel und Alexander Kluge." *Zeitschrift für interkulturelle Germanistik* 8 (2017): 87–104.

Verschave, François-Xavier. *La Françafrique: Le plus long scandale de la République*. Paris: Stock, 2003.

Vološinov, V. N. *Marxism and the Philosophy of Language*. Translated by Ladislav Matejka and I. R. Titunik. Cambridge: Harvard University Press, 1973.

Warminski, Andrzej. *Readings in Interpretation: Hölderlin, Hegel, Heidegger*. Minneapolis: University of Minnesota Press, 1987.

Weber, Max. *Political Writings*. Edited by P. Lassman and R. Speirs. Cambridge: Cambridge University Press, 1994.

Wicks, Robert. *Hegel's Theory of Aesthetic Judgment*. New York: Peter Lang, 1994.

Wigley, Mark. *The Architecture of Deconstruction: Derrida's Haunt*. Cambridge: MIT Press, 1993.

Wilkins, Burleigh T. *Hegel's Philosophy of History*. Ithaca: Cornell University Press, 1974.

Williams, Eric. *Capitalism and Slavery*. Chapel Hill: University of North Carolina Press, 1994.

Williams, Robert. *Recognition: Fichte and Hegel on the Other*. Albany: State University of New York Press, 1992.

Wyss, Beat. *Hegel's Art History and the Critique of Modernity*. Translated by Carlonie D. Satlzwedel. Cambridge: Cambridge University Press, 1999.

Yeomans, Christopher. *Freedom and Reflection: Hegel and the Logic of Agency*. Oxford: Oxford University Press, 2011.

Žižek, Slavoj. *The Sublime Object of Ideology*. London: Verso, 1989.

Žižek, Slavoj. *Less than Nothing: Hegel and the Shadow of Dialectical Materialism*. London: Verso, 2000.

Žižek, Slavoj. *The Parallax View*. Cambridge: MIT Press, 2009.

Žižek, Slavoj. *The Most Sublime Hysteric: Hegel with Lacan*. Cambridge: Polity Press, 2014.

INDEX

Index

Index

Index

Index

Index

Index

Index

vs. sign (*see under* Sign)
sublime 76 (*see also* Sublime)
synthesis with romantic art 41 (*see also* Goethe)
unconscious symbolism 40 n.39, 66, 76
Werkmeister (*see under* Werkmeister)

Tavares, Pierre-Franklin 123 n.15, 139 n.23,
    214 n.4, 255 n.233, 262 n.257, 264 n.266,
    265 n.268
Telos of History 2, 2 n.4, 13, 129 n.13, 132,
    190 n.63, 204, 206, 210, 279
Tieck, Ludwig
    Die verkehrte Welt 150-2
    irony 151, 151 n.81
    and Schlegel 151 n.82
Time
    aesthetic dissolution of 176
    Africa 204-7, 210-1, 270 n.296, 285
    architectonic endurance of form in 57, 82 n.28,
        153 n.89
    architectonic marking of thought in 56-7, 68
    architectonic or poetic delineation of 11, 13,
        17-8, 56-7, 68, 73, 110, 121-3, 138 n.15, 215
    chronological vs. philosophical view of 24-5,
        41-2
    figural mediation of 10
    force of ideality in 224, 263
    freedom and "right" in 10
    in Hegel's system 129 n.13
    idealism 34, 41-2, 179-80
    limit and theory of history 104-117, 121-3, 215
    Memnon 57, 100
    memory vs. recollection, *see* Memory
    perception of 135
    perverse or vulgar understanding of 142, 144-5,
        147, 152-3 n.89, 199, 208 n.138
    philosophy and 117 n.64
    plasticity 152-3 n.89
    pyramid and obelisk 21 n.8, 42
    and recognitive agency 163, 174, 197-8
    reconciliation or forgiveness in 200-1, 215
    slave articulating form in 157, 180
    slavery and personhood 221
    sound as temporal medium of poetry 78, 92,
        100
    state in 238
    telos (*see* Telos of History)
    theory of future, New World 268
    ungraspability of present 5-7
    vs. freedom in absolute knowing 129-33,
        129 n.13, 200-1, 210-1
Toguo, Barthélémy 287-9
Toussaint L'Ouverture 123-4 n.15
Translation
    architecture 64

freedom 279
    of *Knecht* 191 n.66
    paradoxical possibility and impossibility of 279
    perversion 155
    and problems in Hegel studies 20 n.5, 152-3 n.89,
        170 n.56, 180, 184, 191 n.66, 192 n.69,
        234 n.124, 240 n.159, 254, 254 n.232
    pyramidal sign 61, 61 n.43
    and reconciliation 280
    Walter Benjamin 279 n.331
Trope, *see also* Figuration and Symbol
    chiasmus 145-6 (*see also* Chiasmus)
    master-slave dialectic and gender 196
    performativity or force 144-5, 150
    perversion 145 n.51
    sublimity 94
    understanding 150
Troy 62 n.45, 74, 75 n.4
Truth and Reconciliation 280
Tunisia 282

Übersetzung, see Translation
Understanding
    inverted world (*see* Inverted World)
    ironic destabilization of 142, 148-9, 152, 159,
        162, 164, 199
    logos 152
    perversion of subjectivity and objectivity
        144-55, 180, 232, 286
    state based on architectonic of reason 1, 155,
        214-5
    state based on (*see under* State, "State based on
        understanding")
United Fruit Company 245 n.185
United States of America as empire 245 n.185

Vautier, René 273 n.313
Verkehrung, see Perversion
Vermischung, see Miscegeny
*Verstand, see under*standing
Verstandesstaat, see under State, "State based on
    understanding"
Violence
    Africa 206
    agency and recognition 187, 190 n.63
    history, aesthetics, reconciliation 193, 201
    language 185
    of mastery 183, 187, 195
    performativity 5
    pre-historical vs. historical 185 n.44, 198
    state (*see under* State)
    struggle for recognition (*see under* Self-
        Consciousness, *see also* Recognition)
    theory of 12, 197-8
    and theory of power 185, 187

Made in the USA
Middletown, DE
09 September 2023

38265828R00190